LINKING PARTIES WITH PEOPLE?

Linking Parties with People?
Party Membership in Sweden 1960-1997

ANDERS WIDFELDT
University of Aberdeen, UK

Ashgate

Aldershot • Brookfield USA • Singapore • Sydney

Published by
Ashgate Publishing Ltd
Gower House
Croft Road
Aldershot
Hants GU11 3HR
England

Ashgate Publishing Company
Old Post Road
Brookfield
Vermont 05036
USA

British Library Cataloguing in Publication Data
Widfeldt, Anders
　　Linking parties with people? :party membership in Sweden
　　1960-1997
　　1. Political parties - Sweden 2. Party affiliation - Sweden
　　I. Title
　　324.2'1'09485

Library of Congress Catalog Card Number: 98-74934

ISBN 1 84014 758 X

Printed in Great Britain

Contents

List of Symbols and Abbreviations

Symbols:

§   Paragraph.

---   Not applicable (used in some tables, usually means that the organisation or party in question did not exist, or a survey was not conducted, in a given year).

Abbreviations:

A	Total and absolute number of active party members
A/E	Per cent active party members of entire national electorate
A/M	Per cent active party members of entire membership
ave	average
A/V	Per cent active party members of a party's voters
CDU	Christian Democratic Union (Germany)
Centre P	Centre Party (Sweden)
Ch.	Chapter
Chr. Dem.	Christian Democratic Party (Sweden)
EB	Eurobarometer
EC	European Community
ES	Swedish Election Study (-ies)
esp.	especially
EU	European Union
ExC	Executive Committee
f	The following page (p. 1f means pages 1 and 2)
ff	The two following pages (p. 1ff means pages 1, 2 and 3)
Green	Green Party (Sweden)
incl.	including
ind.	individual members
Left P	Left Party (Sweden)
LO	Landsorganisationen (Swedish confederation of blue collar unions)
M	Absolute number of party members
M/E	Per cent party members of entire national electorate
Moderate	Moderate Party (Sweden)
MP	Member of Parliament

Abbreviations (cont.):

M/V	Per cent members of a party's total number of voters
n	Number of cases
n/a	Data not available, or data not found
NC	National Council
NE	National Executive
New D	New Democracy (Swedish party)
no.	Number (other than number of cases)
org.	Organisation
ÖVP	Austrian People's Party
People's	People's Party Liberals (Sweden)
PR	Party Rules
P Rec.	Party Records
q.	question
rep.	Representation, or representative
resp.	Responsible
SCB	Statistics Sweden (*Statistiska Centralbyrån*)
SD	Social Democratic Party (Sweden)
sect.	section
SOM	Society, Opinion, Media (Survey series conducted at Göteborg University)
SPD	Social Democratic Party (Germany)
SPÖ	Socialist Party (Austria)
SSKF	Women's organisation of the Swedish Social Democratic Party
StD	Standard Deviance
Sw.	Swedish
tot.	total (including collective) members
ULF	Swedish living conditions studies made by SCB
VALU	Vallokalsundersökning (Exit poll conducted by Sveriges Television)

NB: some symbols and abbreviations used in tables, which are explained in the comment immediately below the relevant table, are not included here.

List of Figures

List of Tables

Acknowledgements

This book is based on my Ph.D dissertation which was defended at Göteborg University, 20 September 1997. My *opponent* at the *disputation* in Göteborg was Professor Patrick Seyd, University of Sheffield. His comments were thoughtful and balanced, yet challenging, and it was a privilege to be part of the discussion that took place that day.

Jon Pierre has offered unending support and advice. He introduced me to the Party Organization project, led by Richard S. Katz and Peter Mair. Other participants were Luciano Bardi, Lars Bille, Kris Deschouwer, David Farrell, Ruud A. Koole, Leonardo Morlino, Wolfgang Müller, Thomas Poguntke, Jan Sundberg, Lars Svåsand, Paul D. Webb and Hella van der Welde. The work in the project has, in particular, inspired Chapters 3 and 4. The project was funded by the National Science Foundation (USA), grant no. SES-8818439, with additional support provided by the *Forschungsstelle für Gesellshaftliche Entwicklungen* at the University of Mannheim, Germany. The Swedish part of the project was supported by HSFR, the Swedish Social Science and Humanities Research Council.

The support and advice from Sören Holmberg has also been crucial. He encouraged and supported my application as a young scholar to the Beliefs in Governments (BiG) project, funded by the European Science Foundation. Project directors were Max Kaase and Kenneth Newton. I was a member of a subgroup led by Hans-Dieter Klingemann and Dieter Fuchs. Other group members were Kees Aarts, Roberto Biorcio, Giovanna Guidorossi, Ola Listhaug, Renato Mannheimer, Hermann Schmitt, Palle Svensson, Jacques Thomassen, Gábor Tóka, Richard Topf and Matti Wiberg. I am also grateful to the BiG research co-ordinator, Elinor Scarbrough. The work in BiG has particularly inspired Chapters 7 and 8.

My host departments have been Göteborg until 1996 and Aberdeen from 1996 to date. Professor Bo Särlvik, who passed away in January 1998, was a major influence in Göteborg. It was a privilege to be able to benefit from his phenomenal knowledge and experience. In Aberdeen, the support from Professor David Arter has been extremely important.

Jonas Hinnfors, Lennart J. Lundqvist and Sune Persson have made valuable comments on earlier drafts. Martin Bennulf and Per Hedberg have advised me on the statistical analysis and helped me through the sometimes complicated maze of the Swedish Election Studies. Maria Oskarson's generosity with the data from her study on class voting has been crucial for the work on Chapter 7, but her contribution extends much further. Henrik

Oscarsson has been helpful in many ways, mostly (but not only) related to the analysis of survey data. Peter Esaiasson and Mikael Gilljam have been long standing sources of advice and support. Nicholas Aylott, Lynn Bennie, William Maloney and Lisa Trahair have read chapter drafts and made valuable comments. Janet Michaelsen helped prepare the final manuscript. Bodil Agasøster has been very supportive and helpful in a variety of ways.

Besides those mentioned, I am grateful to a great number of people at the Department of Political Science, Göteborg University and the Department of Politics and International Relations, University of Aberdeen. You have given me help and advice, and your friendship has been a constant source of inspiration. A collective round of thanks to you all.

All these persons apart, it would not have been possible to complete the book without the help and co-operation of the Swedish political parties. In my experience, the Swedish parties, and their side organisations, are indeed open organisations, with very kind and helpful members and staff who are always happy to assist political science research. Representatives of all the eight parties included in the book have been very forthcoming when asked for information, and have generously supplied me with the material I have required. The Moderate Party, People's Party Liberals and the Centre Party have let me work in their own archives. The former two, and the Christian Democrats, have also given me access to their depositions at *Riksarkivet* in Stockholm. The Left Party have given access to their depositions at the Labour Movement Archive in Stockholm. Much of the material on the Social Democrats also comes from the Labour Movement Archive. Both *Riksarkivet* and the Labour Movement Archive provide excellent research facilities, and I am indebted to the staff at both places for their patience and help. *Ungdomsstyrelsen* in Stockholm have been very helpful with information about the parties' youth organisations. Lars Häll at Statistics Sweden (SCB) has generously supplied me with data on party membership and activity, and made helpful comments on earlier drafts of Chapter 4.

I would also like to thank all representatives of parties and side organisations who, in the middle of an election campaign, quickly responded to my queries for complementary data in the late summer of 1998. The responsibility for any remaining mistakes rests on me alone.

Aberdeen, November 1998
Anders Widfeldt

1 Democracy and Political Parties

Persuasion in the street

Herbert Tingsten was walking down Barnhusgatan, Stockholm, Sweden. Quite unexpectedly he met one of his former students, who had become a leading local activist in the Social Democratic Party. A conversation began in which Tingsten, who was known to support the party, was asked why he had not joined as a member. His reply was somewhat evasive. He had indeed voted for the party for several years but feared that formal membership would bring too much constraint and commitment. However, the party activist sensed that the defence line was penetrable.

"Rubbish. If you vote for us you might as well join us. You have no reason to deny us the small support your membership would be. My office is just around the corner, come along and we'll have it sorted out in a minute." Tingsten was still reluctant, but eventually decided there was some merit to the argument. He accepted the invitation and became a party member.[1]

This incident from the 1930s is an example of how political parties work in a democratic political system. A vital contribution to democracy by the parties is that they are open and voluntary membership organisations. That will also be the perspective of this study. It will review the debate about party membership in a representative democracy. It will empirically investigate important and democratically relevant aspects of party membership. Finally, it will raise questions about the democratic role of party members and parties as membership organisations.

By recruiting members political parties provide citizens with the opportunity to participate in political activity. It can even be claimed that

---

[1] The incident, here summarised and translated into English by the author, appears in Tingsten 1962:289f. Herbert Tingsten (1896-1973) was a well known personality in the Swedish political debate from the 1930s until the 1960s. He was Professor of Political Science at Stockholm University between 1935 and 1946, and editor of the daily morning newspaper Dagens Nyheter between 1946 and 1959. The person who made the successful recruitment attempt was named Bertil Nyqvist.

parties need to be open and internally democratic membership organisations to fit into a democratic system. Paul Whiteley, Patrick Seyd and Jeremy Richardson, who have done extensive research on the members of British political parties, argue that responsible parties require grass-roots membership. This requirement extends from the parties to the entire political system. They also raise the argument that party membership provides citizens with increased political competence. "(T)he exercise of citizenship rights in liberal democracies involves acquiring information, understanding political problems and participating in political action. Political parties with their dues-paying members, provide one means of facilitating this citizenship".[2] The authors acknowledge that competing institutions exist, and note the recurring arguments about decreasing relevance of parties. They disagree with that, however, and conclude the discussion with an unambiguous declaration: "We believe that party members help keep democracy alive".[3]

Parties use members as a source of recruitment which means that people are more likely to be elected to official posts if they are party members. Party membership also makes it possible for the people to communicate with the élites. A person can communicate with the party élites, either by talking to party members, or by becoming a member. Conversely, party élites can communicate with the public via their members. Susan Scarrow has attributed the members a role as the parties' 'Ambassadors to the community', and Whiteley, Seyd and Richardson speak of the members as the parties' 'eyes and ears'.[4]

The arguments can be summarised into two basic points. First, that party membership provides political decision-makers with contacts with the general public. Second, that party membership is an outlet for political activity.[5] Political parties can promote democracy by involving citizens in political activity. This is in line with a democratic perspective which can be called the 'participatory democracy model'.

According to an alternative perspective, citizens in general are too uneducated and too unsophisticated to have the necessary competence to

---

[2] Whiteley, Seyd and Richardson 1994:7f.

[3] Whiteley, Seyd and Richardson 1994:8.

[4] Scarrow 1991:124. Whiteley, Seyd and Richardson 1994:4. See also Katz 1990:144ff.

[5] Cf. Katz 1990:159.

participate in politics. Instead, democracy should be organised so that they can choose between competing élites. The élites should not be reached via popular participation but held responsible for their government record at regular intervals. This view on democracy, which is largely inspired by Schumpeter, can be labelled the 'competitive élites model'.[6]

The two models have been discussed by Leif Lewin. He proceeds to synthesise them into an interactive democracy model. In the interactive democracy decisions are taken by élites, who compete with each other for power. Lewin argues that it is inevitable that the decisions are taken by élites because at some stage decisions need to be authoritative. Without some kind of élite this is not possible. On the other hand, lack of participation leads to apathy. Thus, while the competitive élites make the decisions, they must make them after a process in which citizens may participate.[7]

The point here is not to argue that Lewin's model should be taken as an ideal. However, it is an example of how political organisations with open membership can fit into other conceptions of democracy than those based on participation as the fundamental principle. Modern democracy is primarily representative. Lewin's line of argument suggests that representation needs not be contradictory to participation. Indeed it can be argued that the two complement, even require, each other. Via elections, political parties provide representation. By being open membership organisations they can also provide participation. In fact, party membership can also be argued to bear some relevance to the representational aspect of democracy. If the members provide communicative channels between the party and the public, they can be said to be representing the public inside the party.

Regardless which democratic model -- or mixture of models -- is preferred, party membership can therefore be argued to be a vital component of democracy. Thus, Herbert Tingsten's entry into the Social Democratic Party can be seen as an example of democracy at work. It is party membership as an aspect of political democracy that will be the perspective of this book. The Swedish parties will be studied with respect to their capacity to, as open and voluntary membership organisations, contribute to the Swedish democracy.

---

[6] Schumpeter 1942/1952.

[7] Lewin 1970. The interactive model is presented in his book on pp. 220-247.

Previous research on party membership

It would not be fair to say that party membership has been overlooked by political scientists. But it is nevertheless surprisingly rare to find studies focused on membership, and the perspectives that have been applied have varied.

One research tradition has approached party membership as an aspect of political participation. As a rule, such studies have had a very wide perspective. Sten Johansson's study on political resources in Sweden is an example. Johansson investigates differences in political participation and resources among social groups. The analysis deals with party membership and activity but also includes variables such as voting turnout, attendance at political meetings, demonstrations and personal contacts with politicians. The conclusion, based on data from the 1960s, was that the political capacity among citizens in Sweden to a significant extent was determined by social status. Vilgot Oscarsson's comparative study on Sweden, the former West Germany, Great Britain and the United States from the same period reinforced this picture. Jörgen Westerståhl and Folke Johansson's study on local government politics in Sweden in the 1970s reported a slightly higher degree of equality in participation. However, they noted that a significant amount of participation took place outside the political parties.[8]

A more recent example is Olof Petersson, Anders Westholm and Göran Blomberg's book published in connection with the Swedish Government Investigation of Power report (*Maktutredningen*). The study is theoretically and empirically very ambitious and covers wide aspects of citizens' resources, power and participation. The results are too complex to summarise here, but the authors detect a development over time towards increased political equality. More people than before have the competence and confidence to actively influence political decisions.[9] The most recent study is by Mikael Gilljam and Sören Holmberg, who report long term trends in political activity; informal and formal, inside and outside the political parties. Their conclusion is that there is some decline in party related activity

---

[8] Johansson 1971, Oscarsson 1976, Westerståhl and Johansson 1981.

[9] Petersson, Westholm and Blomberg 1989.

but that there is no overall decline in total political activity between the 1960s and 1990s.[10]

Outside Sweden, Geraint Parry, George Moyser and Neil Day have analysed participation in local politics in Great Britain. The perspective is quite similar to the mentioned Swedish studies. Their conclusion is that political participation is to a large extent determined by social resources and that Britain has some way to go before being able to fit the label participatory democracy. Similar results are presented in a Danish study by Jörgen Goul Andersen who, unlike Parry et al., bases his conclusion on an observed decline over time.[11]

All of these studies deal with party membership, but hardly give it more than passing attention. Another research tradition which has dealt with party membership is the literature on party organisation. One such aspect is the relationship between membership and élites. This was a key problem already in Michels's classic study on the German Social Democrats, where it was argued that deference and lacking sophistication among the masses determined their subordination to the elite levels in the party. More recently, Jon Pierre has shown how the leadership of the Swedish Social Democratic Party has tried, and largely succeeded, in avoiding letting congress decisions constrain their freedom of action.[12]

Writers who have employed the organisational perspective often regard party membership as part of a leadership strategy. Robert Michels saw the members as a means for success for the party élites. Duverger and Epstein both discussed the importance of party membership in the parties' quest for votes, although their conclusions were diametrically opposite to each other. Duverger saw mass membership as more or less necessary, while Epstein's view was almost exactly the opposite.[13] A recent example of the organisational perspective is Susan Scarrow's study on the memberships of the German SPD and CDU and the British Labour and Conservative parties. Scarrow explicitly declares at the outset that her work deals with parties' perceptions of the strategic value of members; not the democratic relevance

---

[10] Gilljam and Holmberg 1995:175-184.

[11] Parry, Moyser and Day 1992, Goul Andersen 1993.

[12] Michels 1915/1968, Pierre 1986.

[13] Michels 1915/1968, Duverger 1951/1964, Epstein 1967.

of members. Her conclusion is that the party leaderships still see a significant amount of strategic value in their members.[14]

An important organisational aspect is the size of membership. In a number of cases, membership has been used as an indicator of partisanship. An example is Ola Listhaug's book on Norwegian electoral politics between 1957 and 1985, which includes a chapter on party membership. The perspective is to view membership as an extra strong form of attachment to a political party, and the data presented includes not only membership as such but also potential membership, that is people who consider it possible that they some time might join a party.[15] Other, largely descriptive, studies have studied membership trends in different countries and used the observations to draw conclusions about the status and future of political parties.[16]

A related topic is the analysis of reasons behind changes in membership size. Stefano Bartolini's study of the memberships of European socialist parties analyses the impact of background variables such as electoral success and incumbency. Jörgen Elklit's study on Denmark analyses the impact of cost-benefit calculations of citizens, and of demographic changes. Another Danish study, by Lise Togeby, studies the relationship between membership and demography, and also more general patterns of political participation. Angelo Panebianco, in a very influential work on party organisation, focuses on membership size and its relationship with internal party variables such as internal cohesion and power structure.[17]

There are also monographs on individual parties which take party membership into account. Per Albinsson's study of the organisation of the Swedish Moderate Party deals with membership size, the economic relevance of the membership and the formal and informal influence of the members. Carl Gunnar Peterson's study of the youth organisation of the Swedish Social Democratic Party centres on membership influence and the relationship between leading officials and grass roots membership.[18]

---

[14] Scarrow 1991:30. See also Scarrow 1996, which is a published version of the same

The work by Patrick Seyd, Paul Whiteley and Jeremy Richardson has already been mentioned. Their thorough investigations into the British Labour and Conservative parties are in many respects milestones. Partly because the analysis is based on impressive data collections of several thousand party members, which makes it possible to draw more thorough conclusions about the members of an individual party than in any previous study. Also, however, because their theoretical perspective is very wide. They analyse strategic aspects such as the effectiveness of membership activity in election campaigns. They also probe into the incentives for political participation.[19]

Throughout their analysis, they employ a democratic perspective. Their two books are based on the normative assumption that open membership parties are valuable to democracy. Their analysis does not in any way lead them to reconsider this position. On the contrary, their findings are used as evidence to contradict the notions of parties consisting of 'loony leftists' or reactionary right extremists. In this respect they have begun to fill a gap in political research. Previous studies have tended to view membership from the perspective of the party, or as one of several aspects of political participation and mobilisation. Until Seyd and Whiteley's studies, the perspective of party membership as a central aspect of political democracy had been overlooked.[20]

This study, then, will place the democratic perspective at the forefront. Before the empirical chapters, however, the position of political parties in a democratic political system needs to be elaborated. This chapter has argued for the relevance of party membership in party research. The next task is to place these arguments in the context of political parties and their relevance to democracy.

2   Parties and Political Linkage

Party decline?

Political parties are often said to be in a state of crisis, or decline. This argument assumes, explicitly or implicitly, that the parties have a number of roles, tasks or functions to fulfil in a political system. In this chapter, it will be argued that party crisis, or decline, is related to how the parties fulfil their main functions. In turn, it will be argued that a key function of political parties is to provide connections, referred to as linkage, between citizens and the state, and that their members constitute a vital aspect of their ability to do so. The chapter will be concluded with the identification of a number of conditions which the parties will have to meet in order to provide linkage. The then following chapters will empirically investigate how the Swedish parties have performed according to these conditions for linkage between 1960 and 1994.

The claim that political parties are in crisis is not the most original of statements. In the past couple of decades much of the discussion in political science has revolved around this problem.[1] One argument has been that political parties as a phenomenon have become redundant and out of date and should be succeeded by other types of organisations.[2] Others argue that political parties as such could still be relevant but that the existing traditional parties are past their prime and should be succeeded by new parties.[3]

Hans Daalder identifies four main themes in the party crisis debate. First, the view that parties are detrimental to society and therefore not legitimate. This Daalder calls the denial of party argument. Secondly, the argument that some, but not all, parties are bad; the selective rejection of party argument. Here, Daalder concentrates on the classic division between party democracy/mass versus rational efficient/cadre parties where some scholars have argued that the latter parties have a better future than the former. The selective party rejection can, however, also apply to new versus

---

[1] Cf. Katz 1990, Katz and Mair 1992:1f, Lawson and Merkl 1988:3f, Blondel 1991.

[2] E.g. Kitschelt 1990.

[3] E.g. Müller-Rommel 1990.

old parties. The new politics parties which challenge the hegemony, style and principles of old parties are, after all, still parties. They reject old parties, but their alternatives are not to reject Party as a phenomenon, merely to renew that phenomenon. Third, that some party systems are good and others bad; the selective rejection of party system argument. The debate here has centred on the division between two-party and multiparty systems. Fourth, the redundancy of party argument, where parties are seen as outdated relics. They were relevant in a historically specific context, but in a long-term perspective no more than a transient phenomenon.[4]

In a very influential article, Richard Katz and Peter Mair argue that in the party crisis debate, the mass party model is often mistakenly used as the point of departure. Instead, the mass party was merely a passing phase in an ongoing process of party change. This process is only possible to understand if the relationship between the parties and the state is analysed. The Mass Party acted as a link between civil society and the state. The Mass Party was succeeded by the Catch-All Party, which acted as a broker between civil society and the state. The newest party type, the Cartel Party, has left all links with civil society and have penetrated the state to the extent that they have become "semi-state agencies".[5] At the same time there has been a collusion process among the established parties which have formed a cartel. The members of the cartel compete among each other, but only within certain limits. The losers are, partly due to the public subsidies, guaranteed a share of the spoils. The Cartel Parties, Katz and Mair argue, are subject to a challenge, but it is misconceived to call it a challenge against Party (i.e. political parties as a phenomenon). Rather, it is a challenge against the Cartel Parties.[6]

Thus, Katz and Mair do not reject all indications of a party crisis. What they deny is that parties as such are in crisis. They are open to the possibility of severe crisis for certain parties, or groups of parties. Indeed, their view on Cartel Parties is by no means uncritical. Their position touches on what Daalder would call a selective rejection of parties. This selective rejection could include most of the parties in a party system (but note that this is not the same as the rejection of the party system as such, it could be that a multiparty system in crisis would be fine with new or revitalised

---

[4] Daalder 1992. The article is a text version of the 1991 Stein Rokkan Lecture.

[5] Katz and Mair 1995:10-13, 16ff.

[6] Katz and Mair 1995:25.

parties). In this sense Katz and Mair come remarkably close to much of what has been said by those who argue the existence of a party crisis. Even if Party as such, or the structure of a party system, is not redundant or obsolete, the situation in a political system is still quite serious if most parties, especially the most powerful and influential parties, are subject to serious challenge. This is exactly what the emergence of Cartel Parties can lead to.

But how can it be analysed empirically if there is a party crisis? Those who argue the case of a party crisis base their argument on a variety of observations. Anders Håkansson argues that the Swedish parties are in crisis, using decreasing membership, activity, party identification and confidence in political institutions as evidence.[7] Other writers also point to increased electoral volatility and increased support for new parties or non-partisan organisations. Clearly, most signs of distrust in public institutions affect political parties to some extent. Parties are central in modern democracy and are consequently, directly or indirectly, affected by all problems for the democratic system.[8]

However, there is no unanimous agreement that there is a party crisis. It can be argued that despite parties being in decline in some respects, this is not the whole story. Against Håkansson's evidence, for example, it can be said that the parties are still able to mobilise critical resources. The growth of public subsidies to political parties which, after all, are decided by the parties themselves, is an example of how the parties have managed to secure their financial and, hence, organisational survival.[9] Some counter-arguments are based on alternative interpretations of the empirical evidence. Hermann Schmitt and Sören Holmberg have studied the development of party identification in Western Europe up to the 1990s, and find no evidence of a general and linear decline, although it is quite steep in some countries.[10] Others argue that the electoral volatility in West European party systems is

---

[7] Håkansson 1995. See also Bäck 1995, who argues that the Swedish parties are in crisis and suggests that the explanation could be connected to a crisis for the welfare state and representative democracy.

[8] E.g. Dalton, Flanagan and Beck 1984:451, 460, Dalton and Kuechler eds. 1990, Gilljam and Holmberg 1993:169-184, Gilljam and Holmberg 1995:85ff.

[9] Pierre and Widfeldt 1995.

[10] Schmitt and Holmberg 1995.

quite moderate and that the loss of support for some old parties and the rise of new parties are not drastic in a long-term perspective.[11]

Paul Webb argues that there are two basic aspects of party life that should be studied. First, the *legitimacy* of the parties. This he operationalises as the extent of party identification, electoral turnout and support for anti-system parties. The second aspect is *organisational strength*. Among the organisational indicators are the parties' ability to mobilise critical resources, such as finance and staff, and their capacity to use those resources according to the party's purposes. Membership strength is another indicator used by Webb, which he argues is relevant to the legitimacy as well as organisational aspect. Webb proceeds to use the indicators to test the British parties. The conclusion is that there is no unambiguous evidence of a party crisis in Britain. There are discomforting signs, such as a decline in membership and party identification. On the other hand, the British parties are still found to be strong enough to meet crucial demands of the political system such as decision making, recruitment and interest aggregation.[12]

The essence of Webb's argument is that demands such as these are crucial to the understanding of whether a party is in crisis. A party's popular legitimacy and organisational strength affect its ability to fulfil certain *functions* in a political system. Webb's conclusion is that although some doubt can be cast on, especially, the legitimacy of the British parties, they still seem capable of fulfilling crucial functions.[13]

Functions of political parties

The discussion about the functions of parties is not new. Even before the 'crisis of party' debate, the *raison d'être* of political parties has often been described in terms of functions. These functions are assumed to be crucial, or at least highly relevant, to the democratic nature of the political system. The term 'function' is problematic, however. Some writers use it because they employ a functionalist approach, while others do not. G. A. Almond and G. Bingham Powell belong to the former category. Their analysis includes the political system as a whole, in which a set of functions need to be

---

[11] Bartolini and Mair 1990, Maguire 1985.

[12] Webb 1995.

[13] Webb 1995:318f. Henry Bäck's argument that there is a party crisis in Sweden is also based on their problems to fulfil important functions. Bäck 1995.

fulfilled. Political parties perform some, but not all, of these functions. Moreover, parties are more important to some functions than others and, conversely, some of the functions attributed to parties are more central to the system than others.[14]

The functionalist approach is not without problems. One is that its focus is set on the functions as such, and/or the whole system, rather than the actual entities which perform the functions. The functions of parties can thus only be understood in relation to other functions and, above all, the complete set of functions in the whole system. Another criticism against the functionalist perspective is that it has a static or conservative bias, implying equilibrium or harmony.[15]

Paul Webb is aware of these problems and criticisms. Yet, he observes, political scientists remarkably often end up using the language of functionalism when dealing with comparative problems. His conclusion is that the functionalist approach is an invaluable analytical instrument in the context of party decline.[16] It is easy to agree with Webb on this point. The functionalist tradition has supplied concepts and tools which are difficult to overlook in any analysis of politics on a reasonably aggregated level. In practice it is quite difficult to discuss political parties and their relations to democracy without to some extent adopting functionalist language.

Does this mean that the functionalist approach as such is also adopted? Not necessarily. If functionalism is given a 'hard' definition, as a static system with a fixed set of functions which are intertwined in a pre-defined web of interdependence, then it seems as if some functionalist language can be accepted without the whole study being stamped as functionalist. It does not seem reasonable that the mere use of words like 'functions' should be exclusive to such a specific analytical approach. A looser definition, however, would mean that it is quite difficult to avoid being a functionalist as soon as reference is made to the system level. Then, on the other hand, most of the biggest problems with functionalism are avoided.

Thus, the perspective of this study is not one of 'strict functionalism'. It will be assumed that functions can be meaningfully understood on their own. It is not necessary to construct a grand system to discuss individual functions. Nor do all functions relevant to the system have to be taken into account in order to understand any individual function. Rather, the

---

14 Almond and Bingham Powell 1966:29, 114ff.

15 Almond and Bingham Powell 1966:12f.

16 Webb 1995:302.

perspective is one of 'mild functionalism'. Political parties are assumed to be actors which fulfil a number of functions in the system. These functions are important, but not necessarily crucial. There may also be other functions fulfilled by other actors. Thus, the functions fulfilled by parties are not necessarily sufficient to the understanding of the system. But they are sufficient to the understanding of the status of political parties in the system.[17]

But what are the functions of political parties? Many authors have come up with different suggestions and classifications. A summary of the party functions given by a number of political scientists can be found in Figure 2.1 below. The figure is not conclusive, as the authors who appear in it are by no means the only to have made the attempt to identify the functions fulfilled by parties. However, it does illustrate the lack of consensus among different writers.

It will not be attempted here to bring the jungle of party functions into order, even if this would be a justifiable exercise in its own right. A possible reason for the diversity is that the authors have varying purposes with their listing of functions. It may be noted, however, that in some cases, very little space is spent on elaborating and arguing for the choice of functions.

One lesson from the figure is that the majority of functions are in some way related to establishing and maintaining connections between civil society and the state. Such connections are often referred to as political linkage. Linkage is given as a function in its own right by W. E. Wright, but is implicit in many of the other functions, such as representation, interest articulation and aggregation, participation and legitimisation. Linkage can thus be seen as a meta-function of political parties. And the debate about party crisis, or decline, is to a large extent focused on whether there has been a decline in the parties' ability to provide linkage.

---

[17] The use of the word 'actors' leads to another semantic trap. Here, 'actor' is merely used as a means to indicate an agent; somebody or something which does something. In no way does this mean a standpoint on the actor-structure problem, nor does it imply the adoption of the actor-structure approach. Cf. Pierre 1986:21, who refers to parties as structures, but also as actors, in the political system.

Figure 2.1   Functions of political parties, as given by seven political scientists

Almond & B. Powell	Wright	Sartori	Panebianco	von Beyme	Pierre	Duverger
Interest articulation	Goal definition	Channelment	Selection of office holders	Interest articulation and aggregation	Policy formulation	Representation of opinion
Interest aggregation	Representation	Expression	Integration and expression	Goal identification	Candidate nomination	Choice of rulers
Recruitment	Government	Communication	Participation	Elite recruitment and government formation	Legitimisation	Structure of government
Socialisation	Linkage			Mobilisation and socialisation	Socialisation	
				Voter mobilisation		

Sources: Almond and Bingham Powell 1966:29, 73, 98 and 118-121; Wright 1971:20-32; Sartori 1976:37-67; Panebianco 1988:267ff, 312; von Beyme 1985:13; Pierre 1986:21f; Duverger 1951/1964 353ff, 272ff and 392ff.

Political linkage

The concept of linkage appears frequently in political science but its use is somewhat confusing. Most authors use the concept to indicate some sort of a bond between the political establishment and the general public. The term linkage is derived from the word link, meaning something which connects two other parts. A linkage is a system of links or a connecting relationship. In other words something which connects, or establishes a relationship between, two other entities.

But what is political linkage? Just as with party functions, there are several suggestions on offer. In Wright's words, linkage is playing the role "as intermediaries linking citizens with government." Similarly, Hans-Dieter Klingemann and Dieter Fuchs refer to "(T)he linkages between citizens and the state established by political parties and interest groups." V. O. Key speaks of linkage as the "interplay... between mass opinion and government". Richard Katz suggests two types of linkage between citizens and the state: a channel of communication and an outlet for activity. Sigmund Neumann, as quoted by Wright, speaks of links between social forces and ideologies and official government institutions.[18]

An elaborated discussion on the concept of linkage is provided by Kay Lawson. By quoting James Rosenau, she starts out by stating that political links "take place between different levels of aggregation". An aggregational level can be a geographical unit but also an organisation.[19] Lawson also argues that the empirical case studies of the anthology reminds us that political linkage is always between senior and junior levels; "e.g. the individual and the party, the party and the state and the individual and the state".[20] She adds that linkage is a "connection, usually with a connotation of interaction".[21]

Linkage takes place via intermediaries. Examples are plenty: elections, opinion polls and various forms of organisations, among them political parties. Political parties are the most important intermediaries -- they are subsumed in or relevant to all the other examples. According to Lawson, the whole raison d'étre of political parties is to provide linkage.[22]

Lawson identifies four main types of linkage which are relevant for political parties. Participatory, where the party gets citizens actively involved in government related activities. Electoral, where the party can be controlled by the citizens via elections. Clientilistic linkage, where the party is a channel for the exchange of votes for favours or services. And finally directive linkage, where the party is an agent on behalf of the government to control citizens' behaviour, via coercive or educational methods.[23]

The last two types of linkage are problematic. The clientilistic linkage is restricted in two senses. First, it only concerns those among the electorate who are involved in the clientilistic deal, that is, the favours on offer for the exchange of votes. Second, it only refers to the favours or services which are included in the deal. Once in office, the elected decision makers will be totally unrestricted in everything which is not included in the deal. The directive linkage is also a problem. Of the four types outlined by Lawson, it is the only one without any kind of mutuality to it. Thus it is

---

[18] Wright 1971:26; Fuchs and Klingemann 1995:1; Key 1967:411; Katz 1990:159.

[19] Lawson 1988:14f.

[20] Lawson 1988:32.

[21] Lawson 1988:14.

[22] Lawson 1988:14ff.

[23] Lawson 1988:16ff.

questionable whether the clientilistic and directive linkage types are applicable to a democratic political system.

But the other two are directly relevant. The participatory linkage is by many seen as very important in a democracy. Lack of participation in political activities is by many given as an indicator that the democratic system is in crisis.[24] The electoral linkage is also central. All democratic systems, presidential or parliamentary, are ruled by elected office holders or assemblies. These office holders and assemblies are elected representatives which are provided by the political parties. The term would therefore be more useful if it was renamed representative linkage.

Thus, two main types of linkage provided by parties in a democracy have been identified: participatory and representative.[25] In the previous chapter, it was argued that by being open membership organisations, political parties provide an outlet for political activity. However, political parties have become closely associated with representative rather than direct democracy. Indeed, they were often formed as organisations with the purpose to supply citizens with representatives to vote for. Whether starting as groups of already elected parliamentarians or as popular movements outside legislative assemblies, political parties tended to work as primarily representative organisations from the very start. That is a situation which, if anything, has become more accentuated since. The success and failure of a political party is very much judged in relation to its electoral results. Furthermore, most parties tend to be internally organised according to the principle of representation. Internally democratic parties can be likened to representative political systems in miniature.

Although political parties have become closely connected to representation, this is not the whole truth, however. First, there are several cases of parties which adopted the representative principle without whole-heartedly supporting it. Socialist, and especially communist, parties are one example. Their eventual adherence to representative democracy often came as a gradual, sometimes very reluctant process. In many cases, the reasons were mainly tactical. And in recent years, parties given the collective label 'new politics' base a large part of their ideology on scepticism against representation and preference to direct democratic methods.

---

[24] E.g. Dalton 1996, Dalton and Kuechler eds. 1990.

[25] Note that both representation and participation are included among the party functions in Figure 2.1.

Second, it should be noted that the one direct method which has prevailed in the constitutions of several representative democracies, the popular referendum, has in practice proved to be compatible with, rather than an alternative to, the existence of strong political parties. Parties have often actively taken part in referendum campaigns, using their resources to advocate one of the alternatives. Indeed, parties have often worked hard to make a referendum take place.[26]

Third, as was also argued in Chapter 1, the parties can offer direct democratic connections with the ruling élites if they offer citizens the opportunity to participate. Thus, although parties are most commonly associated with representative democracy, there is no inherent conflict between direct democracy and parties. Such a conflict has existed in many historical situations but this does not bear general significance.

Lawson draws some conclusions on how the organisation of a particular party is related to the type of linkage the party prioritises. A party with emphasis on participatory linkage is internally democratic and grass roots oriented. A party which emphasises the representative linkage is organised in more of a top-down fashion: the party leadership is in control of the party and party activists are only used for vote-maximising purposes.[27] The parallel with Wright's distinction between rational-efficient and party-democracy parties is obvious. But many of the writers who distinguish among party types, notably Wright and Epstein, do not make the distinction with a linkage perspective in mind. Their main concern is which type of organisation is the most useful when it comes to maximising the number of votes.[28]

Linkage and democracy

Is it necessary for the parties to be membership organisations to provide political linkage? It should be clarified that by membership we mean formal, but open and voluntary membership. Without this clarification the question would be trivial; no party is completely without members. But the point is that any grown-up person should be able to join if he/she agrees with the ideas of the party.

---

[26] Holmberg and Asp 1984, Butler and Kitzinger 1976, Molin 1965.

[27] Lawson 1988:16f.

[28] Epstein 1967, Wright 1971.

According to the Competitive Elite Democracy Model discussed in Chapter 1, open membership party organisations and grass root participation are counter-productive because they entail the risk of exacerbated social conflict. Ordinary citizens should be able to choose between and elect governments but apart from that be politically passive.[29] According to this reasoning, parties provide linkage by presenting candidates and policies to the voters so that they are better informed when going to the polls. The parties provide representative linkage which, furthermore, is very limited between election campaigns.

But according to the Participatory Democracy Model, open membership parties are valuable. Here, party membership is a means for ordinary citizens to become involved in politics more directly and not only at elections; they can influence the party and prevent it from being entirely ruled by small élites. In this perspective, parties are important to the extent that they offer open, internally democratic membership organisations which anyone interested is free to join; thus they provide participatory linkage. And if any combination between the 'pure' participatory and competitive elite models is allowed, participation becomes a vital part, as exemplified in Lewin's interactive model (see Chapter 1 above).

A party provides participatory linkage to the extent that citizens can influence the party by participating in internal party business rather than merely via the ballot box. A party provides representative linkage to the extent that it takes the interests and opinions of its voters into consideration in its decisions.

In the real world, participatory and representative linkages converge. Parties provide both types, even if it may vary among parties and over time. Internally, parties tend to be organised according to the principle of representation and their activity is to a great extent focused on working in representative institutions. It is however, possible to participate in representative organisations. The more open political organisations and institutions are to public participation, the higher the degree of participation in democracy, even if the organisations or institutions are organised according to the principle of representation and the entire political system is based on the principle of representative democracy.

---

[29] Cf. Schumpeter 1942/1952, Berelson, Lazarsfeld and McPhee 1954/1986:309f and Lewin 1970:19ff.

Conditions for linkage

The remainder of the chapter will outline the structure of this study. A number of conditions for political linkage, relevant to political parties, will be identified. These conditions determine whether a party, as an open and voluntary membership organisation, is able to provide linkage between citizens and the state. The conditions will each be tested empirically.

The first condition can be labelled the *openness* of the party. It should be open to join for all citizens. Some restrictions may be necessary, for example that the members must be adults, that simultaneous membership of another party is forbidden and that the member is obliged to pay dues. But the principle should be that there are no severe restrictions or commitments necessary to become a member; no requirements of competence or activity, for example obligations to engage in pre-defined party activities.

A closed or restricted membership means that the party is only open to select individuals. Such a party could be the original Duvergerian cadre party where membership is only available to selected élites. It could also be a closed party of the 'vanguard', or 'devotee', type where the members are seen as particularly initiated and dedicated people whose task is to lead the masses. Examples have existed on the far left as well as the far right.[30]

Second, the party should allow *membership influence*. Otherwise the fact that it is open for the public to join is of little use. The reasoning is that it gives citizens a wider variety of arenas to express their views and to influence decisions than if the parties were closed organisations. Given the centrality of parties in modern democracies, it enhances popular participation in politics if the citizens can take part in party business.

The openness and membership influence are aspects of the formal organisational structure of the party and can be regarded as prerequisites to both participatory and representative linkage. If a party is not open and with opportunities for all members to have influence, the subsequent conditions are irrelevant. It is not an open membership party and therefore not of interest to this study. These two prerequisites are also indicators of the intentions of the party. The openness of its membership and the degree of internal democracy are determined by the party rules, and can therefore be influenced by the party itself. If either, or both, are not present, it can be

---

[30] Duverger 1951/1964:70-74.

assumed that the party does not want to be an open membership organisation.

It should be pointed out that it is potential rather than actual openness and membership influence that will be investigated. No attempt will be made to test whether the formal preconditions, as defined in the party rules, mean that the parties are *de facto* open and internally democratic. But this empirical investigation into the formal party rules will provide an insight into the intentions of the parties to provide participatory linkage, and whether the conditions for political participation via political parties are at hand.

Thus, the two first conditions are applicable to both participatory and representative linkage. The remaining conditions, however, are specific to one or the other. We begin with the conditions for participatory linkage. The first two are *membership strength* and *activity*. If nobody wants to join the party, or if the members remain passive, it is difficult to see how it can provide participatory linkage. It is there for the taking, but the people do not seem bothered. If the party is open and democratic, this is a failure because it wants to be an organisation based on a large membership. It can also be a failure in other ways, for example because the party needs the revenue from the membership, or the legitimacy of grass roots connections.[31]

The party's members and activists also need to be *socially representative*. If the number of members and activists refers to the ability to attract members at all, this refers to the ability to attract the 'right' members. The reasoning is that the party is failing to provide participatory linkage if the members come from social groups different to the composition of its voters or supporters. This is not to say that social representativeness is a prerequisite to political representation. But it is to say that if the social characteristics of those that join the party are markedly different to those of the party's supporters, the party has failed to provide those societal groups with participatory linkage.

The conditions required for representative linkage are different. Here, it is not the amount of popular participation in a party which is important, but the extent to which the party, as an open membership organisation, represents its voters. Therefore, membership strength and activity are not necessary conditions. The important thing is that the members who are there make sure that the party provides representative linkage. This may seem unsatisfactory, but it should be borne in mind that

---

[31] Susan Scarrow's study shows that the legitimacy aspect turns is a very important reason why leading party officials appreciate the value of the party members. Scarrow 1996.

the study is concerned with both participatory and representative linkage, and the linkage performance of a political party can only be understood in the context of a combination of the two. All is not well if a party provides participatory but not representative linkage, and vice versa.

Social representativeness has already been dealt with in the discussion about participatory linkage. It can also be argued for as an aspect of representative linkage. There are three main arguments.[32] First, the equity argument, which states that all social groups should have equal opportunity to be represented. If a group is underrepresented among party members, it is unfair to that group. Second, the life experience argument, according to which representatives have a better understanding of the needs of people of the same social group because they share similar life experiences. This does not necessarily mean that the representative holds the same opinions as the represented, but the assumption is that the decisions of the former will be based on an understanding of the situation of the latter. Finally, the prerequisite argument, which holds that similarity in social position is a prerequisite to similarity of opinion.[33]

As social representativeness has already been included as a condition for participatory linkage, it will be tested and can therefore be interpreted in representative linkage terms according to the three arguments just mentioned. However, in this study social representativeness will not be considered a condition for representative linkage. The equity argument is already accounted for in the discussion about participatory linkage. The life experience argument can be questioned on grounds of competence. Are people with low education necessarily best represented by other uneducated people? The prerequisite argument is based on an assumption about reality which can be empirically tested. There is little empirical support for the assumption that social representativeness goes hand in hand with opinion representativeness.[34] Thus, the argument is not that social representativeness is an irrelevant as a condition for linkage, but that it is relevant to participatory rather than to representative linkage.

---

[32] Cf. Holmberg and Esaiasson 1988:135f.

[33] Knut Heidar has presented three arguments for the democratic importance of similarity in socio-demographic background between the elite and the electorate: 1) it may encourage participation from low-mobilised groups, 2) it may improve representativeness in terms of opinion and 3) it may contribute to system legitimacy. Heidar 1986:281.

[34] Esaiasson and Holmberg 1996:99f, Widfeldt 1995.

Representativeness in terms of similarity in opinion is by many seen as indispensable in a democratic system which to a great extent is based on representation. Again, counter-arguments tend to be based on the notion of a gap in competence between the representatives and the represented. For example, it can be argued that politicians are better informed about the problems and technicalities of an issue, or that popular opinions are lacking in transitivity; internally conflicting opinions may be simultaneously held by the same person(s). Then again, it can be argued that there has been an increase in the general level of education which has led to increased political competence among the general public. As a consequence opinion representativeness is, if anything, becoming a more relevant to representative linkage.[35] *Opinion representativeness* thus becomes a condition for representative linkage.

The thus outlined conditions for the two kinds of linkage are summarised in Figure 2.2 below. It should be noted that for a party to provide either type of linkage *all* conditions given as necessary in the respective column, have to be met.

Figure 2.2   Conditions for political parties to provide participatory and representative linkage

	Participatory linkage	**Representative linkage**
Openness	necessary	necessary
Internal membership influence	necessary	necessary
Membership strength	necessary	not necessary
Membership activity	necessary	not necessary
Social representativeness	necessary	not necessary
Opinion representativeness	not necessary	necessary

---

[35] This discussion is centred on opinion representativeness as similarity in opinion between representatives and represented at the same time point. This is a simplification, as representation can also involve a time dimension. The representatives can follow the opinions of the represented, but also act as opinion leaders where their opinions will only after some time be adopted by the represented. This will be discussed further, and taken into account in the analysis, in Chapter 8.

The research problem

The purpose of this study is to examine to what extent the Swedish parties have provided participatory and representative linkage between 1960 and 1997. This examination will be structured according to the conditions for linkage given in Figure 2.2. But according to which criteria can linkage performance be assessed? How can we say whether a party has failed to provide linkage? In Lawson and Merkl's mentioned anthology on party failure, some contributors define failure as decreased support for a party. Others set the criterion much harder. According to Mackie and Rose, a party must have disappeared completely to be a failure.[36]

This is a discussion related to the party crisis debate. The concept of crisis would imply that there is a critical level at which, when reached, there is party crisis. Very few attempts have been made to establish where this level is. Most writers tend to use decline and crisis as synonyms. When it is claimed that parties are in crisis, it is usually based on the allegation that parties have declined in some vital aspects over time. This is of course a simplification; a decline is not necessarily sharp enough to reach the level of crisis. In this study, the focus will be set on decline. This does not mean that decline is considered as synonymous with crisis. What it does mean is that the study is focused on decline rather than crisis. The reason for this is the problems with the concept of crisis, and the difficulty in establishing what should be regarded as the critical levels of the conditions for linkage in Figure 2.2, such as membership strength.

The research problem of this study is, consequently, to seek to establish whether there has been a *linkage decline* for the Swedish parties, according to the conditions for linkage in Figure 2.2. Have the parties become less open? Has the membership influence declined? Have the parties lost members and activists? Have the members and activists become less representative? It should be pointed out that decline will be treated as a discrete dichotomy -- decline or no decline. The conclusions in this study will be based on whether there has, or has not, been a decline in the conditions for linkage. More elaborated observations will be made in the separate chapters where the findings will be presented in detail.

The study deals with the Swedish parties. It is acknowledged that the ideal would be a broad comparative study of the linkage performance of

---

[36] Lawson and Merkl, eds., 1988.

political parties. Each chapter will be concluded with a comparative outlook into what is known about relevant developments in parties in other European countries. These observations are not systematic, and primarily included to add to the descriptive value of the study. They could also to some extent serve to control for any possible Swedish bias in the interpretations of the results. Hopefully, however, together with future studies on other nations, this book could still turn out to be of comparative value.

Nevertheless, Sweden is a suitable case for a study like this. The political parties play an important role in the policy process but also have strong traditional connections with civil society. The Swedish society has a reputation for an organisational and collectivist culture, where the parties have been an integral part. The political parties, notably the dominant Social Democrats, have strong traditional connections with organised interests as well as civil society.[37] Sweden is also known for its large public sector and extensive welfare state.[38]

However, in all of these respects the situation has changed. The welfare state has to an increasing extent been criticised and debated since, at least, the early 1980s. In the 1990s, economic difficulties in the shape of huge fiscal deficits and a galloping national debt have led to a dismantling of the welfare state. At the same time, the size and role of the public sector has also been subject to debate and changes. In both these respects, the Social Democratic Party has reassessed much of its traditional policies. In connection herewith, the party has been heavily criticised by its traditional allies among the organised interests.[39]

The Swedish party system has traditionally been regarded as one of the most stable in Europe. But in the 1980s and 1990s this has changed. Since 1988, three new parties have obtained parliamentary status.[40] Voter volatility has increased and party identification has decreased. Popular confidence in politicians has plummeted.[41] The parties themselves have also changed. In the mid 1960s, state subsidies to both the parliamentary and

---

[37] For an elaboration of these arguments, see Pierre and Widfeldt 1994, especially pp. 332-336. See also Berglund and Lindström 1978.

[38] See, for example, Childs 1936/1948, Elder, Thomas and Arter 1988, Heclo and Madsen 1987 and Milner 1990.

[39] Recent developments in the Social Democratic Party are discussed in Arter 1994.

[40] Even if one of them, the populist New Democracy, lost its parliamentary status after one election period, and has since lost all political and electoral significance.

[41] Gilljam and Holmberg 1995:37-45, 66-73, 85ff.

extra-parliamentary organisations were introduced. These subsidies have subsequently increased enormously, and been complemented with local and regional party subsidies.[42] This would suggest that the parties themselves no longer see the same need for members as before, as they are not to the same extent financially dependent on them. Indeed, one of the main factors Katz and Mair claim to be behind the development into Cartel Parties is their increased financial dependence on the state.

The development just sketched reinforces the argument that Sweden is a suitable test case for a study of linkage decline. The expectation would be that there has been some decline in the linkage conditions which appear in Figure 2.2. The subsidies to parties would suggest that the parties have seen no reason to recruit members or to give their members much influence. The decreased party identification and increased distrust in politicians would suggest that people in general are less interested in joining parties. Both these factors suggest that those who, despite everything, are party members, have become less representative of the public.

The time frame is between 1960 and the mid 1990s. Some data stretch up to 1994, in other cases it has been possible to get information up to and including 1997. This time frame covers the research problem of the study quite well. In 1960, the parties, the party system and the Swedish political system all conformed to the 'ideal' or traditional model, and the changes had clearly manifested themselves by the mid 1990s.[43]

A total of eight parties will be considered: The Social Democrats, the Left Party, The Centre Party, the People's Party Liberals, The Moderate Party, The Christian Democrats, the Green Party and New Democracy. These parties are presented in more detail, with their names in Swedish (including any previous names), origins and ideology, in Appendix I. For simplicity, all the studied parties will consistently be referred to under one name, even though some parties have changed names during the research period. The included parties have been chosen because they are the ones who have been represented in the Swedish Riksdag between 1960 and 1994.[44]

---

[42] Gidlund 1991.

[43] In some cases, data limitations mean that the starting point has to be moved forward in time several years.

[44] There are two other parties which could have been added to this list. Citizen's Coalition (*Medborgerlig Samling*) gained three seats in 1964. However, this was a coalition between the Centre, Moderate and People's Party Liberals rather than an independent party. Of their three elected MPs, two immediately joined the party fractions of their respective original

Outline of the study

The empirical evidence of the developments in the conditions for linkage will be presented in five chapters. Chapter 3 deals with the internal structure of the parties. The openness of membership (the amount of restrictions and demands on new and existing members) will be studied, as well as the influence of the rank-and-file members in the party organisations. This will be based on an analysis of the party rules.

Chapter 4 looks into the membership development of the parties and in the nation as a whole. Two types of source will be used: the parties' own membership statistics, and survey data where respondents have been asked whether they are members of a political party and, if yes, which party. A related condition for linkage is the number of active members in a party. This will be the subject of Chapter 5 which, however, does not cover the entire research period, as comparable data only exist from 1979 onwards.

Chapter 6 discusses the relationship between membership development and a number of background factors (party vote, incumbency, election year cycles and membership influence). This chapter is slightly separate from the other empirical chapters, as it does not test any of the conditions for linkage which appear in Figure 2.2. However, it will provide additional information about the development of participatory linkage. Is, for example, a party's participatory linkage closely connected to the party's popularity (as manifested in the party's electoral success)? And do government parties tend to be more or less participatory than opposition parties?

Chapter 7 deals with social representativeness and presents the development among party members and activists in terms of gender, age, education and social class. It will be entirely based on survey data. This is the final chapter dealing with participatory linkage. Chapter 8 will be focused on representative linkage. The evidence presented is the development of ideological representativeness of party members and activists. Again, the source will be survey data.

Finally, Chapter 9 will summarise and systematise the findings from Chapters 3,4,5,7 and 8. Based on the results, it will be determined whether there has been a decline in the linkage performance of the Swedish parties.

---

parties. The second example is the Worker's Party Communists (*Arbetarpartiet Kommunisterna*) which split from the Left Party in 1977 and was joined by two parliamentarians who had been elected as Left Party members. The two seats were lost in the next election in 1979, and the party has never won any seats of its own strength. ,

The conclusion will be made on party level as well as on the national level. The development among the different parties will be used as evidence of whether an individual party has suffered a linkage decline. The combined party evidence will be used to determine whether such a decline can be attributed to the Swedish party system as a whole.

The data will be presented and discussed at the beginning of each chapter. Most of the survey data used will be taken from the Swedish Election Studies. Thus, a great part of this study will be based on secondary analysis of material collected for more general purposes than the study of party membership. Still, the Election Studies provide a unique collection of data which allows a wide variety of secondary analysis. In addition, official party documents will be used. Chapter 3 will primarily be based on the printed party rules. Chapter 4 will partly use annual reports of the parties which include membership figures. The majority of these documents were collected in connection with the comparative Party Organisation project, led by Richard Katz and Peter Mair.

3 The Parties' Internal Structure: Openness and Membership Influence

Introduction

"The most important reason to become a member of a political party is the ambition to influence politics and society".[1] This declaration is to be found in an organisational programme published by the Social Democratic party in 1989, below the headline "Increase membership influence!".[2] Such a view on membership is not unique to the Social Democrats. In an organisational handbook for party activists and employees, the People's Party Liberals state that the party members should be able to directly influence local as well as national politics.[3] At least on the face of it, most major Swedish parties seem to adhere to this view.[4]

This chapter will investigate whether the commitment to membership influence is mere lip service or if it is reflected in the organisational structures of the Swedish parties. The way the parties are organised reflect their ambitions and ability to provide participatory linkage. The normative aspects of the internal structures of political parties have been subjected to much scholarly debate. It is not a controversial statement that the general political system should be democratic. But it does not necessarily follow from this that political parties should be internally democratic.

The debate has been summarised in an article by Jan Assarsson, who has referred to the problem of internal party democracy as 'the micro

---

[1] "*Folk i rörelse*", (Proposal to organisational manifesto presented to 1990 Party Congress), Swedish Social Democratic Party 1989, p. 25.

[2] See note 1 above.

[3] "*Politik i praktiken*", (Organisational handbook, third edition), People's Party Liberals 1984, p. 11.

[4] Left Party: "*Organisationsöversyn, maj 1992*" (internal organisational report) 1992; Green Party: "*Lilla gröna*" (Handbook) 1987, p. 152 and Moderate Party: Albinsson 1986:174f.

problem of macro democracy'.[5] From the academic debate, Assarsson has identified five arguments for and five arguments against democracy being appropriate in party organisations. The first argument for, is that internal party democracy is a way of providing citizens with democratic education and that the parties can act as democratic examples. Second, that a system of accountability for leaders in the parties is a complement to the accountability of political leaders in the general political system. Public debates and discussions inside parties can provide a means to external scrutiny of political leaders. Third, internal democracy will enhance the legitimacy of the parties. Fourth, internally democratic parties can be argued to be the best way of providing citizens with opportunities for political participation. Fifth, it can help provide citizens with interest articulation. Using Hirschman's vocabulary, voters can do little more than exiting from one party to another via the ballot box. Internal party democracy, however, provides a voice mechanism to those who join a party.

The arguments against internal democracy are as follows: First, that it will harm the necessary efficiency of the party leadership. Second, it is argued by adherents to the competitive élite democracy model, that internally democratic parties could constrain the freedom of movement for the party leaderships who are thus unable to compete freely with each other. Third, there can be a conflict between the party leaders' accountability to party members and their accountability to voters. Fourth, it is argued that party activists are often not representative of the public which means that internal democracy could lead to extreme policies. The fifth and final argument is based on the assumption that parties fulfil limited functions in the political system; mainly the structuring of the votes. The functions fulfilled by internally democratic parties, for example policy making and articulation of opinion, should be assumed by other organisations than parties (such as interest organisations and the media) in order for the system to be pluralistic.[6]

Assarsson observes that arguments against internal party democracy tend to be based on a systems perspective, where the emphasis is on interactions between different structures and rather little attention is paid to what takes place inside these structures. Arguments in favour of

---

[5] In Swedish: "*makrodemokratins mikroproblem*", Assarsson 1993:40.

[6] Assarsson 1993:42-53. The arguments, summarised in his article in a figure on p. 50, are not Assarsson's own but from other writers cited by Assarsson.

internal party democracy, on the other hand, tend to be oriented towards the level of the individual.[7]

Democracy in organisations, such as parties, is a peculiar matter with some similarities, but also important differences, to societal democracy. Organisations face similar democratic dilemmas as society, like direct versus representative democracy, and majority rule versus the protection of minorities. At the same time the solutions of these dilemmas must be found in different contexts. An organisation is more free to define its own solution to democratic dilemmas. Many organisations, like commercial industries, do not have to be democratic at all. In political organisations, however, that freedom is constrained. It would be problematic for organisations which work inside a broader democratic context to be undemocratic. There is also freedom in the other direction, however. So long as the deviation from the prevailing style of societal democracy is not perceived as undemocratic, the organisation can, for example, put more emphasis on direct democracy than on representation.

Commercial industries can have a lot in common with political organisations. For example, their respective internal power relations and decision-making processes can often be analogous.[8] There are also obvious similarities between profit-maximising in industries and the vote-maximising often attributed to political parties.

One type of organisation, the trade union, has been subject to a great deal of analysis.[9] Political parties, however have one characteristic which makes them unique among organisations -- they are based on two different and distinguishable groups, their members and their voters. And if a party comes to power, it has to cater for the interests of the whole nation.[10] As a consequence of this, it has been argued that internal party democracy is not compatible with societal democracy, because the party members are not representative.[11] Whether that applies to the Swedish parties will be investigated in Chapter 8 about representative linkage.

Jon Pierre has identified three main schools of thought with regard to the definition of internal party democracy.[12] First, those who focus on

---

[7] Assarsson 1993:50f.

[8] Morgan 1986, esp. p 145.

[9] For example Lewin 1977.

[10] Pierre 1986:57f.

[11] McKenzie 1982:195.

[12] Pierre 1986:57f.

the decision-making process. Robert Michels based his critical arguments on the fact that formally democratic processes were distorted by informal power structures and resources which benefited leading groups. His focus was on the decision making processes in the party and the discrepancy between formal rules and actual power relations. According to Wellhofer and Hennessey, however, one problem with Michels's approach is that he did not see the distinction between members and voters as problematic. From a Marxist perspective, he postulated that the masses were organised in a party whose members thus comprised the masses; those not in the party were class enemies.[13]

The second perspective is related to the first, but concentrates on the contents of the decisions instead of the procedures. The important thing here is whether a certain decision reflects the members' opinions, regardless of how the decision has been taken. The third perspective does not so much concentrate on the decisions as on the representativeness of leading persons. If they are representative, their actions are assumed to be responsive.[14]

Desirable or not, many writers have expressed pessimism with regard to whether internal party democracy is a realistic ambition. Michels is a classic example. His conclusion is almost one of despair: "The oligarchical structure of the building suffocates the basic democratic principle." This oligarchical determinism does not exist despite democracy; instead it is a consequence of democracy. Democratically elected leaders become oligarchs.[15] Despite a largely different perspective, Maurice Duverger agrees with this view to some extent. The leadership of political parties is the same as in other organisations "it is democratic in appearance and oligarchic in reality". Duverger, however, does not deplore this. He merely notes that the practical efficiency of electoral competition gives the party leaderships little choice.[16]

In a critical article, John D. May has powerfully argued against the pessimistic determinism of Michels. A major criticism is that Michels treats democracy as an absolute concept, where an organisation, or a nation, is either democratic or undemocratic -- there are no possible intermediate positions. Thus, Michels's framework does not allow for

---

[13] Wellhofer and Hennessey 1974:280ff.

[14] See also Lewin 1977:79.

[15] Michels 1915/1968:365.

[16] Duverger 1951/1964:133f. The quote is from p. 133.

relative democratisation although, May argues, much of the empirical evidence in Michels's study of the German Social Democratic Party showed that the party had been democratised.[17]

This is not the place to make an authoritative judgement on the advantages and disadvantages of internal party democracy and its relation to societal democracy. However, it is an important factor if the parties are to be able to provide participatory linkage. If party members, as was stated by the Social Democratic Party in the quote at the beginning of this chapter, have joined parties primarily because they want to influence society, then internal party democracy is a necessary requirement.

Democracy is a multi faceted concept, however. Assarsson discusses three possible definitions of democracy and their applicability to political parties: democracy as individual rights and freedoms, direct democracy and representative democracy. He argues that democracy defined as individual rights and freedoms is not applicable to parties. This is because party membership, unlike citizenship, is voluntary. It is possible to exit from a party. If, for example, a party member is constrained in his/her expression of political opinions in the party, it does not stop him/her from expressing those opinions somewhere else, even if it in effect means that the member has to leave the party.[18] The second definition of democracy, direct democracy, is rejected as inapplicable to parties for practical reasons. It is not practically possible to let all members participate in every party decision.[19]

The third democracy definition, however, representative democracy, is considered more applicable. Still, representative democracy is in itself not a straightforward concept. There are three main models of representative democracy; the competitive élite model, the opinion representative leadership model, and the accountable leadership model. Assarsson concludes, somewhat cautiously, that the last of the three models is best suited for political parties.[20]

Again, the concept of democracy has shown its complicated nature. It is very difficult to decide which type of democracy is best suited for political parties. Fortunately, this is a hurdle which can be cleared. In order to analyse the internal structure of the parties, and its relevance to their ability to provide participatory linkage, it is possible to limit the discussion.

---

[17] May 1965:418f.

[18] Assarsson 1993:54.

[19] Assarsson 1993:55.

[20] Assarsson 1993:57-62.

In order for parties to provide participatory linkage, two aspects of party organisation are of particular importance. First, there should be no or few restrictions on membership. If it is very difficult or costly to become or to stay a party member, the parties cannot be assumed to be particularly interested in providing participatory linkage. This will be referred to as the *openness* of the parties.

Second, the members must have some *influence* in the party organisation. Membership influence can be of two kinds. On the one hand, the influence could be limited to the selection of leading party officials. This would be close to the accountability view on representation, where leaders are held to account by the members at the time of their re-election, but where members have no other influence on party matters. However, there is no contradiction in also allowing for some membership influence on matters other than leadership selections. The extent of such influence may vary, as may also the way in which it can take place. However, besides being able to elect the leaders, it can be seen as a complement if the members also have some impact on the leaders' freedom of movement between the internal party elections. This possibility is an important difference between internal party democracy and societal democracy, but can be viewed as an extra right to party members because they voluntarily, and at a cost, have decided to become party members.

Data and method

In line with the entire study the focus will be on development over time. The purpose is to see whether or not there has been a decline in openness and membership influence in the Swedish parties. Both openness and influence will be studied according to a formal, *de jure* definition. With the lengthy time perspective of this study it will not be possible to probe into the real story behind the party rules. There is no doubt that a more profound insight into the real world inside the parties would have provided very valuable additional information. Time and resources have not permitted such an approach, although it is hoped that studies such as those done on the British political parties can soon also be conducted among members of the parties in Sweden.[21]

There are, however, arguments in favour of the formal rules being relevant to the purposes of this study. Richard Katz and Peter Mair have

---

[21] Seyd and Whiteley 1992, Whiteley, Seyd and Richardson 1994.

outlined convincing arguments in favour of the relevance of the formal side of party organisations, which they refer to as the 'official story' of the party in question. First, the official story is important in its own right. While it can be argued that it does not tell the whole story of internal party life, it certainly tells a valid part of the story. The party rules are one of the factors which determine the nature of internal party struggles.

Second, the formal organisation reflects the power balance within the party in the sense that a shift in that balance can be expected to manifest itself as formal organisational changes. Conversely, the party rules constitute a resource in internal party struggles, so that the control of rule-making can become a part of such struggles. "For these reasons", Katz and Mair argue, "a reading of the party rules and statutes, rather like a reading of the formal constitution in a national political system, offers a fundamental and indispensable guide to the character of a given party".[22]

The argument can be extended to the analysis of participatory linkage. If the party rules display a high degree of openness and membership influence it is not a trivial finding, because a) it is an indicator of the intentions of the dominant forces in the party, and b) like all constitutions they define certain procedural criteria which cannot be violated. As Katz and Mair point out, the party rules have often been subject to fierce internal party struggles, which can only be interpreted as the participating factions consider the rules to be important. Furthermore, in nations like Sweden, where parties are subject to very little public legislation or control, there is no formal way of stopping parties from adopting rules with a low degree of openness and a low degree of membership influence, if they so wish.

This means that the evidence presented will almost exclusively be based on the official rules (in Swedish "*partistadgar*") of the respective parties. Other sources will sometimes be referred to for additional information, but the substantive part of this chapter is based on the letter of the rules. It has been possible to locate the rules for every party since 1960 with a few exceptions. The Moderate Party rules of 1950, which were in operation until 1964, have not been found. The nearest document is a proposal from 1949 by an internal committee which includes an outline of new rules to be taken by the 1950 congress. The situation up to 1964 is based on this document and also on Per Albinsson's study of the Moderate

---

[22] Katz and Mair 1992:6f. The quote is on p. 7.

Party.[23] The situation is similar in the People's Party Liberals, where it has not been possible to find official printed party rules before 1964. An internal document from 1960 with proposed rule changes is used instead.

A few presentational details need to be clarified. Party rules in Sweden are presented as a number of so-called 'paragraphs', with the symbol §. A paragraph is usually sub-divided into a number of 'sections'. References in this chapter will be made to PR (short for Party Rules), the paragraph (the symbol § will always be used) and usually also the 'section' (abbreviated 'sect.').

The time frame in this chapter is 1960 to 1994. In line with the purpose of the book, to show the development over time, all relevant substantive rule changes between 1960 and 1994 will be shown. It will also be shown where in the party rules a certain rule can be found throughout the 1960-1994 period, regardless whether it has changed or not. Every time a rule has changed paragraph and/or section, this is shown (even if the wording is unchanged), so that it is possible for the reader to locate the ruling in the rules of the party in question at any time during the research period of this study.

Openness

Openness of membership refers to how easy it is for any citizen to become, and stay, a member of a political party. This is a factor which has sometimes been overlooked in party research. It is taken for granted that anyone willing to pay the dues is welcome as a member. While this is quite true in most parties, a systematic study of what Kenneth Janda refers to as membership requirements is nevertheless worthwhile.[24] It highlights the conditions for involvement in political parties and illustrates the extent to which the parties actually wish to be open to participation from ordinary people. It is not necessarily a foregone conclusion that every party accepts anybody as a member. Indeed, Katz and Mair's edited data handbook on

---

[23] Albinsson had access to the actual party rules from 1950. Despite helpful personal advice from Albinsson, however, I have not been able to locate a copy.

[24] Janda 1980:126f. Janda defines membership requirements as criteria imposed on individuals who wish to take part in the party's activities. In consequence with the rest of this study, requirements of passive members will also be considered. In modern Swedish and other European parties the requirements are set for acceptance as a member and no additional requirements are set for passive members to become active.

party organisations in Europe and the USA reveals that the degree of party openness has not been totally without variation during the period between 1960 and 1990.[25]

Janda has listed four types of membership requirements, with rising severity: no requirements at all, to register as party member, to pay dues to the party and, finally, to go through a probationary period before acceptance.[26] These categories reflect the very wide perspective of Janda's work, which has the purpose to be applicable to the study of all political parties in the world. If we take the modern Western European parties, where formal membership is the rule, Janda's first three requirements become superfluous. This is because they are so basic; the first two can be classed as determining whether the party has formal membership at all and the third is practised by the vast majority of parties.[27] The final of Janda's criteria, however, is more relevant and will be returned to.

The degree of party openness, then, is dependent on the requirements on individuals who wish to become members of the party. These requirements can be divided into two sub-categories. *Obstacles* restrict entry into the party. *Obligations* determine how to remain a member. Obligations can, in turn, be divided into negative (prohibitions, e.g. against fractional activity) and positive (tasks, e.g. to attend party meetings). In practice, obstacles and obligations can be expected to correspond. Parties with high obstacles can be expected to tend to have more severe obligations, and vice versa. It is also possible that a requirement is both an obstacle and an obligation. For example, a ban on membership in other parties is an obstacle because a new member is not accepted if it is revealed that he/she already is a member of another party. At the same time it is also a negative obligation, because if somebody is found out to be a member of more than one party, the consequence is likely to be expulsion.

In the Social Democratic Party the degree of openness has remained quite stable during the 1960-1994 period. The only relevant alteration in the party rules is a minor one: until 1968 members who were not also members of an LO union or the women's organisation were obliged

---

[25] Katz and Mair, eds., 1992.

[26] Janda 1980:126.

[27] A check through Katz and Mair's edited Data Handbook on party organisations in Western Europe (Katz and Mair, eds., 1992) suggests that every party in the included countries did have membership dues throughout the period between 1960 and 1990.

to make an extra contribution to the party's newspaper fund.[28] There have been no obstacles for membership applicants.[29] Obligations exist, but they do not belong to any of the more severe prohibitions or tasks employed by some other European parties. Members are expected to accept the ideological fundaments of the party and are forbidden to take part in propaganda in obvious conflict therewith.[30] Note the wordings: ideological 'fundaments' (rather than the details of the party programme), and 'obvious' conflict. These distinctions do not seem to reveal any intention to curb a diversity of opinion in the party. There are no rules demanding a commitment to party discipline or obedience to party decisions. Multiple party membership is not allowed, nor to appear against the party in public elections. Members are not allowed to behave in a treasonable, or obviously damaging, way against the party, in a systematically disloyal way or in other ways that can cause damage to the party. Finally, it is prohibited to behave in a disloyal manner in an industrial conflict.[31]

All these obligations seem to be designed to protect the party rather than to demand special qualities or commitments of the members. There are no requirements of activity, nor is reference made to behaviour which is not related to party activities (something which is underlined by the specification 'behaviour which obviously causes damage to he party').

The most striking feature is the ruling against 'disloyal' behaviour in industrial conflicts. This is unique among the Swedish parties, and not known to have existed elsewhere in Europe.[32] This obviously means that members who are 'scabs' (act against industrial action) could be expelled from the party. This is indicative of the traditional close links between the party and union branches of the Swedish labour movement, and can be regarded as a negative obligation not directly related to the survival of the party itself. At the same time, there are many other possible obligations,

---

[28] Social Democrats, PR 1956 and 1964, §4 sect. 1.

[29] It has come to the author's knowledge that some local organisations of the Social Democratic party have on occasion made the entry of some new members subject to decision of a meeting of the organisation in question. The party rules, however, have not included any reference to such a procedure during the 1960-1994 period.

[30] Social Democrats, PR 1956 and 1964, §13 sect. 2; PR 1968, 1970 and 1972, §15 sect. 2, PR 1975, 1984 and 1990, §13 sect. 2., and PR 1993, §12 sect. 4.

[31] Social Democrats, PR 1956 and 1964, §13 sect. 4; PR 1968, 1970 and 1972, §15 sect. 4, PR 1975, 1984, 1990, §13 sect. 4 and PR 1993, §12 sect. 4.

[32] Katz and Mair, eds., 1992.

which exist in other European parties, such as compulsory union membership, which the Swedish Social Democrats do not have.[33] On the whole, the obstacles and obligations of the Swedish Social Democratic Party cannot be considered to be very severe.[34]

The situation in the Left Party is somewhat different. This is a party which has undergone several changes during the research period. In 1960, it was still a traditional communist party with organisation and policies quite similar to its Comintern days between 1919 and 1943. After 1967, when the party name was changed from the Communist Party of Sweden to the Left Party Communists, it became a more independent 'Euro-communist' party. In 1990, in the wake of the collapse of the communist regimes in Eastern Europe, the revision went even further. The word 'Communist' was dropped altogether and the party is now called the Left Party. For simplicity, the party will throughout the remainder of this study be referred to under this name, regardless of what the actual name was at the relevant time.

The general development of the Left Party is reflected in the development of its openness. In 1960, there were several severe obstacles and obligations. To join the party, the member had to be recommended by two other members, and a decision by a local organisation meeting was also required.[35] The thus enrolled members had several obligations. They had to be active in the party, obey decisions taken by all party levels, advance their political knowledge and make themselves familiar with the elements of Marxism-Leninism, participate in the organisation of mass actions and to read the party press. There were also a number of more general tasks, like to promote the party policies in everyday life, strengthen the party's connections with the masses, help maintain party unity and to behave in a way which is personally honourable and good for the party.[36]

The list is not totally exhaustive, but gives a clear impression of the type of membership the party wanted: active, conscious, knowledgeable

---

[33] Two examples are the Italian Communists and Socialists (Bardi and Morlino 1992:486f) and the Austrian Socialists (SPÖ) (Müller 1992:50f).

[34] It is possible that the ancillary and affiliated organisations of the party may for some periods have adopted a stricter line. For example, the Social Democratic student's organisation reported in 1969 that some of its members had been expelled for lack of activity. (Social Democratic Party, annual report 1969, p. 65). A year later, the organisation was disbanded. It was re-started in 1990.

[35] Left Party, PR 1957 and 1964, §3 sect. 3.

[36] Left Party, PR 1957 and 1964, §3 sect. 6, 7 and 8.

and disciplined members. The party membership did not have to consist of the masses, it was their task to lead the masses. The similarity with Duverger's 'devotee parties' is striking.[37]

In 1967, when the party's name was changed to the Left Party Communists, the rules were thoroughly revised. In the process, the openness increased. All obstacles and most of the obligations were dropped. What was retained was general commitments to the party programme and rules, and to pay the party dues.[38] However some of the obstacles and obligations later returned. In 1969 entry of new members was again made subject to decision by the respective local organisation, although no recommendation by other members was needed.[39] A change which could be interpreted as a step back towards democratic centralism was implemented in 1972. It was stated in the rules that majority decisions were binding for all members and the decisions by higher party levels were binding for lower levels. There was also a ban on fractional activity.[40] Detailed tasks, such as meeting attendance, activity and studies, which had existed until 1967, were not re-introduced, however.

A major revision of the rules took place at the 1990 party congress, at the same time as the party dropped 'Communist' from the name and started a thorough revision of its ideology. The remaining obstacle against the entry of new members, decision by the committee of the relevant local organisation, was abolished. In fact, the 1990 rules stated that the committee of the local organisation had to immediately execute all applications from new members, unless they had previously been expelled.[41] This sentence was dropped in 1993, but there is still nothing which can be interpreted as an obstacle against new membership applicants.[42] The remaining obligations are few and very general. Members are expected to act on behalf of the party's policies, and in accordance with

---

[37] Duverger 1951/1964:70f.

[38] Left Party, PR 1967, §2 sect. 1-4, §14 sect. 6.

[39] Left Party, PR 1969, 1972, 1975, 1978 and 1985, §2 sect. 4. Between 1978 and 1985, the decision was to be taken by a membership meeting of the local organisation. Before and after that period, the decision was to be taken by the committee of the local organisation.

[40] Left Party, PR 1972, 1975, 1978 and 1985, §1. See also Bäck 1984:91.

[41] Left Party, PR 1990, §2 sect. 2.

[42] Left Party, PR 1993, §2 sect. 2.

the party programme and rules, and not to act in a way which can cause damage to the party.[43] There is no longer an explicit rule against fractions.[44]

In summary, the development of the Left Party has had its twists and turns. In 1960 it was a closed party with high demands on its members. These demands were dramatically reduced in 1967, only to be increased again quite soon, although not to the old level. In 1990 it became a very open party.

The story of the non-socialist parties is more straightforward. The Centre Party can be characterised as a party with high and stable openness. There have been few obstacles or obligations. A general obligation to agree with, and act on behalf of, the purpose of the party has been kept without substantive alterations.[45] In 1969, a still existing rule was introduced, which makes it possible for the party to reject membership applications when "special reasons are at hand".[46]

The People's Party Liberals have had a few more, but not particularly severe, obstacles. Until 1969, members had to be Swedish citizens.[47] From that year, however, it has been possible to join the party for all persons resident in Sweden.[48] Entry of new members has throughout the period been subject to decision by the relevant party level.[49] Since 1964,

---

[43] Left Party, PR 1990, §14 sect. 3; PR 1993, §13 sect. 5.

[44] In reply to a motion to the 1990 congress, the party's executive argued that such a provision could be abused to curb a free and open debate in the party. Left Party Communists, Congress Documents 1990, booklet 5, p. 33, motion F13.

[45] Centre Party, PR 1960, 1966, 1967, 1969, 1971, 1972, 1977 and 1992, §2 sect. 1.

[46] Centre Party, PR 1969, 1971, 1972, 1977 and 1992, §2 sect. 3.

[47] People's Party Liberals, PR 1960, 1964, 1966 and 1967, §5.

[48] People's Party Liberals, PR 1969 §5; 1971, 1974, 1977, 1980, 1983, 1987 and 1990, §2. In 1993 all references to Swedish citizenship or residence was dropped. The wording is now "Everybody with a liberal outlook has the right to become a member of the People's Party Liberals...". PR 1993, §2.

[49] Until 1971, there was an explicit rule that all applications were subject to decision by the local organisation. People's Party Liberals, PR 1960, 1964, 1966, 1968 and 1969, §5. From 1971, there has been a slightly more implicit wording, but the meaning is still clearly that a membership application can be refused. PR 1971, 1974, 1977, 1980, 1983, 1987, 1990 and 1993, §2.

however, it has been ruled that new members should be accepted unless 'special reasons' suggest otherwise.[50]

The obligations have been few and general. Members may not simultaneously be members of other parties. This rule was slackened somewhat in 1978, to allow collectively affiliated Social Democrats to join the People's Party, as it was felt that they may be under social pressure not to use the possibility to opt out of the collective affiliation of union members. The members have also continuously been expected to agree with basic liberal principles and to pay the membership dues.[51]

The Moderate Party has had only one obstacle during the research period. Until 1969, the rules included the wording that the party sought to assemble Swedish people who agreed with the ideas of the party.[52] Since that year, there has been no reference to nationality. It is merely stated that anyone who lives in the area of a regional organisation of the party, and who wishes to promote the interests of the party, obey the party rules and pay the membership dues, is eligible to become a member of the regional party organisation in question and, hence, the national party.[53]

Negative obligations in the Moderate Party consist of a ban on membership of other parties and a commitment not to behave in a way which may cause damage to the party's reputation or goals. These obligations were introduced in 1964 and have remained since, with some minor wording adjustments.[54] In 1969, the ban on membership of other

---

[50] People's Party Liberals, PR 1964, 1966, 1967 and 1969 §5; PR 1971, 1974, 1977, 1980, 1983, 1987, 1990 and 1993, §2. It is possible that wording was first introduced already in 1962.

[51] People's Party Liberals, PR 1964, 1966, 1967 and 1969, §5; PR 1971, 1974, 1977, 1980, 1983, 1987, 1990 and 1993, §2.

[52] Moderate Party, PR 1950 and 1964, Rules for regional party level *(Normalstadgar för förbund)*, §3.

[53] Moderate Party, PR 1969, 1972, 1978, 1984, 1987 and 1993, Rules for regional party level *(Normalstadgar för förbund)*, §3.

[54] Moderate Party, PR 1964, 1969, 1972, 1978, 1984, 1987 and 1993, Rules for regional party level *(Normalstadgar för förbund)*, §3, sect. 1. Until 1993, the wording was "...through his/her actions damage the purposes of the regional party organisation". In 1993 the wording was changed to "...damage the party".

parties was extended to a ban on membership of political organisations competing with the party.[55]

The Christian Democratic Party was formed in 1964. The party had a requirement of Swedish citizenship until 1971,[56] when it was changed to Swedish citizens or people resident in Sweden.[57] Throughout its existence, the party has required its members to adhere to the party rules and programme (changed to the party's purpose instead of programme in 1971).[58] Since 1971, there has been a commitment for members not to act in a way which could damage the reputation of the party.

It is worth noting that, although the party had a reputation as confessional from its formation until the late 1980s, this has never been reflected in the party rules. There is no obligation to belong to a church, or to be a believing Christian.[59] The Christian Democrats have, since the formation, been an open party according to the definitions used here. In terms of obstacles and obligations it is very similar to the other non-socialist parties.

The Green Party was formed in 1981. The first party rules were adopted in 1982. The members are expected to act in accordance with the party programme and rules and to pay the membership dues.[60] They are obliged not to, in an obvious way, work against the purpose of the party.[61] In 1986, a ban on membership of other parties was introduced,[62] but it was dropped again in 1987. In practice, it is not tolerated to be a member of another national party.[63]

---

[55] Moderate Party, PR 1969, 1972, 1978, 1984, 1987 and 1993, Rules for regional party level *(Normalstadgar för förbund)*, §3, sect. 3.

[56] Christian Democratic Party, Interim Rules 1964, PR 1965, §2.

[57] Christian Democratic Party, PR 1971, 1974, 1975, 1978, 1979, 1980, 1984, 1989 and 1994, §2.

[58] Christian Democratic Party, Interim Rules 1964, PR 1965, 1971, 1974, 1975, 1978, 1979, 1980, 1984, 1989 and 1995, §2. In 1975, the Swedish wording was changed from *'syftemål'* to *'målsättning'*. In both cases, the best translation into English would be 'purpose'.

[59] Throughout the existence of the party, the first paragraph of the party rules has stated a general commitment to Christian values.

[60] Green Party, PR 1982, 1984, 1986, 1987, 1988, 1989, 1992 and 1993, §3.

[61] Green Party, PR 1982 and 1984 §18, 1986, 1987, 1988, 1989, 1992 and 1993, §19.

[62] Green Party, PR 1986, §3.

[63] According to party officials, the lack of an explicit ban on multiple membership is to allow members to join local environmentally oriented parties.

The final of the parties included in this study, New Democracy, was formed in 1991. The first party rules were adopted in 1992 and revised a year later. The party has not had any formal obstacles against membership. The 1992 rules included some obligations of a general nature: to promote the goals of the party, to follow the party rules, to pay the dues, not to work for other political organisations and not to act in a way which can damage the party's purpose.[64]

The revision in 1993 complicated the picture. The new rules meant that the membership structure became unique among the Swedish parties. The party had no local organisational level, but instead written contracts with autonomous local parties who had the right to use the party name.[65] The 1993 rules did not at all discuss the membership of the local 'co-parties'. But there was also direct membership of the national party which, among other things, included the right to attend the national party conference.[66]

One reason for the rule change was that the party had had problems with some local organisations, and made several expulsions of individual members.[67] The revised rules made it possible to get rid of trouble-making local organisations rather easily, instead of going through the often traumatic experience of expelling individuals. At the same time, the obligations on members of the national organisation were altered. The ban on working for other political organisations stayed, but was rephrased so that it became forbidden to actively support or work for an organisation which represents views contradicting those of the party. The paragraph about damaging the purpose of the party was changed to "in an obvious way damage the party's reputation, interests or trust among the voters". A new obligation was introduced; not to actively work against the party's programme or policies or their implementation.[68]

It could be argued that the structure of the party according to the rules of 1993, with no local organisations, indicated a decrease of openness. But it was still possible, and in fact at least as easy, to join the central party. The rule changes certainly affected the nature of the party's internal structure, but since it did not become more difficult to become a

---

[64] New Democracy, PR 1992, §2 sect. 6.

[65] New Democracy, PR 1993, §30 and §31.

[66] New Democracy, PR 1993, §1 and §4-7.

[67] Taggart and Widfeldt 1993, Taggart 1993, Taggart 1996.

[68] New Democracy, PR 1993, §33.

member of the party proper, it did not affect the degree of openness, i.e. the number and nature of obstacles and obligations to membership of the party.[69]

To sum up, the Swedish parties have been characterised by a high degree of openness throughout the 1960-1994 period. The only partial exception is the Left Party until 1967 and, to a lesser extent, between 1969 and 1990. In most parties, the level of openness has been stable. The only real exception is the Left Party, where it has increased.

What this means, is that Swedish citizens have throughout the period had several parties which they have been able to join without too much difficulty, and without the membership involving more time and commitment than they choose. This, in turn, has meant that the Swedish citizens have had good opportunities to take part in party activities to the extent that they have wished. Furthermore, with the development towards increased openness of the Left Party, and the emergence of three new and open parties after 1960 borne in mind, the development has, if anything, gone in the direction towards more party openness during the research period.

While the general conclusion can be made rather comfortably, some caveats are appropriate. The analysis is based on the letter of the party rules, not on actual practice in the parties. It could be that some prospective members sense that, in reality, the local party organisers demand more of them than they feel can meet. Failure to meet the demands may not bring formal consequences, but membership might still bring with it informal pressures or unwanted commitments, as illustrated by the hesitation of Herbert Tingsten described in Chapter 1 above.

The other side of the openness coin is the strength of the party organisation. If there is nobody to enrol, and inform, people who are interested in joining, high openness is of little value. There are stories circulating about how local party organisations fail to enrol persons who express interest in becoming a member. If such inertia is widespread in the party, it is in fact a sign of a *de facto* lack of openness.[70]

---

[69] In November 1995, the rules were revised again, to a more traditional organisational structure consisting of local and central party levels. *Expo* (Swedish periodical) 1996 (vol. 2), issue 1. By then, however, the party was an insignificant force in Swedish politics. In the European election in September 1995 the party received 2841 votes.

[70] In 1991, a Swedish journalist tried to join the local organisations of the eight biggest parties in the Malmö area. The intensity of the respective responses was very varying. The

There are two reasons why such considerations are not weighed into the conclusion. First, it is not possible to investigate the practical day-to day life of all parties, especially as problems such as those discussed here manifest themselves at the very lowest party levels. Second, there is reason to re-emphasise the arguments for the relevance of the 'official story' of party organisations, as discussed above. The party rules represent the way the party wants its organisation to look like. It can be assumed that a party with a high degree of openness wants to be open, and if this ambition fails in practice, it is a failure, not a deliberate deception.

Membership influence: an introduction

Openness is a necessary, but not sufficient, criterion for a party to provide participatory linkage. For the linkage concept to be meaningful, there has to be some sort of relevant decision-making at one end of the linkage. If the parties are to provide linkage via participation, then it is not enough that it is reasonably easy to become and remain a member. The member must also be able to have some influence in the party.

The remainder of this chapter will focus on the parties' ability to, as voluntary membership organisations, enable people to influence political decision-making via participation in the party. For this to be possible, rank-and-file members must be able to take part in the parties' internal decision-making. Attention will be paid to the selection of leading party officials and also the possibility for members to have their say in the party. In other words, the accountability of leading party officials to the membership, and the 'voice' facilities for rank-and-file members, will be considered. Again, the focus will be on the parties' formal framework, not the contents of decisions or policies. The analysis will focus on formal rather than real influence. The account will be based on the official party rules.

Another restriction is that the focus will be set on membership influence on central party organs. On the sub-national (local and regional) levels the structures vary among different parties. It is acknowledged that membership influence on local matters is a very important aspect of party life, and that local politics can be an important motivation for people to join political parties. It is a limitation of this study that it focuses on national politics. The limitation is justified by the fact that the format of the

---

Moderate and Left parties were especially late in their reactions to the applications (*Tidningen Z,* no. 15, July 1991).

study, with a 35 year time frame, would be too great if local politics were taken into consideration. Sweden has a high degree of local self government, but national politics are still important and relevant, a fact which justifies a focus on the national party level.

There are two more omissions which must be mentioned. No attention will be paid to the procedures of nominating candidates for public office. This is consistent with the limitation to central party levels. In Sweden, nominations of candidates for the Riksdag are, formally, matters which are decided on sub-national levels. In some parties, central guidelines for nomination procedures have been made, but the regional autonomy is substantial. Unlike in some other European countries, the National Executives of the Swedish parties have no formal authority to intervene at any stage, even if informal attempts have been known to take place.[71]

Second, very little attention will be paid to the role and position of the parliamentary fractions. This party level is problematic because it is accountable to the voters, but also to the party, which nominates the parliamentary candidates before they are elected. The status of the parliamentary fractions is relatively unregulated in the parties but, by and large, they are formally autonomous from the national party organisations. There is no formal way in which the parliamentary fractions can be held accountable by the parties other than the possibility for the constituency party levels not to re-nominate their individual members of the *Riksdag* as candidates in the next election. This study will concentrate on formal membership influence on central party levels which means that the parliamentary fractions will be overlooked.[72]

The national party congress

The national congress is, formally, the most powerful decision-making body in each of the eight investigated Swedish parties.[73] The main duties of

---

[71] Bäck and Möller 1990:115f. A partial exception is the central Nomination Committee introduced by New Democracy in 1993, PR §26-28. Examples of European parties where central party organs can intervene are the major parties in Great Britain (Webb 1992b:862f) and in Austria (Müller 1992:100ff).

[72] For an account of the development of the Swedish Parliamentary fractions, see Isberg 1992.

[73] Social Democrats (Swedish term for congress: *Partikongress*), PR 1956 and 1964, §5 sect. 1; PR 1968, 1970 and 1972, §6 sect. 1; PR 1975, 1987, 1990 and 1993, §4 sect. 1.

the congress are to elect, besides the party leader, at least one other central party organ. It sets and changes the party rules and it decides on party programmes and manifestos. The real story behind this can of course be a different matter. Jon Pierre has, in his study on the congress of the Swedish Social Democratic Party, demonstrated how the party leadership has been very skilful at avoiding undesirable congress decisions, primarily by making the decisions too vague to constrain the freedom of movement for the leaders.[74] Still, the Social Democratic party leadership has on several occasions suffered unexpected and undesired defeats at recent congresses. Other examples where the national congress has played an independent role was when Moderate Party leader Yngve Holmberg was unseated in 1970,[75] and when the Left Party changed to its current name in 1990.

The position of the congress underlines the Swedish parties as organised primarily according to the principle of representative democracy. The most important means by which the party membership can be influential on the central level is via the congress. There are few direct democratic channels. The most important exception to this rule is the possibility of a referendum among the members. Such a facility exists in

---

Centre Party (*Riksstämma*), PR 1960 and 1967, §1; PR 1969, 1971 and 1977, §1; PR 1992, §1. Up to 1977 it was stated that "The congress is the decision-making organ of the national organisation". In the 1992 rules it is stated that "The congress is the highest decision-making organ of the Centre Party". People's Party Liberals (*Landsmöte*), PR 1960, 1964, 1966, 1967, 1969, §8; PR 1971, 1974, 1977, 1980, 1983, 1987, and 1990, §8 sect. a); PR 1993, §6 sect. a). The wording has always been "The supreme organ of the party". Moderate Party (until 1969: *Riksstämma*; after 1969: *Partistämma*), PR 1969 and 1972, §7 sect. 1; PR 1978, §8 sect. 1; PR 1984, 1987 and 1993, §6 sect. 1. Before 1969, it was not explicitly stated anywhere in the rules that the congress *de jure* was the supreme organ. However, Albinsson states that this was the case throughout his research period between 1950 and 1985 (Albinsson 1986:110; see also Winqvist et al. 1972:86). Left Party (*Partikongress*), PR 1957 and 1964, §4 sect. 1; PR 1967, 1969 and 1972, §6 sect. 1; PR 1975, 1978, 1981, 1985 and 1990, §5 sect. 1. PR 1993, §4 sect. 1. Christian Democrats (*Riksting*), PR 1964, §3 sect. 1; PR 1965, §3 sect. 1; PR 1971, §12 sect. 1; PR 1975, 1978, 1979, 1980, 1984 and 1988, §18 sect. 1; PR 1989 and 1993, §18 sect. 1; PR 1994, §18 sect. §1. New Democracy (*Partistämma*), PR 1992, §4 sect. 1; PR 1993, §5. Green Party (*Partikongress*), PR 1982, 1984, 1986, 1987, 1988, 1989, 1992, 1993 and 1994, §6.

[74] Pierre 1986.

[75] Albinsson 1986:96f.

the Social Democratic, Left and Green parties, and New Democracy, but it has rarely been put into use.[76] The criteria for allocation of congress delegates and the rights for all party members at the congress are summarised in Table 3.1. In all parties, congress delegates are allocated to sub-national (usually regional) party units according to their membership size. The rules ensure that every unit is guaranteed at least one delegate. This principle has been applied very widely, with two exceptions.

Before 1964, the Moderate party allocated delegates among the regional organisations on the basis of the number of votes in that area in the most recent 2nd Chamber Riksdag election. Since that year, however, the rules correspond with those of the other parties. The other exception is New Democracy who, in connection with the abolition of all sub-national party levels in 1993, made it possible for every person who has been a dues-paying member for at least four months in succession, to be a delegate with the right to vote. The only extra requirement is to notify attendance in advance. In this respect, New Democracy after the rule change offer the highest degree of potential influence to their members, using a direct democratic method.[77] With this exception, the party congresses are representative organs.

---

[76] Social Democrats, PR 1956 and 1964, §9; PR 1968, 1970 and 1972, §12; PR 1975, 1984, 1987, 1990 and 1993, §10. It has not been practised since 1922 (Winqvist et al. 1972:206). Left Party, PR 1967 §13; PR 1969, §14; PR 1972, 1975, 1978, 1981, 1985 and 1990, §13; PR 1993, §12. The referendum was introduced in connection with the major rule revision in 1967. It is consultative and has, to the best of the author's knowledge, never been put into practice. Green Party, PR 1982 and 1984, §15; PR 1986, 1987 and 1988, §16; PR 1989 §15; PR 1992, 1993 and 1994, §17. The party had a controversial referendum about the abolition of military defence in 1990 (Lundgren 1991:68). New Democracy, PR 1993, §24. The party introduced the possibility of a membership referendum in 1993. It was used, in controversial circumstances, to confirm the election of Vivianne Franzén as party leader in the summer of 1994.

[77] Of course, the new principle can have practical problems. For one thing, the opportunity to attend for all members is not equal, since the distance of travel to the location of the congress is not equal. The new system in New Democracy was practised at the extra Congress in Västerås in August 1994. It was reported to have been quite a chaotic affair. It was alleged that supporters of the new party leader Vivianne Franzén had been 'bussed' to the congress, in order to ensure a majority for her faction in the party. Similar controversies connected with direct democratic methods for decision making have also occurred in other parties, e.g. a Social Democratic meeting in Göteborg in 1934 (Kennerström 1974:99f).

Table 3.1 Allocation of delegates and right to attend national congress, Swedish parties 1960-1994

year	Left Party	Social Democrats	Centre Party	People's Party	Moderate Party	Christian Democrats	Green Party	New Democracy
1960	Local org. (*Arbetarekommuner*) allocated delegates according to membership size. (PR 1957, §8 sect. 3)	350 delegates allocated to regional org. according to membership size. (PR 1956, §5 sect. 1; §6 sect. 1)	Regional org. allocated delegates according to membership size. All members may take part in debates and make proposals. (PR 1960, §20 sect. 2; §26 sect. 3)	Regional org. allocated delegates according to membership size. All members may take part in debates and make proposals. (PR 1960, §8)	200 delegates allocated to regional org. according to no. of votes in most recent election to Riksdag 2nd chamber. (PR 1950, §4)	---	---	---
1964	As above.	As above.	As above.	As above. (PR §8, sect. A and D)	200 delegates allocated to regional org. according to membership size. (PR §4 sect. 1)	Regional org. allocated one delegate each. (Interim rules §3, sect. 1)	---	---
1965	As above.	As above.	As above.	As above.	As above.	Regional org. allocated delegates according to membership size. All members may take part in debates and make proposals in connection with motions. (PR §3 sect. 3 and 5)	---	---
1967	Delegates allocated to regional org. according to membership size. (PR §6 sect. 6)	As above.	As above.	As above.	As above.	As above.	---	---
1968	As above.	As above. (PR §6 sect. 1; §7 sect.1)	As above.	As above.	As above.	As above.	---	---
1969	As above.	As above.	As above. (PR §24 sect. 2; §29 sect. 2)	As above. (PR §8)	As above. Individual members right to attend after pre-notification. (PR §7 sect. 1 and 3)	As above.	---	---
1971	As above.	As above.	As above.	As above. (PR §8 sect. A and E)	As above.	As above. (PR §8 sect. 5; §12 sect. 4)	---	---

3.1	Left Party	Soc. Dem.	Centre Party	People's Party	Moderate	Chr. Dem.	Green Party	New Dem.
1975	As above.	As above. (PR §4 sect. 1; §5 sect. 1)	As above.	As above.	As above.	As above. All members may participate in debates and make proposals; not specified when. (PR §14 sect. 6; §18 sect. 5)	---	---
1978	As above.	As above.	As above.	As above.	As above. (PR §8 sect. 1 and 3)	As above.	---	---
1982	As above.	As above.	As above.	As above.	As above.	As above.	Regional and/or local org. allocated delegates according to membership size. All members may take part in debates and make pro-posals. (PR §6; §14)	---
1984	As above.	As above.	As above.	As above.	As above. (PR §6, sect. 1 and 3)	As above.	As above.	---
1985	As above, but no. of delegates set to 275. (PR §5 sect. 6)	As above.	As above.	As above.	As above.	As above.	As above.	---
1986	As above.	As above.	As above.	As above.	As above.	As above.	As above. (PR §6; §15)	---
1989	As above.	As above.	As above.	As above.	As above.	As above. (PR §14 sect. 6; §18 sect. 6)	As above. (PR §6; §14)	---
1992	As above.	As above.	As above. (PR §18 sect. 2; §23 sect. 2)	As above.	As above.	As above.	As above. (PR §6 sect. 6.4.1 and 6.9)	Local org. get delegates according to membership size. Other members may attend after notification (PR §4, sect. 1 and 5)

3.1	Left Party	Soc. Dem.	Centre Party	People's Party	Moderate	Chr. Dem.	Green Party	New Dem.
1993	As above. (PR §4 sect. 6)	As above.	As above.	As above, but no. of delegates set to 150. (PR §6 sect. A and E)	As above.	As above.	As above.	All who have been members for at least 4 months may participate in debates and make proposals. Members who have notified attendance in advance may also vote. (PR §8; §32)
1994	As above.	As above.	As above.	As above.	As above.	As above. (PR §14 sect. 7; §18 sect. 7)	As above.	As above.

Some parties give all their members the right to take part in congress debates and to make proposals, whereas the right to vote is confined to the delegates. The fact that some parties do not restrict the conference floor to the formal delegates can be interpreted as a direct democratic element in party organisations which otherwise are based on a representative principle. It has existed in the Centre and Liberal parties throughout the research period, and in the Christian Democratic and Green parties since they were formed. While this arrangement does not give the rank-and-file members formal influential power, it does give them a 'voice' opportunity; to express their views to the party leadership. On the whole, the rank-and-file members' possibility to influence the central party via the congress has not changed much. The only exception worth noting is the recent change in New Democracy.

Arguably more important than the right to take part in congress debates, is the right to submit motions. Attendance has its practical limitations and, as has been exemplified in note 77, unlimited right to attend can be controversial. It seems more plausible that individual members have equal opportunities to sit at home and write motions which then are subject to decision on the congress, than that they have an equal chance to personally attend the congress.

The development of the right to submit motions is summarised in Table 3.2. Throughout the research period, all parties, except two, have allowed all members to submit motions to the congress. The first exception was the Moderate Party until 1969. Until then, the regional organisations constituted the lowest party level to have the right to submit motions. An individual member had to have his or her motion accepted by the regional meeting for it to be dealt with by the congress. Since 1969, however, the Moderate party gives all party members the right to submit motions to the congress.[78]

The Social Democrats have a rule which ensures the right for individual members to submit motions to the congress, but all motions can be stopped at the local *Arbetarekommun* level. Every motion is subject to decision by an *Arbetarekommun* meeting which can a) adopt it, b) reject it, in which case it is 'killed' or c) send it to the congress as a 'private' motion which means that the regional organisation in question does not entirely agree with the motion. This rule has remained unchanged throughout the research period. In all other parties, individual members may submit motions to the congress without it being stopped at any level.

In the Left, Centre, Moderate and Christian Democratic parties, regional levels deliberate the motions and issue a recommendation to the congress, but they have no power to stop any motion from being put on the congress agenda. In all parties, the National Executive issues a statement on every motion, which is given to the delegates before the congress, but in no case does it have the right to stop motions.

---

[78] Cf. Albinsson 1986:110f.

Table 3.2   Individual party members' right to propose motions to national congress, Swedish parties 1960-1994

year	Left Party	Social Democrats	Centre Party	People's Party	Moderate Party	Christian Democrats	Green Party	New Democracy
1960	Yes. Basic org. (*grund-organisa-tion*) of the member shall attach statement. NE issues statement to each motion. (PR 1957, §8 sect. 4)	Yes, but local org. (*Arbetare-kommun*) submits motions as adopted or private; can also stop motions. NE issues statement on each motion. (PR 1956, §5 sect. 10 and 12)	Yes. Regional org. shall attach statement. NC prepares congress agenda; in practice motions are deliberated by special congress committees. (PR 1960, §26 sect. 5, §27 sect. 2; Winqvist et al. 1972:144ff)	Yes. If motion involves changes to party programme or party rules, it should be prepared by NE and regional org. (PR 1960, §8)	No. Motions may be submitted by NE, regional org. and congress delegates. (PR 1950, §4; Albinsson 1986:110f)	---	---	---
1964	As above.	As above.	As above.	Yes. All motions should be prepared before the congress by the NE. (PR §8 sect. g. The change may have been introduced in 1962)	As above, plus executive of youth organisation (PR §4 sect. 5)	No rule. (Interim Rules)	---	---
1965	As above.	As above.	As above.	As above.	As above.	Yes. All motions are deliberated by regional org. NE prepares all congress matters. (PR §3 sect. 4; §4 sect. 3)	---	---
1967	As above. (PR §6 sect. 8)	As above.	As above.	As above.	As above.	As above.	---	---
1968	As above.	As above. (PR §6 sect. 10 and 12)	As above.	As above.	As above.	As above.	---	---
1969	As above.	As above.	As above, but NE takes over formal role previously held by NC. (PR §29 sect. 4; §31 sect. 2)	As above.	Yes. All motions are deliberated by regional org. and NE. (PR §7 sect. 6 and 7)	As above.	---	---
1971	As above.	As above.	As above.	As above. (PR §8 sect. h)	As above.	As above. (PR §12 sect. 4; §15 sect. 3)	---	---
1972	As above. (PR §5 sect. 8)	As above.	As above.	As above.	As above.	As above.	---	---
1975	As above.	As above. (PR §4 sect. 14 and 16)	As above.	As above.	As above.	As above. (PR §18 sect. 4; §19 sect. 2)	---	---

3.2	Left Party	Soc. Dem.	Centre Party	People's Party	Moderate	Chr. Dem.	Green Party	New Dem.
1978	As above.	As above.	As above.	As above.	As above. (PR §8 sect. 6 and 7)	As above.	---	---
1982	As above.	As above.	As above.	As above.	As above.	As above.	Yes. Motions deliberated by relevant central party committee. (PR §6; §8-§11)	---
1984	As above.	As above.	As above.	As above.	As above. (PR §6 sect. 6 and 7)	As above. (PR §18 sect. 4; §20 sect. 2)	As above.	---
1992	As above.	As above.	As above. (PR §23 sect. 3; §25 sect. 2)	As above.	As above.	As above.	Yes. Motions deliberated by NE. (PR §6 sect. 6.5.1 and 6.5.3)	Yes. Motions deliberated by NE. (PR §4 sect. 6-7)
1993	As above. (PR §4 sect. 8)	As above. (PR §4 sect. 12 and 14)	As above.	As above. (PR §6 sect. h)	As above.	As above.	As above.	As above. (PR §12; §14)
1994	As above.	As above.	As above.	As above.	As above.	As above.	As above.	As above.

The widespread right to submit motions has been used by the members to an increasing extent over the years. The total number of motions at the party congresses between 1960 and 1991 are presented in Table 3.3. The number of motions dealt with by party congresses has been multiplied since the early 1960s in all parties. The big rise took place between 1960 and 1975, and from then on, the levels in the respective parties have, on the whole, remained fairly stable. With regard to the differences in the rules over time and among different parties, two observations deserve attention. On the one hand, the comparatively restrictive rules in the Social Democratic Party do not stop it from having, on average, by far the highest number of motions for any party. On the other hand, the softening of the Moderate Party rules in 1969 was followed by a notable increase in motions. It is of course not possible to decisively assert whether this is caused by the rule change as such, or to other factors which account for the generally increasing trend among all parties.

The trends in Table 3.3 give some flesh to the formal rules in Table 3.2. The formal possibility for individual members to submit motions to the national congress has been stable in all parties except the Moderates, where it increased in 1969. On the national level, it can be argued that the possibility has increased, as the new parties to have emerged during the period, the Christian Democrats in 1964, the Green party in 1981 and New Democracy in 1991, all have liberal rules in this respect.

Table 3.3 Number of motions to party congresses, Sweden 1960-1998

year	Left Party	Soc.Dem.	Centre	People's Party	Moderate	Chr.Dem.	Green
1960	-	131	n/a	3	7	---	---
1961	n/a	-	16	-	-	---	---
1962	-	-	12	6	13	---	---
1963	-	-	24	-	-	---	---
1964	63	175	28	29	52	0	---
1965	-	-	32	-	36	10	---
1966	-	-	26	53	-	6	---
1967	160	113e	52	52	71	33	---
1968	-	196	41	35	-	29	---
1969	107	404	57	136	12 (+63e)	47	---
1970	-	-	87	-	-	25	---
1971	-	-	110	248	-	36	---
1972	182	474	88	497	127	40	---
1973	-	-	91	-	-	38	---
1974	-	-	183	205	-	47	---
1975	325	1186	222	275	140	57	---
1976	-	-	206	-	-	40	---
1977	-	-	316	367	-	64	---
1978	361	728	250	357	283	61	---
1979	-	-	296	-	-	80	---
1980	-	-	259	356	-	95	---
1981	310	727	327	-	308	138	762
1982	-	-	303	1004	-	87	245
1983	-	-	360	-	-	94	175
1984	-	590	315	324	226	111	275
1985	232	-	317	-	-	124	110
1986	-	-	296	-	-	100	118
1987	336	896	300	316	242	92	129
1988	-	-	268	-	-	126	160
1989	-	-	281	-	-	100	181
1990	268	912	272	440	259	84	157
1991	-	-	228	-	-	129	166
1992	-	-	237	-	-	161	78
1993	417	673	389	273	286	218	84
1994	-	-	223	-	-	167	71
1995	-	-	352	-	-	169	61
1996	543	2341	458	-	-	218	105
1997	-	1824	453	1100	195	156	284
1998	372	-	395	-	-	147	147

Comment: - indicates that no party congress was held that year. "e" indicates that the congress was an extraordinary congress. Several parties have changed their frequency of congress during the research period covered (see Table 3.4 below). Some extraordinary congresses, where deliberating motions has only been of minor importance, or when the only motions debated were originally submitted to an earlier congress, are not included in the table. The table is a complemented and updated version of Table 13.1 in Pierre and Widfeldt 1994:346.

Table 3.3 suggests that the party members to an increasing extent have taken this opportunity, also in the parties where the rules have not been changed over time.[79] Since the congress is the highest decision-making organ in all parties and an important bond between the members and the leadership, the frequency with which they take place is another indicator of membership influence. The more frequent the congress, the more often the members can voice their opinions to the leadership and hold it accountable. The rules for the Swedish parties appear in Table 3.4.

Three Swedish parties hold congresses at least once a year; the Centre Party, the Green Party and the Christian Democrats. This has been without alteration throughout the research period. The other parties have tended to follow the election cycle with their ordinary congresses (ordinary as opposed to extra congress). The Moderate Party held their congress every two years until 1969.[80] In that year the Moderate Party rules were changed so that ordinary congresses were held the year before elections to the unicameral Riksdag, i.e. every three years until 1994. The People's Party held ordinary congresses every two years until 1971, when the frequency was changed to two out of every three years. In 1983, the periodicity was decreased to once every three years. The Social Democrats held their ordinary congress every four years until 1968, when the frequency was increased to every three years. New Democracy stated in the 1992 rules that the congress shall be held every three years. The rules from 1993 state that it should be held once every election period, and there was an explicit provision to cater for the now implemented change of the parliamentary election period from three to four years.

---

[79] The increasing number of motions has led to practical problems at the party congresses. Åsa Lundgren has pointed out that of the 181 motions submitted to the Green Party congress in 1989, there was only time to deal with 41 (Lundgren 1991:70). In the Moderate Party, there have been reactions against the vast number of motions and even suggestions to change the rules so that motions could be stopped at some level, like in the Social Democratic party (Albinsson 1986:111). So far, however, no such change has been implemented.

[80] Until 1964, the Moderate Party held a congress all even years, which coincided with the elections to the Riksdag 2nd chamber or to the regional and local elections. In 1964, the congresses were moved to every odd year, which was years when no elections were held.

Table 3.4   National congress, frequency of meeting, Swedish parties 1960-1994

year	Left Party	Social Democrats	Centre Party	People's Party	Moderate Party	Christian Democrats	Green Party	New Democracy
1960	At least once every 3 years. (PR 1957, §8 sect. 1)	Every 4 years (year of ordinary election to Riksdag 2nd chamber). (PR 1956, §5 sect. 2)	Annually. (PR 1960, §26 sect. 1)	Every 2 years (even years). (PR 1960, §8)	Every 2 years (even years). (PR 1950, §4)	---	---	---
1964	As above.	As above.	As above.	As above.	Every 2 years (odd years). (PR §4 sect. 4)	No rule. (Interim Rules)	---	---
1965	As above.	As above.	As above.	As above.	As above.	Annually. (PR §3 sect. 1)	---	---
1966	As above.	As above.	As above.	Every 2 years (odd years). (PR §8 sect. b)	As above.	As above.	---	---
1967	As above. (PR §6 sect. 2)	As above.	As above.	As above.	As above.	As above.	---	---
1968	As above.	Every 3 years (year before ordinary Riksdag election). (PR §6 sect. 2)	As above.	As above.	As above.	As above.	---	---
1969	As above.	As above.	As above. (PR §29 sect. 1)	As above.	Every 3 years (year before ordinary election). (PR §7 sect. 4)	As above.	---	---
1971	As above.	As above.	As above.	Every 2 in 3 years (years with no ordinary Riksdag election). (PR §8 sect c)	As above.	As above. (PR §12 sect. 2)	---	---
1972	As above. (PR §5 sect. 2)	As above.	As above.	As above.	As above.	As above.	---	---
1975	As above.	As above. (PR §4 sect. 2)	As above.	As above.	As above.	As above. (PR §18 sect. 2)	---	---
1978	As above.	As above.	As above.	As above.	As above. (PR §8 sect. 4)	As above.	---	---
1982	As above.	As above.	As above.	As above.	As above.	As above.	Annually. (PR §6)	---
1983	As above.	As above.	As above.	Every 3 years (year before ordinary Riksdag election). (PR §8 sect. c)	As above.	As above.	As above.	---
1984	As above.	As above.	As above.	As above.	As above. (PR §6 sect. 4)	As above.	As above.	---
1992	As above.	As above.	As above. (PR §23 sect. 1)	As above.	As above.	As above.	As above. (PR §6 sect. 6.2)	Every 3 years (year before ordinary election). (PR §4 sect. 2)

3.4	Left Party	Soc. Dem.	Centre Party	People's Party	Moderate	Chr. Dem.	Green Party	New Dem.
1993	As above. (PR §4 sect. 2)	As above. (Due to national electoral reform this in practice now means every four years). (PR §4 sect. 2)	As above.	At least once every 3 years. (PR §6 sect. c)	As above. (Due to national electoral reform this in practice now means every four years). (PR §6 sect. 4)	As above.	As above.	Every 4 years (once per election period, 3-15 months before election day). (PR §9)
1994	As above.	As above.	As above.	As above.	As above.	As above.	As above.	As above.

There has been no general trend over time with regard to the frequency of ordinary congresses. Two parties have increased the frequency; the Social Democrats in 1968 and the People's Party Liberals in 1971. The latter party reduced the frequency again in 1983, to a lower level than at the beginning of the research period. The Moderate Party decreased the frequency in 1969. These changes were motivated as adjustments to the national election cycle. The Swedish parties can be divided into two groups with respect to the frequency of congress. Three parties hold congress every year, and the remaining five parties follow the election cycle, and have made adjustments when that cycle has changed.[81]

The recent change of the Swedish election cycle from three to four years has had the effect that, without any rule change, party congresses have become less frequent in parties who follow the election cycle. It is not yet clear whether the parties in question will adjust their rules, but some observations can be made. The Social Democrats decided at the 1993 congress to increase the number of extra congresses until the next ordinary congress in 1996. It will then be evaluated whether annual congresses will be codified in the party rules. At the 1993 congress, the Left Party appointed a commission with the task to revise the rules, and the National Executive indicated a positive stance towards annual congresses. The People's Party changed the rules in 1993 so that the congress is now to be held 'at least every three years' instead of, as before, just every three years. The Moderate Party has at the time of writing not planned any adjustment.

---

[81] To follow election cycles still allows for some variations. There are parties which hold their congresses a few months before the election, like the Moderates until 1964, the Liberals until 1966, and the Social Democrats until 1968. Such congresses are naturally focused on the forthcoming election and have been labelled 'manifestation congresses' by Per Albinsson. All these mentioned parties have since changed to years when no election is held, more specifically the year before the election. Such congresses are different in character, and can be labelled 'working congresses' (Albinsson 1986:110). Parties who hold congress every year can of course combine both these types of congress.

The party has long argued that the local/regional and Riksdag elections should be held in separate years, and may wait to change the frequency of the congress until such a reform is reality.[82]

As can be seen in Table 3.5 below, all parties make it possible to call an extra congress. This can be done by the National Executive or, in most cases, by sub-national levels. The exception is the Centre Party, where it can only be done by the National Executive or the National Council (the terms of central party organs are explained later in this chapter). This can be interpreted as limiting the membership influence, but it should be remembered that the party holds annual congresses anyway. In the Christian Democrats, who also hold their congress annually, only the National Executive could call an extra congress until 1994, when the right was extended. It can now be demanded by at least half the number of regional organisations.

However, in the majority of the parties it is possible for lower party levels than the National Executives to call extraordinary congresses. In the Left Party, an extra congress may be called by sub-national organisations with a combined total number of members amounting to 1/3 of the total national party membership. In the Green Party, an extra congress may be called by the National Executive (before 1992 the National Council) or on demand by ten per cent of the party's members. The Social Democratic membership can call an extra congress via a membership referendum. Such a referendum can be initiated by 5 per cent of the party's members. The People's and Moderate parties are the only cases where the right to call an extra congress has changed in a substantively important way during the research period. At the beginning of the 1960s, decisions by central levels was the only possibility, in the People's Party the National Executive and the National Council, and in the Moderate Party the National Executive only.

---

[82] Sources: *Aktuellt i Politiken* (Social Democratic periodical), 1993 congress edition, September 18th (Social Democrats); Left Party, Congress 1993, booklet 4, p. 26 (National Executive answers to motions); People's Party Liberals, PR 1993, §6 sect. C; telephone interview with Moderate Party organising director Claes Weidstam, 10 December 1993.

Table 3.5   Ways of calling extraordinary congress, Swedish parties 1960-1994

year	Left Party	Social Democrats	Centre Party	People's Party	Moderate Party	Christian Democrats	Green Party	New Democracy
1960	National Executive or local org. representing a combined total of 1/3 of party members. (PR 1957, §8 sect. 2)	National Executive or via membership referendum. Such referendum can be called by 5% of total members. (PR 1956, §5 sect. 2; §9 sect. 3)	National Executive or National Council. (PR 1960, §26 sect. 2)	National Executive or 1/3 of National Council (PR 1960, §8)	National Executive. (PR 1950, §4)	---	---	---
1964	As above.	As above.	As above.	As above. (PR §8 sect. c)	As above, plus on demand by 1/3 of no. of regional org. (PR §4 sect. 4)	No rule. (Interim Rules)	---	---
1965	As above.	As above.	As above.	As above.	As above.	National Executive. (PR §3 sect. 2)	---	---
1967	As above. (PR §6 sect. 3)	As above.	As above.	As above.	As above.	As above.	---	---
1968	As above.	As above. (PR §6 sect. 2; §12 sect. 3)	As above.	As above.	As above.	As above.	---	---
1969	As above.	As above.	As above. (PR §29 sect. 1)	As above.	As above. (PR §7 sect. 4)	As above.	---	---
1971	As above.	As above.	As above.	As above; also on demand by executives of 1/3 of no. of regional org. (PR §8 sect. d)	As above.	As above. (PR §12 sect. 3)	---	---
1972	As above. (PR §5 sect. 3)	As above.	As above.	As above.	As above.	As above.	---	---
1974	As above.	As above.	As above.	As above. (PR §8 sect. d)	As above.	As above.	---	---
1975	As above.	As above. (PR §4 sect. 2; §10 sect. 3)	As above.	As above.	As above.	As above. (PR §8 sect. 3)	---	---
1978	As above. Decisions by membership meetings of local org. explicitly required. (PR §5 sect. 3)	As above.	As above.	As above.	As above. (PR §8 sect. 4)	As above.	---	---
1980	As above.	As above.	As above.	As above, but National Council abolished. (PR §8 sect. d)	As above.	As above.	---	---
1982	As above.	As above.	As above.	As above.	As above.	As above.	National Council or on demand by 10% of party membership. (PR §6)	---
1984	As above.	As above.	As above.	As above.	As above. (PR §6 sect. 4)	As above.	As above.	---

3.5	Left Party	Soc. Dem.	Centre Party	People's Party	Moderate	Chr. Dem.	Green Party	New Dem.
1992	As above.	As above.	As above. (PR §23 sect. 1)	As above.	As above.	As above.	National Executive or on demand by 10% of party membership. (PR §7)	National executive or on demand by 1/3 of no. of local org. (PR §4 sect. 3)
1993	As above. (PR §4 sect. 3)	As above.	As above.	As above. (PR §6 sect. d)	As above. (PR §6 sect. 5)	As above.	As above.	As above, but 1/3 of total members required (local org. abolished). (PR §9)
1994	As above.	As above.	As above.	As above.	As above.	National Executive, National Council, congress itself or on demand by at least half of no. of regional org. (PR §18 sect. 3)	As above.	As above.

Now, however, it has become possible for 1/3 of the regional organisations of the two parties to force an extra congress to take place (not to be confused with the Left Party rules where the requirement is that the regional organisations represent a specified proportion of the party membership). The Moderate Party made this change in 1964 and the People's Party in 1971.[83]

New Democracy has a similar rule, but when all sub-national levels were abolished in 1993, the rules changed so that 1/3 of the total members could call an extra congress.

At the end of the research period, sub-national levels have the authority to call an extra congress in each of the investigated parties except the Centre Party. The procedures vary, but it is difficult to assess if any certain ruling is more cumbersome than others. The People's Party's demand that the call must come from the regional executives, can be interpreted as a restraint on membership influence. The same might be said about the Social Democratic method, where the members must first force a referendum, which must then end up with a majority in favour of the extra congress.

---

[83] There is one difference between the Moderate and Liberal parties. The former state that an extra congress will be held on demand from 1/3 of the regional organisations, while the People's party require the executives from 1/3 of the regional organisations to make such a demand. The difference may be a mere formality; indeed the Moderate party rules do not state whether a regional membership meeting is required.

The rule that such a membership referendum can be called by 5 per cent of the membership is in itself problematic. While the proportion of 1/20 is notably lower than the one-third required to call an extra congress in the Left Party and New Democracy, or the 10 per cent required in the Green Party, the size of the Social Democratic party is a factor to be reckoned with. In 1997, the Social Democratic Party reported to have over 188,000 members (including the women's organisation), while the Green Party around 7500. Thus, the support from nearly 10,000 Social Democratic members is needed to call the referendum necessary to demand an extra congress (and then, of course, a majority is needed in the referendum itself), while a mere 800 are required to call an extra Green Party congress. During the times of collective affiliation to the Social Democratic party, when the total membership for several years exceeded one million, the five per cent rule was even more problematic. There was nothing in the rules which said that the five per cent rule applied to individual members only.

Over time, changes have taken place in three parties. The Moderate Party in 1964, the People's Party in 1971 and the Christian Democrats in 1994 have all made their members more influential when it comes to calling an extra congress.

Selection of the party leader

The externally most conspicuous level in a party is not an organ as such, but a person -- the party leader. The leader holds a key position in most parties all over the world, although the formal status may vary. In Germany and the United States, for example, the parties' candidates for the position as *Bundeskansler* or President are, as a rule, not the same persons as the chairpersons of the party organisations. In Sweden, however, the chairperson of the national party organisation is almost without exception the same as the party's main political spokesperson and consequently the party's candidate as *Statsminister* or, if such a position is not realistic, the person who will assume the most central post the party can get, if it is included in government.[84]

Peter Esaiasson has identified three main tasks for the party leader: organising internal party work, acting as the party's representative before

---

[84] For a thorough study on party leadership in Sweden, including a historical background, see Esaiasson 1985.

the voters and making decisions in government and parliament.[85] This is also reflected in the Swedish parties. The party leader chairs other central party organs, such as the National Executive and usually also the Executive Committee. He/she also plays a leading role in parliamentary work, although not always as formal chairperson of the Riksdag group.

Given the centrality of the party leader, the way in which he/she is elected is a valid indicator of the membership influence in a political party. There is, however, no variation among the Swedish parties in this respect. The party leader is elected by the party congress, and this has been so throughout the entire 1960-1994 research period. The only exception is the Left Party, whose National Executive elected the party chairperson until the party rules were revised in 1967.[86] The Green Party has never had a formal party leader. Instead the party has had two spokespersons, one from each gender. This institution developed in practice and was not codified in the party rules until 1992, although spokespersons have in fact been elected by the party congress since 1984.[87]

The rule that the leader is elected by the party congress applies to most parties in other nations as well, but it is not a rule completely without exception. In Great Britain, the Conservative Party leader is elected by the parliamentary party. This was the case also in the Labour Party until 1980. Since then, the leader has been selected by an electoral college, where the constituency organisations have one third of the total votes (the other two thirds are shared between the parliamentary party and affiliated

---

[85] Esaiasson 1985:1.

[86] Social Democrats, PR 1956 and 1964, §7 sect. 1 and 3; PR 1968, 1970 and 1972, §6 sect. 15 and §8 sect. 2; PR 1975, 1987 and 1990, §4 sect. 18 and 20 and §6 sect. 2 and PR 1993, §4 sect. 16 and §6 sect. 2. Centre Party, PR 1960 and 1967, §26 sect. 6.; PR 1969, 1971 and 1977, §29 sect. 5; PR 1992, §23, sect. 5. People's Party Liberals, PR 1960, 1964, 1966, 1967, 1969, §8; PR 1971, 1974, 1977, 1980, 1987, and 1990, §8 sect. g); PR 1993, §6 sect. g). Moderate Party, PR 1950, §4; PR 1964, §4 sect. 9; PR 1969, 1972 and 1974, §7 sect. 11; PR 1978, §8 sect. 11; PR 1984, 1987 and 1993, §6 sect. 11. Left Party, PR 1957 and 1964, §9 sect. 3; PR 1967, 1969 and 1972, §6 sect. 11; PR 1975, 1978, 1981, 1985 and 1990, §5 sect. 11. PR 1993, §4 sect. 12. Christian Democrats, Interim Rules 1964, §3 sect. 3; PR 1965, §3 sect. 6; PR 1971, §12 sect. 5; PR 1975, 1978, 1979, 1980 and 1984, §18 sect. 6; PR 1989, §18 sect. 7; PR 1994, §18 sect. 8. New Democracy, PR 1992, §4 sect. 11; PR 1993, §19.

[87] Pierre and Widfeldt 1992:812. Green Party, PR 1992, 1993 and 1994, §6 sect. 6.7.9.

organisations). The Liberal Democrats, on the other hand, subject the selection of the party leader to a referendum among all party members.[88]

Thus, there has been little change over time, or variance among the parties, when it comes to the selection of Swedish party leaders. But that is only a part of the story. The attention now turns to the selection of other leading party officials.

Selection of inter-congress central party organs

It has already been shown that the national congress is the highest decision-making body in every Swedish party. Between the congresses, all parties have other central organs. They vary in number, competence and size, but every party has at least one organ with formal as well as informal decision-making power. After the congress, these organs constitute the formally most powerful party level, which in practice means that they govern the parties between the congresses. Therefore, the way these organs are appointed is a valid indicator of membership influence. Rank-and-file members are relatively more influential if a central organ is directly elected by the congress or by sub-national levels than if the organ in question is appointed by another central organ. In the latter case, it is only indirectly elected by the congress.

The Swedish parties have given their central organs different labels, but they can be summarised into three levels. The top level, the Executive Committee (ExC), is in practice the most powerful level. Sometimes referred to as the party presidium, it consists of the most important individuals in the party leadership and is quite small in number. The intermediate level, the National Executive (NE), is for some parties the highest decision-making body between congresses. Bigger in size, it might not have the same informal status as the Executive Committee, but consists of élite groups in the party, and is formally superior in terms of decision-making authority. The third level, the National Council (NC), does not exist in every party. Where it exists, it has the function of a mostly advisory 'mini-congress' which maintains contacts between the central party and sub-national party levels.

Before proceeding to the presentations of these organs, the system of *suppleanter* must be explained. Most Swedish organisations (not only

---

[88] Webb 1992a:853f, Fisher 1996:38ff, 71ff and 99. After the Conservative Party's heavy defeat in the 1997 General Election, suggestions were made to involve ordinary party members in the process of selecting John Major's successor as party leader.

political, but also unions, sports clubs etc.) elect two types of members to their decision making bodies. Besides the full members there are also *suppleanter* who act as substitutes in the event of a full member being unable to attend. A *suppleant* is usually allowed (often expected) to attend meetings also when his/her presence is not required due to an absence. The position as a *suppleant* to a National Executive or an Executive Committee of a party is prestigious and involves a lot of work. In the tables below, *suppleanter* appear after the 'plus' sign. Thus, if a National Executive has '28+28 members', it means it has 28 full members and 28 *suppleanter*.

The development of the Executive Committees can be found in Table 3.6 below. Such organs have existed in most parties throughout the 1960-1994 period, with only partial exceptions. The Centre Party has never had an ExC written into the rules, but in practice it has existed since the 1960s, with a forerunner since the 1940s. The Moderate Party had an informal ExC which dealt with party finance and organisational matters until 1969, when a formal organ, similar to those of most other parties, was introduced and codified into the party rules. The Green Party introduced an ExC in 1992. New Democracy had an ExC in the 1992 rules but abolished it a year later.[89]

As a rule, the Executive Committee is elected by the National Executive within itself. The only exception to this is the Social Democrats, where it is directly elected by the congress, separately from the election of the NE. In practice, however, the congress elects part of the ExC in other parties as well. The party leader is, by the letter of the party rules or in practice, pre-designated to *ex officio* be included in the ExC where such exists. In the Centre Party, People's Party Liberals and Christian Democrats two party deputy chairpersons are elected separately by the congress who are as such pre-designated as *ex officio* members of the ExC. The Moderate Party specified that the party chair should be in the ExC until 1993. Since then, the party rules only state that the NE elects the ExC within itself.

---

[89] It is a matter of judgement which of the Executive Committee or the National Executive that actually was abolished. At the same time as the ExC was abolished, the NE was reduced in size (see Table 3.8). The intention of the party seems to have been to get rid of one organisational layer and to combine the roles of the ExC and the NE.

Table 3.6   Central party organs I (Executive Committee, ExC): selection, composition and competence, Swedish parties 1960-1994

year	Left Party	Social Democrats	Centre Party	People's Party	Moderate Party	Christian Democrats	Green Party	New Democracy
1960	*Arbets-utskott.* 6 to 10 members. Elected by NE within itself. Leads party between NE meetings, appoints central party staff, responsible for party enterprises and party finance. Sets salaries for central party staff. (PR 1957, §9 sect. 3)	*Verkställande utskott.* 7+7 members elected directly by congress. Includes Party Leader and Party Secretary (both elected separately). Rep. of women's and youth org. have right to attend. Responsible for day to day and administrative party business; accountable to NE. Responsible for party finance, propaganda and support to regional org. Appoints central party staff and sets their salaries. (PR 1956, §7 sect. 3 and 7; §8)	Not mentioned in PR. Informal presidium consists of Party Leader plus 1st and 2nd deputy party chairs. (Winqvist et al. 1972:150f)	*Arbetsutskott.* Party Leader and 8 other members. Elected by NE within itself. Also includes two officials (*Riks-ombudsman* and Party Secretary). Responsible for day to day party business and executive organ of party. (PR 1960, §10; §11)	*Förvaltnings-utskott.* Not mentioned in PR. Consists of Party Leader, 2 deputy party chairs, chairs of youth and women's org. party officials. Deals with finance and organisational matters. (Albinsson 1986:117f)	---	---	---
1964	As above.	As above.	As above.	As above, but now stated as executive organ of NE instead of whole party. (PR §10; §11)	As above.	*Arbets-utskott.* Party Leader, 2 deputy party chairs, 2 members appointed by NE within itself, up to 3 party officials appointed by NE. (Interim Rules §4)	---	---
1965	As above.	As above.	As above.	As above.	As above.	*Verk-ställande utskott.* Appointed by NE within itself; no further spe-cifications. (PR §4 sect. 4)	---	---
1967	*Verk-ställande utskott.* Party Leader; 6+2 members elected annually by NE within itself. Duties as above. (PR §8 sect. 3; §9)	As above.	*Arbetsutskott.* Minutes of said body from this year found in party archive. Not mentioned in PR.	As above.	As above.	As above.	---	---

3.6	Left Party	Soc. Dem.	Centre Party	People's Party	Moderate	Chr. Dem.	Greens	New Dem.
1968	As above.	As above, but propaganda and support to regional org. not mentioned among duties. (PR §8 sect. 2 and 3; §9)	As above.	As above.	As above.	As above.	---	---
1969	As above, but at most 9 members including Party Leader. (PR §8 sect. 3; §9)	As above.	*Arbetsutskott.* Elected by NE within itself. Not mentioned in PR (however, NE may appoint committees found necessary). (Winqvist et al. 1972:150f, PR §31 sect. 2)	As above.	*Arbetsutskott.* 7 members: Party Leader, chairs of youth and women's org. and four congress elected NE members; the latter four are appointed by NE. Prepares matters for, and executes decisions by, NE, deals with matters too urgent for NE. (PR §9 sect. 4)	As above.	---	---
1971	As above.	As above.	As above.	As above, but *Riks-ombudsman* abolished. (PR §10; §11)	As above.	As above. (PR §15 sect. 4)	---	---
1973	As above.	As above.	First mentioned in party annual report. 6+3 members incl. Party Leader and 2 deputy party chairs.	As above.	As above.	As above.	---	---
1975	As above. (PR §7 sect. 3; §8)	As above, but rep. of party's Christian org. also given the right to attend. Also responsible for NE and congress archives. (PR §6 sect. 2 and 3; §7)	As above.	As above.	As above.	Party Leader and at least 6 other members; the latter appointed by NE within itself. Resp. for party activities, finance, employs party staff, prepares matters for NE. (PR §19 sect. 3; §20)	---	---
1977	As above.	As above.	As above.	Rep. of youth and women's org. given the right to attend. (PR §10; §11)	As above.	As above.	---	---
1978	As above.	As above.	As above.	As above.	As above. (PR §10 sect. 4)	As above.	---	---
1982	As above.	As above.	As above.	As above.	As above.	As above.	None.	---

3.6	Left Party	Soc. Dem.	Centre Party	People's Party	Moderate	Chr. Dem.	Greens	New Dem.
1983	As above.	As above.	As above.	*Partiledning.* 6 to 8 members including Party Leader and Party Secretary. Youth and women's org. no longer represented (instead in newly created Organisation Delegation). (PR §9; §10)	As above.	As above.	None.	---
1984	As above.	As above.	As above.	As above.	As above. (PR §8 sect. 3)	Reduced to Party Leader and 4 other members. Resp. for employing staff moved to NE. (PR §20 sect. 3; §21)	None.	---
1985	As above.	As above.	5+3 members. (Party annual report)	As above.	As above.	As above.	None.	---
1990	As above, but at most 7 members including Party Leader. (PR §6 sect. 3; §7)	As above.	5+4 members. (Party annual report)	As above.	As above.	As above.	None.	---
1992	As above.	As above.	As above. Still not mentioned in PR, but NE may appoint committees found necessary. (PR §25 sect. 2)	As above.	As above.	As above.	*Arbets-utskott.* 2 party spokes-persons and 5 members elected by NE within itself. Prepares matters for NE, executes NE decisions and supports spokes-persons. (PR §11 sect. 11.8-11.11)	*Verk-ställande utskott.* Party Leader plus 4 congress elected NE members; the latter appointed by NE. Prepares matters for NE, executes NE decisions and deals with urgent matters. (PR §4 sect. 3)
1993	As above. (PR §6)	As above.	As above.	As above, but Organisation Delegation abolished. (PR §7; §8)	As above, but Party Leader not explicitly included. Wording on duties simplified. (PR §8 sect. 3)	As above.	As above.	None specified in PR (NE may appoint committees found necessary). (PR §23)

3.6	Left Party	Soc. Dem.	Centre Party	People's Party	Moderate	Chr. Dem.	Greens	New Dem.
1994	As above.	As above.	As above.	As above.	As above.	Party Leader, 2 deputy party chairs and 2+2 members elected by NE within itself. Duties as above. (PR §20 sect. 3; §21)	As above.	As above.

The Executive Committees are small units. That is one of the reasons for having such a level; it should be able to react quickly to political and internal events. It must be able to meet often and at short notice. The typical Swedish ExC consists of about 10 people. The lowest number found between 1960 and 1994 is 5, in the Christian Democratic Party and in New Democracy before the rule change in 1993.[90] The highest total is 14 (half of whom are *suppleanter*) in the Social Democratic Party throughout the research period.

The development of the National Executives is presented in Table 3.8 below. This is in most parties the most powerful organ between congresses (the exceptions are when a third level National Council with decision-making power exists). The National Executives are elected by the party congress. The only partial exception has been the Centre Party, where a minority of the NE was elected by the National Council until 1969. Consisting of more members than the Executive Committees, the National Executives are easier to assemble. However, as can be seen in Table 3.7. immediately overleaf, the actual number of meetings between the two organs differs significantly only in the Social Democrats and the People's Party Liberals.

The division of labour between the ExC and the NE is in short that the NE determines the political direction of the party, while the ExC takes care of more direct matters. Both organs are important power centres in the Swedish parties. Therefore, the way in which they are appointed is a valid indicator of membership influence. Unlike their size and frequency of meeting, however, there has been no variance with respect to how the National Executives are appointed. They have always been directly elected by the congress, with the Centre Party as the only partial exception. But there are differences with the Executive Committees. If this body is in its

---

[90] The Centre Party ExC also had five full members between 1985 and 1990, but there were also three *suppleanter*, who had the right to attend meetings.

entirety directly elected by the congress, the membership influence can be regarded as higher than if it is elected by the NE within itself.

Table 3.7   Number of meetings of the National Executives and Executive Committees, Swedish parties in 1991

	Left Party	Social Democrats	Centre Party	People's Party	Moderate Party	Christian Democrats
National Executive	7	7	11	7	7	8
Executive Committee	n/a	17	12	33	6	8

Sources: Left Party annual report 1990-1992, p. 15; Social Democrats annual report 1990-1992, p. 100; Centre Party annual report 1991, p. 10; People's Party Liberals annual report 1990-1993, p. 3; Moderate Party annual report 1990-1992, p. 12; Christian Democrats annual report 1991/92, p. 4 (the Christian Democratic figures are for the period between June 1991 and May 1992).

The Green Party deserves something of an account of its own. Since the first party rules were adopted in 1982, the party had made a point of having a less hierarchical structure than the traditional parties. Instead of the customary Executive Committee and National Executive, the party had four separate committees with a division of labour among them, all elected annually by the congress. The most well known of the committees was the Political Committee which was responsible for policy formulation and media contacts. The other committees dealt with internal matters and party publications.[91]

This organisational structure became increasingly controversial in the party. In the self-analysis after the election defeat in 1991, it was claimed that the structure with four committees was too slow and cumbersome, and there were suggestions of a change to an organisational structure more in line with the other Swedish parties. The proposals were met with some resistance, but at the 1992 congress the rules were revised so that the party is now traditionally organised with a National Executive elected by the congress, and an Executive Committee which is elected by the NE within itself.

---

[91] See Pierre and Widfeldt 1992:807, 812.

Table 3.8 Central party organs II (National Executive, NE): selection, composition and competence, Swedish parties 1960-1994

year	Left Party	Social Democrats	Centre Party	People's Party	Moderate Party	Christian Democrats	Green Party	New Democracy
1960	*Central-kommitté.* 45+15 members, elected by congress. Leads the party's political and organisational activities between congresses. (PR 1957, §9)	*Partistyrelse.* 28+28 members elected by congress (Party Leader, Party Secretary and ExC elected separately). Rep. of women's and youth org. have right to attend. Leads party in accordance with party programme, party rules and congress decisions. Highest decision making body between congresses. (PR 1956, §7 sect. 1 and 3)	*Partistyrelse.* 17+10 members (Party Leader, 2 deputy party chairs, 5+5 elected by congress, 5+5 elected by NC, 1 rep. each for women's org., youth org., party press and party staff). Responsible for party finance, day to day party business and party propaganda; appoints party staff and prepares matters for NC. (PR 1960, §28)	*Partistyrelse.* 28+11 members (Party Leader, 22+11 members elected by congress, Party secretary and *Riks-ombudsman* appointed by NE, 1 rep. each for Women's and youth org. and party press). Leads party in accordance with party rules and decisions by congress and NC. Executes decisions by, and prepares matters for, congress and NC. (PR 1960, §10)	*Partistyrelse.* 19 members (Party Leader, 2 deputy party chairs, 8 separately elected by congress, women's and youth org., 3 rep. each, Party Secretary and *Riks-ombudsman.* Leads party according to programme, PR and congress decisions, is in touch with regional org., supports and supervises regional, women's and youth org. (PR 1950, §7; Albinsson 1986:119ff)	---	---	---
1964	*Parti-styrelse.* Otherwise as above. (PR §9)	As above.	As above.	As above.	22 members (as above but 10 separately elected by congress; Party Director added). Duties as above plus: plans, leads and co-ordinates party activity; appoints staff and committees found necessary; in touch with parliamentary fraction. (PR §7)	*Rikskommitté.* 18+5 members (Party Leader, 2 deputy party chairs, 15+5 members elected by congress). Leads party between congresses (Interim Rules §4)	---	---

3.8	Left Party	Soc. Dem.	Centre Party	People's Party	Moderate	Chr. Dem.	Greens	New Dem.
1965	As above.	As above.	As above.	As above.	As above.	*Förbunds-styrelse*. 38+25 members (Party Leader, 2 deputy party chairs, 35+28 elected by congress, of which 28+28 allocated to regional org. on a one to one basis; election period is two years so half of the members are elected every year). Leads party between congresses, responsible for party finance and day to day business, prepares matters for congress. (PR §4 sect. 1-3)	---	---
1967	Party Leader, 30+10 elected by congress. Duties as above. (PR §6 sect. 11; §8)	As above.	As above.	As above.	As above.	As above.	---	---
1968	As above.	35+22 . Highest decision making organ between congresses. Otherwise as above. (PR §8 sect. 1-3)	As above.	As above.	As above.	As above.	---	---

3.8	Left Party	Soc. Dem.	Centre Party	People's Party	Moderate	Chr. Dem.	Greens	New Dem.
1969	As above, but 35+10 members including Party Leader. (PR §6 sect. 11; §8)	As above.	18+10 members (Party Leader, 2 deputy party chairs, 10+10 elected by congress, 1 rep. each for women's org., youth org., student's org., party press and party staff). Duties as above, plus: plans, leads and co-ordinates party activity, prepares matters for congress, appoints national and regional committees, in touch with and promotes party press. (PR §31)	As above.	19 members (Party Leader, 2 deputy party chairs, women's and youth org. 3 rep. each). Many others have the right to attend *ex officio*. Duties as above, but specified that NE is accountable to congress and shall plan and lead political, financial and administrative party activity. (PR §9 sect. 1, 3 and 7)	As above.	---	---
1971	As above.	As above.	As above.	27+14 members (as above, but *Riks-ombudsman* abolished and women's, youth and press org. 1+1 each instead of just 1). Duties as above, but prepares matters for, and executes decisions by, congress only. (PR §10)	As above.	*Partistyrelse*. 38+28 members (Party Leader, 2 deputy party chairs, 33+28 elected by congress, incl. 1+1 from each regional org. (elected for two years; 50% up for election every year), Party Secretary (appointed by NE), youth org. 1 rep). Plans, leads and co-ordinates party activity, resp. for party finance, prepares matters for congress, appoints staff and com-mittees (PR §15 sect. 1-3 and 5)	---	---
1972	As above. (PR §5 sect. 11; §7)	As above.	As above, but no rep. for the now abolished Student's org.	As above.	As above.	As above.	---	---
1975	As above.	As above, but rep. of party's Christian org. also right to attend. (PR §6)	As above.	As above.	As above.	As above. (PR §19; §25)	---	---

3.8	Left Party	Soc. Dem.	Centre Party	People's Party	Moderate	Chr. Dem.	Greens	New Dem.
1977	As above.	As above.	As above.	28+15 members (as above, but Student's org gets 1+1 rep). (PR §10)	As above.	As above.	---	---
1978	As above, but 35+15 members including Party Leader. (PR §5 sect. 11; §7)	As above.	As above.	As above.	As above. (PR §10, sect. 1, 3 and 7)	As above, but specified that chairs of regional org. should be at least *suppleanter* of NE. (PR §19)	---	---
1980	As above.	As above.	As above.	As above. (PR §9)	As above.	As above.	---	---
1982	As above.	As above.	As above.	As above.	As above.	As above.	No single organ of this nature. Instead four committees: *Förvaltnings-utskott* (party finance, administration), *Politiskt Utskott* (policy), *Tidnings-utskott* (periodicals, publishing) and *Stadgeutskott* (party rules, organisation) 5-11 members each, elected by congress. (PR §8 - §11)	---
1984	As above.	As above.	As above; one rep for restarted Student's org. given right to attend. (Party annual report)	As above.	As above. (PR §8 sect. 1-3)	17+11 members: Party Leader, 2 deputy party chairs, 11+11 separately elected by congress (election period two years as above). Party Secretary appointed by NE, chairs of women's and youth org. Stated that NE should have wide regional representation. Duties as above, plus prepares matters for newly formed NC. (PR §20)	As above.	---

3.8	Left Party	Soc. Dem.	Centre Party	People's Party	Moderate	Chr. Dem.	Greens	New Dem.
1990	At most 25+8 members including Party Leader. Deals with finances of party and party enterprises. Otherwise as above. (PR §5 sect. 11; §6)	As above.	As above.	29+16 members (as above, but party's immigrant's organisation given 1+1 representative). (PR §10)	As above.	As above.	As above.	---
1992	As above.	As above.	18+6 members. (Party Leader, 2 deputy party chairs, 11+6 members elected by congress, 1 rep. reach for women's, youth and student's org. and party staff). Duties as above. (PR §23 sect. 5; §25)	As above.	As above.	As above.	Partistyrelse. 21 to 27 members (2 party spokespersons plus 19 to 25 members separately elected by congress; at most 1/3 may be members of the Riksdag). Leads party activities, supports spokespersons, convenes, and prepares matters for, congress and NC, promotes party policies with spokespersons as main means, executes congress decisions, responsible for party assets, develops ideological and visionary progress. (PR §11)	Partistyrelse. At least 13 members (Party Leader, 2 deputy party chairs, at least 10 separately elected by congress). May call others without right to vote. Plans and leads political financial and organisational activity; accountable to congress. Appoints committees and staff, in touch with parliamentary fraction, assists and supervises local org., (PR §4 sect. 11; §2 sect. 6)

3.8	Left Party	Soc. Dem.	Centre Party	People's Party	Moderate	Chr. Dem.	Greens	New Dem.
1993	Composition and selection as above. Responsible for execution of congress decisions, political leadership of party, party finance and party enterprises. (PE §4 sect. 12; §5)	As above.	As above.	25 members (Party Leader, 2 deputy party chairs and 21 members separately elected by congress, Party Secretary (appointed by NE). Side organisations (women, youth, students and immigrants) one rep. each without the right to vote). Duties as above. (PR §7)	15 members (Party Leader, 2 deputy party chairs, women's and youth org. one rep. each). May decide to let others attend without the right to vote. Plans and leads policy, finance organisation and campaign activity. Is accountable to congress. Supports regional org. and women's and youth org.; works to ensure that their activity conforms with party ideology. (PR §8 Sect. 2 and 6)	As above.	As above.	8 members (Party Leader, 2 party deputy chairs, 6 members separately elected by congress). Duties as above, plus: prepares matters for congress, and ensures that party members get continuous information about party activity. (PR§19; §23)
1994	As above.	As above.	As above.	As above.	As above.	As above, plus: makes decisions in important national political issues; decides, in co-operation with parliamentary fraction, par-liamentary guidelines for each election period. (PR §20; §26)	As above.	As above.

Third level organs, the National Councils, are fairly large assemblies which can be described as 'mini-congresses'.[92] They are described in Table 3.9 below. At the end of the research period, they exist among all the investigated parties except two: the Social Democrats and New Democracy. The National Councils have undergone several changes between 1960 and 1994. In the Centre, People's and Moderate parties, the NC had some decision-making power until around 1970. The NC assumed some of the role of the congress in years when no congress was held. Even in the Centre Party, where the congress meets every year, the NC elected part of the NE until 1970, something which since that year rests completely

---

[92] In 1993, the Centre Party National Council consisted of a total of 70+103 members (Annual party report).

on the congress. At the end of the 1960s, however, all these parties changed the rules so that the National Council is now primarily an advisory organ. It can still make decisions, but only in issues specifically submitted by the congress or the National Executive. It is not unknown, however, for the NC to receive this temporary authority, and its status as a consultative organ in the party has remained high.[93]

The People's Party Liberals abolished the National Council in 1980. There was, however, some continuity in the sense that a consultative meeting between the NE, parliamentary party and regional representatives was still possible. In 1993, a new National Council was introduced, with a minimum of one meeting per year except years when the congress meets. It was also given a separate section in the party rules (the consultative meeting between 1980 and 1993 had been mentioned in the paragraph for the National Executive). This can be interpreted as emphasising the importance of the NC, although there has been no third level organ with formal decision making power since 1971.

The Christian Democratic and Green parties introduced a National Council with decision-making authority in 1984 and 1982, respectively. In the Christian Democratic Party it is the NC that decides on the plan for forthcoming election campaigns, and decides the party's internal budget. The Green Party, however, reduced the National Council to an advisory organ, when the party was reorganised and the party rules revised in 1992. Between 1982 and 1992, the NC was the highest decision-making organ between congresses. The change was a clear indication of the Green Party's efforts to streamline the organisation. At the same time, it meant that the Christian Democrats are now unique in terms of the power given to the National Council.

The Left Party introduced an advisory NC in 1967. In 1990 it was renamed. It is still advisory, but its importance as a communicative organ between the party leadership and sub-national levels has increased because it has been given a minimum frequency of meeting of at least once a year and can also be called on demand by one third of its own members.

---

[93] Albinsson 1986:125 mentions some cases from the Moderate Party where the NC has continued to make decisions. It has, for example, decided the party's election manifesto and a policy document on education.

Table 3.9   Central party organs III (National Council, NC): selection, composition and competence, Swedish parties 1960-1994 (Social Democrats and New Democracy not included, as they have never had such an organ)

year	Left Party	Centre Party	People's Party	Moderate Party	Christian Democrats	Green Party
1960	None	*Förtroenderåd.* Rep. allocated to regional org., normally 1+1 each. Also Party Leader, 2 deputy party chairs, chairs and 2 deputy chairs of women's and youth org., one rep. each for student's org., party press and party staff. Called by NE or on demand by 1/3 of NC members. Elects 5+5 members to the NE, prepares matters for congress, deliberates political matters together with NE, parliamentary fraction and executives of women's and youth org. (PR 1960, §20 sect. 1; §27)	*Förtroenderåd.* Party Leader, NE, ten members directly elected by congress, regional org. one rep. each. Meets at least once a year and on demand by NE or 15 NC members. Deals with and approves NE annual report. Appoints regional representatives in *Centrala lönenämnden.* Arranges general political debate in years when party congress does not meet. Parliamentary party and executives of women's, youth and press org. also represented on such meetings. (PR §9)	*Partiråd.* Consists of NE, 10 members separately elected by congress, chairs of regional org., chair of press org. Meetings called by NE. One of three organs which lead party (others being congress and NE). Approves NE annual report and auditor's report in years with no congress. (Albinsson 1986:124ff; PR 1950, §3; §6)	---	---
1964	As above.	As above.	As above.	As above, but rep. of youth and women's attend without the right to vote. Called by Party Leader, NE or on demand by 1/3 of NC members. No mention of duties but still stated as leading party organ besides NE and congress. (PR §3; §6)	*Representantskap.* NE plus regional org., two rep. each. Advisory organ. Called by Party Leader and 2 deputy party chairs. (Interim Rules §5)	---
1965	As above.	As above.	As above.	As above.	Abolished.	---
1967	*Rikskonferens.* Rep. allocated to regional org. according to membership. Deals with political and organisational matters. Called by NE. Should meet in election years with no congress. (PR §7)	As above.	As above.	As above.	As above.	---

3.9	Left Party	Centre Party	People's Party	Moderate Party	Christian Democrats	Green Party
1969	*Riks- eller valpolitisk konferens.* Rep. allocated to regional org. after criteria set by NE. Called by NE but no specification on frequency. Duties as above, but explicitly only advisory. (PR §7)	Regional org. represented according to membership; Party Leader and 2 deputy party chairs, two others appointed by NE; 5 rep. each of women's and youth org.; two rep. from student's org.; parl. fraction represented according to its size; party press and party staff 1 rep. each. Meets at least twice a year. Called by NE or 1/3 of NC members. Organ for mutual information and advice between NE, parl. party and regional org. Can decide on matters submitted by NE or congress. (PR §24 sect. 1; §30)	As above.	Composition as above, except: no. of members elected by congress increased to 20; executive of parliamentary party also included. NE may invite other persons. Advisory organ except on matters submitted by congress. Presented with NE annual report in years with no congress. Meets at least once in years with no congress. Called by Party Leader, NE or on demand by 1/3 of no. of regional org. (PR §6; §8)	As above.	---
1971	As above.	As above.	Composition as above, plus rep. of women's, youth and press org. Parliamentary fraction also called to meetings. Organ for information and consultation in political and organisational matters. Deals with NE annual reports in years with no congress. Called by NE or on demand by 15 NC members. (PR §9)	As above.	As above.	---
1972	As above. (PR §6)	As above, but no rep for the abolished student's org. (Party annual report)	As above.	As above.	As above.	---
1977	As above.	As above.	As above, but one rep. also to student's org.	As above.	As above.	---
1978	As above.	As above.	As above.	As above, but head of *Med-borgarskolan* (study org.) also included. (PR §7; §9)	As above.	---

3.9	Left Party	Centre Party	People's Party	Moderate Party	Christian Democrats	Green Party
1980	As above.	As above.	Abolished. Instead, a meeting with NE, parl. fraction and one rep. each from regional org. can be called, either on demand by at least 5 regional org. or by NE. (PR §9)	As above.	As above.	---
1982	As above.	As above.	As above.	As above.	As above.	*Förtroenderåd.* Regional org. have one rep. each. Meets at least once every 4 months. Extra meetings called by *Förvaltnings-utskott, Politiskt utskott* or on demand by at least half of NC members. Highest decision-making organ between congresses. Decides procedural rules for the four central committees. By-elects new members to those committees if needed. (PR §7)
1983	As above.	As above.	As above, but the meeting is named *Representantskap*	As above.	As above.	As above.
1984	As above.	As above.	As above.	Consists of NE and one rep. per regional org. NE may invite other persons. Meets at least once a year except in congress years. Called by Party Leader, NE or on demand by 1/3 of no. of regional org. Proposes candidates for party's election committee (appointed by congress). Can otherwise make decisions only in matters submitted by congress. Deals with political, organisational and financial matters of common interest to the party and the regional org. (PR §7)	*Partifullmäktige.* Regional org. 1+2 rep. each plus additional rep. according to membership, 7+7 members appointed by NE, 7+7 members appointed by parl. fraction (if any), women's and youth org. 2+2 rep. each. Meets when called by NE and on demand by 1/3 of NC members; at least once a year. Deals with matters of principal relevance to party finance, decides party budget, deals with matters of principal importance to party activity, decides on party activity plan, deals with matters raised by members of NE or NC. (PR §19)	As above.
1985	As above.	As above, but re-started Student's org. given five rep. (Party annual report)	As above.	As above.	As above.	As above.

3.9	Left Party	Centre Party	People's Party	Moderate Party	Christian Democrats	Green Party
1986	As above.	As above.	As above.	As above.	As above.	As above, plus: Decides on all programme matters between congresses, co-ordinates *Landsting* election campaigns if needed. Can make decisions with financial conse-quences only after approval by *Förvaltnings-utskott.* (PR §7)
1987	As above.	As above.	As above.	As above.	As above.	As above, but meets at most twice a year. (PR §7)
1989	As above.	As above.	As above.	As above.	As above.	As above, but also approves party budget. (PR §7)
1990	*Partiråd.* Rep. allocated to regional org. according to membership. Full NE mem-bers attend with the right to vote. Called by NE at least once a year. Extra meeting can be called by 1/4 of NC or 1/3 of NE. Advisory to NE on matters of major political significance. (PR §8)	As above.	As above.	As above.	As above.	As above.
1992	As above.	Party press no longer represented. Otherwise as above. (PR §18 sect. 1; §24)	As above.	As above.	As above.	Composition as above. Called by NE at least once a year. Can also be called by parliamentary party. Support for NE and parliamentary party in new and/or controversial issues. Forum for exchange of information and experience. (PR §13)

3.9	Left Party	Centre Party	People's Party	Moderate Party	Christian Democrats	Green Party
1993	As above. (PR §7)	As above.	*Partiråd.* Same as *Representantskap* above, except: also one rep each for women's, youth, student's and immigrant's org. Shall meet at least once in years with no congress. (PR §9)	As above.	As above.	As above.
1994	As above.	As above.	As above.	As above.	May also be called by party auditors. Also deals with matters of principal importance concerning election campaign and decides on campaign plan. Otherwise as above. (PR §19)	As above.

The compositions of the National Councils vary somewhat, but the principles are similar. It is intended as a representative organ where the regional organisations can meet the party leadership. In the Christian Democrats, Left Party and the Centre Party, the regional organisations are allocated delegates according to their respective membership size. In the Christian Democratic Party and the Left Party, each region is guaranteed one representative, plus one in addition for every 1,000 members.[94] The Centre Party allocates one representative to each region per 5,000 members or fraction thereof.[95] In the Green, People's and Moderate Parties each regional organisation gets one representative each. Besides the regional representatives, the parties' side organisations (youth, women, students etc.) are usually represented and the National Executives normally attend.

Where they exist, the National Councils are important institutions. Even though their formal power has decreased in some parties, they are an extra contact source between the leadership and the sub-national party levels. The NC can therefore be seen as a means by which the members can

[94] Christian Democratic Party, PR 1984-1994, §19 sect. 3. In 1992, this meant that, out of the 27 regional organisations, 13 got one, one got two and one got three extra representatives (Christian Democratic Party, annual report 1991/92, p. 20). Left Party, PR 1993, §7 sect. 3. In 1992, this meant that, out of the 23 regional organisations, one got one and one got two extra representatives (Left Party, annual report 1990-1992, p. 13).

[95] Centre Party, PR 1969, 1971, 1972 and 1977, §24 sect. 1; PR 1992, §18 sect. 1. In 1994 this meant that, out of 29 regions, two were qualified for one extra representative (Centre Party, annual report 1994, p. 10).

exert informal influence other than via the congress. When the NC has formal decision making authority, the membership influence increases.

Most parties have central party organs regulated in the party rules other than those described in Tables 3.6, 3.8 and 3.9. The only exceptions are the Centre Party and the Christian Democrats. The Social Democrats have a Programme Commission, which has a defined role in the process when the party programme is revised. It has no decision-making authority, but must be consulted before the National Executive submits proposals of changes to the party programme to the congress. The Programme Commission consists of five full members and as many *suppleanter*, all directly elected by the congress. Its members have always been leading names, including the party leader.[96]

The Left Party introduced a Programme Commission in 1969. Directly elected by the congress, it consists of up to 7 members. Its role is similar to that of the equivalent organ in the Social Democratic Party, but somewhat less strictly defined. In the 1993 rules it is merely stated that the Programme Commission reports continually to the National Executive. It does not consist of as well known members as in the Social Democratic Party, but it was an integral part of the party's ideological reorientation before the 1993 congress.[97] Until 1964, the party also had a so-called Control Committee. This body was quite powerful. It scrutinised the economy of the party, and enterprises related to the party, and was also the final appeal instance in cases of expulsions of members. It consisted of nine members directly elected by the congress.[98]

The People's Party Liberals have had a number of different formal organs over the years. As a rule, they have been appointed by the National Executive and have not had formal decision making authority. Until 1971 it was stipulated that the NE appointed a number of so-called Permanent Delegations which dealt with finance, internal organisation and information. They ceased to be specified in the party rules in 1971 but the

---

[96] *Programkommission.* Winqvist et al. 1972:203. Social Democratic Party, annual report 1990-1992 p. 27, 112 and 218. PR 1956 §5; PR 1968 §10; PR 1975, 1984, 1987, 1990 and 1993 §8.

[97] *Programkommission.* Left Party, PR 1969 §11, 1972, 1975, 1978, 1981, 1985 and 1990, §10; PR 1993, §9. Left Party, annual report 1990-1992, p. 12.

[98] *Kontrollkommitté.* Left Party, PR 1957, §10. In 1964 its financial duties were taken over by the newly introduced party auditors. The ultimate right to, after appeals, expel members was transferred to the congress. PR 1964, §3 sect. 11.

NE has continued to appoint different groups and committees.[99] The party has also had a special committee for the employment and salaries of party functionaries between 1964 and 1977,[100] and a committee for the party's internal organisation between 1983 and 1993.[101]

The Moderate Party had institutionalised conferences among the chairpersons of the regional party organisations between 1978 and 1984. These conferences were soon considered as unnecessary besides the already existing National Council.[102]

Between 1986 and 1989, the Green Party had a co-ordination group, which had the purpose to co-ordinate and exchange information between the four central party committees and was also intended as a link between these committees and the National Council. It consisted of representatives appointed by the National Council and the four central party committees.[103] In 1993, New Democracy introduced a Rules Committee which deals with matters concerning the party rules, and issues such as arbitration in conflicts between the party and its local co-parties.[104] At the same time a Nomination Committee was introduced, which prepares the party's nominations for elections to the Riksdag and international organs.[105] Both these committees are appointed by the National Executive.

Besides the formally defined inter-congress central party organs, every party has a number of informal committees of varying status and importance. These organs deal with external as well as internal party matters. The Moderate Party has a tradition dating back to the 1940s of central committees which focus on issues related to specific occupational groups. They are not formally defined in the party rules except that it is stated that the National Executive appoints committees as found necessary.

---

[99] People's Party Liberals, PR 1960, §12; PR 1964, 1966, 1967 and 1969, §13. Examples of such groups and committees can be found in the party's annual reports, e.g. 1990-1993, p. 9-12.

[100] *Central lönenämnd*, PR 1964, 1966, 1967, 1969, 1971 and 1974, §12. It may have existed earlier.

[101] *Organisationsdelegation*, People's Party Liberals, PR 1983, 1987 and 1990, §10.

[102] Albinsson 1986:124. Moderate Party, PR 1978, §11.

[103] *Samordningsgrupp*. Green Party, PR 1986, 1987 and 1988, §12.

[104] *Stadgekommitté*. New Democracy, PR 1993, §29.

[105] *Nomineringskommitté*. New Democracy, PR 1993, §27.

Their role is advisory and they also have the purpose to organise party activity among their respective occupational groups.[106]

Most parties have from time to time had committees which have studied the party's organisation. There are also many examples of groups and committees which deal with different policy areas. Some of these groups and committees are in practice permanent for many years but there are also ad-hoc groups. As a rule, these committees are appointed by the NE, as a consequence of its competence to appoint the committees it finds necessary.

Three further institutions need to be mentioned. In every party the congress elects auditors who audit the party's accounts during the forthcoming congress period and present their findings to the next congress. The number of auditors is low, usually two or three plus *suppleanter*. The People's Party Liberals, the Moderate Party, the Christian Democrats and New Democracy require that at least one of them is a qualified chartered accountant.[107] The Green Party introduced an

---

[106] In 1992, three such committees existed: *Moderata Centrala Företagarrådet* (self-employed), *Moderata Centrala Jordbrukarrådet* (farmers) and *Moderata Centrala Löntagarrådet* (employees; until 1989 there had been separate committees for white and blue collar employees). Albinsson 1986:128f, Moderate Party annual report 1990-1992 p. 31-34. PR 1964, §7 sect. 3; PR 1969, 1972 and 1974, §9 sect. 7; PR 1978, §8; PR 1984, 1987 and 1993, §5.

[107] The Swedish word for an auditor is *Revisor*. Social Democrats, PR 1956 and 1964, §10, PR 1968, 1970 and 1972, §11; PR 1975, 1984, 1987, 1990 and 1993, §9. Left Party PR 1964, §10; PR 1967 and 1969, §6 sect. 11 and §10; PR 1972, 1975, 1978, 1981, 1985 and 1990, §5 sect. 11 and §9; PR 1993, §4 sect. 12 and §8 (the role of the auditors lay with the Control Committee until 1964). Centre Party, PR 1960 and 1967, §26 sect. 6 and §29; PR 1969, 1971, 1972 and 1977, §29 sect. 5 and §32; PR 1992, §23 sect. 5 and §26. People's Party Liberals, PR 1960, §8 and §13; PR 1964, 1966, 1967 and 1969, §8 sect. f) and §14; PR 1971 and 1974, §8 sect. g) and §13; PR 1977, §8 sect. g) and §12; PR 1980, 1983, 1987 and 1990, §8 sect. g) and §11; PR 1993, §6 sect. g) and §10. Moderate Party, PR 1950, §4 and §9; PR 1964, §4 sect. 9 and §9; PR 1969 and 1972, §7 sect. 11 and §11; PR 1978, §8 sect. 11 and §13, PR 1987 and 1993, §6 sect. 11 and §10. Christian Democrats Interim Rules 1964, §3 sect. 3; PR 1965, §3 sect. 6 and §6; PR 1971. §12 sect. 5 and §14; PR 1975, §18 sect. 6 and §12; PR 1984, 1985, 1986 and 1988, §18 sect. 6 and §22; PR 1989, 1990, 1993 and 1994, §18 sect. 7 and §22. New Democracy PR 1992, §4 sect. 11 and §9; PR 1993, §19 and §35.

innovation in 1992, in the shape of an auditing committee consisting of seven members, all elected by the congress.[108]

The work of the auditors is normally of an administrative rather than political nature. The duty of the auditors is to scrutinise the management of the central party for which the National Executives are formally responsible. Therefore, in situations when parties have been in crisis and the auditors have found reasons to criticise the management of the party, this has tended to have political consequences. In the Moderate Party (until 1993) and New Democracy, the auditors are divided into economic and general auditors. The former deal with the financial management of the party, while the latter look into more general aspects, including a scrutiny of whether leading organs in the party have acted in accordance with the party programme and party rules during the previous congress period.

In parties where no division of responsibility exists among the auditors, the congress may elect a *décharge* committee which looks into the non-financial aspects of the activities of leading party organs (usually the National Executive and Executive Committee) since the previous congress. The *décharge* committee is usually not codified in the party rules, but its report to the congress is nevertheless an important item on the congress agenda.[109]

Finally, every party has an Election Committee, also elected by the congress. The committee prepares internal elections and proposes candidates to every post to be elected at the next congress (except the Election Committee itself). The Election Committees consist of between 5 and up to 11 members; the highest number of members can be found in the Left, Green and Moderate Parties.[110] The congress is not formally bound by

---

[108] *Revisionsnämnd.* Green Party, PR 1992 and 1993, §8. Previously, the party had a more traditional format of 2+2 auditors. PR 1982 and 1984, §13; PR 1986, 1987 and 1988, §14; PR 1989, §13.

[109] The *décharge* committee (in Swedish also referred to as *granskningsutskott*) in the Social Democratic Party is discussed by Pierre 1986:99ff. See also Winqvist et al. 1972:272f about the Left Party. It is codified in the party rules of the People's Party Liberals where it consists of seven members: PR 1964, 1966 and 1967, §8 sect. f); PR 1969, §8; PR 1971, 1974, 1977, 1980, 1983, 1987 and 1990, §8 sect. g); PR 1993, §6 sect. g).

[110] *Valberedning.* Left Party, PR 1967 and 1969, §6 sect. 13; PR 1972, §5 sect. 13; PR 1975, 1978, 1981, 1985 and 1990, §5 sect. 12; PR 1993, §4 sect. 13. Social Democrats, PR 1968, 1970 and 1972, §6 sect. 16; PR 1975, 1984, 1987, 1990, §4 sect. 18 and PR 1993, §4 sect. 16. Centre Party, PR 1969, 1971, 1972, and 1977, §29 sect. 5; PR 1992, §23 sect. 5.

the proposals of the Election Committee but in practice its proposals carry a lot of weight, because its members have usually checked the possibility of its candidates being accepted. The Election Committee is often a venue for in-fighting, but also for important compromises between party factions. A notable case when the Election Committee played a decisive role was in November and December 1985, when it was revealed that the Election Committee of the Centre Party had decided against proposing re-election of Thorbjörn Fälldin as party leader at the 1986 congress. Fälldin, who earlier had declared his intentions to stay, resigned when he became aware of the position of the Election Committee.[111] Another example of the potential importance of the Election Committee is the Moderate Party, which suffered as series of leadership battles between 1961 and 1970.[112]

The main purpose of this rundown of central party organs has been to shed more light on the membership influence on the central party levels. The evidence presented is quite cumbersome but does give some insight into the development of membership influence. The National Executives are very important bodies in all the Swedish parties. With the Centre Party until 1969 as the only (and partial) exception, they have always been directly elected by the congress in every party. The Executive Committees, however, are elected by the National Executives within themselves, with the Social Democrats as the only exception. In this respect, therefore, the Social Democratic members have more influence on the ExC because it is more directly linked to the congress than in the other parties. The Green Party can actually be said to have somewhat decreased membership influence in this respect when they in 1992 introduced a traditional National Executive which elects an Executive Committee within itself. The

---

People's Party Liberals, PR 1960, §8; PR 1964, 1966 and 1967, §8 sect. f); PR 1969, §8; PR 1971, 1977, 1980, 1983, 1987 and 1990, §8 sect. g) and i); PR 1993, §6 sect. g) and i). Moderate Party, PR 1950, §4; PR 1964, §4 sect. 9; PR 1969 and 1972, §7 sect. 8 and 11; PR 1978, §8 sect. 8 and 11; PR 1984, 1987 and 1993, §6 sect. 8 and 11. Christian Democrats Interim Rules 1964, §3 sect. 3; PR 1965, §3 sect. 6 and §5; PR 1971, §12 sect. 5 and §13; PR 1975, §18 sect. 6 and §22; PR 1984, §18 sect. 6 and §23; PR 1989, §18 sect. 7 and §23; PR 1994, §18 sect. 8 and §23. Green Party, PR 1982 and 1984, §12; PR 1986, 1987 and 1988, §13; PR 1989, §12; PR 1992, 1993 and 1994, §6 sect. 6.7.13 and §9. New Democracy, PR 1992, §4 sect. 8; PR 1993, §15.

[111] Björn Elmbrant's biography on Fälldin has a detailed account of the events, in which the Election Committee played a central part. Elmbrant 1991:268-286.

[112] For the background and course of these events, see Albinsson 1986, especially pp. 90 and 96.

previous comparable party level, the four central party committees, were all directly elected by the congress.

The National Council can also be regarded as promoting membership influence. Besides the congress, it provides a communicative bond between central party organs and sub-national party levels. It is particularly important in the Christian Democratic Party, where it has formal decision-making powers. In the Left, Centre, Moderate, People's, and since 1992 also Green, parties it is primarily an advisory and consultative organ. It is still, however, important as a source of communication between different party levels, and may at times make decisions in matters specifically delegated to it.

It has been argued that the Social Democrats compensate for the lack of a National Council with their National Executive which is larger than in other parties.[113] The combined total of 57 members (35 plus 22 *suppleanter*) is indeed large compared to the other studied parties. The nearest are the Left, Christian Democratic and People's parties with NE's consisting of between 20 and 30 members depending on whether *suppleanter* are counted. A comparison between the Social Democratic National Executive, and the National Councils in some other parties, gives further depth to this argument. The largest NC's can be found in the Centre Party and the Christian Democrats. In 1994 the Centre Party NC consisted of a total of 69 members (not including the *suppleanter* which totalled over 100), 45 of which were appointed by the regional organisations.[114] The Christian Democratic NC has around 45 members appointed by the regional party levels.[115] Thus the Social Democratic NE is indeed comparable to the NC's of most parties, although not larger than all of them. On the other hand, it could be pointed out that the Social Democratic NE is elected by the congress, and sits throughout the entire congress period. The NC's, however, are elected directly by the regional organisations and its members renewed every year, also in parties such as the Moderate Party, People's Party Liberals and the Left Party where the congress does not meet every year. Thus, the NC's are more closely linked to the sub-national levels between congresses than the Social Democratic NE, something which could be taken as evidence of more membership influence.

---

113 Winqvist et al. 1972:204.

114 Centre Party, annual report 1993, pp. 4-8.

115 This is based on the party rules and the membership strength of the regional organisations in 1992 (Christian Democrats, annual report 1992, p. 20).

Conclusion and comparative outlook

The evidence presented in this chapter must be tied together. It has been argued that the openness of the parties is high, does not vary among different parties and has been virtually stable over time. With membership influence, however, the picture is more diverse. The reasoning in this chapter is that membership influence varies according to the following criteria:

a) if membership referenda are possible, membership influence is higher than if this is not the case;
b) the more frequently the national congress meets, the higher the membership influence;
c) if individual members can submit motions to the congress without restrictions, membership influence is higher than if this is not the case;
d) if all members are allowed to participate in the debates at the congress, membership influence is higher than if this is not the case;
e) if there is an inter-congress representative organ, i.e. a National Council, membership influence is higher than if this is not the case; especially if the NC has decision making authority;
f) the higher the proportion of central inter-congress organs which are directly elected by the congress, the higher the membership influence.

The problem is of course that the parties do not fit into a logical transitive scale. The Social Democrats, for example, is the only party whose entire Executive Committee is directly elected by the congress. On the other hand, the party lacks a National Council and the frequency of the congress is low compared to some other parties. To get an overall picture, an additive index has been constructed. The items of the index are presented in Table 3.10.

Item A, the right for sub-national party levels to call a membership referendum, is an indicator of direct democracy. It is based on the evidence presented in footnote 76 above. The Greens and Social Democrats have always given their members the possibility of a referendum, while the Left Party and New Democracy introduced it in 1967 and 1993, respectively.

Table 3.10   An additive index of membership influence in political parties

A. Possibility for sub-national party levels to call membership referendum
* yes   1
* no   0

B. Frequency of national congress:
* at least every year   2
* at least every 2 years   1
* less often   0

C. Right for sub-national party levels to call extra congress:
* yes   1
* no   0

D. Right for individual members to send motions to national congress:
* yes   2
* yes, but can be stopped by intermediate level   1
* no   0

E. Right for all party members to take part in congress debates:
* yes   1
* no   0

F. Inter-congress representative organ (National Council):
* Exists, with decision making authority   2
* Exists, but normally without decision making authority   1
* Does not exist   0

G. Number of other decision-making central organs (National Executive, Executive Committee and their equivalents) directly elected by national congress or sub-national levels:
* all   2
* one   1
* none   0

The next item, the frequency of the national congress, has had a lot of variation among the parties. The empirical evidence can be found in Table 3.4. The variation, together with the fact that it is a very important means by which members via their delegates can hold the leadership accountable, the item has been trichotomised and given a maximum value of two. The Green, Centre and Christian Democratic parties consistently score maximum points here, holding their congress annually. The Social Democrats and the Left Party are all found on the other extreme throughout the research period. The Moderates and People's Party Liberals display a negative development, scoring a zero from 1969 and 1983 respectively.

Item C, right for sub-national party levels to call an extra congress, is based on Table 3.5. This has continuously been possible in the Social Democratic, Left and Green parties and New Democracy. The Moderate Party, People's Party Liberals and Christian Democrats introduced such a reform in 1964, 1971 and 1994 respectively, while the Centre Party is the only party to score a zero at the end of the research period.

The right for individuals to send motions to the congress has been trichotomised. This is justified by the fact that the right to submit motions can be qualified by the possibility for the regional levels to stop the motion going all the way to the congress. It is, furthermore, an important possibility for rank and file members to influence the decisions made by the most powerful level in the party; the congress. Therefore its weight of 2 is reasonable. The evidence party by party appears in Table 3.2. Every party except the Social Democrats and the Moderate Party consistently score maximum points on this variable. In the former case, the score is reduced from 2 to 1 because of the fact that sub-national party levels can stop motions from reaching the congress. The Moderate Party gave no direct right for individual members to propose motions until 1969, but from then on all members have had this right without restrictions.

Another aspect of the party congress is taken care of in item E. Parties who give every member the right to take part in congress debates, based on Table 3.1, have been given a score of 1 and parties where this is not possible a score of zero. The Green, Centre, Christian Democratic and People's Party all score on this item, while New Democracy's rule revision in 1993 moved them from zero to 1. Like item A, this is an indicator which has some direct democratic aspects.

The next item deals with the National Council and is based on Table 3.9. This large representative organ is considered an important bond between central and sub-national party levels and has been given a maximum weight of 2. The middle score of 1 is given to parties who have such an organ but without formally defined decision making authority. The Green Party scored full points on this item until 1992, when it reduced the decision-making authority of the NC. The Christian Democratic Party has scored full points since their NC was introduced in 1984. The People's Party Liberals, Centre and Moderate parties have all moved from 2 points in 1960 to 1 point since around 1970 when they reduced the decision making authority of the NC. The Left Party, on the other hand, went from a score of zero to 1 when such a level was introduced in 1967.

Item G concerns the selection of other central level decision-making organs, primarily the National Executive and the Executive Committee. The scoring is based on the evidence in Tables 3.6 and 3.8. If all of these organs are directly elected by the congress, a score of 2 is awarded. If only one of them is directly elected by the congress, the score is set to one. In cases where none of them is directly elected by the congress, the score is zero. Every party has always scored at least 1 on this item. Only one party has consistently scored maximum points, however, namely the Social Democrats, where the party rules have always stated that the Executive Committee is separately elected at the congress. The Green Party also scored full points on this item between 1982 and 1992, when the party had four central committees which were all directly elected by the congress. The reform where a more traditional format with a National Executive and an Executive Committee was implemented meant that the score went down to 1, because the ExC is elected by the NE. All other parties have consistently scored 1 on this item because the NE is elected by the congress and the ExC by the NE within itself.[116]

The scores thus given, together with the total scores, are presented year by year and party by party in Table 3.11 below. There are cases of increased as well as decreased membership influence, but also of stability. The Social Democratic Party is the only example of the latter. It has remained absolutely stable on every indicator throughout the research period. All other parties have experienced some changes, even if the fluctuations have mostly been quite modest.

The clearest case of increased membership influence is the Christian Democrats. In its first year of existence, 1964, the party amassed a total index score of four. However, this was before the party had had time to organise itself properly and it is more reasonable to count 1965, when

---

[116] A problem is how to deal with the Centre and Moderate parties. In the Centre Party, the Executive Committee has existed *de facto* for many years, but has never been codified in the party rules. The existence of the ExC can be said to have been recognised by the congress when it approved the formation of an ExC in 1969. However, some sort of presidium had *de facto* existed since the 1940s (Winqvist et al.:150f). Another problem is that since 1985, more than half of its members with voting rights consist of the Party Leader and the two deputy party chairs who have been separately elected by the congress. However, since the congress formally does not have anything to do with the ExC except the *ex post* approval of the NE's annual report, where the ExC is mentioned, the party will be given a score of 1 (the NE but not ExC directly elected by the congress) throughout the research period. The same score is consistently given to the Moderate Party, whose ExC was not codified until 1969 but which had *de facto* existed well before 1960 (Albinsson 1986:117ff).

the first permanent party rules were taken, as the real starting point. From that year the party remained at a score of six for nearly two decades. But the revision of the party rules in 1984 meant that the party's total score increased by two points. This was because a National Council with decision making authority was introduced which resulted in a leap from zero to 2 on item F. Ten years later, the score increased again because it became possible for sub-national levels to demand an extra congress.

There are increasing trends also for the Left and Moderate parties and New Democracy. The Left Party increase took place in 1967, when it became possible for sub-national party levels to call a membership referendum and a consultative National Council was introduced. The Moderate Party increased its score in 1964 when sub-national party levels got the right to demand an extra congress. There were further changes in connection with the profound revision of the party rules in 1969. The score increased from 0 to 2 on item D, right for individual members to propose motions to the congress. However, this was offset by the fact that the congress frequency decreased, and that the National Council lost most of its decision making powers. Thus, the aggregate score remained stable, at 5, and has done so since. New Democracy went up between 1992 and 1993 because of the introduction of a membership referendum and that all party members were given full rights to participate in the national congress. The score also increased because there is now only one central party organ between congresses, the National Executive, which means that every central inter-congress organ is directly elected by the congress.

Decreasing trends are found in three cases. The Centre Party went down one point in 1969 when the pre-defined decision making authority of the National Council was removed. Otherwise the party has remained stable on all items. The People's Party Liberals implemented two changes in 1971. Sub-national party levels were given the authority to demand an extra congress, but at the same time the National Council was downgraded to a mainly advisory organ. Therefore, the aggregate index score remained stable. In 1983, however, it sank one point because the frequency of the congress decreased. Finally, the Green Party index decreased when the party was reorganised in 1992. First, because the newly introduced Executive Committee is elected by the National Executive within itself which means that no longer are all of the most central inter-congress organs directly elected by the congress. Second, because the National Council was changed from a decision-making to mainly an advisory and consultative organ.

Table 3.11 Membership influence index, Swedish parties 1960-1994

year	Left Party	Social Dem.	Centre Party	People's Party	Moderate Party	Christian Democrats	Green Party	New Democracy	sum	mean
1960	0012001 **4**	1011002 **5**	0202121 **8**	0102121 **7**	0100021 **4**	-	-	-	28	5.6
1961	0012001 **4**	1011002 **5**	0202121 **8**	0102121 **7**	0100021 **4**	-	-	-	28	5.6
1962	0012001 **4**	1011002 **5**	0202121 **8**	0102121 **7**	0100021 **4**	-	-	-	28	5.6
1963	0012001 **4**	1011002 **5**	0202121 **8**	0102121 **7**	0100021 **4**	-	-	-	28	5.6
1964	0012001 **4**	1011002 **5**	0202121 **8**	0102121 **7**	0110021 **5**	0200011 **4**	-	-	33	5.5
1965	0012001 **4**	1011002 **5**	0202121 **8**	0102121 **7**	0110021 **5**	0202101 **6**	-	-	35	5.8
1966	0012001 **4**	1011002 **5**	0202121 **8**	0102121 **7**	0110021 **5**	0202101 **6**	-	-	35	5.8
1967	1012011 **6**	1011002 **5**	0202121 **8**	0102121 **7**	0110021 **5**	0202101 **6**	-	-	37	6.2
1968	1012011 **6**	1011002 **5**	0202121 **8**	0102121 **7**	0110021 **5**	0202101 **6**	-	-	37	6.2
1969	1012011 **6**	1011002 **5**	0202111 **7**	0102121 **7**	0012011 **5**	0202101 **6**	-	-	36	6
1970	1012011 **6**	1011002 **5**	0202111 **7**	0102121 **7**	0012011 **5**	0202101 **6**	-	-	36	6
1971	1012011 **6**	1011002 **5**	0202111 **7**	0112111 **7**	0012011 **5**	0202101 **6**	-	-	36	6
1972	1012011 **6**	1011002 **5**	0202111 **7**	0112111 **7**	0012011 **5**	0202101 **6**	-	-	36	6
1973	1012011 **6**	1011002 **5**	0202111 **7**	0112111 **7**	0012011 **5**	0202101 **6**	-	-	36	6
1974	1012011 **6**	1011002 **5**	0202111 **7**	0112111 **7**	0012011 **5**	0202101 **6**	-	-	36	6
1975	1012011 **6**	1011002 **5**	0202111 **7**	0112111 **7**	0012011 **5**	0202101 **6**	-	-	36	6
1976	1012011 **6**	1011002 **5**	0202111 **7**	0112111 **7**	0012011 **5**	0202101 **6**	-	-	36	6
1977	1012011 **6**	1011002 **5**	0202111 **7**	0112111 **7**	0012011 **5**	0202101 **6**	-	-	36	6
1978	1012011 **6**	1011002 **5**	0202111 **7**	0112111 **7**	0012011 **5**	0202101 **6**	-	-	36	6
1979	1012011 **6**	1011002 **5**	0202111 **7**	0112111 **7**	0012011 **5**	0202101 **6**	-	-	36	6
1980	1012011 **6**	1011002 **5**	0202111 **7**	0112111 **7**	0012011 **5**	0202101 **6**	-	-	36	6
1981	1012011 **6**	1011002 **5**	0202111 **7**	0112111 **7**	0012011 **5**	0202101 **6**	-	-	36	6
1982	1012011 **6**	1011002 **5**	0202111 **7**	0112111 **7**	0012011 **5**	0202101 **6**	1212122 **11**	-	47	6.7
1983	1012011 **6**	1011002 **5**	0202111 **7**	0012111 **6**	0012011 **5**	0202101 **6**	1212122 **11**	-	46	6.6
1984	1012011 **6**	1011002 **5**	0202111 **7**	0012111 **6**	0012011 **5**	0202121 **8**	1212122 **11**	-	48	6.9
1985	1012011 **6**	1011002 **5**	0202111 **7**	0012111 **6**	0012011 **5**	0202121 **8**	1212122 **11**	-	48	6.9
1986	1012011 **6**	1011002 **5**	0202111 **7**	0012111 **6**	0012011 **5**	0202121 **8**	1212122 **11**	-	48	6.9
1987	1012011 **6**	1011002 **5**	0202111 **7**	0012111 **6**	0012011 **5**	0202121 **8**	1212122 **11**	-	48	6.9
1988	1012011 **6**	1011002 **5**	0202111 **7**	0012111 **6**	0012011 **5**	0202121 **8**	1212122 **11**	-	48	6.9
1989	1012011 **6**	1011002 **5**	0202111 **7**	0012111 **6**	0012011 **5**	0202121 **8**	1212122 **11**	-	48	6.9
1990	1012011 **6**	1011002 **5**	0202111 **7**	0012111 **6**	0012011 **5**	0202121 **8**	1212122 **11**	-	48	6.9
1991	1012011 **6**	1011002 **5**	0202111 **7**	0012111 **6**	0012011 **5**	0202121 **8**	1212122 **11**	-	48	6.9
1992	1012011 **6**	1011002 **5**	0202111 **7**	0012111 **6**	0012011 **5**	0202121 **8**	1212111 **9**	0012001 **4**	50	6.3
1993	1012011 **6**	1011002 **5**	0202111 **7**	0012111 **6**	0012011 **5**	0202121 **8**	1212111 **9**	1012102 **7**	53	6.6
1994	1012011 **6**	1011002 **5**	0202111 **7**	0012111 **6**	0012011 **5**	0212121 **9**	1212111 **9**	1012102 **7**	54	6.8

Comment: The entries represent the scores from the index presented in Table 3.10 above. The first digit represents the score on item A, and so on. The eighth digit, in bold after the space, represents the added total index for the respective party in the respective year.

The decrease in the Green Party index, and the increase in the Christian Democrats, means that the two parties now share the top position. Until the recent changes in both parties, the Greens were without comparison the party with the highest degree of formal membership influence. The Green Party's internal structure allows the members to voice their opinions and hold the leaders accountable in a variety of ways. The congress is held annually. Between the congresses there is a National Council with regional representation which had a pre-defined decision making authority until 1992. The party members can call a membership referendum as well as an extra congress and they can, without formal restrictions, propose motions to the congress and take part in the congress debates. The party meets a number of different criteria of membership influence and democracy.

It is worth noting that, while the Green Party is known for its advocacy of direct democracy, much of its rules can also be regarded as well in line with representative democratic principles. The party's structure includes direct democratic procedures such as the membership referendum, which has also been used. But there are also important representative elements. The high frequency of the congress with annual re-elections of spokespersons and the National Executive means that the members have facilities to constantly hold the party leadership accountable. The National Council, which consists of delegates from the regional organisations, is a representative organ which balances the authority of the National Executive and Executive Committee.

This description now also fits the Christian Democratic Party quite well. In 1994, they are level on points with the Greens. The differences between the two parties cancel out. The Christian Democrats have no possibility of a membership referendum, but the Greens have reduced the authority of the National Council.

The lowest scores can be found in the Moderate and Social Democratic parties, while the Left and Centre and People's Party Liberals are in intermediate positions. Thus, there is no systematic pattern with regard to organisational or ideological party types. Of the traditional movement based parties, the Social Democrats and the Centre Party, neither scores very high. The Social Democrats have not lived up to the pledge quoted at the beginning of this chapter, and are in fact joint bottom together with the Moderate Party for the majority of the 1960-1994 period. The Left Party has a tradition in the labour movement, but is today mostly considered a 'New Politics' party. As such, it is interesting to note how much lower the party scores compared to the Green Party.

The main purpose of the exercise in this chapter, however, is to study the trends over time. Between 1960 and 1994 the aggregate index has gone up in four parties (Left Party, Moderate Party, Christian Democrats and New Democracy). The index has decreased in three cases (Centre Party, People's Party Liberals and the Green Party). It has been stable in the Social Democrats. Thus, there is no overall trend in any direction.

On the national level, the average index has increased over time. It was 5.6 between 1960 and 1963, but has been between 6 and 6.9 in the 1980s and 1990s. It can therefore be concluded, that there is no overall or general decrease in membership influence in the Swedish party system. The increased average is partly caused by the entry of new parties. Both the Christian Democrats and the Green Party have made net contributions to the average index, although the Christian Democrats did not score particularly high on the index until 1984. However, the aggregate index of five traditional parties (Left Party, Social Democrats, Centre Party, People's Party Liberals and the Moderate Party) has also increased somewhat; from 28 (average 5.6) in 1960 to 29 (average 5.8) in 1994.

From a European perspective, there are two things which can be said about the findings of this chapter. The Swedish development of increased or at least stable membership influence is very much in line with the situation elsewhere in Europe. Second, the membership influence in the Swedish parties is high, if not unique, compared to other Western European countries.

In Katz and Mair's edited anthology "How Parties Organize", Peter Mair argues that the combined evidence from 11 European countries suggests no signs of party members becoming marginalised, and that "many parties still consider membership to be of value".[117] In Belgium, for example, any changes concerning the party congresses have been in the direction towards increased participation.[118] However, the situation is not entirely clear cut, and there are examples to the contrary. In Austria, for example, the frequency of congress has decreased in several parties, while the election periods for the National Executives have increased.[119]

---

[117] Mair 1994:14.

[118] Deschouwer 1994:100. See also Bille 1994:142 about the Danish case.

[119] Müller 1994:69. In Sweden, the election periods of the National Executives never extends beyond the period between two ordinary congresses except in the Christian

Indeed, the evidence in the volume suggests that the Swedish parties have, at least, a competitive degree of membership influence according to the indicators used here. In Great Britain, the national congresses of all the major parties meet every year but their respective authority is questionable. In the Conservative Party, for example, it has no formal power whatsoever.[120]

The conclusion of this chapter must be made with care, however. The first caveat is the limitation of studying formal influence. Many writers in the Katz and Mair volume have noted increased informal power of leading party organs. Thomas Poguntke has argued that a large share of the power distribution in a party stems from factors such as material resources and, in addition, immaterial resources such as electoral appeal and media access. Thus, the formal framework of the party rules may be considered insufficient.[121]

Another limitation is the omissions of some important aspects of party life. The parliamentary fractions have not been considered. Clearly, the leadership of a political party has to take this level into account at least as much as the extra-parliamentary party organisation. This is noted by several authors in Katz and Mair's volume. In Sweden, for example, it is argued that the parliamentary fractions in the Swedish parties have a high and, if anything, increasing degree of autonomy towards the national party organisations, and are increasingly influential over the party leaderships.[122]

The candidate nomination procedures, and local and regional politics, are also left out. These limitations are not negligible. What they mean is that the final word is not said about the structure, internal democracy or even membership influence in the Swedish political parties. The finding that formal membership influence on central party levels has not decreased is therefore not trivial, however. Party members in Sweden are not powerless. They have unseated party leaders. They often play an important role when new leaders are elected. The amount of time and effort spent by leading politicians before their parties' congresses says something about the importance they attribute to their members. The commitment to membership influence, in the party documents cited in the beginning of this

---

Democrats where the NE members are elected for two year periods and the congress takes place every year. However, half of the NE is renewed every year.

[120] Webb 1994:110.

[121] Poguntke 1994:207ff.

[122] Pierre and Widfeldt 1994:349ff.

chapter, cannot be neglected. The evidence just presented, indicates that this appreciation of the members is, at least, not only lip service.

Just like in the days of Robert Michels, the parties are led by leaders. These leaders are powerful. As is suggested in Jon Pierre's cited study of the Social Democrats, they can press congress decisions in the direction they want to. But even if this is true, the fact that they spend all this time and effort in trying to appease and influence the members shows that the rank-and file members of the Swedish parties are still a factor to be reckoned with. The ordinary members may not rule the parties, but they have the means to check and balance those who do.

4 Development of Membership Strength

Introduction

Organisational size has often been taken as evidence of whether parties are in decline or not.[1] The parties themselves also perceive large membership as important. In the annual reports presented to the 1993 Congress of the Social Democratic Party, there were reports of recruitment campaigns every year since the previous congress in 1990.[2] This concern is not unique to the Social Democrats. Congress documents of other parties frequently include mentions of membership recruitment campaigns. The membership development is always given some kind of attention; increases are noted with delight, and declines deplored. Particularly successful individual recruiters of new members are often rewarded.[3] This chapter intends to investigate how the Swedish parties have succeeded in their membership recruitment efforts.

The development of party membership has been given quite a lot of attention in previous research. However, it has sometimes been in passing, as part of a wider overview. Examples are the government initiated Swedish Power Investigation (*Maktutredningen*) and the Danish investigation of citizenship, which both refer to party membership as one of several

---

[1] E.g. Dalton, Flanagan and Beck 1984:460, von Beyme 1985:186, 367f, Kitschelt 1990:206.

[2] Social Democratic Party, 1993 Congress, annual report (*Verksamhetsberättelse 1990-1992*) pp. 39f (1990), 139f (1991) and 225 (1992).

[3] In recent years, another three parties besides the Social Democrats have mentioned active membership recruitment campaigns in their annual reports: People's Party Liberals, 1993 Congress (*Landsmöte*), verksamhetsberättelse 1990-1993, p. 4, Moderate Party, 1993 Congress (*Partistämma*), verksamhetsberättelse, p. 27, Christian Democratic Party, 1993 Congress (*Riksting*), verksamhetsberättelse 1992/93, p. 9. Other parties do not mention recruitment campaigns as such, but note their membership development and make comments which clearly show that they wish to have many members: Centre Party, Congress (*Riksstämma*) 1995, *Verksamhetsberättelse* 1994, p. 33, Left Party 1993 Congress, volume 5, *Partistyrelsens verksamhetsberättelse 1990-1992*, p. 12. For an example of rewards to individual recruiters, see *Aktuellt i Politiken* (Social Democratic periodical), 20 September 1993 (Party Congress issue).

indicators of political participation.[4] This is a fully reasonable approach, given the wide perspective of those studies. Here, however, the focus is explicitly set on the parties. Membership strength, on both party and national levels, is an indicator of the parties' ability to provide participatory linkage.

The statement that membership development has been dealt with in passing does not tell the whole truth. Stefano Bartolini has made an extensive study on the membership development of socialist parties in the post-war era. Klaus von Beyme's work on parties in Western Europe outlines the overall development of membership. The most recent, and also most thorough, contribution is Katz and Mair's account which includes most major parties in eleven European countries between 1960 and 1990. The article is based on Katz and Mair's edited data handbook on party organisations, which includes detailed tabular information about the membership development in those eleven countries. Among several country-specific studies, Ola Listhaug has done a thorough investigation on party membership in Norway between 1957 and 1985.[5]

The contribution of this chapter will be to provide a systematic account of the development over time of party membership on the national level as well among individual parties. In previous Swedish and international research, the findings are not broken down by party, but focused on the aggregate national level. Such results are of course relevant, but differences among parties are also important. Do parties to the left or to the right succeed best in attracting members and activists? Is there a difference between old and new parties? The last question is worth considering because the 'crisis of parties' debate often assumes that old organisations are being out-competed by new ones. Some, but by no means all, of the new organisations are parties: green, 'new left' or 'left-libertarian'.[6] In this perspective, the ability of new parties to attract members is of interest. Are parties which represent an ideological and organisational challenge more successful in recruiting members than the old parties that they challenge?

---

[4] Petersson, Westholm and Blomberg 1989, Goul Andersen 1993. Another example is Johansson 1971, which was part of the so-called 'Low Income Investigation'.

[5] Bartolini 1985, von Beyme 1985, Katz, Mair et al. 1992 (EJPR), Katz and Mair eds. 1992 (Data Handbook), Listhaug 1989. In Listhaug's study, which provides an extensive analysis of the development of political behaviour in Norway, a complete chapter is focused on party membership.

[6] E.g. Kitschelt 1990, Müller-Rommel 1990.

In line with the perspective of the whole book, this chapter will concentrate on the development of party membership over time. The purpose is not to judge whether a certain number or proportion of members is 'good enough'. Evidence will be presented which allows comparisons between parties and with other countries. In relation to the whole study, however, the most important question is the trends: decline or no decline.

A decline in membership, or activism, is not necessarily the same thing as party decline. Parties can still fulfil many of the functions attributed to them without a large number of members.[7] It is, however, difficult to see how declining membership is compatible with the parties' ability to provide participatory linkage. It is theoretically conceivable that participatory linkage could be possible with other organisational forms than traditional membership. That possibility would appear as purely theoretical, however, since the Swedish -- and European -- parties have chosen to base their organisations on formal membership.

Membership development alone is an imprecise indicator of the extent to which parties provide participatory linkage. It is not a sufficient criterion; passive members are not participating. However, it can be argued to be necessary. In order to participate in party activities, it is necessary to be a member. The development of party activism will be studied in the next chapter.

Data and method

Measuring party membership is not an entirely straightforward exercise. There are three particularly important problems: how to define a party member, which data to use and which measure that is the most appropriate. The first problem is how to define a party member. Most parties have 'side organisations' which organise youths, women and sometimes also other groups. Some such organisations have a complete membership overlap with the 'mother party'; others are separated. The former are referred to as ancillary organisations, the others we call affiliated organisations.[8]

---

[7] Cf. the discussion in Chapter 2 above.

[8] See Katz and Mair 1992:17.

Figure 4.1 Ancillary and affiliated organisations of the Swedish parties 1960-1997

Party	Women's organisation	Youth organisation	Other organisations
Left Party	none	*Demokratisk Ungdom*, DU (-1967). *Vänsterns Ungdomsförbund*, VUF (1967-1970). *Kommunistisk Ungdom*, KU (1973-1991). *Ung Vänster*, UV (1991-). Affiliated. Party had no youth org. 1970-1973.	*Sveriges Socialistiska Pionjärer*, SSP. Children's organisation. Affiliated. Formed circa 1978. Became non-partisan organisation in 1992. *
Social Democrats	*Sveriges Socialdemokratiska Kvinnoförbund*, SSKF. Ancillary.	*Sveriges Socialdemokratiska Ungdomsförbund*, SSU. Affiliated.	*Sveriges Kristna Social-demokraters Förbund*, SKSF. Also referred to as *Broderskap*. Christian organisation. Ancillary. *Sveriges Social-demokratiska Student-förbund*, SSSF. University students. Affiliated. Out of existence 1970-1990.
Centre Party	*Svenska Landsbygdens Kvinnoförbund*, SLKF (-1962). *Centerns Kvinnoförbund*, CKF (1962-). Affiliated.	*Svenska Landsbygdens Ungdomsförbund*, SLU (-1962). *Centerns Ungdomsförbund*, CUF (1962-). Affiliated.	*Centerns Studentförbund*, CSF. (1961-1971). University students. Affiliated. Existed as part of youth organisation until 1961. *Centerns Högskoleförbund*, CHF (1984-). University students. Affiliated. Out of existence 1972-1984.
People's Party Liberals	*Folkpartiets Kvinnoförbund*, FPK. Affiliated. Had no formal membership registration between 1964 and 1982.	*Folkpartiets Ungdomsförbund*, FPU (-1990). *Liberala Ungdomsförbundet*, LUF (1990-). Affiliated.	*Liberala Studentförbundet*, LSF. University students. Affiliated. Out of existence 1971-1974. *Liberala Invandrarförbundet*, LIF (1988-). Immigrants. Affiliated. Formed 1988.
Moderate Party	*Högerns Kvinnoförbund*, HKF (-1969). *Moderata Kvinno-förbundet*, MKF (1969-1997). Ancillary. *Moderatkvinnor (1997-)*. Network (no longer separate side organisation).	*Högerns Ungdomsförbund*, HUF (-1969). *Moderata Ungdomsförbundet*, MUF (1969-). Ancillary.	none**
Christian Democrats	*Kristen Demokratisk Samlings Kvinnoförbund*, KDS-K (1982-1987). *Kristemokratiska Samhällspartiets Kvinnoförbund*, KdS-K (1987-1996). *Kristdemokratiska Kvinno-förbundet*, KD-K (1996-). Affiliated. Formed 1982.	*Kristen Demokratisk Ungdom*, KDU (1966-1987). *Kristdemokratiska Ungdomsförbundet*, KDU (1987-). Affiliated. Formed 1966.	*Kristdemokratiska Seniorförbundet*, K-S. Pensioners (open for people aged 55 and over). Affiliated. Formed 1992.
Green Party	none	*Grön Ungdom*, GU (1986-). Ancillary. Formed 1986.	none
New Democracy	none	none	none

Comment: Ancillary = complete membership overlap with party. Affiliated = no such complete overlap (there may be a partial overlap). *): There has existed a students' organisation linked to the Left Party (*Kommunistiska Högskoleförbundet*). **): There is a students' organisation with ideological links to the Moderate Party (*Fria Högerstudenters Förbund*, previously *Fria Moderata Studentförbundet*); however, it claims to have no formal party ties.

The ancillary and affiliated organisations of the Swedish parties appear in Figure 4.1. above. It should be noted that the formal distinction between ancillary and affiliated does not necessarily indicate a difference in political 'closeness' between the organisation and the party. Most of the organisations in Figure 4.1 make a point of being independent from the mother party, and any variations among the parties in this respect are not necessarily according to the complete membership overlap distinction; ancillary organisations are not necessarily more loyal to the party than affiliated organisations.[9] The distinction of membership overlap can also be deceptive in a formal way. Most affiliated organisations have a substantial partial membership overlap with the party. This is because local branches of the side organisations may simultaneously belong to the main party, but also because individuals may be members of an affiliated organisation and the main party at the same time.

What, then, is the best method to ensure comparability among the parties? Should we count direct members of the main party only, or also members of the side organisations? The first option has been used in most previously published research. It is also the most plausible considering the perspective of this study, where parties are seen as providers of linkage between citizens and the state. It is not the side organisations that provide candidates for public office, and it is not the side organisations that represent the citizens in public decision-making.

A decision to include only direct members leads to problems with the Swedish parties, however. In the Moderate Party, all female members were automatically enrolled as members of the women's organisation until 1984. Thus, the direct members (direct meaning total party membership minus members of ancillary organisations) until that time were only male. This means that the 'direct membership' figures are not comparable within the Moderate party over time, nor is it comparable with other parties. If the Moderate women's organisation is included, the same must be done for every party (where such an organisation exists), to ensure comparability among parties.

If the purpose is to stay as close to the 'direct membership' criterion as possible, the inclusion of 'side organisation' members should be kept to a

---

[9] The ancillary Social Democratic Women's organisation (SSKF) has often been noted for criticising the party leadership. SSKF has been described as a major factor behind the fact that Sweden decided not to introduce nuclear weapons in the 1950s/early 60s. See Molin 1989.

minimum. Since they do not provide comparability problems similar to the women's organisations, no youth, students', Christian or any other party connected organisations will be included. Thus, direct members, plus members of the women's organisations, ancillary or affiliated, will be treated as party members in this chapter.

Another problem related to the definition of a party member is that of the collectively affiliated members of the Social Democratic Party, also referred to as corporate membership.[10] Beginning in 1898, the Swedish Social Democrats enrolled members of LO, the federation of blue collar unions.[11] The collective affiliation was subject to decision by the local unions. In the beginning, the decisions were taken at open membership meetings, where all members of the local unions had the right to vote. However, a reformation process began in the 1950s, when local unions were amalgamated into what in effect were regional units (in Swedish *storavdelningar*). In these larger units, the decisions were often taken at representative meetings (*'representantskap'*).[12]

After a decision to introduce collective party membership had been taken by a local union, all its members became members of the local Social Democratic *Arbetarekommun*. In 1908, it became possible for individual members to opt out of the collective membership. However, while the collective party affiliation of the union remained until another decision was taken, individual opt-outs had to be renewed every year.[13]

Collective membership was subjected to intense debate, outside as well as inside the party. It has been argued that it is undemocratic to enrol members to a party collectively, and that the right to opt out has often been ineffective because many union members have failed to use it due to fear of repercussions. The debate grew in intensity in the 1980s, and the 1987 Social Democratic congress decided to abolish collective membership.[14] The

---

[10] See Katz and Mair 1992:17.

[11] Thermeanius 1933:74. Until 1900, it was obligatory for all local units of the LO (Confederation of blue-collar unions) to be affiliated with the party. From then on, it has been voluntary.

[12] Hagård 1966:30-36.

[13] Thermeanius 1933:74. Hagård 1966:36-40.

[14] Gidlund 1989:299-303. For a historical background, see also Hagård 1966:40-85. The Social Democratic congress decision in 1987 was influenced by the fact that the Left Party Communists had started to indicate that they were willing to support initiatives from the non-socialist parties to legislate against collective party membership. The 1987 congress

dismantling of the system was gradual, and was completed at the end of 1990.

Collective membership is not unique to Sweden. It also exists in the Labour parties of Great Britain and the Republic of Ireland. The Norwegian Labour Party, however, followed the Swedish example and decided to abolish collective membership in 1992.[15]

It goes without saying that collective members are problematic when it comes to assessing the membership of the Swedish Social Democrats. Not all of the collective members can be expected to have been committed, or even consenting, members of the party. At the same time, it is questionable if subtracting all collective members from the analysis solves the problem. It seems plausible, for example, that some collective members would have enrolled as individual members if that was the only option.[16] This is not to say that all collective members could be treated as equal to individual members. Some of them should, but we do not know who, or how many. In this study, both individual members and the totality of Social Democratic members, including those collectively affiliated, will be considered to the extent that data allow.

The second major problem when measuring party membership is which type of data to use. There are two possible sources: Party Records (the

---

decided to introduce a new type of corporate membership by which local trade unions became affiliated with the party as organisations. This has also been criticised as undemocratic on the grounds that interest organisations should not be parts of party organisations. However, the 'organisational membership' does not affect this study, since it does not mean that the individual union members become party members. Under the new system, it is theoretically possible for a local union to be affiliated with the party without one single of its members joining the party; this they will have to do individually.

[15] Svåsand 1994:315; von Beyme 1985:194ff. For a discussion on the British case, see Webb 1992a:15-19 and Seyd and Whiteley 1992, Chapter 2.

[16] This has also been argued by Birger Hagård, see Hagård 1966:28. Some light can be shed on this problem using the data from the Swedish Election Studies, which since 1968 have distinguished between individual and collective members. The data show that the vast majority of collective members are supporters of the Social Democratic party. In all studies more than three-quarters (in all studies except 1979 over 80 per cent) of them have reported to vote for the Social Democrats. However, the proportions have tended to be lower than among the individual members where the proportion voting Social Democratic have been around 95 per cent.

parties' own statistics) and survey data, taken from surveys where respondents have been asked whether they are members of a political party.

Both sources have validity problems. Party Records are based on the local organisations' reports, which are sent to the central party, sometimes via intermediate levels. There is an obvious risk of administrative inaccuracies, but in addition most parties have structural incentives for lower levels to inflate the figures. This is because representation to regional and central congresses as a rule is based on membership figures. At the same time, however, there are also financial incentives not artificially inflate the membership figures, because the higher levels charge a proportion of the membership fee for every member.

The incentive not to inflate the membership figures is illustrated by the Moderate Party, where no membership fees were charged by the central party before 1965. After this change had been implemented, the membership figures reported by the party declined drastically. It has been suggested that this can be explained by the fact that the members now started to cost money; hence there was an incentive for local organisations to keep their records 'tidy' from members who had failed to pay their dues.[17]

Another problem with Party Records is the risk for double counting. Double counting can take place if a) a collectively affiliated member is

---

[17] The administrative problems are discussed by von Beyme 1985:183. The example from the Swedish Moderate party is taken from Albinsson 1986:39. Another factor, which can be expected to have worked in the opposite direction, was introduced almost simultaneously. When the party rules were revised in 1964, representation to the party congress was changed so that it was based on the number of members. It had previously been based on the party's proportion of votes in the constituency corresponding to the regional organisation in question in the most recent election to the 2nd Chamber of the Riksdag (see Table 3.1 above). Albinsson reports that this second change was intended as an incentive to intensify the recruitment of new members. On the face of it, it seems as if the effect of the introduction of membership dues to the central party more than outweighed that of the representation reform. One possibility is that both had consequences; that the cost factor meant that obsolete members were cleared out of the records while the representation factor meant that recruitment efforts were increased -- it seems plausible that the former effect would be more immediate than the latter.

Another factor, which could be an incentive to inflate membership figures, is the fact that some public subsidies -- local and central -- to organisations are based on the number of members. The effect on political parties in Sweden can be expected to be limited, however. Subsidies based on membership strength are only given to youth organisations. It has affected the youth organisations of every Swedish political party, but since they are not included in this study, the effect can be expected to be limited here.

simultaneously individually affiliated,[18] b) if a member of an ancillary organisation has also, separately, joined the 'mother party'[19] and c) if a member decides to join more than one local organisation in the same party. In each case, the likely reason is that the member in question is very committed to the party and there is no reason why parties should keep an eye on this -- as long as all relevant membership dues are paid.

Thus, Party Records contain factors which can inflate the level of membership, but also factors which could work in the opposite direction. Survey data also have problems. Besides well known difficulties such as sampling and statistical probability that all survey data carry, there is one difficulty with particular relevance to the measurement of party membership. Party members can be expected to be disproportionately politically interested and aware, and hence less likely to refuse to participate in a survey. Therefore, it seems likely that they are over-represented among those in the sample who agree to be interviewed.[20] Another problem is that of the collective Social Democratic members. When faced by a question whether they were members of a party, some collective members may not have been aware of, or wished to acknowledge, their membership.[21]

---

[18] For a discussion of this problem, see Hagård 1966:22ff.

[19] In this study, where the main analysis will be based on the combined total of direct membership and the membership of the women's organisation (if any), this reasoning also applies if the women's organisation is affiliated.

[20] Jörgen Goul Andersen places particular emphasis on this problem. He states that "the party records are hardly exaggerated. However, information from citizens themselves is", using the reason mentioned for over-representation of party members among respondents as an argument (Goul Andersen 1993:52). While it is easy to agree with that part of his argument, it seems somewhat rash not to discuss any of the possible problems with the parties' records. The representation problem mentioned in the text above is applicable to most Danish parties. The membership strength of sub-national party levels has at least some bearing on the allocation of national congress delegates in all major parties except the Conservatives, the Progress Party and, before 1985, the Christian People's Party (see Bille 1992).

[21] There is, at least potentially, also the possibility that some may have believed that they were collective members when in fact they were not. The proportion of LO union members that were collectively affiliated with the Social Democratic Party was never even close to 100 per cent. Data do not exist from every year, but the highest proportion found by Hagård is 45 per cent in 1912. Since then, the available information has varied between 30 and 39 per cent of the total LO membership (Hagård 1966:22, Social Democrats organisational

To study the development of membership strength, both Party Records and survey data will be used. This will give the most thorough foundation for conclusions, but the intention is also to evaluate the validity of the respective sources. It should be pointed out, however, that Party Records can only be used as an indicator of membership levels. Later chapters on activism and representativeness will be based on survey data only.

Another difference between Party Records and survey data is that the former source has a bigger number of time points. As a rule (although not without exception) the parties have reported their membership figures every year, while survey data of course exist only from years when surveys have been conducted. For the majority of the time period of this study, the Swedish Election Studies is the only available survey source. However, the Election Studies of 1973, 1976 and 1982 did not include questions on party membership. Since 1986, the SOM Studies have asked questions about party membership every year. In addition, Statistics Sweden (SCB) have asked questions about party membership annually since the 1970s (see further below in this chapter).

The third major problem when measuring party membership is which measures, or parameters, that are the most suitable. Richard Katz and Peter Mair distinguish three measures.[22] First, *the raw membership count (M)*, which reports the total number of members in a party or a nation in absolute figures. This measure has two limitations. It does not hold the potential 'membership pool' constant among countries and over time, and it requires Party Records data.

Second, *the proportion members of a party's voters (M/V)*. The M/V count has often been used as an indicator of organisational strength.[23] Katz and Mair are very sceptical about it, because it is based on the erroneous assumption that parties have stable electorates. They argue that an increasing M/V ratio can just as well be explained by a decreasing number of voters as an increasing number of members. In fact, research indicates that

---

report 1975). In the 1980s, LO had a total of circa 2 million members. (Bäck 1984:117, Bäck and Möller 1990:146). The highest total number of Social Democratic members ever reported was around 1.2 million between 1980 and 1986, some 25-30 per cent of whom were individual members.

22 The three measures discussed are based on Katz and Mair et al. 1992:330ff.

23 E.g. von Beyme 1985:170, 180ff, Back and Berglund 1978:95ff, Thermeanius 1933:195, Bartolini 1985:186ff and Albinsson 1986:41f.

the former is usually the case. On the party level, membership levels tend to be much more stable than votes.[24]

The third measure, which is preferred and used by Katz and Mair, is *the proportion members of the national electorate (M/E)*. The M/E count is more appropriate for comparisons among countries and over time, because the development of the electorate is much more stable than that of a party's voters.[25] A problem is that M/E figures can be very small, especially for individual parties. Another problem, which can be used as an argument in favour of the M/V count, is that a party cannot be expected to be able to recruit members among voters for other parties. Thus, the whole electorate not a realistic impression of a party's potential membership pool.

The last argument can be met with the counter-argument that we need not take the realistic membership potential into account. What we need to find out is the degree of organisational penetration into the adult population, i.e. the electorate. Thus, the stability and better comparability of the M/E measure outweigh its problems, and the conclusions will primarily be based on that measure. The M count will also be referred to because of its descriptive value.

The ambition has been to collect data up to as recent a point as possible. Party Records, SCB and SOM data have been collected up to and including 1997, but the remaining sources stretch only to 1994.

Development of membership strength: Party Records

The membership development (M), based on Party Records, appears in Figures 4.2 and 4.3 (the raw figures can be found in Appendix II). The most striking observation in Figure 4.2 is the dominance of the Social Democrats. This is due to the party's overwhelming amount of total (individual plus collective) members, which affects the scale of the graph, making the trends of other parties hard to distinguish. Figure 4.3 only includes individual Social Democrats. The party remains dominant, albeit less overwhelmingly

---

[24] This argument is substantiated by Bartolini's study on the memberships of socialist parties, see Bartolini 1985:192.

[25] This is also argued by Per Albinsson (Albinsson 1986:43). For the sake of clarity, it should be mentioned that on the aggregate national level, the M/V and M/E counts converge, although not to 100 per cent, as non-voters are included among the electorate but not among a party's voters.

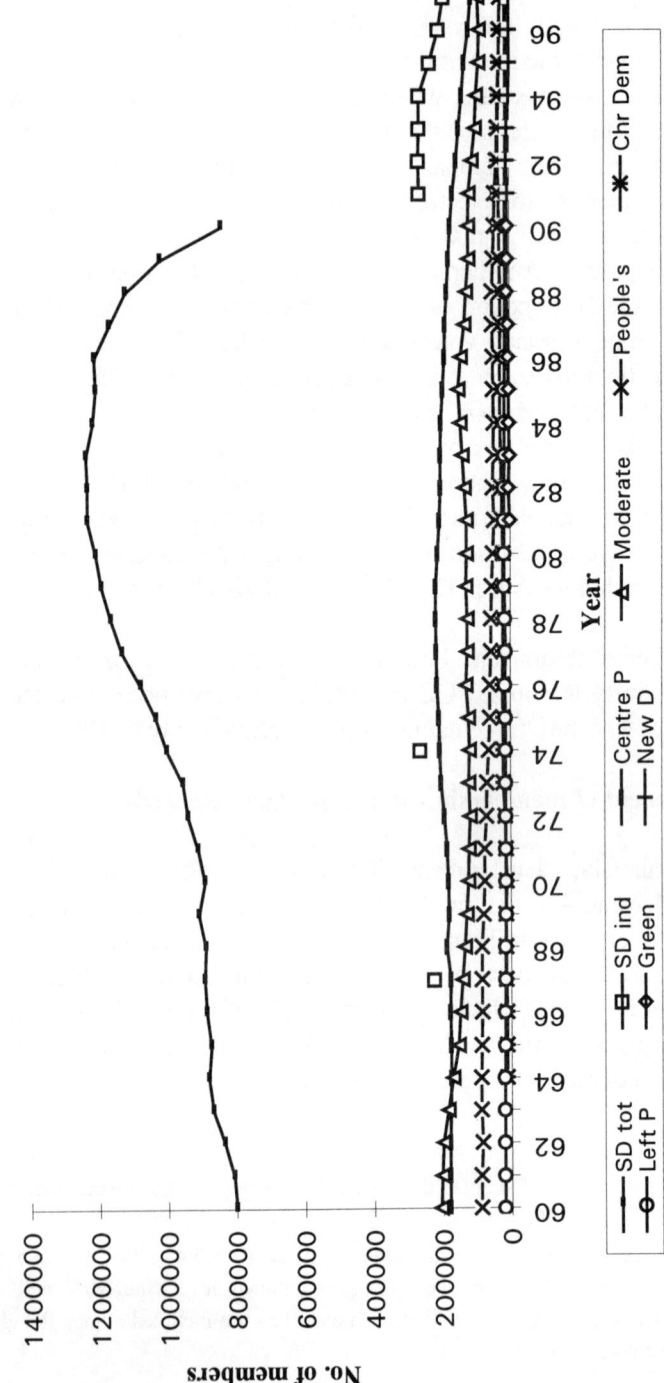

Figure 4.2. Party membership in Sweden 1960–1997. Absolute number of total (including collective) members, including membership of parties' women's organisations (if any). Source: Party records.

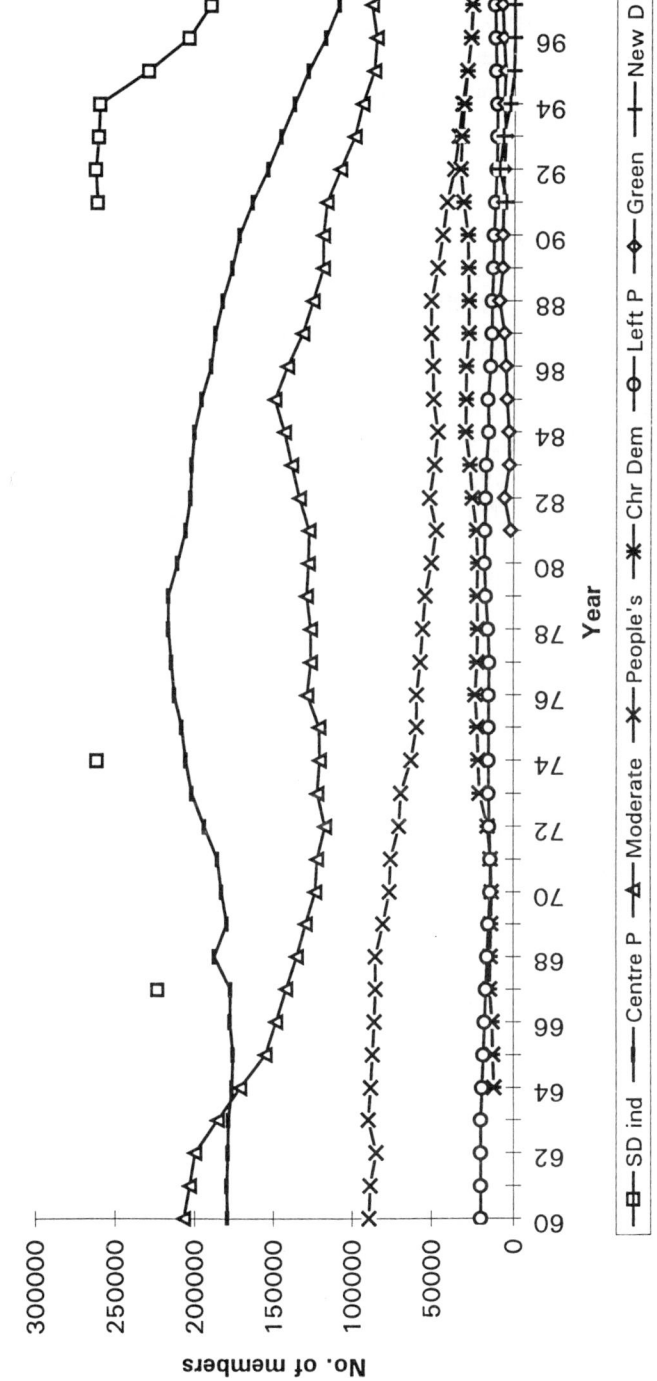

Figure 4.3. Party membership in Sweden 1960-1997. Absolute number of individual members, including membership of parties' women's organisations (if any). Source: Party records

so. If it is true, as was argued above, that the number of 'genuine' Social Democratic members is bigger than the number of formal individual members, the dominance in the 1960s and 70s was clearer than what is apparent in Figure 4.3.

One problem with the Social Democratic figures is that membership statistics which separate collective and individual members are only available at two time points during the research period; in 1967 and 1974. Although the level went up between those two years, this is not enough to speak of a trend in any direction. The party's total membership trends can hardly be expected to be a valid indicator of the individual membership development. On the few occasions where separated figures are available, around three-quarters of the total membership have been reported as collective.[26] That means that the collective members account for most of the variation of the total membership which, hence, is more dependent on agreements between local party units and trade unions than on successful membership recruitment and retention.

Nevertheless, the massive total number of Social Democratic members until the end of the 1980s is striking. Between 1971 and 1989 it was in excess of one million. The peak was reached in 1983, with 1.23 million, equivalent to around 15 per cent of the entire Swedish population. A major reason behind these impressive figures is the development among the LO unions where local unions were amalgamated into larger regional *storavdelningar*. This meant that each decision of collective affiliation affected a much larger number of union members than before, when decisions were taken by smaller units. Another factor which may have increased the importance of collective membership is the urbanisation process. Collective membership was more widespread in towns and cities than in rural areas.[27]

After the abolition of collective membership in 1990, the total number of members was in the region of 260,000. This is in fact almost identical to the number of individual members in 1974. It should be reiterated that the number of individual members from the times of collective membership probably is lower than the number of 'genuine' members.

---

[26] *Utveckling av organisation och verksamhet.* Social Democratic party commission on organisational issues, report to the 26th party congress, 1975; p. 28. The publication reports membership figures broken down by collective and individual in 1948 (67 per cent collective), 1957 (71 per cent), 1967 (75 per cent) and 1974 (73 per cent).

[27] Hagård 1966:30-36.

Therefore, the apparent stability between 1974 and 1991 can just as well be interpreted as a decline. Even if this speculation is accepted, we do not know when and how quickly the decline took place, or how steep it was, since we do not know from which level the decline started. The decline was temporarily halted in 1991, but since 1994 there has been a sharp fall in membership. The 1997 figure of 188,904 is the lowest known number of individual members of the party since WWII.

For the majority of the research period, the Centre Party has been the second largest of the Swedish parties. The only exception is the first three years in the 1960s, when the Moderate Party reported a larger membership. The Centre Party membership rose steadily from the late 1960s, and peaked at 216,000 in 1978 and 1979; an all time high in the history of the party. From then on, however, there has been a continuous decline. In 1997 the membership was almost exactly half of the peak level from the late 1970s. The position as the second largest party does not seem to be under threat, however, as the trend is also negative for the closest competitors, the Moderate Party.

The Moderate Party has experienced a development reminiscent of a roller-coaster ride. The figures of over 200,000 in the early 1960s represented an all time peak in the history of the party.[28] A decline from over 200,000 in the early 1960s to 117,000 a decade later was followed by a revival which reached a climax in the mid 1980s. The levels from the early 1960s have never been reached again, however. After 1984, a new decline began. After 1990 the membership has sunk to levels unprecedented in the research period; in 1993 to below 100,000. A small recovery in 1997 does not alter the overall picture of a decline.

The People's Party Liberals has suffered an almost continuous slide since 1960, when the membership was nearly 90,000. There was a fairly sharp dip in the 1970s, which was halted in the 1980s but followed by a new decline after 1988. In 1997 the membership had dropped to 32,000.[29]

---

[28] Albinsson 1986:40. Note, however, that the figures from the early 1960s may have been exaggerated. See p. 106 above.

[29] From 1982, the affiliated women's organisation of the People's Party started to register its own members for the first time since the early 1960s, which partly explains a small increase between 1981 and 1982. The organisation's membership has varied between 1800 and 5000.

The Left Party membership was halved, from nearly 20,000 to less than 11,000, between 1960 and 1993. It has not been a continuous trend. There was a revival in the 1970s, but since 1980 the development has been unambiguously negative. The slide was halted in 1994, but in 1997 the recovery was still modest, to just under 12,000. The Green Party had nearly 2000 members in its year of formation in 1981. In 1988, the year of the party's electoral breakthrough, it reached an all time high of 8857. It then stabilised at just below 7000 members; in 1997 there had been a small increase to 7500.

It is difficult to ascertain the exact membership of New Democracy. It has been claimed that the party's membership statistics disappeared in connection with defections during the party's internal splits in 1994. Different sources have indicated membership figures from 3000 up to 11,000 between its formation in 1991 and 1994.[30] One of the persons who left the party, John Holck-Bergman, has made some statistics available which suggest that the party had a maximum of just over 9000 members in 1992. According to Holck-Bergman's figures, the membership then declined steeply, to around 2500 members in 1994.[31] There is no information about the membership after 1995, but it is certain to be negligible.

The Christian Democratic party was formed in 1964, when it counted 12,000 members. Since then, the party has managed to more than double its membership. In 1992 the total membership peaked at 33,000. There was a subsequent decline, to just under 26,000 in 1997.[32]

---

[30] *Göteborgs-Posten* reported a figure of 3000 at the beginning of 1994 (*Göteborgs-Posten*, 5 June 1994). Party Leader Ian Wachtmeister claimed a membership of 8000 in a radio interview in 1993 (Swedish National Radio, *Studio 1*, February 1993). In a telephone conversation with the author on 23 March 1995, Kristina Wahlberg from New Democracy's central office gave the information that the membership reports from local party units were missing from all years since 1991, but that the party at one stage had 11,000 members. An additional problem with New Democracy is the rule change in 1993, which meant that there were no local party units, only members directly affiliated with the central party. See p. 46 above.

[31] Fax message from John Holck-Bergman to Dr. Paul Taggart, University of Sussex, 3 August 1995. The fax claims that the membership had sunk to 445 in 1995. I am indebted to Paul Taggart for these figures.

[32] The affiliated Christian Democratic women's organisation was formed in 1982, which serves to somewhat increase the figures from then on. Its membership has varied between 1700 and 3700.

The Christian Democratic development nevertheless provides an exception. All other parties except the Greens had less members in 1997 than at the outset (outset meaning 1960 or, if later, the year of formation). While trends have not been continuous, the general picture of the membership development of the Swedish parties, based on the M count and the parties' own statistics, is one of decline.

The numbers which are the basis for Figures 4.2 and 4.3 can be translated into M/E percentages. This is done by dividing the M figures with the electorate for the given year. In years when no election was held, sliding means from the two nearest 'surrounding' election years have been used as divisor. The figures appear in Table 4.1.

The trends of the table are not notably different to those in the figures. The Swedish electorate has grown slowly but steadily throughout the research period, from just under 5 million in 1960, to 6.6 million in 1998. This means that increases in the M count will be somewhat deflated in the M/E count. In other words, M/E is more conservative than the M count. For the smaller parties it is also more difficult to discover trends in the M/E count, unless more than one decimal is shown in the table. This applies to the Left and Green parties, and New Democracy.

Table 4.1 adds important information to Figures 4.2 and 4.3. According to the M count, individual Social Democratic membership was similar in 1991 compared to 1974, the previous year from which data exist. The M/E count, however, shows that in terms of proportion of the electorate, individual Social Democratic membership declined slightly during the same period. Between 1967 and 1991, the M/E count showed no change, while the M count increased. In 1994, M/E was only marginally lower than in 1967, while the M count was clearly higher. In 1997, however, both counts had declined to the lowest levels in the table. The M/E count for total (including collective) members peaked somewhat earlier than the M count.

In the Centre Party, the M/E trend is different to the M trend. As can be seen in Figure 4.3, the M development is curvilinear with a peak in the late 1970s. The M/E trend, however, has two peaks and two troughs. The first peak, in the early 1960s, had an M/E percentage of 3.6 which is almost identical to the second peak in the late 1970s. In between, there had been a modest decrease with a bottom level of 3.2 in 1969-70. In other words, the stability and subsequent slight increase of the M count during this period was drowned by the increasing size of the electorate. From 1978-79, however, the

Table 4.1   Party membership strength in Sweden 1960-1997. Per cent party members (including members of women's organisations) of electorate (M/E). Based on Party Records

year	Left	SD tot	SD ind	Centre	People's	Moderate	Chr. Dem.	Green	New D
1960	0.4	16.1	n/a	3.6	1.8	4.2	---	---	---
1961	0.4*	16.2	n/a	3.6	1.8	4.1*	---	---	---
1962	0.4*	16.6	n/a	3.6	1.7	4.0	---	---	---
1963	0.4	17.1	n/a	3.5	1.8	3.7*	---	---	---
1964	0.4*	17.3	n/a	3.5	1.7	3.4	0.2	---	---
1965	0.4*	16.7	n/a	3.4	1.7	3.0	0.2*	---	---
1966	0.3	16.6	n/a	3.3	1.6	2.8*	0.2	---	---
1967	0.3*	16.5	4.1	3.3	1.6	2.6*	0.3	---	---
1968	0.3	16.3	n/a	3.4	1.6	2.5	0.3	---	---
1969	0.3*	16.3	n/a	3.2	1.5	2.3	0.2	---	---
1970	0.3	15.8	n/a	3.2	1.4	2.2	0.2	---	---
1971	0.3	16.1	n/a	3.3	1.3	2.2	0.3	---	---
1972	0.3*	16.6	n/a	3.4	1.2	2.1	0.3	---	---
1973	0.3	16.7	n/a	3.6	1.2	2.1	0.4	---	---
1974	0.3	17.3	4.5	3.6	1.1	2.1	0.4	---	---
1975	0.3*	17.6	n/a	3.5	1.0	2.1	0.4	---	---
1976	0.3	18.1	n/a	3.6	1.0	2.2	0.4	---	---
1977	0.3	18.9	n/a	3.6	1.0	2.1	0.4	---	---
1978	0.3	19.3	n/a	3.6	0.9	2.1	0.4	---	---
1979	0.3	19.7	n/a	3.6	0.9	2.1	0.4	---	---
1980	0.3	19.9	n/a	3.5	0.8	2.1	0.4	---	---
1981	0.3	20.2	n/a	3.4	0.8	2.1	0.4	0.0	---
1982	0.3	20.1	n/a	3.3	0.8	2.2	0.4	0.1	---
1983	0.3	20.0	n/a	3.3	0.8	2.2	0.4	0.0	---
1984	0.3	19.5	n/a	3.2	0.8	2.3	0.5	0.0	---
1985	0.3	19.3	n/a	3.1	0.8	2.4	0.5	0.1	---
1986	0.2	19.2	n/a	3.0	0.8	2.2	0.5	0.1	---
1987	0.2	18.5	n/a	3.0	0.8	2.1	0.4	0.1	---
1988	0.2	17.6	n/a	2.9	0.8	2.0	0.4	0.1	---
1989	0.2	16.0	n/a	2.8	0.7	1.9	0.4	0.1	---
1990	0.2	13.1	n/a	2.7	0.7*	1.9	0.4	0.1	---
1991	0.2	4.1	4.1	2.5	0.6	1.8	0.5	0.1	0.1
1992	0.2	4.1	4.1	2.4	0.6	1.7	0.5	0.1	0.1
1993	0.2	4.0	4.0	2.2	0.5	1.5	0.5	0.1	0.1
1994	0.2	4.0	4.0	2.1	0.5	1.4	0.5	0.1	0.0
1995	0.2	3.5	3.5	2.0	0.4	1.3	0.4	0.1	0.0
1996	0.2	3.1	3.1	1.8	0.4	1.3	0.4	0.1	0.0
1997	0.2	2.9	2.9	1.6	0.4	1.3	0.4	0.1	0.0

Comment: All entries are based on the parties' own statistics. The M figures have been divided by the national electorate. In years when no election has been held, sliding means of the two nearest 'surrounding' election years have been used. Entries marked * indicate that the figure is artificial. The membership figure for the party and/or women's organisation for that year is not available and the figure is based on a 'notional' membership figure which is a average of the figures for the two nearest 'surrounding ' years where membership figures are available.

trends converged and both counts show continuous declines until the end of the research period.

For the remaining parties, the M/E trends are fairly similar to the M trends. There are some deviations in the detailed fluctuations, but the overall developments are similar. The Moderate Party went down sharply in the 1960s, recovered in the 70s to reach a second peak in the mid 80s (which was lower than in the early 60s), followed by a decline into the 1990s. The People's Party has experienced an almost continuous decline throughout the research period, with only short lived and minor recoveries. The development has also been negative for the Left Party -- the M/E slide was temporarily halted in the late 70s and early 80s --, while the Greens have remained fairly stable since the mid 1980s. The Christian Democrats are still the exception. The M count was more than doubled, from 12,000 to 25,000, between 1964 and 1997. This is also enough to constitute an increase if the growth of the electorate is taken into consideration. The M/E percentage of 0.4 in 1997 is twice as high as in the 1960s.

The first finding of this chapter is thus that Party Records indicate a membership decline for most parties during the 1960-1994 period. The Christian Democrats and, to some extent, the Green Party are the only exceptions. The Left, Centre, Moderate and People's parties had M/E percentages in 1997 which were less than half of what they had been in the early 60s. The Social Democratic M/E in 1997 was just under 2/3 of the individual M/E in 1974. The recent trend is very negative for the party, with a drop of 1.1 percentage point between 1994 and 1997.

Development of membership strength: survey data

There are several Swedish surveys which at one time or another have asked respondents whether they are members of a political party. The longest time series is provided by the Swedish Election Studies. The first available time point is the first ever Election Study from 1956, and it reaches up to the most recent election.[33]

The question technique, however, has varied somewhat over time. The 1956 Election Study did not ask party members which party they were members of. This means that the members will have to be broken down by party vote or party sympathy in order to find out the membership strength of

---

[33] It has not been possible to include data from the 1998 Election Study here.

the different parties. Thus, the 1956 figures broken down by party are not comparable with the subsequent studies.[34] From 1960, however, those who have answered yes to the party membership question have been asked the follow-up question of which party they are members.

The first three Election Studies did not distinguish among collective and individual members of the Social Democratic Party. Between 1968 and 1988, respondents who answered 'Social Democrats' to the question of which party they are members were asked a second follow-up question whether they are collective or individual members, or both at the same time. From 1979 onwards, respondents have also been asked whether they are members of other political organisations. This includes ancillary and affiliated party organisations, such as youth or women's organisations.[35]

Statistics Sweden (SCB) have conducted studies of living conditions since 1976. The SCB studies have always included questions on party membership, but without a follow-up question of which party the respondents are members. Another source is the SOM (Society, Opinion, Media) Studies, which have been conducted by Göteborg University every year since 1986. SOM data are based on mail questionnaires, in contrast to the other mentioned studies which are all based on in-person interviews. Like the SCB Studies and the 1956 Election Study, the SOM questionnaires have not included a follow-up question about which party the respondents are members of; nor have they been asked whether they are individual or collective members.

The account will primarily be based on Election Studies data for a number of reasons. First, it provides the longest time series. Second, no systematic study of party membership has been done using data from the Swedish Election Studies. Analyses of party membership using SCB data have been published before, although the perspective has been wider than just party membership.[36] Third, Election Studies have, since 1960, asked respondents which party they are members of, which is not the case with the SCB and the SOM Studies. This means that members need not be broken down by more indirect variables such as party sympathy or vote. The other

---

[34] Data from 1956 will not be used in this study, because of the general time frame which starts in 1960.

[35] The wordings of questions have varied somewhat over time, although the wording has been identical since 1979. English translations of every Swedish Election Study are available from the Department of Political Science, Göteborg University.

[36] SCB 1994, SCB 1996.

studies will be referred to when summarising the long term trends of total party membership on the aggregate national level.

The M/E percentages broken down by party, based on data from the Swedish Election Studies, are reported in Table 4.2. Several of the differences between parties and over time are within the margin of error. It is often difficult to speak of clear trends. Even if one ignores the fact that many of the variations in the table are not statistically significant, and takes the nominal figures at face value, trends are difficult to find. It can, however, be concluded that the Centre and Moderate parties have suffered declines. In neither case has it been continuous, but the difference between the beginning and the end of the research period indicates a long term loss of members. This is in line with the Party Records reported in Table 4.1.

The case of the People's Party, however, for which Party Records indicate a nearly continuous decline, is somewhat less clear when Election Studies data are used. There is a decline between the 1960s and the 1990s according to both sources.[37] Yet, while the Party Records indicate a clearly decreasing long term trend (with brief interruptions) also in the 1970s, 1980s and 1990s, Election Studies data indicate very little variation after 1970. The long term development, however, is unambiguously negative.

A methodologically important observation from Table 4.2 is that survey data tend to give similar M/E percentages to those based on Party Records. The exact short term fluctuations do not always go in the same direction, but for most parties a comparison between Tables 4.1 and 4.2 indicate that both data sources give similar M/E percentages at any given time point. With the exception of the Social Democrats, it is rare for any party to have a difference of more than one percentage point any year -- often the differences are much smaller than that. The rank ordering of the parties, according to their relative membership sizes, also remain the same, with a few occasional exceptions.

---

[37] The difference in Table 4.2 between 1.5 per cent in 1960 and 0.8 per cent in 1994 is significant on the .05 but not the .01 level. However, the difference between 1964 and 1994 is significant also on the .01 level.

Table 4.2   Party membership strength in Sweden 1960-1994. Per cent party members (including members of women's organisations) of electorate (M/E). Swedish Election Studies data

Year	Left	SD tot	SD ind	Centre	People's	Moderate	Chr. Dem.	Green	New Dem.
1960	0.3	8.5	---	3.9	1.5	3.5	---	---	---
1964	0.2	8.7	---	3.6	1.9	2.5	0.2	---	---
1968	0.2	8.4	3.5	3.4	1.6	2.1	0.2	---	---
1970	0.5	5.9	3.6	3.0	0.8	2.4	0.1	---	---
1979	0.4	8.5	4.8	3.8	0.9	2.1	0.2	---	---
1980	0.4	7.2	3.9	3.2	0.8	1.7	0.2	---	---
1985	0.2	8.4	4.6	3.0	0.6	2.4	0.6	0.3	---
1988	0.3	6.3	5.4	3.0	0.5	2.1	0.4	0.3	---
1991	0.2	---	4.1	2.5	0.8	1.3	0.3	0.1	0.3
1994	0.2	---	4.9	2.0	0.8	1.5	0.2	0.1	0.0

Comment: Data are taken from the Swedish Election Studies all years except 1980, when data are taken from the Referendum Study. 1960: q. 100, n=1461. 1964: q. 115, n=2849. 1968: q. 85, n=2855. 1970 (sample categories K70 and T70 only): q. 41, n=1316. 1979: q. 36A, n=2678. 1980: q. 41, n=1552. 1985: q. 47A, n=2778. 1988: q. 49A, n=2662. 1991:q. 52A, n=2599. 1994: q. 51A, n=2527.

The Social Democrats are the only, partial, exception. Up to 1994, individual Social Democratic membership remained in the region of four per cent according to both sources. There are, however, big discrepancies in the Social Democratic M/E percentages for total (including collective) members. The party's own records report a much higher proportion of total members than the Election Studies. The highest total Social Democratic M/E percentage ever recorded by an Election Study is 8.7 in 1964, while the highest corresponding figure according to Party Records is 20.1 per cent in 1982.

Differently put, the highest total number of Social Democratic members reported by the party itself is over 1.2 million, while the M/E percentage of 8.7 recorded by survey data in 1964 is equivalent to about 443,000.[38] Thus, the caveats about collective members in survey data

---

[38] The figure 443,000 is calculated as 8.7 per cent of the actual electorate in 1964 (5,095,850).

mentioned above, which suggest that collective members are underestimated in surveys, are corroborated.[39]

The Christian Democratic Party displays figures somewhat contrary to the largely positive development according to Party Records. Election Studies data suggest a continuous decline since 1985. The Green Party is also ambiguous displaying a marginally decreasing trend which is in contradiction to the party's own records. There is no easy explanation to these discrepancies. The Christian Democrats have, by their own standards, a remarkably high M/E of 0.6 based on survey data in 1985. Without it, very little is left of the negative trend. Furthermore, all the M/E percentages for these two parties in both Table 4.1 and 4.2 are smaller than one full per cent and all variations are very marginal in any case. Table 4.2 does, however, suggest that there is some cause for caution before acclaiming a positive trend for the Christian Democrats.

The findings on the party level can now be summarised. The majority of the Swedish parties have suffered a membership decline in the 1960-1997 period, according to both Party Records and Election Studies data. The reduction in membership is quite unambiguous for the Centre and Moderate parties, and also for the People's Party Liberals. The Left Party has also suffered a decline, although it is difficult to corroborate this with Election Studies data. The Social Democrats have suffered a sharp decline since 1994.

If we accept the suggestion that collective Social Democratic members included a number of 'genuine' members, who would have enrolled individually had that been the only option, the decline started even earlier. According to the 1960 and 1964 Election Studies, about 8 per cent of the electorate claimed to be Social Democratic members. At the same time, the party's own records claimed a total membership equivalent to an M/E percentage of between 16 and 17. Eight per cent could therefore be taken as an indirect estimate of the 'genuine' membership level of the party at the time: at least this many were aware of, and prepared to acknowledge, their membership. If this, admittedly loose, assumption is accepted, Table 4.2

---

[39] Election Studies data indicate that, of all members of the Social Democratic Party, between 40 and 60 per cent were individual members (except in 1988 when the dismantling of collective membership had begun and the proportion individual members was 87 per cent). This can be compared with the proportions of around 70-75 per cent from the known time points based on Party Records (see note 26 above).

suggests a Social Democratic membership decline from 8.7 to 4.9 per cent between 1960 and 1994. It cannot be denied that this is a speculative combination of numbers. The case for a Social Democratic membership decline between 1960 and 1994 is reasonably strong. The exact rate of the decline, however, is unknown. The clear decline according to Party Records after 1995 corroborates this conclusion.

The two parties which to some extent contradict the general pattern of decline are the Christian Democratic and Green parties. The evidence concerning the former is somewhat contradictory, with an increasing trend according to Party Records until 1992, and then a relatively limited decline, and a longer decline according to the Election Studies. If the formation year of 1981 is not taken into account, stability is the best description of the Green Party.

At the end of the research period, the two parties traditionally characterised as mass parties, the Social Democrats and the Centre Party, hold their respective positions as the two biggest membership parties. This may be a predictable, but not trivial, result. As has already been pointed out, the desire to recruit many members is by no means confined to socialist parties, or parties with movement origins. There has been an organisational convergence among the Swedish parties since the Second World War in the direction towards the mass, or party democracy, type. This convergence has taken place in the shape of the parties' intentions, as manifested in recruitment campaigns, rule changes etc. and not necessarily in the degree of success of those intentions.[40] The findings of this chapter so far, show that these intentions have not been successful. Tradition is still a crucial factor behind membership strength among parties in Sweden.

While the traditional 'mass' parties have maintained their relative positions in the party system, they have not been able to maintain their memberships. They are not alone in this predicament. All the old and established parties have lost members. At the same time, it is interesting to note that the emergence of new parties has not compensated for this membership loss. Any new party will of course provide a contribution to the total membership, but the emergence of the Christian Democrats, the Green Party and New Democracy has come nowhere near to making up for the membership losses for the older parties.

This observation is relevant to one of the arguments raised in the 'decline of parties' debate, which says that old parties fail to attract members

---

[40] For an elaboration of this argument, see Pierre and Widfeldt 1994:336ff.

who prefer new types of organisations. Of course, this study does not give a full answer to that proposition, because the majority of the new type organisations are not parties. Still, it is a relevant observation that the new parties have not been particularly successful in membership recruitment. The three parties of any lasting political significance to have emerged since the beginning of the research period represent three very different types. The Christian Democrats have developed into something of a mainstream Swedish 'bourgeois' party with a fairly traditional organisation. The Green Party is a 'New Social Movement' or 'Left Libertarian' party, based on ideals of direct democracy and grass root influence, even if the organisation has been somewhat 'streamlined' in recent years. New Democracy, on the other hand, is organised according to what might be called neo-liberal ideas, with few organisational layers and emphasis on quick decision-making.[41]

None of these parties have come close to making up for the membership losses of the traditional parties. Admittedly, it may be unreasonable to expect anything else, but it does suggest that new types of parties do not necessarily provide an alternative to old parties. It is worth remembering that of the three new parties, the one which has been most successful in recruiting members is the Christian Democratic Party which, unlike the Greens and New Democracy, does not represent an organisational challenge to the older parties. The failure of the Greens and New Democracy can, in turn, be interpreted as a serious question mark against the ability of political parties to provide participatory linkage. The pessimistic conclusion is that neither new party types, nor organisational renewal, is the answer to the decline.

Aggregate national party membership

The end of the previous section has more or less already stated that there has been an overall decline in party membership in Sweden between 1960 and 1997. The conclusion was based on an overall assessment based on the membership development among different parties. It will now be complemented with the development of aggregate party membership on the national level. This section will draw on more sources than the Election Studies. The survey data sources mentioned above, which have not

---

[41] Taggart and Widfeldt 1993, Taggart 1993, Taggart 1996.

distinguished among members of different parties, are suitable for the measure of aggregate membership and will provide additional evidence.

The total M/E percentages for all party members, based on Party Records and available survey data sources, appear in Table 4.3. Data from a total of five different sources are presented in the table. Where possible, total (including collective) and individual M/E percentages are presented separately. It should be noted that no survey data sources, except the Election Studies from 1968 onwards, distinguish among collective and individual members.

Party Records (the first two columns in the table) indicate a membership decline. Individual membership has dropped from an M/E of 12.1 in 1967 to less than seven per cent in 1997. Total membership fluctuated around a quarter of the electorate until the late 1980s, when the Social Democratic abolition of collective membership meant that it started to decline rapidly to 19 per cent in the last year of existence of collective membership in 1990.

According to the Election Studies, individual membership has fluctuated within a range of 12.1 per cent in 1979, and 9.8 in 1991. For total members, decline is the best way of describing the development; the highest level of 17.8 in 1960 has never been reached since. This is in fact the highest M/E total ever recorded by any survey data source.[42] If, as has been suggested above, the total M/E percentage based on survey data is a better estimate of genuine party membership than the inclusion of only explicitly individual members (because the total figures include collective but genuine Social Democratic members), then the Election Studies suggest an overwhelming membership decline. There is a decline also in individual membership, but the M/E percentage of 9.9 in 1994 was a mere 1.2 points lower than in 1968.

The SOM data series starts in 1986, and cannot answer the question whether party membership is in a long term decline. During the 1986-1997 period, the M/E count has developed negatively. There was a statistically significant drop between 1991 and 1992, and the level has stayed below 11 per cent since. The lowest M/E figure was recorded at the most recent time point, in 1997.

---

[42] The 1956 Election Study reports a total M/E percentage of 17.4.

Table 4.3 **Aggregate party membership strength in Sweden 1960-1997, according to different sources. Per cent of electorate (M/E)**

year	P Rec. ind.	P Rec. tot.	ES ind.	ES tot.	SOM	Power inv.	SCB
1960	n/a	26.1	n/a	17.8	---	---	---
1961	n/a	26.0	---	---	---	---	---
1962	n/a	26.3	---	---	---	---	---
1963	n/a	26.1	---	---	---	---	---
1964	n/a	26.5	n/a	17.4	---	---	---
1965	n/a	25.3	---	---	---	---	---
1966	n/a	24.9	---	---	---	---	---
1967	12.1	24.6	---	---	---	---	---
1968	n/a	24.3	11.1	16.0	---	12.7	---
1969	n/a	23.9	---	---	---	---	---
1970	n/a	23.0	10.5	13.0	---	---	---
1971	n/a	23.3	---	---	---	---	---
1972	n/a	23.8	---	---	---	---	---
1973	n/a	24.3	---	---	---	---	---
1974	11.9	24.7	---	---	---	13.7	---
1975	n/a	24.9	---	---	---	---	---
1976	n/a	25.5	---	---	---	---	13.6
1977	n/a	26.2	---	---	---	---	---
1978	n/a	26.6	---	---	---	---	13.2
1979	n/a	27.0	12.1	15.5	---	---	14.2
1980	n/a	26.9	10.2	13.6	---	---	14.5
1981	n/a	27.1	---	---	---	13.9	13.3
1982	n/a	27.2	---	---	---	---	14.1
1983	n/a	27.0	---	---	---	---	15.0
1984	n/a	26.6	---	---	---	---	15.7
1985	n/a	26.3	11.9	15.8	---	---	14.5
1986	n/a	26.1	---	---	12.1	---	13.4
1987	n/a	25.1	---	---	13.1	14.8	13.1
1988	n/a	24.1	11.7	12.6	12.6	---	13.0
1989	n/a	22.1	---	---	11.9	---	12.3
1990	n/a	19.1	---	---	11.9	---	11.4
1991	9.9	---	9.8	---	13.2	---	10.3
1992	9.6	---	---	---	10.4	---	11.1
1993	9.2	---	---	---	10.8	---	9.8
1994	8.8	---	9.9	---	10.2	---	8.9
1995	7.9	---	---	---	9.7	---	n/a
1996	7.3	---	---	---	n/a	---	9.7
1997	6.9	---	---	---	9.5	---	8.2

Comment: P Rec. ind.= Party Records, individual members only. P Rec. tot.= Party Records, collective members included. See also comment under Table 4.1. ES ind.= Swedish Election Studies, individual members only. ES tot.= Swedish Election Studies, including collective members (in 1960 and 1964 party members were not asked about individual/collective membership). See also comment under Table 4.2. SOM=Society, Opinion, Media; studies by the SOM institute, Göteborg University. No distinction is made between collective and individual membership. 1986: q. 51, n=1624. 1987: q. 45, n=1673. 1988: q. 43, n=1643. 1989: q. 43 n=1578. 1990: q. 45, n=1582. 1991: q. 46 n=1573. 1992: q. 54, n=1889. 1993: q. 61, n=1857. 1994: q. 63, n=1792. 1995: q. 62, n=1777. 1997: q. 60, n=1754. Method: mail questionnaires. Power inv. = Swedish Power Investigation (*Maktutredningen*); a Commission of Inquiry launched by the Swedish government, to investigate power and democracy in Sweden, from which several reports were published. Column entries are taken from a report titled "The Power of Citizens" (*Medborgarnas makt*), p. 336 (Petersson et al. 1989). No distinction is made between collective and individual members. Method: in-person interviews. While the figures are taken directly from Petersson et al. 1989, the data from 1968, 1974 and 1981 originate from the Level of Living Studies (*Levnadsnivåundersökningarna*) by the Swedish Institute for Social Research at Stockholm University (see Erikson and Åberg, eds., 1984, and Andersson 1984). SCB=Living Conditions Studies (*Undersökningar av levnadsförhållanden, ULF*), made by Statistics Sweden (*Statistiska Centralbyrån, SCB*). The figures have been kindly supplied by Lars Häll, SCB. 1976: n=11,144. 1978: n=10,307. 1979: n=9,468. 1980: n=7,261. 1981: n=7,703. 1982: n=7,290. 1983: n=6,663. 1984: n=7,211. 1985: n=6,585. 1986: n=4,774. 1987: n=7,052. 1988: n=6,514. 1989: n=6,781. 1990: n=6,191. 1991: n=5,827. 1992: n=5,980. 1993: n=6,190. 1994: n=6,001, 1996: n=5,880, 1997: n=5,806. See also SCB report series *Levnadsförhållanden*, especially reports no. 86 and 90 (SCB 1994 and SCB 1996). No distinction between collective and individual members. Method: in-person interviews.

In the Swedish Investigation of Power and Democracy, Petersson, Westholm and Blomberg report a continuous increase between 1968 and 1987. However, this data series says nothing about the development in the 1990s, which is when most of the decline indicated by other sources took place. Indeed, the ULF studies of living conditions conducted by SCB (Statistics Sweden) offer conflicting evidence. The M/E level was more than 1.5 percentage points lower and, furthermore, in a state of decline in 1987. The decline started in 1985 and continued until 1991. There were temporary halts in 1992 and 1996, but the 1997 M/E of 8.2 is unprecedented. The overall development in the SCB column is curvilinear, with a peak in 1985, but in the long term there is a clear decline. It is difficult to compare this with any other source, because none has as many time points in the same period.[43] The decline in the late 1980s and the 1990s, however, corresponds with evidence from SOM and the Election Studies.

On the whole, decline is the best way of describing membership development in Sweden during the 1960-1997 period. All data sources indicate that a smaller proportion of the electorate were party members in the 1990s than in the 1960s. According to Party Records, the decline has continued at an increasing rate since 1994. However, the evidence is not unambiguous. The rate of the decline varies according to source, and whether a distinction between individual and collective members is made.

The total M/E percentage, including collective membership when it existed, has declined. For Party Records this is almost trivial, since the collective Social Democratic membership is certain to have exaggerated the number of 'genuine' members. The decline shown by Election Studies data is more convincing because it started from a lower level; as has been argued before, total membership based on surveys could be taken as a better estimate of the real membership level.

If only explicitly individual members are taken into account, the evidence is less clear. Here, Party Records convey a clearer message of decline than the Election Studies. According to the former, the proportion of the electorate that were individual party members went down by 3.3 M/E points between 1967 and 1994 (5.2 points if the time frame is extended to 1997), while the Election Studies indicate a decrease of 1.2 points between 1968 and 1994. Translated into M figures, the Election Studies in fact indicate an increase of the absolute number of individual members from

---

[43] Total membership according to Party Records is an exception but, as has been argued before, they are not comparable with survey data.

605,000 in 1968 to 643,000 in 1994. Party Records, on the other hand, report a decrease from 661,000 in 1967 to 572,000 in 1994, and to 456,000 in 1997.

Thus, the extent of the decline is a matter of interpretation. That decline is still a defensible conclusion rests on two arguments. First, the increased 'membership pool', the electorate, should be taken into account. Second, during the times when collective membership existed, explicit individual membership did not represent the level of 'genuine' membership. If those two arguments are accepted, a membership decline in Sweden between the 1960s and 1990s is the most reasonable conclusion, even allowing for the less clear decline according to the Election Studies.

Table 4.3 can also be used as an evaluation of the different sources. The table includes Party Records, including and excluding collective members. It also includes four different survey sources, one of which has separated among individual and collective members. The already made observation, that Party Records including collective members gives the highest membership levels, is re-emphasised. It does not seem too bold to assume that the figures reported in the second column in Table 4.3 are exaggerations of the 'genuine' membership. This, however, does not mean that it represents a substantial exaggeration of reality. There is no known reason to doubt that the Social Democratic collective membership was large enough in terms of actually enrolled members to constitute the bulk of the large total M/E percentages reported in the 'P Rec. tot.' column. The problem is that an unknown, probably substantial, number of collective members would not have been party members if collective membership had not existed.

Survey data can be assumed to give a better estimation of 'genuine' membership because collective members who do not accept, or are not aware of, their membership will not be recorded as members in a survey. In the Election Studies, Social Democratic members were asked whether they were collectively or individually enrolled after they had first answered that they were a) party members of b) the Social Democratic party. If they answered 'no' to the initial question whether they were party members, no further questions related to party membership were asked. Thus, the total M/E percentages from the Election Studies can be expected to be nearer the truth with regard to 'genuine', but not necessarily actual, membership including collective members.

At the same time, the table indicates that some of the validity problems attributed to Party Records may have been exaggerated. The discrepancies are mostly quite small between individual party membership according to the Election Studies and Party Records respectively. This is especially notable in the 1990s, when no collective membership exists to distort the picture. Thus, the suspicion that party organisations have incentives to inflate membership levels is not supported by a comparison between Party Records and Election Studies data.

SOM data can be expected to somewhat inflate the M/E percentages. The general problem of members being over-represented among respondents, because they are less likely to decline to participate in surveys, seems likely to be bigger with SOM data than with Election Studies data. This is due to the fact that the SOM studies have a lower response rate.[44] The table supports this assumption: on every comparable time point, SOM indicates a higher M/E percentage than the corresponding Election Study. Especially so in 1991, when the difference was more than three percentage points. In other corresponding years, however, the differences have been small.

The methodological conclusion is that Goul Andersen was somewhat rash in his dismissal of the validity of survey data as indicators of party membership strength. It could be that his caveat explains the comparatively high M/E levels reported by SOM and SCB. However, the close correspondence for individual membership between Party Records and the Election Studies suggest that Party Records and surveys, based on in-person interviews and with carefully designed questions, validate each other. The somewhat tentative methodological conclusion is thus that a) the problems of double counting and administrative slackness of Party Records should not be exaggerated, and b) the problem of potential over-representation of members in surveys is comparatively limited in in-person interviews.

Conclusion and comparative outlook

It has just been argued that party membership in Sweden has declined between 1960 and 1997. Does this mean that the Swedish parties are in a membership crisis? The question is of course dependent on how the concept of crisis is defined. There has been a decline in party membership in

---

[44] The response rate of the SOM studies has varied between 66 and 71 per cent (Rönström 1995:291). The Election Studies have had response rates ranging from over 90 per cent in the 50s and 60s to around 75 per cent in the 1990s (Gilljam and Holmberg 1993:11).

Sweden in the 1990s. Party Records, ULF/SCB and SOM data indicate that this decline has been accentuated from 1995 onwards, to the lowest levels since 1960, the beginning of the time frame of this book.

There is of course no criterion which can determine whether a given level of party membership is 'acceptable' or not. The perspective of this study is longitudinal, and the main question is whether there has been a decline over time. One relevant point of reference is, however, to make international comparisons. It should be noted that these comparisons will not affect the conclusion of this chapter. The comparative outlook has the more modest purpose of putting the Swedish development into perspective.

The most comprehensive comparative account of membership development has been made by Richard Katz and Peter Mair with others. In a journal article, they have published tables of M/E percentages for eleven European countries between 1960 and 1990.[45] The tables are based on Party Records, as published in a data handbook on party organisations, edited by Katz and Mair.[46] The data handbook reports all available membership figures, including those for corporate (i.e. collective), ancillary and affiliated membership, for the majority of politically important parties in most West European democracies. Katz and Mair have only included direct and individual members. Their data are presented in Table 4.4. Because of the small number of time points for individual membership, both total and individual membership for Sweden are reported. In order to make the Swedish figures comparable with those of other countries, women's organisations are now not included for the Swedish parties.

The table should be interpreted with caution. In most countries there are definition problems, especially in terms of how to treat corporate, affiliate and ancillary members. The decision was to bring the figures down to the highest possible degree of 'directness' which means minimising membership types such as corporate, affiliate and ancillary. It is not possible to consistently follow this principle.

The few available time points for individual membership in Sweden is one problem. Another problematic case is the large Austrian catholic ÖVP party, whose direct membership is virtually negligible. Instead the bulk of the members join indirectly via three major organisations: the Farmer's,

---

[45] Katz, Mair et al. 1992.
[46] Katz and Mair, eds., 1992.

Table 4.4 Party membership strength in 11 European countries 1960-1991. Per cent party members of electorate (M/E). Based on Party Records

Year	A	B	DK	SF	D	IRL	I	NL	N	GB	S tot	S ind
1960		21.1									22.0	
1961		7.8			2.5				15.5		22.0	
1962	26.2			18.9							22.2	
1963							12.7	9.4			22.6	
1964			18.5							9.4	22.7	
1965		7.4			2.8				15.9		21.6	
1966	26.0		16.7	18.6						9.1	21.2	
1967								6.2			21.1	8.7
1968		7.8	15.8				12.0				20.7	
1969					3.1				15.2		20.5	
1970	25.9			17.1						8.0	19.8	
1971	26.0	8.0	13.5					4.2			20.2	
1972				16.7	3.7		12.8	3.8			20.7	
1973			11.0						13.4		21.1	
1974		8.8								6.0	21.1	8.7
1975	25.6		10.5	15.3							22.0	
1976					4.5		10.5				22.4	
1977		9.5	8.4			1.2*		4.0	14.5		23.0	
1978		9.4									23.6	
1979	25.4		7.7	14.9			9.8			5.3	23.9	
1980					4.5						23.8	
1981		9.1	7.6			1.8*		4.0	15.5		23.8	
1982						1.6*		4.0			24.1	
1983	24.1			14.0	4.4		9.4			3.9	23.9	
1984			7.2								23.9	
1985		8.7							15.8		23.6	
1986	22.6							3.2			23.3	
1987		9.1	6.8	12.9	4.2	5.5	9.7			3.3	22.5	
1988			6.5								21.7	
1989					5.3			2.7	13.5		19.8	
1990	21.8										17.0	
1991												7.7

Comment: This is an amended version of Table 5.1 in Widfeldt 1995. The table is based on Katz, Mair et al. 1992 which in turn is based on the membership tables in the data handbook on party organisations (Katz and Mair, eds., 1992). Ancillary, affiliated and corporate membership are not included, except in the Swedish 'total' column, which includes collective members of the Social Democratic Party. The figures in the Swedish 'total' column deviate from those in Katz and Mair, eds. 1992, because the Christian Democratic membership is included which is not the case in the data handbook. A=Austria, B=Belgium, DK=Denmark, SF=Finland, D=Germany, IRL=Ireland, I=Italy, NL=Netherlands, N=Norway, GB=Great Britain, S tot.=Sweden, including collective members, S ind.=Sweden including individual members only.

Employers and Employees and the Business leagues.[47] In Norway, Britain and Ireland only direct members are included.

The first observation from the table is that party membership has remained much more stable in Sweden than in several other countries. Denmark has suffered an enormous membership loss since 1960, and the Netherlands, Norway, Britain, Finland, Austria and Italy have also lost members. Positive trends can be observed in Belgium and, to some extent, (West) Germany.[48] As has been shown in earlier sections, the Swedish decline has to a large extent taken place in the 1990s, a period from which comparative data are not yet available. Thus, the conclusion in the previous section, which indicated a Swedish decline, is not directly comparable with the data presented in Table 4.4. Although comprehensive data are not yet available there are some indications that the recent negative Swedish trend is not unique in Western Europe.

The Swedish membership levels are competitive, but not exceptionally high. If collective members are included, the Swedish M/E percentages are overwhelmingly higher than the majority of countries (although it must be remembered that the comparison would be different if collective members in Norway, Britain and Ireland were included). Yet, Austrian membership has never been far behind Sweden. In the 1960s and 70s the Austrian M/E percentages were in fact clearly higher. Individual Swedish figures are very much in the middle order. Belgium overtook the Swedish individual M/E percentage in the mid 1970s. The Finnish figures have always been higher (neither Finland nor Belgium have collective membership) and the same applies to Norway. Even if the assumption of the bare individual figures being an underestimation of 'genuine' membership is accepted, the Swedish M/E figures are by no means unique in an international comparison.

This is supported by a similar comparison based on survey data presented in Table 4.5. Because of lack of data, it is not meaningful to speak of long term trends in most countries, although the Norwegian stability corroborates Table 4.4. So does the, albeit modest, German increase and also the declines in the Netherlands, Britain and Finland. The Swedish decline in

---

[47] Müller 1992:35f, 46ff, Müller 1994:56-68.

[48] The seemingly positive trend in Ireland is explained by the fact that the largest membership party, Fianna Fail, did not report any membership figures until the late 1980s (Farrell 1992).

Table 4.5 Party membership strength in 15 European countries 1960-1991. Per cent members of electorate (M/E). Based on survey data

Year	B	DK	SF	D	IRE	I	NL	N	GB	F	LUX	GR	E	P	S tot	S ind
1960															18	
1961																
1962																
1963								9								
1964								10							17	
1965							14									
1966																
1967																
1968															16	11
1969				4			14	6								
1970															13	10
1971							12									
1972				4			9									
1973			19				14									
1974									7							
1975																
1976																
1977							8	13								
1978															16	11
1979		12													14	10
1980																
1981		11					9	14								
1982			16				7									
1983	5	5		8	4	7	10		7	4	9	8				
1984																
1985							14								16	12
1986							8									
1987			14					6								
1988	7	13		7	4	10	7		6	4	11	6	3	2	13	12
1989	9	8		6	4	7	7	12	5	4	9	12	3	3		
1990		10														
1991			11													10

Comment: This is an amended version of Table 5.2 in Widfeldt 1995. The table includes M/E percentages, not including corporate (i.e. collective), affiliate or ancillary membership. Sources: **Sweden:** National Election Studies (all years). **Norway:** Listhaug 1989, Table 9.1 (1965-1985), National Election Study (1989). **Denmark:** National Election Study (1981), Eurobarometers (EB) 19 (1983), 30 (1988) and 32 (1989), Goul Andersen 1993, Table 3.4 (1979 and 1990). **Finland:** Four party Gallup survey (1973-1987), National Election Study (1991). **Netherlands:** Van Deth and Horstman 1989, p. 45, (1971-1982, 1986), EB 19 (1983), 30 (1988) and 32 (1989). **Great Britain:** Crewe, Day and Fox 1991, Table 3.1.(1963-1987), EB 30 and 32 (1988 and 1989). **Germany:** National Election Studies (1969, 1972), EB 19 (1983), 30 (1988) and 32 (1989). **All other countries:** EB 19 (1983), 30 (1988) and 32 (1989). In years when both Eurobarometer and national survey data are available, the latter have been chosen for the relevant countries. B=Belgium, DK=Denmark, SF=Finland, D=Germany, I=Italy, NL=Netherlands, N=Norway, UK=United Kingdom, F=France, LUX=Luxembourg, GR=Greece, E=Spain, P=Portugal, S tot.=Sweden, including collective members, S ind.=Sweden including individual members only.

terms of explicit individual M/E percentage is not drastic by international comparison. Again, however, if it is accepted that the total M/E figure based on survey data is the best estimate of 'genuine' membership, the Swedish decline is among the sharpest in Europe, equalled only by Finland.

The Swedish membership level compares somewhat more favourably to other countries than according to Party Records. There is a Nordic dominance which has persisted throughout the 1960-1990 period. All four Nordic countries in the table have suffered a decline (although the Norwegian decline has been modest), but Norway, Sweden and Finland have maintained a position ahead of the continent and the British Isles. Sweden has always defended a position in this top layer in Western Europe, although it has not always dominated within the layer in question.

To sum up, the Swedish membership decline seems modest, or at least not extreme, by international standards. The M/E levels in Sweden compare well with most other countries, especially when based on survey data. If, however, the general impression given by other research has been one of Sweden being in a dominant position, matched only by Austria, Tables 4.4 and 4.5 call for caution.

Previous studies, all based on Party Records, have tended to show a Swedish/Austrian dominance. Bartolini, who focuses exclusively on Socialist parties, reports that the Swedish Social Democrats was the biggest membership party in terms of M/E percentages between the mid 1940s and the mid 1970s (where his study ends), and that they in fact took the leading European position even in the M count around 1970. Katz, Mair and others' tables give a similar picture which also applies to the total national membership (cf. Table 4.4). von Beyme, whose evidence is more scattered (M and M/V but not M/E percentages are reported) indicates a similar situation.

Another point worth remembering is the steep membership decline in Sweden in the 1990s, which is not covered in Tables 4.5 and 4.5. Systematic comparative evidence from after 1990 is not yet available, but there are many indications that there has been a general membership decline in Western Europe. It is not possible to assertively state whether the recent decline has meant that party membership in Sweden is now on par with most other countries, or whether declines elsewhere mean that Sweden retains a comparatively high position. There is some room for an educated guess, however.

The data reported in this chapter are based on more sources than previous studies. In addition, an attempt has been made to take the problems of collective membership into account. The findings suggest that there could be some question marks regarding Sweden's alleged position as one of the most membership intensive Western democracies. This was the case already before 1990, and there is no reason to expect that Sweden's relative position has been strengthened in the 1990s.

Going back to the main perspective of this book, the most important lesson is that there has been a membership decline in Sweden. The decline has taken place on the national level as well as among the majority of parties, and has accelerated in the 1990s. In the following chapter, it will be investigated whether the membership decline has been accompanied by a decline in party activity.

5 Development of Membership Activity

Introduction

The total number of members does not tell the whole story. Passive members are not perfect indicators of participatory linkage. Formal membership is a lower step on the participatory ladder than party activity. Passive members constitute a potential for activity and, hence, participation, but there is no saying to what extent this potential is fulfilled. Jörgen Goul Andersen has put it bluntly: "The important thing is not if the parties lose their members but if they lose *active* members".[1]

Although Goul Andersen is one of the relatively few to present separate data on membership and activism, the quote discloses a perspective which is quite common in party research; that membership is regarded as an indicator of activism rather than something important in its own right. This is primarily because data on membership are easier to find than data on activity (see further below). Several studies which study membership do so as an 'emergency operationalisation' of activism. Stefano Bartolini, for example, issues the disclaimer that the proportion activists of total members is assumed to be constant over time and among different countries, implying that activism is in fact what he tries to measure.[2]

An alternative perspective is to award passive membership some importance. Passive membership still indicates close affinity to the party. To become and stay a passive member discloses a sense of belonging, and can at least be considered as an extra strong form of party identification. It indicates a first -- if not complete -- step towards actual participation. The act of paying the party dues can also be seen as an act of participation, at least as much as the less frequent act of voting, which is often used as an indicator of political participation.

The arguments for passive membership as an indicator of participation are of course even more valid for activity. An activist

---

[1] Goul Andersen 1993:53. Emphasis in original.

[2] Bartolini 1985:178. Berglund and Wörlund 1990:27 also use membership strength as indicator of the parties' capacity to recruit votes via organisational strength.

represents the ultimate in party identification. The amount of party activism indicates the extent to which the parties *do* provide participatory linkage (implying that passive membership is merely potential participation). If one wants to influence political decisions, party activity -- not mere payment of dues -- is necessary.[3]

Thus, the argument here is not that mere membership is as important and valid an indicator of participatory linkage as activity, but that it is important and that it is valid. Membership and activity are both indicators of participatory linkage in their own separate right. Therefore, there is reason to keep membership and activism analytically separate. This is not intended as criticism against all those who have used membership as an indicator of activity. Lack of more precise data has meant that there has often been no alternative. If at all possible, however, better indicators should be used.

Previous research has tended to underestimate the complexity of the relationship between membership and activism. The problem has been addressed by Angelo Panebianco. He argues against what he claims is a 'widely' held view that there is an inverse relationship between party size (i.e. membership) and (actual) participation. This, he contends, rests on two assumptions: that small parties are more participatory than bigger parties and that changes in size lead to inverse changes in participation. Panebianco raises important objections on both counts. The case of the Italian communists, the PCI, belies the assumption of an inverse relationship between size and participation; when its size declined in the 1950s, so did participation. And while new parties are often able to mobilise their members, the reason is not the small size but the fact that the party is new. Panebianco's conclusion is not affirmative. His main point is that other, intervening factors mean that there is no direct and general correlation between size and participation.[4] It will not be possible to probe deeply into

---

[3] This opens for a possibility which will not be addressed in this study but which is worth some consideration. The turn from influencing via parties to influencing via other organisations is possible while retaining membership of a party. Such party members are, presumably, passive in the party. However, it is even possible that individual citizens are simultaneously active in parties and other organisations -- but that the other membership is more directly oriented towards influencing decisions while the party activity is symbolic or of a social nature.

[4] Panebianco 1988:187f. He also refers to Mancur Olson's theory of rational involvement (and non-involvement) and contends that participation may be high also in big groups, provided they distribute enough selective incentives.

these complex interrelationships here. However, some observations will be made.

The main purpose of this chapter is to investigate the development of party activity in Sweden. It might as well be said right away that data on activity are more scarce than for membership, which means that any conclusions will have to be made more carefully. At the same time, this chapter will provide useful additional information to the findings in Chapter 4, especially if the declaration just made is borne in mind; that activism can be seen as an indicator of participatory linkage which is analytically separated from mere membership. A second purpose is to address the relationship between membership and activity. Is there any relationship at all, and if so, in what direction?

Data and method

As was observed in the previous section, party organisational research has tended to focus on membership rather than activity. Most studies have data on the former but not on the latter. An exception is Goul Andersen's study on Denmark. Other exceptions are Seyd and Whiteley's studies on the British Labour and Conservative parties. Unlike Goul Andersen, however, Seyd and Whiteley do not have the data to make comparisons over time. The reason for the lack of information about party activity is the data situation. Party Records do not distinguish between active and passive members. Survey data, on the other hand, sometimes include questions about party activity besides membership.

In Sweden, the data situation is comparatively favourable. Data about party activity have been collected in three survey series. The Election Studies have included questions about party activity in 1956, 1960, 1968, 1979, 1985, 1988, 1991 and 1994. The SOM Studies have collected data about activity in the annual surveys since 1986. The studies made by Statistics Sweden (SCB) are also relevant. The annual Living Conditions Studies (ULF) have asked questions about activity in their surveys in 1976 and from 1978 to date.

While the data situation differs from that of party membership, the other two problems discussed in the previous chapter have their analogies in party activity. First, which measure, or parameter, is the most appropriate. Second, the definition, or operationalisation, of an active member.

The possible parameters to measure activity are A (raw number of activists), A/V (per cent activists of a party's voters) and A/E (per cent activists of the entire electorate). Only the last mentioned will be used, because there are no data for the A count (other than if the A/E percentage, based on survey data, is recalculated into absolute numbers) and because A/V has the same problems as those discussed in connection with M/V. However, there is one further measure which is substantively important, the proportion of activists among the total members (A/M). This parameter, which can also be called 'activist density' is an indicator of the relationship between membership and activity. If this relationship is constant, then A/M is stable. If, on the other hand, A/M changes over time, then the relationship between membership and activism can be deduced if it is compared to the development of A/E.

Of course the A/M measure does not tell the whole story, as we know nothing about inter-movements between activity and passivity on the individual level. However, even if the evidence is not conclusive, A/M figures can be used as an indicator of whether the parties have inner cores of activists, which would be the plausible interpretation if A/M is going up when M/E is going down.

How to operationalise an active member is a difficult problem. Whiteley, Seyd and Richardson argue that party activism should not be considered a dichotomous variable. Instead activity is a continuum, with occasional participation at one end and frequent involvement in different sorts of activities at the other.[5] However, their study is based on purposely collected data on party members which makes such distinctions possible. This study, which relies on secondary analysis of 'general' data, has to make do with what is available. Surveys have varied in the wordings of questions, with respect to how activity is operationalised, and also with respect to whether distinctions of more than one level of activity are made.

In some surveys there is no specification of activity at all. Respondents are asked whether they consider themselves as active in their respective party or political organisation, without further specification in the question. Such wordings were used in the 1956 and 1960 Election Studies and in all the ULF studies.

As a rule, however, some sort of specification is included in the question. Two main types of operationalisations have been used. First, attendance at meetings. Since 1979, the Election Studies have added the

---

[5] Whiteley, Seyd and Richardson 1994:101ff.

sentence "By active I mean attending meetings a few times a year" to the initial question whether respondents are active in the political organisation or organisations of which they are members.

The SOM studies distinguish among two levels of activity. The lower activity level is to have attended a meeting during the past six months. The higher level, which is the second of the main types of operationalisations, is to have some sort of commission (or appointed position; Sw. *"uppdrag"*) in the political organisation. This distinction has been the same, with identical wordings, from the first SOM study in 1986 to date.

The 1964 and 1968 Election Studies used an operationalisation which in a way collapsed the meeting attendance and the appointed position criteria into one, and instructed interviewers to consider respondents who had commissions in the organisations or attended most (Sw. *"för det mesta"*) meetings. This is stricter than the criterion for meeting attendance used in the Election Studies from 1979 onwards, where it is sufficient to have attended a few meetings during the past year.[6]

The ULF studies do not specify what is meant by party activity. They have consistently used the wording "Do you actively participate in the activities of the party (youth organisation/women's organisation)?", thus letting respondents themselves define activity. At the same time, however, the ULF questionnaires include a question about whether respondents have attended a meeting organised by a political party, or political youth or women's organisation, during the past 12 months. Respondents have also been asked two follow-up questions; how many times they have attended such meetings and whether they have made spoken interventions at any such meeting. It should be noted that these questions are asked before the

---

[6] The 1964 Election Study does not give information about party activity, because it does not distinguish between activity in parties and other organisations. It was only asked in how many organisations respondents were active (although political parties and organisations were included among those organisations). The 1968 Election Study is worded in a very general way and asks respondents whether they consider themselves as active in any organisation or association. In each Election Study, the question about activity is asked immediately after the question about party membership. 1968 is the only study where the question is asked to all respondents, not only to those who have answered that they are members of a political party or organisation. The question is open-ended and the coding is very detailed and includes political parties and political organisations; up to five organisations per respondent are coded.

questions about party membership and party activity. They do not require that respondents have to be members to have attended or spoken at meetings. It is of course possible to attend and speak at party meetings open to the public without being a member of the party. The ULF studies have also asked whether members have commissions in their party, but only in five out of the 17 studies completed so far.

The data clearly have limitations when it comes to making comparisons over time. The Election Studies provide the only data that separate between activists in different parties. On the other hand, they have the limitations that they do not distinguish among different levels of activity, and that comparisons over time can only start in 1979. SOM and ULF data can separate among different activity levels but do not separate between members of different parties. In time they reach back to 1986 and 1976, respectively.

Thus, on the party level, we can investigate the development between 1979 and 1994 (SOM and ULF data have been collected until 1997). Data from before 1979 have some value, however, as they give information about the relative differences among the parties in a given year. In that sense, the time series can be extended back to 1960. On the aggregate national level, the longest comparable time series is provided by ULF data.

Development of membership activity on party level

The A/E levels by party are reported in Table 5.1 below. The results should be treated with caution. A problem with the A/E measure is that, by definition, A/E percentages will be at least as small as the already small M/E percentages; in practice much smaller. This is a problem when the entire electorate is used as the percentage base, but as was argued in the previous chapter, no better percentage base exists. The differences and fluctuations in the table are mostly too small to be statistically significant.

Second, the changes in the constructions and wordings of questions mean that comparisons over time can start only from 1979. From then on, the operationalisation of activity has been consistent and fairly generous. The 1960 question left it to the respondent to decide whether he/she was active. In 1968 there was an explicit, and comparatively strict, guideline. The table has been split to indicate the differences in operationalisation.

Table 5.1 **Per cent active party members of electorate (A/E), Sweden 1960-1994**

year	Left Party	Soc. Dem.	Centre	People's	Moderate	Chr. Dem.	Green	New Dem.
1960	0.1	1.8	1.3	0.1	0.5	---	---	---
1968	0.1	1.5	1.0	0.1	0.4	0.0	---	---
1979	0.3	3.3	1.7	0.3	0.7	0.1	---	---
1985	0.1	2.7	1.2	0.4	0.6	0.3	0.3	---
1988	0.2	1.9	1.3	0.2	0.5	0.3	0.2	---
1991	0.0	1.4	1.2	0.3	0.5	0.1	0.0	0.2
1994	0.1	1.9	0.8	0.4	0.6	0.0	0.1	0.0

Comment: Data are taken from the Swedish Election Studies. Method: in-person interviews. In 1960, respondents who had answered that they were party members, were asked "Do you consider yourself as one of the active members of...?" (q. 101). In 1968, all respondents were asked "Do you consider yourself as an *active* member of some organisations or association?" with a specification added as an interviewer's instruction: "Active = attends most meetings and/or has commissions in the association." Respondents were then asked in which organisation(s) they were active (q. 87A and B). From 1979 onwards the wordings are comparable. In 1979 (q. 36B) respondents who have answered that they are members of a political party and/or political organisation were asked: "Are you active in the political organisation of which you are a member? By active I mean attending meetings a few times per year." From 1985 onwards, respondents who have answered that they are members of a political party and/or political organisation, have been asked: "Are you active in ... (name of party/organisation)? By active I mean attending meetings a few times per year." 1985: q. 47B. 1988: q. 49B. 1991 q. 52B. 1994: q. 51B. The percentage bases consist of the following number of cases: 1960: 1461. 1968: 2854. 1979: 2675. 1985: 2768. 1988: 2654. 1991: 2597. 1994: 2527. Social Democratic figures until 1988 include collective members who claim to be active. Active members of women's organisations (if any) are included for all parties from 1979 onwards.

Despite the caveats, some interesting information can be extracted from the table. Most importantly, it can be concluded that the Social Democratic dominance in terms of membership is also reflected in activity. The party claims the highest A/E percentage in every year represented in the table -- in this respect the table gives information back to 1960. The second highest number of activists can be found in the Centre Party. These two parties have always been in the top two positions, and always in the same order. The Social Democratic lead is very narrow in certain years, notably in 1991, but the differences are statistically significant in 1979, 1985 and in 1994.[7]

---

[7] According to a one tailed Z test, the difference in A/E percentage between the Social Democrats and the Centre Party is significant on the .01 level in 1979, 1988 and 1994. The difference is significant on the .05 level in 1968 and 1988.

Among the remaining parties, the Moderates are constantly in third place. It is worth noting that, unlike in membership, the Moderates have never actually surpassed the A/E level of the Centre Party, although the difference narrowed drastically in 1994.[8] Then follows a third group. The People's Party Liberals are fourth in 1985, 1991 and 1994 but in other years they are equalled or surpassed by the Christian Democrats or the Left Party. The Green Party and New Democracy have also on occasion reached A/E levels comparable with the People's Party Liberals, Christian Democrats and the Left Party. The contribution to party activity by the newer parties has not been substantial, however. The observation in the previous chapter, that new parties have not had an impact on party membership, also applies to party activity.

The discrepancies in the constructions of questions mean that all conclusions regarding time trends will have to be based on the more limited period between 1979 and 1994. During that period, there has been a decline in the two leading parties, the Social Democrats and the Centre Party. The Social Democrats suffered a continuous decline until 1991. The 1994 figure is a marginal increase, which suggests that the tide had at least been stemmed. Nevertheless, the 1994 A/E is 1.4 percentage points below the 1979 level; a decrease of more than 40 per cent. The Centre Party has also experienced a decline which, unlike the Social Democrats, was not halted between 1991 and 1994. In 1994 the A/E figure was more than halved compared to 1979.

For the other parties, interpretations are very difficult. The A/E percentages are very small, all fluctuations very limited and they do not follow any trends. The only defensible conclusion is conservative: the activism level appears to have remained stable among the remaining parties. However, in this respect Table 5.1 says almost as much about the crudeness of the A/E measure on party level as it does about actual change, or lack of change.

While Table 5.1 gives little room for far reaching conclusions, some observations can be made. First, the leading positions of the Social Democrats and, in second place, the Centre Party. Second, that the A/E level has declined for both these two parties between 1979 and 1994. Thus far, the observations are similar to the findings about membership strength in the

---

[8] According to the same one tailed Z test, the difference in A/E between the Centre and Moderate parties is significant on the .05 level in 1960 and on the .01 level in 1968, 1979, 1985, 1988 and 1991.

previous chapter, an observation which is relevant in its own right. The third observation from the table is that, although the two biggest parties have suffered an activism decline, there is not sufficient evidence to speak of a general decline, which has affected all, or most, parties. In this respect, the development of activism is not consistent with the findings at party level with regard to membership, where a decline was observed in most parties. This is true even if the time frame for membership development is restricted to the same as that of activity, 1979 through 1994.

The conclusion of no proven general decline is not decisive. First, it is of course highly relevant to find a proven decrease in the two largest parties. Second, the nature of available data and measures means that credible trends in any direction will be difficult to find. It is possible that more refined methods would have registered a decline in more parties but this is no more than a guess. The nominal A/E figures suggest that one might suspect a decline in the Left Party, Christian Democrats, Green Party and New Democracy. The People's Party Liberals seem to be characterised by a stable activity level. More far reaching statements are not possible -- the statements above have been made with trembling hands.

Methodologically, it seems as if the differences in wording of questions have some effect on the results. The most restrictive operationalisation of activity, in 1968, results in notably lower A/E percentages than the surrounding time points for most parties. The lack of explicit criteria for activity in 1960 results in intermediate levels, while the slackened operationalisation in 1979 is followed by increased percentages. Of course, *ceteris paribus* do not apply to such conclusions since we do not know how much the time factor has affected the results. It still seems plausible to assume that the methodological changes have had some effect.

The fluctuations in party activity seem to have been limited in most parties. Does this also apply to the activist density, the A/M percentages? The answer can be found in Table 5.2 below. Since the percentage base here is the total number of members instead of, as in the previous table, the entire electorate, the percentages are mostly based on very few cases. For this reason, the Left, Green and Christian Democratic Parties have been left out, as these parties have never had a total of more than 17 members in any Election Study. Even after the smaller parties have been removed, the number of cases is often very low, as seen in brackets after each entry. Thus, a warning is justified against far reaching conclusions based on the percentages.

Table 5.2   Per cent activists of party members (A/M), Sweden 1960-1994

year	SD total	SD ind.	Centre	People's	Moderate
1960	22.0 (123)	-	32.1 (56)	9.1 (22)	13.7 (51)
1968	17.5 (240)	33.3 (99)	29.9 (97)	4.4 (45)	19.4 (62)
1979	39.7 (219)	55.4 (130)	47.9 (96)	37.5 (24)	32.7 (55)
1985	33.3 (222)	50.8 (124)	42.5 (80)	52.6 (19)	26.2 (65)
1988	31.1 (164)	33.3 (141)	51.5 (68)	50.0 (12)	21.4 (56)
1991	-	33.6 (107)	46.3 (67)	35.0 (20)	40.0 (35)
1994	-	37.6 (125)	41.2 (51)	47.4 (19)	36.8 (38)

Comment: Data are taken from the Swedish Election Studies all years. The operationalisation of an active member is the same between 1979 and 1994 but was different in 1960 and 1968. See further comment under Table 5.1. The figures in brackets indicate the number of cases (i.e. members) on which the percentages are based. The A/M figures for individual Social Democratic members do not include collective members in the percentage or the percentage base.

Nevertheless, the table contains some interesting and surprising results. The traditional mass parties, the Social Democrats and the Centre Party, display the highest A/M levels until 1979. These parties have also been dominant in terms of membership (M/E) and activity (A/E). Despite the comparatively large memberships, there have been enough activists in these parties to also give them leading positions in A/M percentages. Thus, these two parties have displayed important mass party characteristics. This observation only takes individual Social Democratic membership into account. Not surprisingly, the party's A/M percentage goes down if collective members are included in the percentage base.

After 1979, however, something happened. The Social Democratic activism density declined, especially drastically between 1985 and 1988. It should be noted that there is no reason to suspect a methodological artefact here, as the construction of questions is identical in all years between 1979 and 1994. The Centre Party has experienced a curvilinear development during the same period, with shifts within a relatively limited range. At the same time, however, the People's and Moderate parties' A/M percentages have increased. Thus, in the 1990s, the two traditional mass parties no longer dominate in terms of activism density. Instead, the highest A/M figure in 1994 is claimed by the People's Party Liberals. What has happened is that all parties have lost members, but only the Social Democrats and the Centre Party have suffered a statistically corroborated decline in activity. As a consequence, the relative differences in A/M have narrowed.

The implications for the party organisations are quite interesting. The traditional mass party had many members but also many activists, thus dominating according to all the measures of membership and activism. In this respect, there has been a convergence among the parties. Until 1979, the Social Democrats and the Centre Party were able to extract more activity out of their organisations than the other parties. In 1960, when admittedly the operationalisation of activity was different, the relative differences in A/M were clear (in the Social Democratic case, the A/M percentage is likely to have been even higher if a distinction between individual and collective members had been possible). In 1979 the differences were still fairly clear. Today, the Centre Party and the Social Democrats have no such relative advantage. They still have more members and activists than the other parties, but they are no longer better at extracting activity out of the given membership base.

The issue of the relationship between membership and activism has to be addressed with care. Available evidence does not suggest that membership and activity go hand in hand. During the 1979-1994 period, individual Social Democratic membership was fairly stable, while activity went down. Consequently, A/M also declined. In the Centre Party, on the other hand, both membership and activity decreased during the same period; at roughly the same rate.[9] Consequently, A/M remained quite stable.

Thus, there is no evidence to suggest that parties in general tend to have a hard core of activists, or that loss of members means that the remaining members are, or become, more committed than those who leave. There may be some weak support for such an assumption in the People's Party Liberals and the Moderate Party.[10] But as the Social Democratic case shows, it is just as possible that activity suffers worse than membership. On

---

[9] The M/E for the Centre Party went from 3.8 in 1979 to 2.0 in 1994; a decrease of just under 50 per cent (see Table 4.2). During the same period, A/E went from 1.7 to 0.8; a decrease of just over 50 per cent.

[10] Election Studies data do not indicate a significant decline in membership for the People's Party Liberals between 1979 and 1994 (see Table 4.2). If, however, the very sharp membership decline according to Party Records during the same period (Table 4.1) is accepted as true, then the stable A/E levels in Table 5.1 would suggest that the party has a core of very committed members, or is constantly able to mobilise a steady number of activists. It would, however, be a bit bold to accept the party's stable A/E figures according to Election Studies data, and at the same time reject the party's stable M/E figures, which are based on the same data.

the other hand, the Centre Party case shows that it is also quite possible that the developments of membership and activity to go hand in hand; as is illustrated by the combined evidence from Tables 4.2, 5.1 and 5.2. In conclusion, therefore, there is no evidence of a general and systematic relationship between trends in membership and activity on the party level.

Development of membership activity on aggregate national level

The data presented so far are sketchy. Because the activists are so few, all variations have been within very small percentages. However, if all activists are put together, the foundation will be stronger. The A/M and A/E percentages on the aggregate national level are reported in Table 5.3. The entries are based on the same questions as before, which again means that comparisons over time can only start from 1979. In order to simplify comparisons with the development of membership, the individual and total M/E figures are also included in the table.

The changes in operationalisations of activity mean that the nearly identical A/E levels in 1960 and 1994 probably do not reflect reality. The period between 1979 and 1994 is characterised by a decline which, however, was halted in 1994. So is this a serious decline or not? It can be said that the loss of less than two percentage points between 1979 and 1991 is modest. On the other hand, the proportion of activists of the Swedish electorate sunk by almost 40 per cent during the same period. Translated into absolute numbers, this means that just over 390,000 people were active in parties in 1979, compared to circa 250,000 in the 1990s.[11] Membership has also declined between 1979 and 1994, but not at the same rate. Consequently, the A/M percentages have gone down. A close look at the table reveals that until 1988, the decline in activity was sharper than that in membership. Hence, A/M continuously went down. From 1988, however, A/M has been stable. This is because the changes in M/E and A/E have followed each other, in direction as well as rate.

---

[11] More specifically, around 244,000 people were active in 1991, compared to 259,000 in 1994. This can be seen as an artificial 'A' measure; the raw absolute number of activists. The figures are recalculations, where the A/E percentages have been multiplied by the actual electorate for the respective years.

Table 5.3 **Development of party membership and activity in Sweden, 1960-1994. Election Studies data. Percentages**

year	M/E ind.	M/E tot.	A/E	A/M ind.	A/M tot
1960	-	17.8 (1461)	3.9 (1456)	-	22.1 (258)
1968	11.1 (2855)	16.0 (2856)	3.2 (2854)	25.6 (316)	19.8 (455)
1979	12.1 (2678)	15.5 (2678)	6.5 (2675)	49.2 (324)	41.9 (413)
1985	11.9 (2778)	15.8 (2778)	5.7 (2768)	44.8 (328)	37.1 (426)
1988	11.7 (2662)	12.6 (2662)	4.7 (2654)	39.4 (307)	37.9 (330)
1991	9.8 (2599)	-	3.8 (2597)	39.1 (253)	-
1994	9.9 (2527)	-	4.0 (2527)	39.8 (251)	-

Comment: M/E ind. = per cent individual members of total electorate. M/E tot. = per cent members of total electorate, including collectively affiliated Social Democrats. A/E= per cent active members of total electorate. A/M ind. = per cent activists of total individual members. A/M tot. = per cent activists of total members, including collectively affiliated Social Democrats. The operationalisation of an active member is the same between 1979 and 1994 but was different in 1960 and 1968. See comment under Table 5.1. The figures in brackets indicate the number of cases (M/E and A/E = electorate, A/M = members) that constitute the percentage base for each entry. Until 1988, the A/E figures include collectively affiliated members who claim to be active. The A/M figures for individual members do not include collective members in the percentage or the percentage base. Data are taken from the Swedish Election Studies all years (see also comments under Tables 4.3 and 5.1).

The evidence suggests a positive relationship between membership and activity on the national level in the sense that changes tend to go in the same direction. Both have decreased during the 1979-1994 period, and the nominal short term changes also converge. But the rate of change does not always correspond. The relative decrease in activity is greater than in membership and the decline in activity began earlier than the decrease in membership. It should also be remembered that the relationship between membership and activity is not uniform among different parties, as was observed when Table 5.2 was discussed.

Data collected by the SOM institute at Göteborg University make it possible to distinguish various levels of activity. Since 1986, respondents have been asked if they are members of a party and have been to a meeting during the past six months. They have also been asked if they have any appointed position (commission) in the party. The results appear in Table 5.4. As in Table 5.3, the M/E figures are included for illustrative purposes.

Table 5.4   Development of party membership and activity in Sweden, 1986-1997. SOM data. Percentages

year	M/E	Attended party meeting	Commission in party	A/M
1986	12.1 (1624)	3.8 (1624)	2.6 (1624)	31.5 (197)
1987	13.1 (1673)	5.9 (1673)	3.3 (1673)	44.7 (219)
1988	12.6 (1643)	4.0 (1643)	2.6 (1643)	31.9 (207)
1989	11.9 (1578)	5.4 (1578)	3.0 (1578)	46.0 (187)
1990	11.9 (1582)	3.6 (1582)	2.3 (1582)	30.2 (189)
1991	13.2 (1573)	5.8 (1573)	3.4 (1573)	44.4 (207)
1992	10.4 (1889)	3.2 (1889)	2.0 (1889)	30.6 (196)
1993	10.8 (1857)	3.3 (1857)	1.7 (1857)	30.5 (200)
1994	10.2 (1792)	3.6 (1792)	2.0 (1792)	34.1 (179)
1995	9.7 (1777)	3.0 (1777)	1.6 (1777)	30.6 (173)
1996	n/a	n/a	n/a	n/a
1997	9.5 (1754)	3.8 (1754)	1.9 (1754)	39.5 (167)

Comment: M/E = per cent members of entire electorate. Attended party meeting = members who have been to a party meeting in past 6 months. Commissions in party = members who have some commission (appointed position) in the party. A/M = per cent activists (including all who have indicated any kind of activity) of total members. Data from the SOM (Society, Opinion, Media) Studies at Göteborg University. 1986: q. 51; 1987: q. 45; 1988: q. 43; 1989: q. 43; 1990: q. 45; 1991: q. 46; 1992: q. 54; 1993: q. 61; 1994: q. 63. 1995: q. 62. 1997: q. 60. Method: mail questionnaires. Respondents have been asked if they are members of a number of organisations (normally also including sports clubs and environmentalist organisations). Party membership specified as including membership of youth and/or women's organisations. Respondents have been asked if they are members, members and have attended a meeting during the past six months or members and have some type of commission in the organisation. Respondents with more than one level of activity (i.e. has attended a meeting during the past six months and has some type of commission) have been coded as the highest activity level. Members with commissions (4th column) are included among members who have attended a meeting during past 6 months (3rd column). Figures in brackets = number of cases that constitute the percentage base for each entry. In the 2nd, 3rd and 4th columns this means the electorate and in the 5th column it means all party members.

The third and fourth columns in the table are different A/E measures. In the third column, the operationalisation of activity is similar to that of the Election Studies. However, the SOM operationalisation is arguably somewhat stricter, since it defines activity as having attended a meeting during the past half year while the Election Studies define activity as attending meetings a few times a year. A comparison between the A/E levels in Tables 5.3 and 5.4 does not suggest that this difference in operationalisation has any important effect. In 1988 and 1994, Election Studies data indicate marginally higher A/E, levels but in 1991 the SOM Study reports a level which is two percentage points higher than in the

Election Study of the same year.[12] The next column, members with commissions in the parties, predictably reports lower levels than the A/E percentages based on Election Studies, although in 1991 the difference is very small.

In Table 5.3 it was shown that, according to the Election Studies, party activity declined between 1979 and 1994. SOM data, which exist for a shorter time period, bear weaker evidence of a decline. According to both operationalisations of activity, attending meetings and having commissions in the party, the activity level fluctuates back and forth. There are cases of rises and declines from year to year, but most differences are very small and there is little systematic development. Indeed, the proportion of members who have attended a meeting during the past half year is identical in 1986 and 1997. With a bit of stretching, however, it is possible to detect a weak tendency for the percentages to be slightly lower in the 1990s than in the 1980s. Since 1992, the proportion of members who have attended meetings have stayed below four per cent which only happened in one year in between 1986 and 1989.

The proportion of members with commissions has also fluctuated back and forth. Here, however, a negative development is slightly easier to detect. The percentages after 1992 are the lowest throughout the 1986-1997 period. However, we are still dealing with small differences and there is not enough evidence to speak of a sharp long-term decline.

SOM data do not suggest much of a relationship between membership and activity. In the long term (that is, between 1986 and 1997), there has been a clear, if not massive, decline in membership, but activity, defined as meeting attendance, is characterised by mostly trendless fluctuation. As a consequence, there has not been a clear trend in the development of A/M. Looking at the short term fluctuations, it is more common for M/E and the two different A/E counts to move in the same direction from year to year than the opposite. However, there are exceptions, such as between 1988 and 1989, to some extent 1993 and 1994 and 1995 and 1997. Consequently, the development of A/M is very reminiscent of a roller coaster ride.[13]

---

[12] The 1991 SOM Study also reports an exceptionally high membership (M/E) level (see Table 4.3). There is no ready explanation for this.

[13] It should be emphasised that the A/M percentages consist of all members who have indicated some sort of activity, that is both those who have attended a meeting during the

Table 5.5   Development of party membership (per cent members of electorate, M/E), party activity (per cent activists of electorate, A/E) and attendance at party meetings (per cent of electorate who have attended a party meeting in the past year) in Sweden, 1976-1997. SCB data

year	M/E	A/E	party meeting
1976	13.6	n/a	7.3
1978	13.2	4.7	7.3
1979	14.2	4.3	8.2
1980	14.5	4.5	8.6
1981	13.3	3.8	8.0
1982	14.1	3.7	8.9
1983	15.0	4.1	8.7
1984	15.7	3.9	9.8
1985	14.5	3.7	8.3
1986	13.4	n/a	8.1
1987	13.1	n/a	6.6
1988	13.0	3.6	7.6
1989	12.3	3.0	7.6
1990	11.4	2.5	6.1
1991	10.3	2.8	5.6
1992	11.1	2.7	7.4
1993	9.8	2.4	5.5
1994	8.9	2.6	5.8
1995	n/a	n/a	n/a
1996	9.7	2.2	5.0
1997	8.2	2.0	4.6

Comment: Party meeting = attended party meeting in the past year. Data are taken from the Living Conditions Studies (*Undersökningar av levnadsförhållanden, ULF*), made by Statistics Sweden (*Statistiska Centralbyrån, SCB*). The figures have been kindly supplied by Lars Häll, SCB. 1976: n=11,144. 1978: n=10,307. 1979: n=9,468. 1980: n=7,261. 1981: n=7,703. 1982: n=7,290. 1983: n=6,663. 1984: n=7,211. 1985: n=6,585. 1986: n=4,774. 1987: n=7,052. 1988: n=6,514. 1989: n=6,781. 1990: n=6,191. 1991: n=5,827. 1992: n=5,980. 1993: n=6,190. 1994: n=6,001. 1996: n=5,880. 1997: n=5,806. See also SCB report series *Levnadsförhållanden*, especially reports no. 86 and 90 (SCB 1994 and SCB 1996). Method: in-person interviews.

past six months and those who have commissions in the party. In other words, the same members as are included in the third column in the table.

SCB data, presented in Table 5.5 above, reinforce the overall impression of a decline in party activism. The A/E percentage declined from 4.7 in 1978, to 2.0 in 1997. The 1978 level has never again been reached. The decline is not continuous, but the long-term trend is undeniable. In 1990, the figure went below three per cent for the first time, and has stayed there since.[14]

The development of attendance at party meetings has been curvilinear. The highest proportion came in 1984, when almost one in ten Swedish citizens claimed to have attended a party meeting. Since then, however, there has been a fairly clear, if not uninterrupted, decline. In the 1990s this decline has sunk below the level of the 1970s. Thus, there has been a long-term decline here too.[15]

SCB data do not give support to the existence of a systematic relationship between membership and activity. The long-term trends of membership, activity and meeting attendance are all negative, in the sense that the most recent time points represent all time lows. However, the short-term fluctuations from year to year do not follow any systematic pattern; they converge just as often as they diverge.

Conclusion

The overall conclusion in this chapter is that party activity has suffered a decline. It is not proven to be uniform among all parties, and it is not possible to accurately trace the long-term development all the way back to 1960. Still, both Election Studies and SCB data show that the long-term trend since the late 1970s has been negative. According to the Election Studies, activism has gone down by one-third, or some 130,000 people, between 1979 and 1994. If the increased electorate is taken into account, the decrease is almost 40 per cent; from an A/E of 6.5 to 4.0. SCB data reinforce this observation. Between 1978 and 1997, the ULF Studies report a

---

[14] See also Häll 1996:10f.

[15] The remarkably high percentages of people having attended a party meeting, compared to Election Studies and SOM data, can be explained by the fact that it is possible for non-members to be included in this category in the SCB studies. In the SCB studies, respondents are asked whether they have attended a party meeting before they are asked whether they are party members or activists whereas in the SOM studies the order is reversed, and the question explicitly refers only to party members.

decrease in A/E from just under five per cent, to 2.0 per cent. The decline is not to the same extent supported by SOM data, but this may be because of the more limited time frame between 1986 and 1997.

Thus, the decrease in potential activism, total membership, which was found in the last chapter, has been accompanied by a decrease in actual activism. In fact, as the decreased A/M percentages on the aggregate national level show (see Table 5.3), the decline in activism has been sharper than that of membership. A smaller proportion of the electorate, but also of the total number of members, are active in the 1990s than they were in the late 1970s.

Unlike the chapter on membership, data to allow international comparisons are scarce. Goul Andersen's Danish study reports a very marginal decrease in party activity, from 6.1 per cent in 1979 to 5.8 per cent in 1990. In that perspective, the Swedish decline appears as accentuated. In 1979, the proportion of party activists in Sweden was only marginally lower than in Denmark (6.5 against 6.9 per cent). In the early 1990s the gap had grown to two full percentage points (3.8 per cent in Sweden in 1991 compared to 5.8 per cent in Denmark in 1990).[16]

The implications for the Swedish parties are not positive. Their ability to channel political participation is declining. This decline is a problem for the parties, regardless of whether it is explained by an overall decline in political participation, or that participation takes other forms than via parties. The coming of new parties has not affected this process. Their entry has not affected activism, just as it has not notably affected membership.

It should be noted that most of the data in this chapter have employed a very generous operationalisation of activity, towards the passive end of the activity continuum discussed by Whiteley, Seyd and Richardson. It is possible that the trend could have been more negative if the operationalisation of activity had been stricter. The relatively modest decline in the proportion of members with commissions in the party organisations (Table 5.4, SOM data) does not corroborate this suspicion, however. The levels are, quite predictably, lower, but the rate of decline is not exceptional compared to the declines in A/E reported in this chapter.

The main issue addressed in this study is whether there has been any long term change in the Swedish parties' ability to provide participatory linkage. The findings in this and the previous chapter constitute the first part of the answer to this question: two of the conditions for linkage suggest that

---

[16] The Danish figures are from Goul Andersen 1993:53.

there must be some question marks with respect to the parties' ability to provide participatory linkage. The social composition of the members can also be taken as an indicator of this type of linkage, and this aspect will be addressed in Chapter 7.

The account so far has had a descriptive tendency. No attempts have been made to explain the development of membership and activism. That is fully consistent with the main purpose of this study. However, the relationship between the development of membership and other variables will not be left totally unattended. Before we proceed to the social representativeness of the Swedish party members, some possible relationships will be discussed.

6 Relationship Between Party Size and Background Factors

Introduction

Thus far, membership and activism have been discussed on their own, without reference to other factors. Of course, they are not isolated phenomena. There are reasons why people join and become active in parties just as there are reasons why people leave parties or stay away altogether. Most political parties of a reasonable size are in an almost constant state of inflow and outflow of members. Sometimes there is a net gain, sometimes a net loss. The purpose of this chapter is to examine the extent to which a number of background factors are related to the organisational strength of political parties.

Membership figures vary according to a number of factors, or forces, which can be divided into four categories. *External* forces, which are outside the party. Examples are economic and general political development. *Internal* forces, which are processes inside the parties themselves, such as internal conflicts and the role of personalities. *Pull* forces, which attract members to political parties and, finally, push forces, that repel members from the parties. These forces can be combined into a four-fold model, as shown in Figure 6.1 below.

Figure 6.1 Possible forces behind membership development

	INTERNAL	EXTERNAL
PUSH	1	3
PULL	2	4

Examples of internal push forces (box 1) are internal party problems such as disillusionment with leading party officers and/or the party's policies, or bitter internal conflicts. Internal pull forces (box 2) include, for example, an emphasis by the party on membership recruitment, or that the party's policies or internal activities are perceived as positive.

External factors are often connected to the political climate. Generally speaking, the existence or non-existence of important political issues or conflicts can be expected to have an effect on membership. If the political system is polarised and conflict-ridden, the incentives to join a party can be expected to be high. External pull forces (box 4) are operating. Conversely, in times of low polarisation we can speak of external push forces (box 3).

It should be noted that different and conflicting forces may operate simultaneously. Consider, for example, a situation where the party system is depolarised with few divisive political issues but some or several parties provide attractive social activities or material incentives. In such circumstances, external push and internal pull forces co-exist, and whether membership goes up or down depends on which forces are the strongest.

The factors just discussed are not an exhaustive list. It is not possible to investigate all possible factors that may be related to membership development. There are, however, some factors which can be expected to have an impact and for which good data are available. Four such factors will be considered. They all relate to the taxonomy in Figure 6.1, but do not claim to be a full scale operationalisation of the whole figure. Rather, they are some possible examples which can be derived from the four boxes.

The first three, votes, incumbency and election years, are external, while the fourth, formal membership influence, is internal. They may all work in both directions; that is, they may be push or pull factors. This may vary according to the direction in which they develop, for example whether a party gains or loses votes, but even with that aspect held constant, it is an open question whether they are exclusively push or pull forces.

The first factor, party vote, has been given quite a lot of attention in previous research. Stefano Bartolini put forward the hypothesis that party vote correlates with membership, but he did not state whether the relationship was supposed to be positive or negative. Electoral success can work positively, because it creates a 'bandwagon effect' to the organisational benefit of the party. At the same time, electoral defeat could also be followed by a membership increase, because the party intensifies membership recruitment as a response to the electoral setback. This possibility has been discussed by Palle Svensson, and used as a hypothesis by Bartolini. The reasoning is that mass parties respond to disturbances in the environment by expanding their membership support.[1]

Second, Bartolini also discusses the relationship between incumbency and membership.[2] The resemblance to party vote is quite close. Electorally successful parties could be expected to be in government more often than unsuccessful parties. The relationship is not exact, however. Especially not if trends in votes are taken into consideration. There are several examples of parties which have stayed in government, on their own or as part of a coalition, despite a loss of votes. There are also examples of parties losing governmental status despite vote gains, for example the Swedish Moderate Party in 1994. Incumbency is therefore a crude factor. It may be regarded as a measure of party success -- and, hence, analogous to party vote -- an assumption which is a simplification. It is also possible to argue that the fact that a party is or is not in government may have an effect on its own, between elections. Such an analysis should ideally take further aspects into account, such as the performance and the popularity of the government. Such factors cannot be addressed here, but Bartolini's hypothesis will be tested.

Third, Bartolini raises the hypothesis that membership increases during, or immediately after, election years. The reasoning is that the campaign raises extra interest in politics, which has the side-effect of increased willingness to become members.[3] Unlike party votes, this factor would affect membership regardless of the outcome of the election and should, hence, increase during and immediately after election years. The difference between this and the other factors is that, if true, the election years hypothesis would mean a cyclical development. In Sweden, where election dates are pre-defined, local and national elections are held on the same date

---

[1] Bartolini 1985:194f, 196ff. Svensson 1974. A possible alternative or complement to party vote is party identification. The reasoning is similar to party vote, but since partisanship is more stable than voting it should be expected to be more strongly and positively correlated with membership; one would expect that joining a party is preceded by a process of increased attachment to the party. The problem with this in the Swedish case is that party identification is not easily separable from party vote; the correlation between the two has constantly been extremely strong.

[2] Bartolini 1985:198f.

[3] Bartolini 1985:195f.

(since 1970) and parliamentary dissolutions are extremely rare, these cycles would be regular and predictable.

The only internal factor that will be investigated is membership influence. A key reason why parties attract members is that they are providers of participatory linkage, i.e. that people can influence political decisions by participating in parties. According to this reasoning members are more attracted to party membership if the parties give them some influence, and vice versa. Hirschman's famous distinction between *Exit* and *Voice* is relevant here. The expectation is that there is an inverse relationship between Exit and Voice. If the members are given Voice opportunity, they can be expected to stay in the party or be interested in joining it. Conversely, if the Voice opportunity is low or declining, the potential for Exit increases. It should be noted that Hirschman's framework does not apply to the entire reasoning in this chapter. The membership development discussed below depends not only on the extent of Exit, but to at least as large an extent on people *joining* parties. 'Entry' is something that Hirschman does not consider.[4]

Previous research has tended to regard development of membership and activism as a dependent variable. It should be pointed out that it is equally possible to turn the causality around and discuss the effect of membership on other factors. Party votes and, ultimately, incumbency, are important examples. Among the reasons why parties recruit members is that they may be considered as potential vote-getters.[5] Consequently, membership increase could be expected to have a positive effect on votes. Sten Berglund and Ingemar Wörlund have found a positive relationship between organisational strength and votes in a study on the Liberal and Social Democratic parties in northern Sweden.[6] Partick Seyd and Paul Whiteley found similar effects for the Labour Party in Great Britain; there is an effect of membership strength and a stronger effect of activism on party vote. Writing in 1992, the authors concluded that the Labour Party would be well advised to promote party membership in order to improve its electoral performances.[7]

---

[4] Hirschman 1970, see especially pp. 82-86.

[5] This is a key finding in Susan Scarrow's research on the major parties in Great Britain and (West) Germany. See Scarrow 1991 and Scarrow 1996.

[6] Berglund and Wörlund 1990:286ff.

[7] Seyd and Whiteley 1992:186-190, 199.

In this chapter the focus is on the co-variation between membership development and the other chosen factors. Thus, the general perspective is not to regard the development of membership and activity as a dependent, nor independent variable. Although some of the discussion of the findings will be in causal terms, the purpose is somewhat less ambitious: to discuss whether the chosen background factors have a systematic relationship with membership and activism, and whether this relationship is positive or negative.

Bartolini assumes that the proportion of activists among the entire membership is constant, which means that membership and activism trends are identical. This is an assumption which he himself admits is questionable but it indicates that he considers activism to be the main focus of interest.[8] As was shown in Chapter 5, Bartolini's assumption is not supported by Swedish data. Hirschman, on the other hand, makes it quite clear that passive membership is still membership of an organisation. Passivity may precede and lead to Exit, but it is the actual and formal Exit which is the crucial stage.[9] Thus, the relationship between the chosen factors and activity is every bit as interesting as that with membership. Due to the scarcity of comparable data on activity, however, the discussion will mostly concentrate on membership.

Although collective membership of the Social Democratic Party will be given some attention, most of the discussion will be based on trends in individual membership. As was explained in Chapter 4, collective membership depends primarily on agreements between the Social Democratic Party and the trade unions, and on organisational changes within the unions, rather than on successful membership recruitment. The background factors could have an effect on the number of people who wish to 'opt out' of collective membership. However, the number of people to have used this opportunity is not likely to have been high enough to influence the net changes in a significant way.

The references to membership and activity levels will be based on the evidence presented in Chapters 4 and 5. The membership levels based on Party Records can be found in Table 4.1 (M/E) and Appendix II (M). Membership levels referred to based on Election Studies Data can be found in Table 4.2 (M/E). Activity levels referred to will be based on Table 5.1 (A/E).

---

[8] Bartolini 1985:178.

[9] Hirschman 1970:38f.

Votes

This section will compare the development of party membership and activism with the number of votes received. The votes for the relevant Swedish parties, in absolute and relative numbers, can be found in Appendix III. The largest Swedish party in terms of votes as well as members, the Social Democrats, is the most difficult to judge because of the collective membership and the very few years for which individual membership data are available. However, there is little to suggest any systematic relationship between the development of the party's individual membership and its electoral fortunes. Between 1967 and 1974, the M figure rose from 222,950 to 260,778, and the M/E percentage rose from 4.1 to 4.5 per cent of the electorate.[10]

The 1967 membership figure is squeezed between the 42.2 per cent received in the regional elections in 1966, at the time party's worst performance since the 1930s, and the election to the second chamber of the Riksdag in 1968, where the party gained a massive 50.1 per cent of the vote. Thus, it makes a lot of difference whether the 1966 or 1968 election is chosen as starting point when the membership development between 1967 and 1974 is compared with the electoral development. After 1968, the Social Democratic proportion of the vote dropped continuously until 1976 when it bottomed at 42.7 per cent, only marginally higher than in 1966. Thus, it is not possible to ascertain whether the membership increase between 1967 and 1974 is followed by an increase in votes.[11] For the trends to have gone in a similar direction, a drastic membership increase between 1967 and 1968 followed by a gradual decrease to the 1974 level would have had to have taken place. This is unlikely, given the circumstantial evidence that the total

---

[10] Membership figures based on Party Records are only available in 1967, 1974 and from 1991 onwards. M = absolute number of members, M/E = per cent party members of total national electorate. See Chapter 4 above.

[11] The absolute number of Social Democratic votes in 1976 was in fact an increase compared to 1973. Compared to earlier years it was bettered only in 1968. The reason for this anomaly is that the electorate increased by about 256,000 due to the voting age being lowered from 20 to 18 years (Broomé and Eklundh 1973:46). In absolute terms, the Social Democratic electoral decline reached its low point in 1973. However, this does not affect the reasoning above. Both the 1973 and 1976 results were improvements on the 1966 result in absolute votes as well as percentages (thus following the membership development). Conversely, both the 1973 and 1976 results were worse than the 1968 result in absolute votes as well as percentages (thus not following the membership development).

membership (including collective members) decreased, both counted as M and as M/E, between 1967 and 1968.

The next available time point for individual membership based on Party Records is 1991, after collective membership was abolished. In absolute terms, the 1991 membership figure of 260,346 was virtually identical to that of 1974; but the increased electorate meant that the M/E figure sank from 4.5 to 4.1 per cent. During that period, Social Democratic electoral fortunes varied, peaking in 1982 with 45.6 per cent, followed by a gradual decline to 1991, when the party recorded its lowest election result since 1928, of 37.7 per cent. Thus, the apparent individual membership stability, or slight decrease in proportion of the electorate, between 1974 and 1991 was accompanied by substantial fluctuations in terms of votes. Even though the lack of information during the 17 year period makes far reaching conclusions impossible, the 1991 election result was considerably lower than 1973 as well as 1976. Thus, the apparent membership stability between 1974 and 1991 does not suggest a relationship between membership and votes. This is emphasised by the development after 1991. Between 1991 and 1994, the number of members remained stable (a slight rise in 1992 followed by marginal decreases in 1993 and 1994; the 1994 M figure of 259,108 was 1,238 lower than 1991), and the M/E percentage decreased marginally from 4.1 to 4. At the same time, the party's votes surged from 37.7 to 45.2 per cent. The virtual membership stability during the same period belies any sort of relationship between members and votes.

Nor do the M/E figures based on Election Studies data display a clear relationship with the party's electoral fortunes. The percentage of members of the electorate rose from 3.5 in 1968 to 4.9 in 1979, when the electoral support developed in the opposite direction. The M/E percentage also rose between 1985 and 1988, while the votes went down. On the other hand, there was an M/E increase from 4.1 to 4.9 per cent between 1991 and 1994 which coincided with the electoral development from 37.7 to 45.2 per cent between the same years. Although lack of data makes assertive conclusions impossible, the general observation is that there is no evidence of a relationship, positive or negative, between the development of individual membership and votes in the Social Democratic Party.

The remaining parties are easier to judge because their membership figures are available for most years. The Centre Party has experienced highly fluctuating electoral support between 1960 and 1994. After a stable period in the first half of the 1960s, the party enjoyed a highly successful spell between 1966 and 1973, when the votes increased from 13.7 to 25.1 per cent. This was followed by a continuous and increasingly sharp decline.[12] The 1994 result of 7.7 per cent was the lowest in the party's history. The membership has undergone a similar development but it has not mirrored the electoral fluctuations. At first, both membership and votes followed a positive trend. However, the convergence was broken in 1973, when the electoral fortunes began to decline but membership continued to develop positively. The membership peaked in 1978-1979, while the 1979 election was disappointing for the party; a decrease compared to 1976 from 24.1 to 18.1 per cent.

Since 1980, however, the membership and electoral trends have again gone in the same direction. The M and M/E counts have dropped substantially and almost continuously, which has also happened to the votes. Thus, there is more support for a relationship between votes and membership in the Centre Party than in the Social Democrats. The difference is that the membership decline started about five years later than the electoral decline. Differently put, the membership increase peaked later.[13]

The Moderate Party experienced a largely negative electoral trend during the 1960s. The 1960 result of 16.5 per cent was a loss compared to 1958. In 1970, the electoral support had declined to 11.5 per cent. The membership also dropped during the same period. In 1960, the party itself reported total figures of over 200,000; over four per cent of the electorate. A decade later, the M/E percentage according to the party's own records had been halved. Election Studies data also indicate a decline during the same period, from 3.5 to 2.4 per cent. Thus, membership and electoral support followed the same trend between 1960 and 1970.

In 1973, an electoral recovery started for the party. The share of the national vote progressed in successive elections between 1973 and 1982. In 1982 the party received 23.6 per cent of the vote; more than twice as much as the low point in 1970. During this successful period the membership

---

[12] The decline has not been entirely continuous if the electoral alliance with the Christian Democrats in the 1985 election is taken into account. If the votes for Christian Democrat lists in 1985 are subtracted from the total number of votes to the alliance, called the Centre, the 1988 result was an improvement on 1985 (Gilljam 1990:27).

[13] If only absolute numbers are considered, the membership and electoral peaks were closer in time. Despite the loss in percentage terms, the 1976 election represented a peak in terms of absolute votes for the Centre Party. This was partly because the electorate grew by a quarter of a million (see also note 11 above). The membership peak came in 1978, when the party reported 216,142 members and an M/E of 3.6.

remained quite stable. According to Party Records, the M/E percentage shifted between 2.1 and 2.2 in the 1970s and early 1980s. Election Studies data indicate similar levels; 2.4 in 1970 and 2.1 in 1979.[14] Membership began to improve after 1982, however. In 1985, when the party suffered a modest loss of votes, the M/E percentage was 2.4 per cent according to both Party Records and the Election Study. This was clearly below the levels of the early 1960s, but it signified a second membership peak which has not been reached since. Thus, just like the case of the Centre Party in the late 1970s, the membership peak came after the electoral peak.

The decline in electoral support turned out to be temporary. There was a further loss of votes in 1988 -- not large enough to seriously threaten the position as the second biggest party in Sweden -- but a significant recovery in 1991 and a marginal increase also in 1994. Throughout the 1986-1994 period, however, the party's membership suffered a relatively continuous and very sharp decline. In the same year as the highly successful 1991 election the Election Study indicated an all time low M/E percentage of 1.3. There was a slight, but not statistically significant, recovery in 1994. The Party Records, on the other hand, indicate a continuous decline after 1990 to an all time low level of 1.4 per cent. In absolute figures, the party's membership sank below 100,000 for the first time in 1993.

The Moderate Party offers less evidence than the Centre Party to support the hypothesis of a relationship between votes and membership development. The trends coincide during the 1960s (simultaneous decline), late 1970s and early 1980s (simultaneous rise) and also in the late 1980s (simultaneous decline). On the other hand, the membership was slow to follow the electoral recovery which began in 1973. The most conspicuous deviation is the sharp membership decline in the 1990s which has coincided with electoral gains both in 1991 and 1994.

The People's Party Liberals has suffered an almost continuous decline in party membership between 1960 and 1994. There have been short-lived recoveries, invariably followed by even greater losses. In 1960, the party reported 89,528 members. 34 years later, the figure was 31,891. As a proportion of the electorate, the decline is from 1.8 per cent in 1960 to 0.5 in 1994. The Election Studies also indicate a loss over time, although the trend is not quite so continuous. The party's election results, meanwhile, have

---

14 The 1982 Election Study did not include a question on party membership. The 1980 Referendum Study indicate an M/E level of 1.7 per cent for the party. However, this study reports conspicuously low membership levels for several parties and also for the whole nation.

fluctuated enormously. The Liberals are the Swedish party with the biggest loss as well as greatest gain of votes between two successive elections. However, the long term electoral trend for the party is also clearly negative. The results between 1960 and 1970 have never been equalled since, and both the 1991 and 1994 elections were calamitous for the party. Thus, the long term trends in votes and membership have coincided.

While the party's electoral support and membership strength have developed in the same direction, the short term fluctuations are not identical. Membership has declined steadily and the electoral support has gone up and down. The trends went in the same direction during the 1960s; the party lost voters as well as members albeit at a rate which, with the benefit of hindsight, was relatively modest.[15] Since the 1960s, the party has made electoral gains in 1970, 1976 and especially in 1985 when the party went from 5.9 to 14.2 per cent. The latter occasion is the greatest gain in percentage points between parliamentary elections by a Swedish party since the 1940s. The 1970 and 1976 successes were not accompanied or followed by any notable membership increases. In 1970, the membership trend was unmistakably negative. In 1976 there was in fact a marginal increase in the absolute number of members, but in the following year, the membership went down again; in M/E terms there was stability between 1975 and 1977. The remarkably successful 1985 election was also accompanied by a slight increase in membership. The gains in absolute numbers were never enough to push the M/E figure up by even 0.1 percentage point, however, and the 1985 and 1988 Election Studies do not indicate any membership increases; in fact rather the opposite. The occasions when the electoral trends have coincided have been when the latter has been negative. This is only to be expected, since the membership trend has almost always been negative.[16] Thus, there is

---

[15] The negative electoral trend in the 1960s should not be over-interpreted. In the 1964, 1966 and 1968 elections, the party took part in joint lists with the Centre Party, or the Centre and Moderate parties in some constituencies. It is not possible to separate the parties' votes in these areas. If the parties had contested each constituency on its own in these elections, the total result would have been better for every party.

[16] 1982 could be seen as an exception. In that year, the party's share of the vote was almost halved compared to the previous election in 1979, while the M figure was an increase compared to 1981. However, this is explained by the fact that the party's Women's organisation started its own membership register this year which means that the members of the organisation are added to the total party membership figures from 1982 onwards. The M figure for the party, excluding the Women's organisation, was 46,891 in 1982, a loss of 665 members compared to 1981. Compared to the previous election in 1979, the M figure

conflicting evidence for the People's Party Liberals. The long term trends converge in a negative direction, but the short term trends sometimes diverge.

The remaining parties have comparatively small memberships and it is therefore difficult to compare trends. However, some observations can be made. Since the M/E percentages for these parties are extremely small, only the M figures, based on Party Records, will be used as point of comparison. The Left Party has had election results fluctuating between 3 and 6.4 per cent since 1960, with no real long term trends. During the same period, membership has declined, although the development has not been continuous. In the early 1960s, the party had nearly 20,000 members, a level which has not been reached since. In the regional elections of 1966, the party received 6.4 per cent of the votes, the best election result since the 1940s and the best throughout the 1960 - 1994 research period. At the same time, the party's membership had decreased to 17,000. The membership decline continued until 1970. A membership revival then followed, which peaked at 18,000 members in 1980. Since then, membership has decreased to around 10,000. In 1994, the party received 6.2 per cent of the votes in the parliamentary election. At the same time, the membership was 10,700; in fact a marginal increase on 1993 but the second lowest between 1960 and 1994 and over 1000 less than in 1991 when the election was considerably less successful. The general impression of the Left Party is that the membership figures have followed long trends but the election results have fluctuated back and forth quite freely.

As was noted in Chapter 4, the Christian Democratic Party is almost unique in Sweden in that it has enjoyed a largely positive membership development since its formation in 1964 (the positive trend was halted in 1992). Electorally, the party remained at a stable level between 1.4 and 1.9 per cent until 1982. From that year the party made electoral gains with increasing force, a trend which culminated in 1991 with a result of 7.1 per cent. During this period, the membership also increased, from about 22,000 in 1980 to 33,000 in 1992. However, the membership increase had begun earlier. The long term trend was always positive from the year the party was formed, and negative deviations were small and temporary. This means that the electoral and membership trends have tended to coincide in the party. The rate of change may not have been exactly the same but the directions have

for 1982 was a decrease regardless whether the women's organisation is included or not. Excluding the women's organisation, the party was in the middle of a continuous loss of members (M figures, based on party records) in 1982. The trend had started in 1976 and lasted until the temporary recovery in 1985.

tended to coincide. There are partial exceptions, like between 1970 and 1973, when the election result was identical but membership rose considerably, and between 1973 and 1976, when membership again rose but the share of the national vote went down. On the whole, however, the trends have tended to coincide. Between 1979 and 1991 both trends were clearly positive and they also both started to decline between 1991 and 1994. The Christian Democrats is thus the party which, arguably, offers most support to the hypothesis of a relationship between membership and votes.

The two remaining parties have very few members and have existed for a very short period of time which means that there is only foundation for some minor observations. The Green Party recorded its largest membership so far, 8,857, in the year of the party's most successful election in 1988. The 1991 election, where the party lost its parliamentary status, was accompanied by a very modest membership loss. The membership decline continued in 1992 and 1993 and although the membership increased again in 1994, when Parliamentary status was regained, it was still lower than three years before. New Democracy's electoral debacle in 1994 coincided with the lowest membership reported. However, this membership figure is difficult to judge because of the abolition of local organisations in 1993 which meant that members of the local so-called co-operation parties are not considered as members of the national party.

The short term trends (that is, from election to election) of membership and votes have been summarised in Table 6.1. The table is based on comparisons of the absolute number of votes and absolute number of members (the M count) from election to election. The election results are from parliamentary elections, except in 1962 and 1966, when the results are from the elections to the regional *landsting* and cities who were not included in a *landsting* area.

In more than half of the total number of cases, the changes have gone in the same direction. Thus, there is some, if not overwhelming, support for the hypothesis of a positive relationship between membership and votes. The party where changes have converged to the highest extent is the Centre Party, but convergences are more common than divergences in the majority of parties.

Table 6.1   Do membership and votes change in the same direction? Comparisons between electoral and membership changes between elections. Sweden 1960-1994

	Converging changes	Diverging changes	Total cases
Left Party	5	6	11
Social Democrats (tot. members)	4	7	11
Social Democrats (ind. members)	0	1	1
Centre Party	10	3	13
People's Party Liberals	8	5	13
Moderate Party	7	4	11
Christian Democrats	7	4	11
Green Party	3	1	4
New Democracy	1	0	1
Total	45	31	76

Comment: Changes in the absolute numbers of votes and members between consecutive election years have been compared. If members and votes have changed in the same direction the trends have converged, and vice versa. The time points are 1960 (election to parliamentary 2nd chamber), 1962 (regional elections), 1964 (election to parliamentary 2nd chamber), 1966 (regional elections), 1968 (election to parliamentary 2nd chamber), and the elections to the unicameral parliament in 1970, 1973, 1976, 1979, 1982, 1985, 1988, 1991 and 1994. The membership data are the total number of members (M) according to the parties' own records (see Appendix II). When applicable, members of women's organisations are included in the membership figures. The total number of cases is less than the possible number of election periods for the Left Party, due to missing membership data in 1962 and 1964. The only time individual Social Democratic membership can be compared between two consecutive elections is between 1991 and 1994. The election results for the Moderate, Centre and People's Party Liberals in 1964, 1966 and 1968 are affected by the fact that the parties presented joint lists in some constituencies. The relevant entries in the table are based on the results of 'pure' party lists only. In the 1985 election, the Centre Party and the Christian Democrats formed an electoral alliance. The relevant entries in the table are based on reconstructions of the parties' votes, taken from Gilljam 1990:28.

On the whole, however, there is no evidence of a general and systematic relationship, positive or negative, short term or long term, between the developments of membership and electoral support for the Swedish parties. Does this also apply to activism? It is not an easy question to answer. Data limitations restrict the time frame to the period between 1979 and 1994, and the extremely small A/E percentages mean that there are few parties where the fluctuations are substantial enough to discuss time trends.[17] During the 1979 to 1994 period, only the Social Democrats and the Centre Party have had A/E percentages of over 1, which means that the discussion will be restricted to these two parties.

---

[17] A/E = per cent activists of the entire electorate. See Chapter 5.

The Social Democrats saw their A/E percentage more than halved between 1979 and 1991, followed by a minor recovery in 1994. The changes in A/E between individual time points are small, but there is an unmistakable trend. During this period the party has experienced changing electoral fortunes, with no systematic relationship to the activity decline. The 1985 election result was an improvement on 1979 (although it was a decrease compared to 1982, when the Election Study did not include questions on party membership and activity), and the 1988 result was almost identical to that of 1979. On the face of it, the electoral and activist trends followed the same path between 1988 and 1994. The shifts in activism (A/E was 1.9 in 1988, 1.4 in 1991 and again 1.9 in 1994) were not statistically significant, however, and the period between 1988 and 1994 can just as well be described as a one of stability. It certainly does not reflect the massive electoral fluctuations during the same period.

The Centre Party provides stronger evidence. The long term development of the A/E measure is negative. The electoral development has largely followed this trend. The shifts in A/E between individual time points are very small -- indeed, there was more or less absolute stability between 1985 and 1991 -- and the negative electoral trend was temporarily broken in 1988, which means that the strength of the relationship between members and votes should not be overstated. Still, the overall trends between 1979 and 1994 are similar.

Again, the evidence is conflicting among different parties. There is some justification to speak of a positive relationship between activism and votes in the Centre Party (positive meaning that the trends go in the same direction -- both trends are of course negative), but in the Social Democratic case there is no support for a relationship in any direction.

Incumbency

Bartolini's analysis of the relationship between incumbency and membership development is based on data from several countries.[18] In Sweden, the relatively few changes in government composition between 1960 and 1994 make it difficult to probe deeply into this problem. In the following, only formal government participation will be considered as incumbency, not mere co-operation on parliamentary level. Of the eight parties considered in this

---

[18] Bartolini 1985:198f.

study, five have at some time taken part in governments: the Social Democrats, the People's Party Liberals, the Centre, Moderate and the Christian Democratic parties.

The Social Democratic dominance of Swedish governments since the 1930s is well known. The party has been in government from 1936 to date, except between 1976 and 1982, and between 1991 and 1994. Because of the scarcity of data of individual membership, it is not possible to make much out of any relationship between the party being in or out of government and its membership development. A few observations can be made, however. The historic event in 1976, when the party was ousted from government for the first time in 40 years, was met by an increase in the number of total members, as reported in the party's own records. It is not possible to determine whether this was mainly due to an increase in the number of collective members or successful recruitment of individual members. Even if the increase consists mainly of collective members, it could be interpreted as a response by the party leadership -- and also by the unions loyal to the party -- to the new government situation. Against this could be said that the total membership, both in absolute numbers as well as in proportion of the electorate, had been increasing throughout the 1970s, before the non-socialist coalition government took office. The increase peaked in 1983, one year after the party had regained office. Therefore, the trend in total membership does not entirely fit the government changes. Election Studies data are only available from 1979 during the 1976-1982 opposition period. The individual membership amounted to an M/E of 4.8 in that year which is an increase on 1968 and 1970. This offers some, albeit limited, support to the assumption that the party responded to the unusual situation of being in opposition with increased recruitment of individual members.

The next period in opposition was between 1991 and 1994. This happened immediately after the party had abandoned collective membership. For reasons discussed in Chapter 4, the Party Records after 1990 are not easily comparable to earlier figures based on Party Records, individual or total. However, Party Records indicate that there was little change in membership during the three years of the Moderate led government. Thus, any prediction of the loss of governmental status having an effect on membership -- positive as an organisational response, or negative due to membership frustration -- is not supported. Election Studies data do not indicate any important changes in M/E between the 1982-1991 incumbency period and the 1991-1994 opposition periods. Of course, Election Studies are only conducted in election years, something which means that there is no information about the development between elections. Nevertheless, available evidence from neither survey data, nor Party Records, suggests a systematic relationship in any direction.

Of the non-socialist parties, the People's Party Liberals has the highest number of years in government between 1960 and 1994. The party has taken part in coalition governments between 1976 and 1978, 1979 and 1982 and between 1991 and 1994. The party also formed a minority government on its own between 1978 and 1979.

The Liberals illustrate the fact that incumbency and electoral success do not go hand in hand. When the party entered the four party coalition in 1991, the election result of 9.1 per cent was at the time the second worst in the party's history. There is little to suggest that the party's changes in governmental status had any relationship with its membership development. As has been noted above, the party has suffered a nearly continuous membership decline throughout the research period. The small and temporary recoveries have not taken place when the party has been in government, nor immediately before or after these periods. The 1976-1982 period when the party was continuously in government, as part of coalitions or on its own, was marked by a fairly sizeable loss of members according to the party's own records. The same is true of the 1991-1994 government period. This is not sufficient to speak of a negative relationship between the party's government participation and membership, however, because the membership decline has also taken place when the party has been out of government.

The Centre Party appeared in coalition governments between 1976 and 1978, 1979 and 1982 and between 1991 and 1994. The first of these governments coincided with the party's membership peak, but the membership had already begun to decline when the party lost its governmental status in 1982. Participation in the 1991-1994 government did not halt an increasingly rapid membership slide. Again, there is little to suggest a systematic relationship between incumbency and membership.

The same applies to the Moderate Party, who participated in government coalitions between 1976 and 1978, 1978 to 1981 and 1991 to 1994. When the party entered government for the first time since World War II, the membership had been on the increase for a few years, a recovery after a severe decline in the 1960s and early 1970s. The recovery peaked in 1976, the year of the entry into government, and the membership remained relatively stable after that. After the Moderate Party had left a coalition government for the second time in 1981, another period of membership increase followed, which peaked in 1985. This increase took place when the party was in opposition. From then on, the party's membership has declined rapidly. The participation in a non-socialist coalition government between 1991 and 1994, with Moderate Carl Bildt as Prime Minister, did not have a visible effect on this development.

While it is true that the party's participation in two governments in the late 1970s and early 1980s happened during a period of positive membership development, the increase started before and continued after the incumbency. 1991-1994, when the party held the Prime Minister position, coincided with a severe membership decline.

The fifth and final party to have participated in government is the Christian Democrats, who took part in the four party coalition between 1991 and 1994. This coincided with the party's membership peak in 1992 and 1992, but the membership level declined somewhat in 1993 and 1994.

Scarcity of data makes it virtually impossible to analyse the relationship between activism and incumbency. Available data for the Centre Party and the Social Democrats do not suggest any correlation. The Centre Party's highest A/E percentage came in 1979, when the party was in government, and the Social Democrats recorded their highest A/E in the same year, when the party was in opposition.

The relatively small turnover in governments and government parties during the 1960-1994 period makes firm conclusions very difficult. An important additional problem is the lack of comparable data over time for the most frequent government party, the Social Democrats. Still, available data for the other parties do not suggest any systematic tendencies. Parties have lost members while in government, something which happened to three of the four parties of the 1991-1994 coalition. There are also cases of the opposite, like the Centre Party in the late 1970s and the Christian Democrats in the 1990s. Nor is there a general tendency for parties to lose or gain members just after they have left government. The Moderates had a positive development after 1981, but the Centre Party fared negatively after 1982. All in all, there is no evidence of a systematic relationship between incumbency and membership.

Election years

One of Bartolini's hypotheses is that membership should go up in connection with elections, because the increased political activity in the campaign arouses political interest.[19] To test this hypothesis, data from inter-election years are needed. This means that Party Records will be utilised because Election Studies data exist only from election years.

There are other problems when testing the election year hypothesis. It is possible that any membership inflow due to the increased interest during an election campaign may not show in the membership statistics until the following year. However, it is not possible to know to which extent this is the case.[20] A related problem is the short election periods in Sweden until 1994. Until 1970, a nationwide election was held every two years, and between 1970 and 1994 every three years. Thus, the membership statistics can be affected by an election -- previous or forthcoming -- almost every year.

In spite of these problems, Table 6.2 attempts to test the election year hypothesis. The parties' membership figures in election years are compared with the immediately preceding year. Due to the fact that membership figures are missing certain years for some parties, the table does not cover the 1962-1994 period in its entirety. Nevertheless, it is quite apparent that there is little support for the election year hypothesis. In the People's Party Liberals and the Centre Party, where membership figures exist without gaps, it has in fact been more common for the membership to decline in election years. As can be seen at the bottom of the table, the total number of cases for all parties are quite evenly split between increases and decreases.

If true, the election year hypothesis would mean that the combined membership of all parties would increase in election years. The lack of information of individual Social Democratic membership means that Party Records allow the hypothesis to be tested on the aggregate national level only in 1994. In that year, total membership declined by over 20,000 compared to 1993 (592,913 to 572,013). M/E went down from 9.2 to 8.8.

Survey data cannot rescue the election year hypothesis (see Table 4.3). According to the ULF Studies by SCB, the hypothesis is supported in connection with the 1979 and 1982 elections, but not since. The SOM

---

[19] Bartolini 1985:195f.

[20] The membership statistics of the Swedish parties are from 31 December every year, except in the Christian Democratic Party whose statistics are from May every year.

Studies support the hypothesis in 1991 but not in 1988 and 1994. SOM data on activity (Table 5.4) indicate that activity rose in 1991 (but sank again in 1992) and 1994, but not in 1988. SCB data (Table 5.5) indicate limited increased in activity only in the election years of 1991 and 1994.[21]

To be precise, Bartolini has formulated the Election Year hypothesis: "The number of members increases during election years and, possibly, during the year following that of an election. Then the membership tends to decrease until a new election year".[22] This would mean that Table 6.2 is not a full test of the hypothesis, because it does not account for the year following the election. A problem with this is that until 1970, this coincides with the point of comparison for the next election, as there were only two years between national elections.

Table 6.2   Do parties get more members in election years?
Comparisons between membership level in years when
nationwide elections have been held and previous years.
Sweden 1962-1994

	No. of increases	No. of decreases	Total cases
Left Party	2	4	6
Social Democrats (tot. members)	7	4	11
Social Democrats (ind. members)	0	1	1
Centre Party	5	8	13
People's Party Liberals	5	8	13
Moderate Party	5	4	9
Christian Democrats	5	5	10
Green Party	4	1	5
New Democracy	0	1	1
total	33	36	69

Comment: The absolute number of members according to Party Records (See Appendix I) in election years has been compared to the membership the immediately preceding year. When applicable, members of women's organisations are included in the membership figures. The time points are 1962 (regional elections), 1964 (election to parliamentary 2nd chamber), 1966 (regional elections), 1968 (election to parliamentary 2nd chamber), and the elections to the unicameral parliament in 1970, 1973, 1976, 1979, 1982, 1985, 1988, 1991 and 1994. Due to missing membership data certain years, the total number of cases is smaller than the possible maximum for some parties.

---

[21] It should be noted that Election Studies data can not be used here, as they only exist from election years.

[22] Bartolini 1985:195.

In Table 6.3, the membership figures from election years have been compared with the figures from the immediately following year. Here, the support for the hypothesis is even weaker. Out of a possible 72, the election year hypothesis is supported in 30 cases. The figures for the People's Party Liberals and the Moderate Party are remarkable. Membership has gone up in years immediately following election years twice and once, respectively. Thus, the number of times the hypothesis is supported for these parties in Table 6.2 (i.e. election year compared with previous year) suggests that election years may, after all, have some independent effect, because of the tendency for membership in these parties to go down just after elections. But this observation does not rescue Bartolini's hypothesis, because membership development in Sweden does not follow cyclical trends.

Table 6.3   Do parties get more members after elections?
Comparisons between membership levels in years when
nationwide elections have been held and following years.
Sweden 1960-1991

	No. of increases	No. of decreases	Total cases
Left Party	3	5	8
Social Democrats (tot. members)	10	2	12
Social Democrats (ind. members)	1	0	1
Centre Party	5	8	13
People's Party Liberals	2	11	13
Moderate Party	1	9	10
Christian Democrats	6	4	10
Green Party	1	3	4
New Democracy	1	0	1
total	30	42	72

Comment: The absolute number of members according to Party Records (See Appendix I) in election years have been compared to the membership the immediately following year. When applicable, members of women's organisations are included in the membership figures. The time points are 1960 (election to parliamentary 2nd chamber), 1962 (regional elections), 1964 (election to parliamentary 2nd chamber), 1966 (regional elections), 1968 (election to parliamentary 2nd chamber), and the elections to the unicameral parliament in 1970, 1973, 1976, 1979, 1982, 1985, 1988 and 1991. Due to missing membership data certain years, the total number of cases is smaller than the possible maximum for some parties.

Instead of following election year cycles, membership trends among Swedish parties tend to be long term. This is exemplified by the rise in the Centre Party in the 1960s and 1970s, the rise in the Christian Democrats throughout the majority of the research period, the continuous decline in the People's Party Liberals and the widespread decline among most parties in the late 1980s and 1990s. In none of these cases there is anything to suggest that negative trends are broken, or slowed down, in or immediately after, election years. Nor is there any evidence suggesting that positive trends are speeded up in or just after national elections. Similarly, during periods of stability, like for the Social Democrats between 1991 and 1994, there is no indication that the stability is broken by an election year.

The lack of cyclical membership development is almost totally general among the Swedish parties. Only the Green Party is a limited exception. From the party's formation in 1981 until the most recent available data in 1994, every election year except 1991 has seen at least some increase in the party's membership in comparison with the previous year.

On the whole, however, the Swedish parties offer little support for the hypothesis about membership fluctuating according to election cycles. There are indeed cases where membership has risen in, and immediately after, election years but for the hypothesis to be true, election cycles would have to have an independent effect, which is not true when the rise is primarily a part of a more long-term general trend.

One reason why election years seem to have no effect could be that elections are so close together in Sweden that the parties are almost constantly either feeling the effects of the last election, or preparing for the next. It could be that the election cycles would have a more noticeable effect in countries where national elections are held less frequently. However, Stefano Bartolini's own data show that the hypothesis is not supported by Great Britain, where elections are less frequent than in Sweden. Thus, the fact that election periods in Sweden have been extended from three to four years after 1994, might not make much difference.

Membership influence

If political influence is an incentive for people to become party members, then it would be expected that parties with more opportunities for membership influence should find it easier to attract members. Likewise, changes over time in a single party could be expected to have an impact. It could be argued that membership influence has only a limited effect on membership recruitment. Prospective members cannot be expected to check the internal procedures in the party before joining. Nevertheless, many people join because they know people who are already members in a party, and may also have a general perception of the party's internal situation. It is therefore not unreasonable to assume that the degree of membership influence could make a difference to someone who is considering joining a party.

The other side of the coin is that, even if new members may not always have much information about the influence possibilities before they join, they will sooner or later become aware of the actual opportunities. If too disappointed, several members can be expected to leave the party. As Hirschman said: "(T)he decision whether to exit will often be taken in the light of the prospects for the effective use of voice".[23] Thus, even if membership influence has a limited effect on recruitment it could still be expected to have an effect on membership retention and, hence, on membership figures.

The index constructed at the end of Chapter 3 (Tables 3.10 and 3.11) has been used as indicator of membership influence. As has been pointed out, the index has its limitations. It only takes formal influence, as defined in the party rules, into consideration and it does not take local politics into account. The arguments why the index is still a valid -- if not totally satisfactory -- indicator have already been given in Chapter 3 but are, in summary, that the formal rules of a party are the party's own constitution, and as such they are considered as binding by all levels in the party. The fact that the formulation and changes of formal rules of a party are often the subject of heated debates suggests that they are considered relevant.

There is, however, little evidence that membership influence has any effect on membership. If we first look at the relative sizes of the parties, there is no correlation whatsoever between membership size and membership influence. The party with the highest influence index between 1982 and 1992, the Green Party, is the second smallest of all parties included in this study. And the Social Democrats which, whether collective members are included or not, is the biggest membership party have throughout the research period had an influence index of five, which after 1967 has been joint bottom of all the analysed parties (except in 1992 when New Democracy had an aggregate index of four). It can also be noted that the People's Party Liberals have consistently had a higher index score than the Moderates, but in terms of membership the Moderates have always been bigger. The Centre Party index was eight until 1968, and has since stayed at seven. This is higher than the Social Democrats, who have more members.

---

[23] Hirschman 1970:37.

At the same time the index is lower than that of the Green Party and, since 1984, also the Christian Democrats, both of which have much fewer members.

The other way to illustrate the (lack of) effect of membership influence on membership size is to compare developments over time within the same parties. The aggregate index has decreased since the 1960s in the Centre Party, People's Party Liberals and the Green Party. In the Centre Party, the index went down from eight to seven in 1969, because the National Council lost its pre-defined decision making authority. The following decade was characterised by an increase in membership which peaked around 1978-79. Thus, membership size and membership influence went in opposite directions in the late 1960s and the 1970s. In the 1980s and 1990s the party has lost a lot of members, but the index has remained stable. Thus, the long term developments in membership and influence converge but the short, or medium, term fluctuations do not.

The People's Party Liberals is a similar case. The party's membership has declined throughout the 1960-1994 period. The influence index changed once, from seven to six in 1983, because the frequency of the meeting of the party congress was reduced. But in the short term, the decrease in the index was followed by a recovery in membership (albeit limited and temporary), in connection with the successful 1985 election and the so-called 'Westerberg effect' (coined after the popularity of party leader Bengt Westerberg).

The membership influence in the Green Party decreased in 1992, when an Executive Committee not directly elected by congress was introduced, and the authority of the National Council was reduced. Party Records suggest that the party's membership has fluctuated back and forth since 1992, but there was a positive trend in 1996 and 1997.

The party with the clearest trend towards an increased influence index since the 1960s is the Christian Democrats. In 1964, the party had an index of four, which in 1994 had increased to nine, together with the Greens the joint highest index of all parties. The increase in the influence index has been followed by a long term increase in membership. The Christian Democrats is the clearest case where both trends converge in the long term. In the short term, however, it can be noted that the increase of the influence index score from six to eight in 1984 was followed by a five year period of membership stagnation. Again, the long term trends go in the same direction, but the short term fluctuations do not always follow the same pattern.[24]

The other cases where the influence index has increased are the Moderate and Left parties. In both cases the long term trends have gone in opposite directions; the influence has increased and membership decreased. This is true also in a shorter time-frame. The Moderate Party index increased in 1964 (sub-national party levels were given the right to call an extraordinary party congress), when the party was in the middle of a sharp decline in membership. Likewise, the Left Party index increased in 1967. Sub-national levels were given the right to call a membership referendum, and a National Council was introduced (the party's openness also increased, something which is not seen in the index). However, this happened during a period of negative membership development.

The Social Democrats is the only party whose index has remained stable throughout the period. In fact, not one of the seven items has changed at all. Because of the collective membership, it is difficult to assert the party's long term membership development. It is also difficult to pinpoint short term changes, because individual membership is only available for a handful of the years between 1960 and 1994. However, it was argued in Chapter 4 that the long term development of the party's membership has been negative. This is because the apparent stability in individual membership is likely to hide an actual outflow of members, since some collective members would have joined individually if that had been the only possibility. This would mean that stability in membership influence has been followed by a decrease in membership, especially bearing in mind the decline after 1994.

There are some instances which could be taken as support for the hypothesis of a positive relationship between the developments of membership influence and membership strength. The long term trends converge in the Christian Democratic and Liberal parties. In the Moderate and Left parties, however, the trends diverge. Thus, there is no evidence of a general and systematic relationship.

There is also conflicting evidence when it comes to a general relationship between membership size and the amount of membership influence. The Centre Party has scored fairly high on the index as well as always having been competitive in terms of membership. At the end of the

---

[24] The increase of the index score from eight to nine in 1994 took place when the party's membership began to decline. The decline continued in 1995, 1996 and 1997.

period, however, the Centre Party is outscored on the index by the Green Party and the Christian Democrats; in fact also matched by New Democracy.

Potentially more interesting in the context of membership influence, is the relationship with activity. Is it the active members that are affected by the internal structure of a party? If the opportunities for members to influence the party is reduced, is it the active members who react first, and most strongly? The lack of comparable data on party activity means that the possibility to study this relationship is very limited, however. The two parties with the largest A/E percentages, the Social Democrats and the Centre Party, have had no variations in their influence index between 1979 and 1994, the period when comparisons of activity over time are possible. During this period, the activity level has decreased in both parties. In other parties, the A/E percentages are too small to make meaningful comparisons with the influence index possible. The very limited evidence does not suggest any systematic relationship between activity and membership influence.

Conclusion and comparative outlook

Bartolini subjected his hypotheses to empirical tests for the socialist parties in 12 European countries. He found a tendency for membership to converge with election results, although the convergence was greater before World War I. He did not find a systematic relationship between incumbency and membership. Nor is there a general tendency for membership to increase in connection with national elections.[25]

In this chapter, no variable has been found to have a strong and general relationship with membership development. On the face of it, votes correlate very strongly with membership. A single correlation analysis, of all membership figures and election results between 1960 and 1994 for all Swedish parties, would result in a very high coefficient. This is simply because electorally big parties tend to have many more members than parties with fewer votes. If the same procedure is done for the individual parties, there are cases with strong positive correlations, notably the Centre Party and the People's Party Liberals. However, the Moderate Party has a negative correlation, because it had its largest membership in the 1960s when it was electorally inferior to what it has been in the 1980s and 1990s. Thus, there is no general relationship among different parties.

---

[25] Bartolini 1985:191-199.

Incumbency also has instances of fairly strong correlations. They are negative for the People's and Moderate parties, because these parties had more members in the 1960s when they were never in government, but positive for the Christian Democrats because they reached their membership peak when they were in government between 1991 and 1994. It is impossible to analyse the Social Democrats because of the scarcity of data on individual membership. The fact that the party with by far most years in government cannot be satisfactorily analysed, obviously makes all conclusions tentative.

The influence index correlates negatively with membership for the Moderate Party, where membership strength and membership influence have developed in opposite directions. In the Christian Democratic Party, on the other hand, the index has increased over time, as has membership. The same applies to the People's Party Liberals with the difference that both trends have been negative. Elsewhere, no relationships are found.

Thus, there are individual parties where some of the background variables appear to have a strong correlation with membership. There is, however, no evidence of a general relationship which cuts across the party system. Where background factors do correlate with membership, the direction of the correlations vary. For example, election results correlate positively with membership in the People's Party Liberals (both have decreased) but negatively in the Moderate Party (membership has decreased but party votes have increased).

To sum up, there is some correlation between membership strength and some of the background factors. On the other hand, the account in this chapter should make it apparent that there is very little evidence of a relationship between membership trends and the trends of the studied background factors.

Two of the studied variables have displayed any relationship at all with membership strength: party votes and, to a weaker extent, incumbency. There is also limited evidence to suggest a weak relationship, between trends party votes and membership development. Referring to the introductory section of this chapter, these are external variables. The only internal variable analysed, the influence index, shows no signs of a relationship with membership trends or size. This is of course not the exhaustive answer to the question whether membership varies primarily according to external or internal party factors. Other internal factors such as real, rather than formal, membership influence, the role of individual personalities, the ability of local party organisations to create meaningful membership activities and the general atmosphere in local party organisations could be expected to be closely related to membership size and development.

The analysis could benefit if it was broken down geographically. Internal factors such as real membership influence could be broken down to local analyses to really investigate their true relationship with membership. This also applies to external factors, such as party vote; even incumbency (in the form of the party's position in local politics) could be broken down to small local levels to allow a thorough analysis of their relationship with membership development in the respective area. The evidence used in this chapter is not enough to suggest that external factors explain membership development and internal factors do not. On the national level, however, there is some justification to conclude that external factors appear to have some limited relationship. The only tested internal factor does not.

If the distinction between external and internal factors is related to the strength of a relationship between two variables, the distinction between push and pull refers to the direction. The same factor, for example votes, can be a push factor for some parties; that is, a positive trend in votes co-varies with decreasing party membership. In another party, the same trend can coincide with a positive membership development in which case party vote is a pull factor. It can also vary over time in the same party, although the more it changes in the same party, the less meaningful it becomes to speak in terms of push or pull at all.

Seen this way, party vote is a pull factor for the Centre Party, People's Party Liberals, the Christian Democrats and the Green Party, while it is a push factor for the Moderate Party. Incumbency is a pull factor for the Christian Democrats but a push factor for the Liberals and Moderates. Membership influence is a push factor for the Moderates but a pull factor for the Christian Democrats and the People's Party Liberals. These characterisations are all simplifications, however. They are based on comparisons of long-term trends, and do not take into account the degree of co-variance in the short-term fluctuations. According to the long-term trends, none of the investigated variables have proven to have a systematic and general relationship with membership development in any direction. The co-variations that have been found go in different directions for different parties; sometimes the relationship is positive, sometimes it is negative. Thus, even if some fairly strong relationships do exist, none of the investigated variables has been shown to have a systematic and general relationship with membership development.

Where does this place Sweden in a European context? Bartolini found evidence of a relationship between membership and votes: they tend to converge rather than diverge. However, the relationship was not found to be deterministic and had decreased over time.[26] In another quantitative study, the effect of membership on some other variables has been studied in 11 European countries.[27] Party vote was found to have the biggest explanatory power. Incumbency and election year cycles were not found to have very strong effects at all. However, the effect of party vote was comparatively weak in Sweden. It was absolutely zero in the United Kingdom, but together with Finland, Sweden displayed the lowest effect of votes on membership. The highest effects were found in the Netherlands and West Germany.[28] Thus, the findings in this chapter are in accordance with what has been found in earlier research. There is some relationship between votes and membership, but it is not systematic, the trends do not always converge, and it is not general across the different parties. Nor is the relationship strong in a comparative context. Incumbency correlates with membership strength on the aggregate level, but that is explained by the dominance of the Social Democrats. None of the other background factors can be found to have any systematic and general relationship with party vote at all.

Where does this leave the parties? A possible consequence of John D. May's 'Special Law of Curvilinear Disparity' is, that parties which are popular with the public, are likely to be pursuing policies which alienate their members, because they tend to be more radical that the voters.[29] In such circumstances, the members could be expected to leave the party, and others would be less likely to join. The empirical case most in line with this reasoning is the Moderate Party, which has been electorally successful during the 1990s, and was the dominant party in a coalition government between 1991 and 1994. Yet, during this period the membership according to the party's own records declined continuously. According to this reasoning, the membership decline could be explained by the party's difficult political position. Although dominant, the Moderates were not alone in the government which, furthermore, did not command an outright parliamentary

---

[26] Bartolini 1985:194.

[27] Webb and Widfeldt 1996. In that study, membership development is treated as a dependent variable, which is not the case here.

[28] Data are from before the German unification.

[29] May 1973. 'May's Law' is further discussed in Chapter 8 below.

majority. Therefore, the party was not able to fully pursue its policies. This, in turn, may have alienated actual and potential members. The less radical voters, however, were not too unhappy. The Moderate Party's result in the 1994 election was a slight improvement on 1991, and the fact that the government was forced to leave was due to losses of the other coalition parties. Thus, the party's restrained policies may have enjoyed a stable popularity among the electorate but less so among the members.

For the findings to offer general support for this reasoning, however, there would be an inverse relationship between membership and votes. This is not the case. The Centre and People's parties both have on the whole positive relationships between membership and votes, and internationally the relationship is also usually positive. It is more common to find a positive than a negative relationship between votes and membership. Alternatively, it could be argued in the Moderate case that it was the constraints of the minority government that alienated the members, and therefore that the most important factor behind the membership outflow has been incumbency rather than votes. Against this it can be said that the party's membership did not decline when the party was in government in the 1970s and early 80s. Perhaps it could be argued that the especially difficult situation for the Bildt government between 1991 and 1994, with a serious crisis for the Swedish economy and a very unstable parliamentary platform for the government, was the main reason for alienation and discontent among party members. But examples of positive membership development during periods in government for other parties, as well as in other periods for the Moderates, reinforces that there is no general relationship between incumbency and membership.

None of the investigated background factors has been shown to have a strong and systematic relationship with membership development. This does of course not mean that the parties' ability to provide participatory linkage varies at random. It does, however, seem as if a number of factors, which at first seemed plausible, are unable to account for one condition for participatory linkage, namely the parties' ability to recruit and keep members.

7 Social Representativeness of Party Members and Activists

Introduction

The next two chapters will deal with the representativeness of party members. This chapter examines social representativeness and Chapter 8 is focused on representativeness in terms of opinion. The purpose will be to investigate whether the members are less representative in the 1990s than before. They will be compared to the general public and the voters of their respective parties.

As was explained in Chapter 2, social representativeness is in this study treated as a condition for participatory, rather than representative, linkage. Chapters 4 and 5 have addressed the development of the number of members and activists. The answer was negative: there has been a decline. Thus, two necessary conditions for participatory linkage have not been met. This chapter will attempt to answer whether there has been any change in the parties' ability to recruit the 'right' people. The main question is: Are significant social and demographic groups to an increasing extent left outside the party organisations?

It is also possible to look at social representativeness as an aspect of political representation. This tends to be the perspective when, for example, the social composition of parliamentarians is studied.[1] But is social representativeness at all important? For centuries, the arguments have raged about the relations between representatives and the represented. A key issue has been the relationship between representation and representativeness. Representativeness, i.e. likeness between representatives and the represented, has sometimes been treated as the same thing as representation. But such a view is not without problems. According to Hanna F. Pitkin, it fails to take any kind of activity into account. At most, it assumes that activity will be the consequence if the representative meets the criterion of likeness. It also fails to address the issue of accountability. If the representative meets the criteria of likeness, there are no ways in which he/she can be held accountable; "A man can only be held accountable for what he has done, not for what he is."[2]

---

[1] See note 4 below.

[2] Pitkin 1967:75f. Quote taken from p. 76.

Pitkin concludes her thorough investigation into the etymological, practical, cultural and political aspects of representation with a definition which carefully includes activity. Representation is defined as "acting in the interest of the represented, in a manner responsive to them".[3]

Nevertheless, several empirical studies on political representation have focused their attention on various criteria of likeness rather than on what the representatives actually do.[4] This does not mean that the writers in question have neglected the problem of representation versus representativeness. First, it may be argued that various criteria of likeness can be taken as indicators of representation, i.e. that the representative is more likely to act according to Pitkin's definition if he/she meets those criteria. Second, likeness can be regarded as a value in and by itself. It can be argued that the multitude and diversity of a nation's citizens should be reflected in decision-making bodies. The second argument, however, is a step away from Pitkin's definition of representation and based more on societal equity as an ideal.

Whether directly connected to the concept of representation or not, representativeness can thus be regarded as a relevant aspect of the relationship between representatives and represented. Political science research has so far tended to concentrate on voters as the represented and elected office holders as the representatives. The relationship between party members and the public does have important parallels, however. This argument is based on two assumptions. First, that decisions made internally by parties are important in the policy-making process. Second, that the parties are internally democratic. If some, if not total, credibility can be attributed to these assumptions, then party members have some, albeit indirect, influence on public decisions and, hence, they are of interest as representatives. Thus, political parties can provide representative linkage by being open and democratic membership organisations.

Both assumptions have problems. In practice, party representatives in local and central governments and legislatures are not able to consult their party every time they act as representatives. Nor are they formally bound by party decisions. The final decisions taken by public bodies are more often

---

[3] Pitkin 1967:209.

[4] E.g. Holmberg 1974, Holmberg and Esaiasson 1988, Esaiasson and Holmberg 1996, Holmberg 1996a and Roth 1996 (parliamentarians as representatives); Dalton 1996 Chapter 11 and Rohrschneider 1991 (party elites as representatives).

than not influenced by other factors, such as agreements with other parties and legal or 'bureaucratic' constraints.

At the same time, it is not implausible to assume that decisions taken at party congresses, etc. have some influence on the eventual policy outcome. Jon Pierre's somewhat discouraging findings on the Swedish Social Democrats, where the party leadership was found to do its utmost to avoid being back-tied by decisions by the party congress, could be interpreted that way.[5] If congress decisions were irrelevant, why would the party leadership bother to put so much effort into trying to influence them in the desired direction?

Another factor not to be forgotten, is that the party representatives who participate in public decisions are selected by the party. In a country like Sweden, where the election system has allowed a minimum of personal voting, the nomination procedures in parties are crucial factors behind who is elected into public office.[6] Thus the rank-and-file members of a political party are part of an organisational context in which their ability to have their say on decisions is constrained. But because they are a part of that context, they can also constrain the freedom of movement for the party leadership.

The second assumption, that parties are internally democratic, is also problematic. The development of formal membership influence was mapped out in Chapter 3. The finding was that membership influence has improved or remained stable between 1960 and 1994. This finding has limitations; above all it does not probe into the practical world behind the formal party rules. Very limited evidence exists with regard to how influential rank-and-file members really are in the Swedish parties. Second, it is limited to the study of membership influence instead of the more complex concept of democracy. Furthermore, it departs from the situation as it was in 1960, and does not try to establish a sort of model of what is required for a members to be considered to have influence, let alone for the party to be called democratic. Another problem is that influence on the local level is not taken into account. Nevertheless, the evidence presented in Chapter 3 suggests that ordinary members have at least some influence on party decisions.

Thus, even if they do not have quite as central a position as elected office holders, it is possible to view party members as representatives of the

---

[5] Pierre 1986:257ff. This conclusion is also expressed in the English summary of his study, see p. 282f.

[6] Petersson 1994:146, Pierre 1990:89ff.

public. In this perspective, the relationship between members and the public can be considered a case of political representation. An alternative approach is the equity argument. Given the centrality of political parties in modern democracies, it is a problem if they do not meet criterion of likeness between representatives and represented.

Political representation is thus a relevant aspect of party membership. This chapter will deal with social representativeness, a variable whose centrality not unquestionable. Many would argue that representativeness in terms of opinion is more relevant. Those who also advocate social representativeness often do so on the assumption that it is a prerequisite to opinion representativeness (and, further along the chain, representation). Whether this in fact is the case with regard to Swedish party members will be discussed at the end of next chapter, when we know more about social and opinion representativeness.

Arguments can also be raised in favour of social representativeness as relevant in its own right. It can be argued, in Burkean fashion, that long-term interests of the represented are not necessarily consistent with their opinions, which tend to be short-term.[7] In the same vein, it can be claimed that the representatives are better informed to make decisions than those that they represent, but at the same time that the representatives need to have reasonably similar life experiences to those of the represented. The chances of this being the case are greater if they are socially representative. This has been referred to as the 'complementary experience' argument.[8]

Thus, the parties' social representativeness can be viewed as relevant to the parties' ability to provide representative linkage. As was argued in Chapter 2, however, social representativeness is not a necessary condition for representative linkage. Many of the arguments for the relevance of social representativeness are also applicable to opinion representativeness. Furthermore, if opinion representativeness is high, some of the arguments for social representativeness become redundant. It can be argued that it does not matter if a social group is under-represented, as long as the opinions of that group are represented. Therefore, the question whether there has been representative linkage decline will be answered in Chapter 8.

Social representativeness is a necessary condition for participatory linkage, however. Openness, membership influence, membership strength and activity, the subjects of Chapters 3, 4 and 5, are necessary, but not

---

[7] Pitkin 1967:181ff.

[8] Oskarson and Wängnerud 1995b:199ff.

sufficient, conditions. If members and activists are socially unrepresentative it means that parts of society are not participating.[9]

The argument for the relevance of social representativeness can be extended further. It may, for example, have a bearing on the legitimacy of the parties.[10] If the parties prove to consist primarily of élite groups, it would probably reinforce the criticism against parties and politicians that they are out of touch with the public. There is also a communicative aspect to party membership. The members can be seen as communicative bonds between party leaders and the public, even as 'political ambassadors' of the parties.[11] They can communicate from the public into the party, as what may be called 'palps', and they can also communicate in the opposite direction, as 'megaphones'.[12] Their ability to do so is greatly impaired if they are not socially representative, because there would be smaller chances of communication with the under-represented social groups. This has implications for the democratic process as a whole, as communication is a central aspect of democracy. In addition, communication problems can also have adverse effects for the parties in their quest for votes.[13]

The equity argument has already been mentioned. It can be argued that it has a value in its own right that the parties, which play such an important role in modern democracies -- not least in Sweden -- reflect the social composition of the nation. If the parties reflect the social composition of their own voters, the party system should reflect the composition of the electorate.[14] Finally, it can be argued that there is a conflict of interest between different social groups. This would mean that under-represented groups would be adversely affected by political decisions made by organs dominated by opposing social groups. This argument is particularly prevalent in the debate about gender equality but can also be applied to

---

[9] This perspective is prevalent in research on political participation. Examples are Parry, Moyser and Day 1992:232-237, Westerståhl and Johansson 1981:50-61 and Petersson, Westholm and Blomberg 1989, especially Chapters 6 and 10.

[10] Oskarson and Wängnerud 1995b:199ff.

[11] Scarrow 1991:124.

[12] Whiteley, Seyd and Richardson refer to the members as "both the party's standard-bearers and its eyes and ears". Whiteley, Seyd and Richardson 1994:4.

[13] Seyd and Whiteley 1992:37.

[14] This argument is raised in a study on the representativeness of Swedish parliamentarians, Holmberg and Esaiasson 1988:136.

possible conflicts of interest between working class and middle class, young and old and so on.[15]

Data and method

Five social, or demographic, variables will be used: gender, age, education, social class and social group. Together they provide a comprehensive picture of the social composition of party members and activists, and an adequate foundation for comparison with the general public. Gender and age represent social conflict dimensions the importance of which has, if anything, increased over time. Education and class are indicators of social status. Even if it is sometimes argued in the public debate that class differences are decreasing and, at least, changing in nature, there is quite convincing evidence that they are not obsolete. The theoretical and normative aspects of each variable will be elaborated in the respective sections.

The main question to be answered is: have differences between members and the public increased over time? The focus will be set on the size rather than on the direction (for example, if women are over- or under-represented among party members) of the differences between members/activists and the public. That is not to say that the direction of differences is irrelevant. It will be noted and discussed, and the tables will be presented in enough detail for the reader to be able to probe further into these aspects. But for the purpose of this study, it is of secondary importance whether party members are disproportionately male or female, young or old, highly or poorly educated, working class or middle class -- the discrepancy as such indicates a lack of representativeness.

On the system level, all party members and activists in Sweden will be compared to the electorate. On the party level, a party's members and activists will be compared to the party's own voters. The comparisons will be made between the actual social composition of members/activists and the electorate/party voters at the same time point, not with any 'ideal' distribution. On the national level this is a limited problem, because the electorate can be expected to be 'equitably' distributed. On the party level, however, it almost goes without saying that social profiles of different parties vary, among voters as well as members. The tables will be presented in enough detail to enable comparisons between parties and the electorate, and some such observations will be discussed. However, it is already well proven

---

[15] See Oskarson and Wängnerud 1995b, especially pp. 199f and 222f.

that different parties have different social profiles on the electoral level, a fact that remains true to this day.[16] In this chapter it will be attempted to find out whether a party's members are different to the party's voters in this respect. Are the social profiles accentuated or are they diminished? And, to reiterate the main question: have the members become more or less socially representative over time?

The account will be based on data from the Swedish Election Studies. As has become apparent in Chapters 4 and 5, the absolute number of members, especially active members, among the respondents is low in most Election Studies. The number of cases are enough at the aggregate national level, but some parties have far too few members to allow far reaching conclusions, let alone breaking down into different social groups. Therefore, only three parties will be dealt with; the Social Democrats, the Centre Party and the Moderate (Conservative) Party.[17] For some years, the figures in the tables will still be based on disturbingly few cases, but, with the exception of Moderate activists, the statistical foundation will mostly be reasonably solid. To increase the number of cases, members of youth as well as women's organisations are included among the members from 1979, when this becomes possible. This means that the results in the tables will not be exactly comparable over time; the data situation does not allow inclusion of members of side organisations before 1979. The inclusion women's and, especially, youth organisation members has a limited effect on the number of cases, however, and the long-term trends are still reasonably comparable.[18]

The other side of the comparison, with what to compare the members, has also been subject to some consideration. On the aggregate national level, the natural comparison material is the entire electorate. On the

---

[16] For convincing, thorough and empirical arguments to this effect, see Oskarson 1994.

[17] The figures on the aggregate national level, however, also include members of other parties.

[18] In a study on the representativeness of 37 different European parties, based on four merged consecutive Eurobarometer studies, a criterion of a merged total of at least 30 members was used when determining which parties would be included (Widfeldt 1995). Among the remaining Swedish parties, only the People's Party Liberals fit this criterion, and only in the 1964 and 1968 Election Studies. These statistical limitations bring with them a problem: it means that only parties with relatively many members can be studied. There are several reasons why smaller parties could be of interest. They often play important roles in policy making, often in pivotal positions, and some of them are 'new left' or 'new politics' parties which are seen as a challenge to the political establishment.

party level it is slightly less straightforward. Both party voters and party identifiers could be suitable. This is not a big problem in the Swedish case, however. The difference between party voters and party sympathisers is mostly very small, because the two go very much hand in hand. Voters have been chosen as unit of comparison. The reason for this is that in 1960 and 1964, only one half of the sample was asked about party sympathy as opposed to party vote. Thus, the time series about party vote is slightly more consistent.[19]

To sum up, the electorate and party voters will be compared with party members. Three membership strata, or membership categories, will be used: total members (individual plus collective members), individual members and active members. It should be pointed out that all party members are always included in the comparison categories. Thus, members are compared to the entire electorate, and all voters of a party, not merely with non-members.

Gender representativeness

Politics has often been criticised as male dominated. The title of the book "We Have Been Waiting Long Enough", which investigates various aspects and cases of women and politics in the Nordic countries, is but one evidence of the intensity of the debate.[20] It is not difficult to find empirical support for this criticism. On the parliamentary level, no legislature in the world has been known to have consisted of an equal proportion men and women.[21] Similar evidence has also been found inside the political parties, where existing research indicates that the vast majority of European parties are

---

[19] In almost all Election Studies since 1960 (1970 being the sole exception), the pre-election half of the sample was asked about party vote in a separate mail questionnaire sent out after the election. Those answers were combined with the answers from the post-election sample to constitute a coherent party vote variable. Party sympathy refers to responses to the question 'Which party do you like best', which has been asked separately from questions about vote and vote intention. This question has primarily been used to determine the direction of party identification. It can also be used to analyse tactical voting. In the mentioned comparative study of party members in Europe, party identification is used instead of party vote (Widfeldt 1995). This is appropriate in studies where data are not only taken from election years. It is problematic to ask respondents of who they would vote for if the question is not asked in connection with an actual election.

[20] Dahlerup 1989.

[21] Norris 1987:116, Norris 1993:309f.

male dominated on the membership level.[22] In recent years, some scholars have noted changes in the direction towards increased equality, not least in Sweden.[23] The general conclusion, however, must still be that even in Sweden there is some way to go before the gender distribution of the population is reflected in the political system.

Arguments in favour of the relevance of gender as a criterion for representativeness are well known and plenty. The debate has been summarised by Maria Oskarson and Lena Wängnerud, who identify three main arguments: legitimacy, complementary experience and conflict of interest.[24] These arguments, already mentioned above, can all be used in favour of the relevance of social representativeness in general, but are particularly often referred to in gender-oriented research.

The findings in this section will make some contribution to that discussion. If the general picture of male domination in politics is reinforced among the party members, it has consequences for the representativeness of the parties. It also has important implications for the participatory aspect of the social composition of party membership discussed above. It would mean that the parties fail, or neglect, to involve women in their organisations, thus misrepresenting a large and important societal group. This would be especially remarkable, considering the fact that Sweden has been noted for having come comparatively far in gender equality. The 40.4 per cent of women in the Swedish Riksdag after the 1994 election made it the most equal legislature in the world.[25]

The percentage distribution of males and females among members, activists and voters is presented in Table 7.1. The table is large, and could appear to be somewhat hard to digest. Interpreting the table is easier if attention is paid to the difference columns which indicate the differences in percentage points in gender distribution between members and activists, and voters. A negative difference means that men are over-represented among the

---

[22] Widfeldt 1995:147-151.

[23] Sainsbury 1993, Bergqvist 1994.

[24] Oskarson and Wängnerud 1995b. For a summary in Swedish of the debate within feminism and about gender and politics, see also Oskarson and Wängnerud 1995a.

[25] The exact proportion women in the Riksdag has not remained the same since the 1994 election, due to factors such as deaths, resignations, election into the EU parliament, governmental appointments, etc. In the 1995/96 Riksdag year, the proportion women had increased to 43 per cent.

members and activists. An asterisk means that there is a difference between the percentages which is significant on the .05 level or higher. It should not take very long to find that party membership is dominated by men, as is shown by the overwhelming amount of negative differences between members and voters. This applies to all time points, on the national level as well as in the three included parties. It is also applies to all membership categories: total (including collective), individual and active members. There are some exceptions, notably among the activists in the Centre and Moderate parties, but they are mostly based on so few cases that they should be interpreted with care.

On the aggregate national level, comparisons between members and the electorate are easy because the latter has for obvious reasons been evenly split. Total, including collective, party members in Sweden have consisted of between 62 and 70 per cent men, while the domination is slightly smaller among individual members. The most plausible explanation is that collective members have tended to come from male-dominated trade unions. Among individual members, the smallest recorded gender differences is 59 per cent men and 41 per cent women in 1970, 1985, 1991 and 1994. The over-representation of men has been smaller among activists than among individual members all years except 1985. In 1991 and 1994 the active members have in fact become more or less fully gender representative of the electorate.

Thus, on the national level, two observations are particularly important. First, that party members have tended to consist of a disproportionate number of men, compared to the electorate. Second, that there is a tendency for the representativeness to increase from massive male domination among total members, via an intermediate level among individual members, down to the comparatively equal gender distribution among the active members.

On the party level, interpretations will be slightly more complex. We are now comparing within parties with different and changing gender profiles instead of with the evenly divided electorate. The Social Democratic membership has consistently been dominated by men, if an ideal 50-50 distribution is taken as reference point. Between 57 and 71 per cent of individual and active members have been male during the research period. Thus, men have dominated all three membership categories, and at all time points.

Table 7.1   Gender distribution of Swedish electorate, party voters, party members and activists, 1960-1994. Percentages

Nation

	electorate			tot. members				ind. members				active members			
	m	f	n	m	f	diff.	n	m	f	diff.	n	m	f	diff.	n
1960	48	52	1466	67	33	-19*	260	*data not available*				65	35	-17*	57
1964	51	49	2849	67	33	-16*	496	*data not available*				*data not available*			
1968	51	49	2892	70	30	-19*	450	63	37	-12*	311	57	43	- 6	98
1970	50	50	1322	63	37	-13*	171	59	41	- 9*	138	*data not available*			
1979	51	49	2905	67	33	-16*	431	64	36	-13*	341	57	43	- 6	178
1985	50	50	2944	62	38	-12*	447	59	41	- 9*	343	65	35	-15*	164
1988	52	48	2845	65	35	-13*	341	65	35	-13*	318	63	37	-11*	127
1991	51	49	2729	*no coll. members*				59	41	- 8*	265	51	49	0	101
1994	51	49	3378	*no coll. members*				59	41	- 8*	263	53	47	- 2	103

Social Democrats

	voters			tot. members				ind. members				active members			
	m	f	n	m	f	diff.	n	m	f	diff.	n	m	f	diff.	n
1960	47	53	663	70	30	-23*	124	*data not available*				59	41	-12	27
1964	53	47	1248	77	23	-24*	248	*data not available*				*data not available*			
1968	52	48	1435	81	19	-29*	236	71	29	-19*	97	65	35	-13*	46
1970	50	50	559	69	31	-19*	78	60	40	-10	47	*data not available*			
1979	51	49	1183	71	29	-20*	221	66	34	-15*	131	61	39	-10*	87
1985	48	52	1166	65	35	-17*	233	58	42	-10*	129	61	39	-13*	76
1988	49	51	1093	65	35	-16*	171	66	34	-17*	148	65	35	-16*	51
1991	51	49	889	*no coll. members*				63	37	-12*	110	67	33	-16*	36
1994	54	46	1075	*no coll. members*				66	34	-12*	129	57	43	- 3	47

Centre Party

	voters			members				active members			
	m	f	n	m	f	diff.	n	m	f	diff.	n
1960	51	49	194	63	37	-12	57	56	44	- 5	18
1964	59	41	359	60	40	- 1	103	*data not available*			
1968	57	43	464	57	43	0	95	42	58	15	31
1970	49	51	268	56	44	- 7	39	*data not available*			
1979	45	55	442	64	36	-19*	102	57	43	-12	49
1985	52	48	283	64	36	-12*	83	77	23	-25*	35
1988	52	48	284	63	37	-11	68	51	49	1	35
1991	46	54	208	56	44	-10	68	39	61	7	31
1994	45	55	200	51	49	- 6	53	52	48	- 7	23

Moderate Party

	voters			members				active members			
	m	f	n	m	f	diff.	n	m	f	diff.	n
1960	50	50	181	61	39	-11	51	86	14	-36*	7
1964	42	58	265	46	54	- 4	72	*data not available*			
1968	47	53	278	57	43	-10	61	50	50	- 3	12
1970	57	43	113	56	44	1	32	*data not available*			
1979	58	42	526	65	35	- 7	60	61	39	- 3	18
1985	59	41	527	58	42	1	69	68	32	- 9	19
1988	58	42	401	59	41	- 1	58	62	38	- 4	13
1991	57	43	520	52	48	5	42	38	62	19	16
1994	60	40	477	60	40	0	43	47	53	13	15

Comment: Source: Swedish Election Studies. m = male, f = female. 'diff.' = difference in percentage points between a membership stratum (total, individual or active) and electorate or party voters. Positive difference = women are over-represented among members, and vice versa. (*) = difference is significant on .05 level or higher (one-tailed Z test). Members include members of women's and youth org. (if any) from 1979 onwards. Members are included in electorate and party voters.

The picture largely remains the same if the gender fluctuations among the Social Democratic voters are taken into account. The party's voters had a majority of women in 1960, 1985 and 1988, and a majority of men all other years (except 1970 when the distribution was exactly 50-50). However, the male dominance among the voters has seldom been close to that in any of the membership categories. During the majority of time points the differences between voters and members have been statistically significant. The smallest difference was in 1994, when 54 per cent of the party's voters were male, compared to 57 per cent of the party's active members. All other years the difference has been at least ten percentage points between the voters and each of the three membership strata.

The Centre Party membership has also been male-dominated, although somewhat less markedly so than in the Social Democrats. The proportion of males was 63 per cent in the beginning of the research period but sank continuously, to reach 56 per cent in 1970. In 1979, the men were again as dominant as in 1960, something which is remarkable as 1979 is the year when the data starts to explicitly include members of the women's organisations. In the 1990s, however, the discrepancy decreased drastically, and in 1994 the Centre Party members were in fact almost totally evenly distributed. The active Centre members have also mostly been dominated by men but with two exceptions; in 1968 and 1991.

The Centre Party voters have fluctuated between male and female majorities. The men outnumbered the women in the 1960s and 1980s but the opposite applies to the 1970s and 1990s. If the members are compared to the voters, the Social Democratic pattern of male over-representation is largely repeated. Female voters outnumbered male voters on four out of nine time points; note the rather clear differences in 1979, 1991 and 1994. This means that the comparatively even gender distribution among the members in the 1990s nevertheless constitutes a male over-representation if a comparison is made with the party's voters at the same time.

The Moderate Party membership has been dominated by men on every time point except in 1964. The size of this difference has varied quite freely. The proportion of 60 per cent males and 40 per cent females in 1994, compared with the 52-48 distribution three years earlier, give an indication of the lack of stability. There is no visible trend in any direction; the size of the gender difference in 1994 is almost identical to what it was 34 years earlier. The figures on active Moderate members are based on too few cases to allow any assertive conclusions; the apparent shift towards a much higher female proportion in the 1990s must be interpreted with caution. On the electoral level, the Moderate party has gone through quite a transformation in terms of gender distribution during the research period. In the 1960s there was female majority, but the Moderate Party of the 1990s is very much a 'men's party'. Thus, the party's membership, which has a history of male dominance, is more representative of the voters in the 1990s than in it was the 1960s.

If the gender distribution among party members compared to an ideal 50-50 distribution, the conclusion of this section is negative. The entirety of the Swedish party membership as well as the three largest membership parties by themselves are, and have been, dominated by men. With the exception of the Centre Party members, there is not much to suggest that total equality among party members is around the corner, although there is possibly a weak tendency towards somewhat increased equality. The general situation is that Swedish party membership has been dominated by men since the 1960s and that the extent of this domination has, by and large, remained constant.

The situation is somewhat different if we focus on the active members, however. As a rule, the male domination has tended not to be as strong among activists as among the totality of active and passive members, and the gender distribution in the 1990s is in fact quite close to full equality on the aggregate national level as well as among all the three studied parties.

Another point worth noting is that among individual members, the only membership category where it is possible to compare all three parties from the 1960s through the 1990s, the party with the smallest overall gender differences is the Moderate Party. Interestingly, this gender equality is not reflected everywhere in the party's organisation. At the time of the extra party congress held by the Moderate Party in 1995, one-third of the National Executive members were women.[26] After the 1994 Riksdag election, 27 per cent of the party's parliamentary fraction were women, the lowest female proportion of the seven Riksdag parties.[27]

---

[26] *Extra Partistämma, Stockholm 1995, stämmohandlingar* (Printed Congress Document), p. 13.

[27] Since the first election to the unicameral Riksdag in 1970, the Moderate Party has been the party with the lowest proportion of elected women after every election except in 1991. Before 1970, however, it did happen that other parties had a lower representation of women. Bergqvist 1994:35f and 40-43.

If the point of comparison is not the ideal 50-50 distribution, but the actual gender distribution among the voters, there are a few more positive findings. Most years, members and activists in the Moderate and Centre parties are quite representative of their voters, with few cases of statistically significant differences. The situation is more problematic in the Social Democrats, however. There are few cases of clear trends in any direction. Tendencies towards increased representativeness can be found in several instances, but they are almost never conclusive. The only case where there can be a suspicion of decreased representativeness is among Moderate activists but this is based on very shaky statistical evidence. If the size of the difference between members and voters are compared between the first and last available time points, the members tend to be more representative at the end than at the beginning of the research period. What can be concluded is that there is no evidence of a general decline in gender representativeness among Swedish party members.

From a gender perspective, the situation among the party members is not satisfactory. Men dominate among the members on the national level as well as among all parties. If the totally equal 50-50 distribution is considered the ideal, the most equal party during the 1960-1994 period has on average been the Moderates, while the Social Democrats is the most male dominated. The party with the clearest recent development towards gender equality among the members is the Centre Party.

The active members are, on the whole, more evenly distributed than the totality of members. The activists have, furthermore, developed towards a more even distribution than before. This gives some room for a slightly more positive interpretation, since the generous operationalisation of activity in the Election Studies means that it is only the active members that can influence decisions made in the parties. It also indicates that a higher percentage of women who join political parties are willing to become active than men. A caveat must be issued against this conclusion, however. Some of the active female members are coded as members of women's organisations rather than the parties themselves. Thus, they are not necessarily involved in decisions taken by the main party organisations. It should also be noted that the active members are not perfectly evenly distributed; the 1994 figure of 53 per cent males signifies a small decrease in equality compared with 1991.

As has already been noted, the Swedish parliament has developed towards increased equality, and is among the most gender equal in the world. Christina Bergqvist's research has shown that other political élite groups in Sweden have also tended to develop towards increased equality. This applies to, for example, the national executives of the major political parties, governmental posts and regional authorities.[28] The more equal distribution among activists than members as a whole may be viewed in this perspective. It could be that, instead of beginning among the grass roots before spreading up to the élite level, gender equality goes in the other direction. A related point is that several Swedish parties have introduced formal or informal gender quotas to internal posts as well as nominations for public elections.[29] So far, it appears that it has proved difficult to extend these efforts to membership recruitment.

If it is true that equality begins at the top, then the results in this section could mean that gender equality is about to reach the activists, but still has some way to go before it starts to affect party members in general. The case of the Moderate Party shows that there is no evidence that strong female representation on the membership level leads to higher equality on the élite level. The Centre Party can also be used to illustrate this point. The numerical strength of the women's organisation is notable and has long traditions, and in 1994 the party's members and activists were very evenly distributed. Yet, this has not helped to keep the gender balance of the party's Riksdag group comparable to most other parties.[30]

Returning to the main perspective of this study, however, the conclusion is that the gender situation, at least, no worse than it has been in the past. The parties are about as representative -- or unrepresentative -- of their voters in the 1990s as they were in the 1960s.

Age representativeness

One of the recurring critical stereotypes of politics is that it is dominated by middle-aged men. The previous section has shown that one part of the stereotype is, by and large, applicable to party membership in Sweden. Age representativeness has not been given quite the same attention as gender but it has been referred to in some studies on representation. Existing research

---

[28] Bergqvist 1994:71, 201-206.

[29] Bergqvist 1994:68ff. Cf. Norris 1993:320.

[30] After the 1994 election, the Centre Party had the second lowest female representation in the Riksdag, with 37 per cent women (the Riksdag in Figures 1994/95). See also Bergqvist 1994:70ff.

tends to confirm the latter part of the stereotype; political representatives tend to be middle-aged to a disproportionate extent.[31]

Such a situation is not unanimously regarded as alarming, at least not to the same extent as in the case of gender. Politics are often complex and complicated and it can be argued that older people are better equipped to make the often difficult decisions. Another, sometimes forgotten, difference between age and gender is that older people have been young, while there are extremely few men who have been women. Obviously, there are counter-arguments against this. At any given time in history, the situation for young people is not identical to what it was for older people when they were young. Indeed, the three main arguments for social representativeness are all applicable to age. The alienation and lack of involvement of younger people is considered a big problem in politics. Indeed, under-representation of old people can be regarded as just as problematic. They have specific problems which often are politically central, like pensions, health and care of the elderly. The formation of pensioner's parties in some European countries in recent years suggest that it is not unthinkable to consider age as potential source of conflict of interest.

To compare age distributions over time is somewhat problematic, because the Swedish Election Studies have consisted of samples which have followed the changes in eligibility to vote. Several successive changes were decided in the 1960s and 70s. In 1960, the age limit was in practice 22 years. The current limit of 18 years has been in operation since the 1976 election. On the other end of the scale, the Election Studies have employed an upper age limit of 80 years in their samples.[32]

The age variable will be presented in two ways: first with mean ages and then with the respondents divided into a trichotomy of young, middle-aged and old. The mean ages for the electorate, party voters and the three membership categories are presented in Table 7.2 below. The table confirms

---

[31] E.g. Esaiasson and Holmberg 1988:136f, Westerståhl and Johansson 1981:112.

[32] In 1960, it was required to have reached the age of 21 during the year preceding the election. In 1965 it was changed to the age of 20 and in 1969 to 19 during the preceding year. Finally, in 1974 it was lowered to the current limit of 18 years. At the same time, it was now stipulated that the age limit needs only to have been reached on the date of the election. Thus, the first election where the current age limit was in operation was in 1976; the first time point in this study is 1979. The Election Studies have used an upper age limit of 80 years every time except in 1968 when the sample included respondents aged up to 85 years. To enhance comparability with other years, all respondents in 1968 aged between 81 and 85 have been removed.

the suspicion that party politics is dominated by the middle-aged. It should be noted that this still true after 1979, when members of youth organisations are included in the figures. The lowest average age for any membership stratum on any time point is 45 years for total (including collective) Social Democratic members in 1985. As a rule, the average age for members is around 50, or often higher.

On the national level, there has been a tendency for the average age of individual and active members to increase over time. For individual members, the average age of 53.4 in 1994 is the highest during the research period. It is not a case of a constant increase; since 1968 the trend for individual members is curvilinear. But the lower average age in 1979 compared to 1968 and 1970 is partly explained by the fact that the sample now includes respondents down to the age of 18, and that from this year members of youth organisations are included in the figures. This means that the average ages from the 1960s are higher than would have been the case if exactly comparable data had been available. Therefore, the increased average age in the 1990s compared to the 1970s and 1980s is all the more notable.

Because of the comparability problems, it is plausible to assume that the seemingly curvilinear trend between 1968 and 1994 hides a general trend towards increasing average age. The development between 1979 and 1994 is indisputable.

Among the parties, the Centre Party has undergone the most remarkable development. In 1960, Centre Party members were on average 46.6 years old. In 1994 the party had become by far the oldest with an average age of over 58. The rise has been almost perfectly continuous over the years. Centre Party activists have also become older over time, but not at the same rate, and there has been little change after 1985.

Individual members of the Social Democratic Party display a curvilinear development, similar to that of the aggregate number of individual members in the nation. The average age sank in the 1970s and 1980s but rose again quite steeply in the 1990s, to unprecedented levels. Active Social Democrats also became older in the 1990s, while the average age of the total (including collective) members sank in the 1980s, before collective membership was abolished. Members of the Moderate Party have fluctuated back and forth. There is no trend in any direction. The average age of 47.5 in 1991 was the lowest during the research period. Three years later it had risen by over four years and was the highest since 1970.

Table 7.2   Mean age of Swedish electorate, party voters, party members and activists, 1960-1994

Nation

	electorate			total members				ind. members				active members			
	mean	StD	n	mean	StD	diff.	n	mean	StD	diff.	n	mean	StD	diff.	n
1960	46.6	14.9	1466	48.3	12.7	1.7*	260	*data not available*				47.8	11.5	1.2	57
1964	47.8	15.7	2849	50.4	13.6	2.6*	496	*data not available*				*data not available*			
1968	46.4	16.3	2892	50.7	13.7	4.3*	450	51.6	13.0	5.2*	311	50.7	11.8	4.3*	98
1970	46.6	16.4	1322	52.4	13.9	5.8*	171	52.8	13.4	6.2*	138	*data not available*			
1979	45.8	17.1	2905	48.0	15.7	2.2*	431	49.4	15.8	3.6*	341	49.1	15.1	3.3*	178
1985	44.9	17.0	2944	47.2	16.5	2.3*	447	48.9	16.5	4.0*	343	48.5	16.0	3.6*	164
1988	44.9	17.0	2845	49.3	15.8	4.4*	341	49.8	16.0	4.9*	318	51.8	15.6	6.9*	127
1991	44.9	17.2	2730	*no collective members*				52.6	16.0	7.7*	265	54.9	15.4	10.0*	101
1994	45.3	17.4	3378	*no collective members*				53.4	16.4	8.1*	263	52.7	15.8	7.4*	103

Social Democrats

	voters			total members				ind. members				active members			
	mean	StD	n	mean	StD	diff.	n	mean	StD	diff.	n	mean	StD	diff.	n
1960	44.4	13.9	663	47.0	12.6	2.6*	124	*data not available*				46.5	11.6	2.1	27
1964	47.9	15.1	1248	50.2	13.3	2.3*	248	*data not available*				*data not available*			
1968	46.5	15.9	1435	50.3	14.5	3.8*	236	52.9	13.3	6.4*	97	51.7	11.4	5.2*	46
1970	45.6	15.6	559	53.1	12.5	7.5*	78	53.7	11.0	8.1*	47	*data not available*			
1979	47.1	16.8	1183	46.0	14.5	-1.1	221	48.4	14.5	1.3	131	48.0	13.9	0.9	87
1985	45.9	17.2	1166	45.0	15.8	-0.9	233	47.7	15.7	1.8	129	47.5	15.0	1.6	76
1988	46.8	17.2	1093	46.4	14.9	-0.4	171	47.1	15.2	0.3	148	50.2	14.3	3.4*	51
1991	47.8	16.7	890	*no collective members*				53.6	14.5	5.8*	110	57.9	12.5	10.1*	36
1994	46.3	16.7	1075	*no collective members*				52.4	15.5	6.1*	129	53.4	14.1	7.1*	47

Centre Party

	voters			members				active members			
	mean	StD	n	mean	StD	diff.	n	mean	StD	diff.	n
1960	47.9	14.6	194	46.6	13.1	- 1.3	57	47.4	11.4	-0.5	18
1964	48.5	14.3	359	49.9	12.9	1.4	103	*data not available*			
1968	47.0	15.5	464	50.1	12.6	3.1*	95	50.5	9.4	3.5	31
1970	46.5	16.7	268	50.1	14.7	3.6	39	*data not available*			
1979	47.5	17.1	442	50.3	15.2	2.8	102	50.1	15.2	2.6	49
1985	48.2	17.3	283	53.2	15.7	5.0*	83	55.4	15.3	7.2*	35
1988	47.6	16.9	284	53.7	15.7	6.1*	68	55.1	16.2	7.5*	35
1991	49.3	16.7	208	53.9	14.7	4.6*	68	55.2	15.1	5.9*	31
1994	48.1	18.4	200	58.2	15.5	10.1*	53	55.3	17.5	7.2*	23

Moderate Party

	voters			members				active members			
	mean	StD	n	mean	StD	diff.	n	mean	StD	diff.	n
1960	48.9	15.2	181	52.1	13.1	3.2	51	50.4	14.4	1.5	7
1964	50.4	16.0	265	51.0	14.0	0.6	72	*data not available*			
1968	48.7	16.1	278	51.9	13.6	3.2	61	46.1	13.0	-2.6	12
1970	48.5	16.1	113	53.4	14.6	4.9	32	*data not available*			
1979	46.7	16.1	526	50.3	17.5	3.6	60	52.9	17.6	6.2	18
1985	44.4	16.7	527	48.7	16.9	4.3*	69	47.8	18.0	3.4	19
1988	45.4	17.1	401	50.9	17.0	5.5*	58	52.6	19.4	7.2	13
1991	43.3	17.1	520	47.5	19.7	4.2	42	47.8	19.1	4.5	16
1994	45.6	17.4	477	51.8	18.7	6.2*	43	48.5	17.5	2.9	15

Comment: Sources: Swedish Election Studies, all years. StD = standard deviance. 'Diff.' = difference in mean age between the membership stratum (total, individual and active members respectively) and the electorate or a party's voters. Positive difference = members older than the voters, and vice versa. Asterisk (*) = difference between the two averages is significant at the .05 level or higher (T test for significance between two means). Members include members of women's and youth organisations (if any) from 1979 onwards. Members are included among electorate and party voters.

Individual members tend to have the highest average age, followed by active members and then total members. All these categories usually (but not always) have a higher average age than both the electorate and the parties' voters. The two latter have almost never reached an average of 50. Since the voting age was lowered to 18, the average age of the electorate has been around 45. Party members in the whole country, as well as among the three studied parties, are on average usually around 50 or older.

It has already been pointed out that the figures from between 1960 and 1970 are not exactly comparable to those from 1979 to 1994. To compare the figures from 1968 (the first time when individual members can be separated) and the end of the research period, the data from 1994 have been manipulated. Members of youth and women's organisations, and all respondents aged below 21, have been removed. These figures, henceforth referred to as the 'manipulated data', are not included in Table 7.2. Quite naturally, this operation means that the means increase. The average age of all party members in the nation goes up from 53.4 to 54.7 years. A comparison with the 'unmanipulated' figures in Table 7.2 underlines the already made observation that party members have become older. Even without the manipulation, the aggregate total of individual members was on average older in 1994 than on any previous time point. Similarly, the average age of all active members goes up to 53.3 (compared to 52.7 in Table 7.2). On the party level, the average age of the members rises for all three parties. The manipulated figure for Social Democratic members is 53.2 (compared to the unmanipulated figure of 52.4), for Centre Party members 60.4 (compared to 58.2) and for Moderate Party members 54.8 (51.8). The general observation that party members have become older over time is strengthened.

So far the account has been restricted to the development of average age on its own. In order to study the development of age representativeness, the age of the voters on the same time point is used as reference point. Thus, the focus now shifts to the difference in mean age between members and voters in a given year (as shown in the 'diff.' columns), and how the size of that difference has developed over time.

The most striking feature is the massive number of positive differences, meaning that the members are older than the voters. This applies to all but six of the 74 possible comparisons in Table 7.2. The only partial exception is the Social Democratic total members, who were slightly younger than the party's voters between 1979 and 1988. On the whole, however, the evidence is overwhelming: party members and party activists are older than the electorate and the voters of their respective parties. It is also apparent that the differences between members and voters have increased over time. In 1968, the difference in average age between the aggregate of individual members and the electorate was 5.2 years. In 1994 the difference had risen to over 8 years.[33] The active members have also become clearly less representative of the voters. What has happened is that the average age of the electorate has decreased somewhat over time, mainly due to the lowering of the voting age. At the same time the individual and the active members have become older. The trend towards decreasing representativeness is clear. The total members have fluctuated with no general trend (possibly a slight increase) between 1960 and 1988. However, if we assume that the individual and active members are the most important for the purposes of this study, decreasing representativeness is the general finding.

The Social Democratic members do not follow the national development. This is worth noting, as they are the largest membership party and, hence, constitute a large part of all Swedish party members. The individual members display a curvilinear pattern. They developed towards decidedly higher representativeness from the 1960s to the 1980s, but in the 1990s they moved back, almost to the level of 1968.[34] The active members, however, follow the national trend somewhat more closely, and are clearly less representative in the 1990s than before.[35] The total (including collective) Social Democratic members are the *enfant terribles* of the whole of Table 7.2. They were clearly more representative in the late 1970s and 1980s than earlier, thus constituting the only clear case of increased representativeness.

The Centre Party members have become decidedly less representative over time. In 1994, the members were on average more than

---

[33] Using the manipulated data, the difference between individual members and the electorate is 7.8 years compared to 8.1 in the table. The exclusion of young respondents and members of youth organisations means that the average age of members goes up, but the exclusion of young respondents from the sample of course means that so does the average age of the electorate.

[34] This is true also if the manipulated data are considered. According to the manipulated data, Social Democratic voters were on average 47.9 years old, compared to the members' average age of 53.2. This is a difference of 5.3 years which is less than the differences in 1968 and 1970 and also smaller than the original difference of 6.1 years shown in the table.

[35] It should be remembered that there is less point in 'manipulating' the figures for active members because the operationalisation of activity is not the same before 1979.

10 years older than the party's voters.[36] The active members have developed in the same direction, although they have remained quite stable since 1985. The Moderate members also follow the national pattern of decreased representativeness, although slightly less markedly so than the Centre Party, and the activists show no decrease at all. In summary, however, Swedish party members and activists have clearly become less age representative over time. The average age of the party members and activists has virtually always been higher than that of the general public, but the size of this difference has increased.

In Table 7.3, the age composition of the members and voters has been trichotomised into three age groups. The young group includes those aged up to 30 years.[37] The middle category is between 31 and 60 and the 'old' group is between 61 and 80. The table is included mainly for additional illustrative purposes, and therefore does not specify the differences between the various membership categories.

That the middle group is dominant everywhere is only natural because it encompasses the widest age range. The main purpose of the table is instead to give better information about the representation of the young and old groups, which is not possible when using the mean figures.

The young group is under-represented almost everywhere. This applies to the national level as well as the three parties. Due to the lowering of the voting age, the relative size of the youngest group has increased among the electorate. There has been an increase also among members and activists, but it has been slower, still leaving young people under-represented. In relative terms, there is no great difference among the parties; young people are quite simply badly represented in party organisations in general. This has not been offset by the inclusion of members of youth organisations, and the lower age limit, from 1979 onwards.[38]

---

[36] Based on the manipulated data, the difference in 1994 was 10.6 years (members 60.4 and voters 49.8).

[37] The lower limit of the youngest age category varies because of the changes in voting age. In 1960 and 1964 it is 22 years. In 1968 it is 21 and in 1970 20 years. From 1979 onwards it is 18 years.

[38] It should be pointed out that the Tables in this and the next chapter do not include all members of the parties' youth organisations. A fair amount of their members are aged below 18 and thus not included in the Election Study samples.

Table 7.3   Age group distribution of Swedish electorate, party voters, party members and activists, 1960-1994. Percentages

Nation

	electorate				total members				ind. members				active members			
	young	mid	old	n	young	mid	old	n	young	mid	old	n	young	mid	old	n
1960	18	62	20	1466	10	74	16	260	*no data available*				7	82	11	57
1964	18	58	24	2849	9	67	24	496	*no data available*				*no data available*			
1968	23	54	23	2892	11	63	26	450	7	67	26	311	7	69	24	98
1970	23	53	24	1322	8	63	29	171	7	64	29	138	*no data available*			
1979	24	52	24	2905	14	63	23	431	12	61	27	341	10	64	26	178
1985	24	53	23	2944	18	57	25	447	15	57	28	343	13	61	26	164
1988	25	52	23	2845	14	57	29	341	14	55	31	318	11	54	35	127
1991	26	52	22	2730	*no coll. members*				11	53	36	265	8	50	42	101
1994	26	51	23	3378	*no coll. members*				11	52	37	263	11	56	33	103

Social Democrats

	voters				total members				ind. members				active members			
	young	mid	old	n	young	mid	old	n	young	mid	old	n	young	mid	old	n
1960	20	65	15	663	11	74	15	124	*no data available*				7	85	8	27
1964	15	62	23	1248	10	66	24	248	*no data available*				*no data available*			
1968	22	55	23	1435	14	57	29	236	9	59	32	97	6	70	24	46
1970	24	56	20	559	4	64	32	78	2	66	32	47	*no data available*			
1979	21	53	26	1183	14	68	18	221	10	67	23	131	8	70	22	87
1985	22	53	25	1166	21	59	20	233	15	60	25	129	16	62	22	76
1988	22	51	27	1093	16	62	22	171	16	60	24	148	8	65	27	51
1991	19	55	26	890	*no collective members*				10	54	36	110	6	50	44	36
1994	22	54	24	1075	*no collective members*				11	56	33	129	6	62	32	47

Centre Party

	voters				members				active members			
	young	mid	old	n	young	mid	old	n	young	mid	old	n
1960	13	66	21	194	14	70	16	57	11	78	11	18
1964	13	64	23	359	7	71	22	103	*no data available*			
1968	19	59	22	464	8	71	21	95	3	78	19	31
1970	22	55	23	268	13	64	23	39	*no data available*			
1979	21	49	30	442	10	63	27	102	10	61	29	49
1985	20	51	29	283	10	56	34	83	6	60	34	35
1988	21	51	28	284	9	51	40	68	11	46	43	35
1991	16	54	30	208	6	57	37	68	3	55	42	31
1994	23	48	29	200	8	43	49	53	13	43	44	23

Moderate Party

	voters				members				active members			
	young	mid	old	n	young	mid	old	n	young	mid	old	n
1960	16	62	22	181	8	69	23	51	0	71	29	7
1964	15	53	32	265	10	64	26	72	*no data available*			
1968	19	56	25	278	5	67	28	61	8	75	17	12
1970	20	53	27	113	6	63	31	32	*no data available*			
1979	17	61	22	526	15	57	28	60	11	56	33	18
1985	26	53	21	527	14	57	29	69	16	53	31	19
1988	25	52	23	401	12	52	36	58	15	39	46	13
1991	31	49	20	520	24	45	31	42	19	50	31	16
1994	26	50	24	477	14	49	37	43	13	60	27	15

Comment: Sources: Swedish Election Studies, all years. Young 1960-1964: 22-30. Young 1968: 21-30. Young 1970: 20-30. Young 1979-1994: 18-30. Mid = middle aged (31-60 all years). Old: 61-80 all years. Members include members of women's and youth organisations (if any) from 1979 onwards. Members are included among electorate and party voters.

The youngest age group did grow among the membership categories after 1979, but it is still on the whole under-represented. Since the late 1960s, about one-quarter of the electorate has been 30 or below, but never more than 15 per cent of the national aggregate of individual members have been in that age category. The under-representation is even clearer among the active members.

The oldest age group has a different story. On the national level, it has been slightly over-represented among individual members on most time points (not to the same extent among total members, where the percentage has mostly been very similar to that of the electorate). The differences in percentage points have increased in later years, leaving the old group clearly over-represented among the members in the 1980s and 1990s. This pattern is repeated, in fact accentuated, among the active members. In 1994, 33 per cent of all active party members were aged between 61 and 80, compared to 23 per cent of the electorate.

On the party level, the national pattern has largely been followed. The over-representation of the old is very clear in the 1990s, especially in the Centre Party, but in earlier years the differences in percentage terms between the parties' respective voters and members have tended to be quite small; there are also cases of the oldest age group having been under-represented, for example among individual Social Democratic members in 1979 and 1988, Centre Party members in 1960, 1964 and 1979 and Moderate members in 1964.

The middle group is a little bit too crude to be really meaningful. It has mostly been quite proportionately represented, sometimes over-represented, among the members. Among the active members it has clearly been over-represented, although the extent has decreased in recent years. Again, the situation is similar in the three parties.

The party members' age representativeness has similarities but also important differences to what was found about gender. The members are not representative in terms of gender, but this has been so throughout the research period. The age variable has developed towards decreasing representativeness, which is of particular relevance for the overall purpose of this study.

Is this good or bad? From a participatory perspective, the findings in this section cannot be regarded as anything but detrimental. The membership stock is becoming older; young people are clearly being under-represented and the older over-represented. Unlike the case of gender, this situation is the same among activists as well as all individual party members. The fact that the average age has been rising suggests that the parties are having increasing difficulties recruiting members and activists from the younger generations. In this way, young people seem to be turning their backs on the parties. If this trend cannot be halted, political parties could soon be entering a participatory deficit among younger people, which will become increasingly difficult to remedy.

From an equity perspective, it must be considered a problem that the quarter of the nation's population aged between 18 and 30 is so clearly under-represented and that the difference in average age is increasing. It is already a well-established fact that political élites are not age representative. This may or may not be serious enough, but if even grass root participants are not representative, the parties may be losing their legitimacy with the younger generations. If this is not remedied, and future generations remain under-represented while the currently young cannot be converted, the Swedish parties are likely to be facing a serious problems.

On the other hand, the fact that the oldest age group is becoming increasingly over-represented has its own political implications. In Sweden, older people have from time to time been very critical against political decisions concerning areas such as pensions and care of the elderly. In the 1990s at least two pensioner's parties have been formed.[39] Even if these parties so far have been unsuccessful, there are recurring signs that not only the young, but also the old may be seeing themselves as involved in a social conflict of interest. But the findings from Tables 7.2 and 7.3 suggest that the older people are not badly represented in the parties. If any age group in Sweden has reason to feel under-represented, it is the young.

In the Swedish Parliament, the dominance of the middle-aged group is even more accentuated than among party members. Both the youngest and oldest age groups are clearly under-represented compared to the electorate. This is in itself not difficult to explain. It takes time to be able to compete seriously for election as a Member of Parliament and the parties usually expect their parliamentarians to retire after they have reached the pension age of 65. Nevertheless, the average age of the members of the Swedish Riksdag after the 1994 election was 48.7 (50.6 in 1991). Thus, while the parliament

---

[39] Two pensioners parties took part, without success, in the Swedish elections in 1991 and 1994. A new pensioner's party was launched in the summer of 1996 (Göteborgs-Posten 20 June 1996).

is not representative of the youngest and oldest age groups, it is on average more age representative than the party organisations.[40]

From a representational perspective, the results of this section are more open to interpretation. The key issue is whether age is an important criterion of representation. To return to Pitkin's definition, can older people be expected not to act according to the interests of, and in a manner responsive to, younger people? The answer can depend on various assumptions. It may, for example, be argued that with age comes experience and an increasing ability to make difficult judgements in a balanced way while still appreciating and considering the interests of younger people. At the same time, life experiences of older people may be so different to those of young generations that the representatives will not be able to fully appreciate the concerns of the younger persons among those that they represent.

Educational representativeness

The first two variables that have been probed into are of demographic rather than directly social nature. The focus now shifts to variables which are more directly related to social status. The most common approach in social science research is to regard education as an indicator of class.

The correlation between educational level and status, income and living standard is well known. Social class, based on occupational categories, will be studied in the next section. According to a slightly different perspective, however, education as such has important cultural and social implications, so much so that educational differences could develop into a conflict of interest. This conflict may be directly related to educational issues but also to media and culture politics. Seen this way, education can be regarded as a social cleavage in its own right.

In research on party attachment, education is a controversial issue. Many scholars have hypothesised education as a predisposition for political activity and organisational membership. The reasoning is that education is a personal resource which can be expected to be positively correlated to party involvement.[41] According to this view, party membership is something of an élite phenomenon. On the other hand, it has been argued that people with

---

[40] The figures on parliamentarians are taken from The Riksdag in Figures 1994/95 (distributed by Riksdagens Förvaltningskontor), p. 4.

[41] Listhaug 1989:191-199.

better education have no need for traditional party activities. Instead, they use other more effective means for their political ends. This line of reasoning is especially prevalent in the 'decline of party' debate. An example is a much cited work by Dalton, Flanagan and Beck. They present a model, openly labelled functionalist, which predicts a general partisan dealignment among citizens at large. The main reason given is the increasing level of education and, hence, sophistication.[42] According to this view, party membership is a means for underprivileged groups to promote their interests.

To compare educational levels over as long a time period as between 1960 and 1994 is problematic. During this period, an educational explosion has taken place. A person with a *studentexamen* (the educational level required for eligibility for university studies) was considered highly educated in 1960. Since then, the number of people to have obtained this level has multiplied. In the process, its status has diminished. Today, it is very unusual for students to leave school after the obligatory nine-year comprehensive education. The number of people to attend university-level education has also increased enormously. This of course means that the proportion of highly educated people has increased among the party members and activists. But the problem addressed in this section is if this has happened at the same rate as among the voters. According to the argument of Dalton, Flanagan and Beck, the educational explosion cannot be expected to be reflected among party members to the same extent. Instead, the highly educated would be constantly under-represented among the members. According to the opposite, more traditional view, party members can be expected to be disproportionately well educated.

The Swedish Election Studies have always made very detailed codings of educational levels. The comparability over time is problematic, however. This is because the educational system has changed considerably during the research period but also because of variations in coding principles. To simplify the data, and to make comparisons over time reasonably meaningful, the educational levels have been collapsed into two main categories. The high education category includes those who have obtained finished a three or four year *gymnasium* education and/or have attended university or equivalent education. All others have been put into the 'low plus middle' category. Therefore, the latter category is very diverse. It includes older people whose only education is the old obligatory six year *folkskola* as well as those with two year *gymnasium* education which is

---

[42] Dalton, Flanagan and Beck 1984:460f, Listhaug 1989:191.

sufficient to be eligible for some university courses (but those who have proceeded to university are included in the 'high' category). Still, it will make it possible to study the development of the really highly educated and the differences between party members and the voters in this respect. Following the discussion above, this is the most relevant aspect of the educational representativeness of party members.

The percentage distributions of the educational dichotomy among members and voters appears in Table 7.4. The table is constructed in the same way as Table 7.1 on gender. Positive differences indicate that there are more highly educated among the members than among the voters, and vice versa. The overall development of the educational level of the Swedish population is apparent in the upper left section of the table which shows the distribution among the electorate as a whole. The trend is unmistakable: the general educational level has increased substantially. In 1960, seven per cent met the criterion for the top educational level. After a continuous increase, the corresponding proportion in 1994 was 39 per cent of the electorate. In this light, the fact that the educational level among the members has increased is trivial. The interesting point is comparisons with the voters at a given time point; whether it has increased to the same extent and with the same speed as among the electorate and the parties' respective voters.

On the national level, all three membership strata have followed the general trend quite closely. The differences between members and the electorate are seldom statistically significant. There is a weak tendency for individual members to have changed from being somewhat more highly educated than the electorate in the 1960s and 1970s to being slightly less well educated in the 1980s and 1990s. However, the differences are always small and the general observation must be that party members have followed the same trend as the general public. This also applies to active and total (including collective) members.

The voters of all the three studied parties have followed the general educational explosion. Nevertheless, the individual parties have different educational profiles. The Moderates have always had a bigger proportion of highly educated voters than the electorate as a whole, while the situation in the Centre Party and the Social Democrats is the opposite. Of the two latter parties, the Centre Party has tended to have slightly bigger proportions of highly educated voters than the Social Democrats, although the differences have been very small in the 1990s.

Table 7.4 Educational levels of Swedish electorate, party voters, party members and activists, 1960-1994. Percentages

Nation

	electorate			total members				ind. members				active members			
	low+mid	high	n	low+mid	high	diff.	n	low+mid	high	diff.	n	low+mid	high	diff.	n
1960	93	7	1464	91	9	2	260	*no data available*				91	9	2	57
1964	93	7	2842	93	7	0	494	*no data available*				*no data available*			
1968	90	10	2892	92	8	-2	450	89	11	1	311	91	9	-1	98
1970	91	9	1318	90	10	1	171	88	12	3	138	*no data available*			
1979	80	20	2816	80	20	0	429	76	24	4*	339	79	21	1	176
1985	73	27	2770	76	24	-3	446	70	30	3	342	69	31	4	163
1988	70	30	2668	75	25	-5*	338	73	27	-3	315	69	31	1	125
1991	66	34	2602	*no collective members*				68	32	-2	261	67	33	-1	99
1994	61	39	2528	*no collective members*				65	35	-4	263	61	39	0	103

Social Democrats

	voters			total members				ind. members				active members			
	low+mid	high	n	low+mid	high	diff.	n	low+mid	high	diff.	n	low+mid	high	diff.	n
1960	98	2	662	99	1	-1	124	*no data available*				100	0	-2	27
1964	98	2	1245	97	3	1	246	*no data available*				*no data available*			
1968	96	4	1435	96	4	0	236	92	8	4*	97	93	7	3	46
1970	97	3	559	96	4	1	78	94	6	3	47	*no data available*			
1979	90	10	1151	90	10	0	221	85	15	5*	131	85	15	5	87
1985	85	15	1101	87	13	-2	233	82	18	3	129	80	20	5	76
1988	83	17	1042	87	13	-4	169	86	14	-3	146	82	18	1	49
1991	78	22	853	*no collective members*				75	25	3	107	77	23	1	35
1994	71	29	1022	*no collective members*				76	24	-5	129	77	23	-6	47

Centre Party

	voters			members				active members			
	low+mid	high	n	low+mid	high	diff.	n	low+mid	high	diff.	n
1960	98	2	194	100	0	- 2	57	100	0	- 2	18
1964	97	3	359	98	2	- 1	103	*no data available*			
1968	91	9	464	98	2	- 7*	95	100	0	- 9*	31
1970	93	7	268	100	0	- 7*	39	*no data available*			
1979	85	15	432	89	11	- 4	101	88	12	- 3	48
1985	81	19	267	89	11	- 8*	83	94	6	-13*	35
1988	74	26	273	87	13	-13*	68	86	14	-12	35
1991	75	25	200	90	10	-15*	67	83	17	- 8	30
1994	72	28	187	85	15	-13*	53	83	17	-11	23

Moderate Party

	voters			members				active members			
	low+mid	high	n	low+mid	high	diff.	n	low+mid	high	diff.	n
1960	76	24	181	59	41	17*	51	29	71	47*	7
1964	74	26	265	74	26	0	72	*no data available*			
1968	72	28	278	70	30	2	61	67	33	5	12
1970	70	30	112	66	34	4	32	*no data available*			
1979	62	38	511	44	56	18*	59	59	41	3	17
1985	58	42	506	39	61	19*	69	26	74	32*	19
1988	50	50	378	44	56	6	57	31	69	19	13
1991	50	50	501	33	67	17*	42	31	69	19	16
1994	46	54	456	28	72	18*	43	13	87	33*	15

Comment: Source: Swedish Election Studies. 'High' = attended upper secondary education or higher. 'Low+mid' = lower than 'high' category. 'Diff.' = difference in percentage points between membership stratum and electorate or a party's voters. Positive difference = 'high' over-represented among members, and vice versa. (*) = diff. between percentages significant on .05 level or higher (one-tailed Z test). Members include women's and youth organisations (if any) from 1979 onwards. Members are included among electorate and party voters.

On the membership level, the Centre Party has constantly been the least educated of the three investigated parties, if only individual members are taken into consideration. On every time point that a distinction between individual and collective members is possible, Centre Party members have been less educated than individual Social Democratic members, even if the differences have sometimes been small. Thus, the relative educational profiles of the two parties on the electoral level are reversed on the membership level. This also applies to the activists of the two parties. Social Democratic activists have had a higher overall educational level than their Centre counterparts every year except 1960. The Moderate Party, on the other hand, has constantly had the most educated members and activists as well as voters.

Compared to the respective parties' voters, the educationally most representative party members can be found in the Social Democratic Party. The differences in percentage points with the party's voters are seldom significant. The party's individual members have tended to be somewhat more highly educated than the voters, but this may have started to change in recent years, judging by the negative differences in 1988 and 1994. All differences are small, however, and the party's members have followed the same trend as the party's voters. There are no trends in the representativeness, possibly with the exception of a slight decline among total members.

If the differences between members and voters are small in the Social Democratic Party, they are more substantial in the other two studied parties. But the direction of the differences is not the same. In the Moderate Party, the members are more highly educated than the voters and in the Centre Party it is the other way round. In Centre Party, the differences have increased over time. The members were quite representative of the voters in 1960 and 1964. The proportion highly educated started to increase among Centre Party voters from 1968. The members followed, but more slowly and have become less and less representative. Centre Party activists have also consistently been somewhat less educated than the voters but there is no trend in their degree of representativeness.

The observation that Moderate members are disproportionally well educated does not apply to every year in Table 7.4. The difference has sometimes been large but is not significant in four out of nine time points. In 1964 the percentage distribution was in fact identical between members and voters. The differences tend to be higher in the 1990s than in the 1960s. This pattern of decreased representativeness is disturbed by the large difference in 1960 and the small difference in 1988. It is therefore not quite justified to speak of an overall decline in educational representativeness in the Moderate Party.

As was noted in the beginning of this section, there are conflicting views on the relationship between education and party membership. On the one hand, it has been argued that higher education is a resource which makes party membership redundant. On the other hand, it has been argued that high education is a resource which makes party membership more likely. Previous research has tended to support the latter view. Ola Listhaug concludes in his study on Norwegian party members that the hypothesis of an inverse relationship between educational level and party membership is refuted. Instead he writes that education is a personal resource which correlates positively with membership. Other research have reinforced this observation.[43] However, the findings reported in this section partly contradict those results. In fact, neither of the mentioned hypotheses about the relationship between education and party membership is supported. The totality of party members and activists in Sweden have consistently been fairly representative of the electorate in terms of education. The picture varies somewhat among the different parties, but the differences between members and voters go in conflicting directions. The highly educated are over-represented among Moderate members but under-represented among members of the Centre Party.

Seen this way, there is no general and systematic relationship between education and membership. But this is not a full refutation of Dalton, Flanagan and Beck's theory. As was argued in Chapters 4 and 5, party membership and activity in Sweden has declined since the 1960s. During the same period, the general educational level has increased drastically. Thus, it is possible to argue that increased educational sophistication on the aggregate level has an adverse effect on party membership and activity.

At the same time, however, this does not mean that party members and activists tend be less educated than the general public. As is shown in Table 7.4, this is so only in the Centre Party. While Dalton, Flanagan and Beck base much of their reasoning on developments at the macro level, that the generality of citizens is becoming more educated and sophisticated, the

---

[43] Widfeldt 1995:156-160, Listhaug 1989, Seyd and Whiteley 1992, Whiteley, Seyd and Richardson 1994, Johansson 1971, Oscarsson 1976, Häll 1996.

core of the reasoning ought to have consequences also on the individual level. If more sophisticated citizens need parties less, why are they not more clearly under-represented among party members? It could be that the recent development, at least in the Social Democrats and the Centre Party, are pointing in this direction. For Dalton, Flanagan and Beck's reasoning to hold, however, the highly educated ought to be under-represented among party members and activists in general.

Class and group representativeness

Class is a vital component in a discussion about social representativeness. It is a well known perspective to regard differences between social classes as a major source of political and social conflict. Even if the composition and size of the classes have changed, and even if class is not quite as important as it once was, it remains a key factor in the structuring of party systems and voting behaviour. This is most certainly so in Sweden. As Maria Oskarson has expressed it, "Class voting is still a reality in Sweden."[44]

Like education, the social composition of the Swedish electorate has changed over time. The proportion of working class voters has decreased and the middle class has increased. This development is not nearly as drastic as in the case of education, however. Thus, it is not to the same extent a foregone conclusion that the members have followed the societal trend and, of course, not that they have done so to the same extent. On the party level, it is well known that different parties have different social profiles on the electoral level, especially so in terms of social class. Yet, while class voting remains a key factor in Swedish electoral behaviour, and is still high by international standards, its explanatory power behind voting has decreased over time.[45] It is therefore of additional interest whether the members and activists follow the general development of the voters of their respective parties, or if the parties' traditional social profiles persist longer among the members and activists.

The operationalisation of social class is a complex business. This study will use objective data, where respondents have been asked to indicate

---

[44] Oskarson 1994:233.

[45] Oskarson 1994 is a thorough investigation of the changing nature of class voting in Sweden between 1956 and 1991. Gilljam and Holmberg 1995:98-105 cover the development until 1994.

their current or former occupation. The very detailed information thus extracted is then reduced into occupational categories which, in turn, can be categorised into classes. In other words, the respondents' subjective image of their class belonging is not taken into account.

The long research period of this study brings comparability problems. The working class in Sweden has changed from being chiefly workers in the production sector, to today's situation in which a substantial proportion is employed in the service sector. Hand in hand with this development, the proportion employed by the public sector has increased substantially. A similar development has taken place in the middle class.[46]

Space limitations mean that it will not be possible to account for all these shifts. The operationalisations of class will have to be rather crude. Two variables will be used: class and group. Class, the crudest of the two, uses a simple dichotomisation between working class and middle class. The group variable uses the same singular definition of the working class, but the middle class has been split into three separate categories: salaried employees, self-employed and farmers. The farmers has decreased significantly in proportion but are still of interest, because they remain an important support base for the Centre Party. Students are excluded altogether from both the class and group variables.[47]

The percentage distributions of the class variable appear in Table 7.5. As is readily seen in the top left corner of the table (Nation, electorate), the working class was in a majority among the electorate in the 1960s, but has since been overtaken by the middle class. The shift took place in the 1970s. In 1976 the proportions of working class and middle class were identical (this cannot be seen in the table).[48] However, it can be can be seen in the table that the middle class has been bigger since 1979.

---

[46] Oskarson 1994:77f.

[47] Farmers include only those who own their own farms. Farmhands etc. are coded as working class. The working class category is identical in the class and group categorisations. Both categorisations are based on an eight-fold occupation variable used in the Swedish Election Studies. Maria Oskarson has been responsible for the re-coding of the 1956-1964 Election Studies to create variables which are comparable over time. See further Oskarson 1994:30f. Oskarson has also created set-ups for the 1968 and 1970 Election Studies, to make the variables comparable across time. The occupational codes used in the 1973 through 1994 Election Studies are identical, and have been used as model for the re-coding of the earlier studies.

[48] Oskarson 1994:56.

Table 7.5 Social class distribution of Swedish electorate, party voters, party members and activists, 1960-1994. Percentages

Nation

	electorate			total members				ind. members				active members			
	work	mid	n	work	mid	diff.	n	work	mid	diff.	n	work	mid	diff.	n
1960	56	44	1342	50	50	6*	244	*no data available*				53	47	3	53
1964	51	49	2803	48	52	3	491	*no data available*				*no data available*			
1968	53	47	2785	50	50	3	446	31	69	22*	307	47	53	6	97
1970	55	45	1262	46	54	9*	168	37	63	18*	135	*no data available*			
1979	47	53	2696	42	58	5*	417	32	68	15*	331	36	64	11*	174
1985	43	57	2636	42	58	1	431	29	71	14*	330	30	70	13*	155
1988	43	57	2530	42	58	1	327	39	61	4	304	29	71	14*	120
1991	41	59	2444	*no collective members*				37	63	4	258	33	67	8	98
1994	41	59	2294	*no collective members*				33	67	8*	248	38	62	3	98

Social Democrats

	voters			total members				ind. members				active members			
	work	mid	n	work	mid	diff.	n	work	mid	diff.	n	work	mid	diff.	n
1960	76	24	613	80	20	-4	116	*no data available*				80	20	-4	25
1964	71	29	1242	80	20	-9*	248	*no data available*				*no data available*			
1968	71	29	1398	80	20	-9*	234	61	39	10*	95	80	20	-9	46
1970	70	30	546	71	29	-1	77	61	39	9	46	*no data available*			
1979	67	33	1123	61	39	6*	216	48	52	19*	130	49	51	18*	86
1985	60	40	1074	65	35	-5	225	51	49	9*	124	46	54	14*	72
1988	57	43	1010	63	37	-6	166	61	39	-4	143	51	49	6	49
1991	55	45	820	*no collective members*				54	46	1	109	47	53	8	36
1994	52	48	956	*no collective members*				49	51	3	124	48	52	4	46

Centre Party

	voters			members				active members			
	work	mid	n	work	mid	diff.	n	work	mid	diff.	n
1960	35	65	181	22	78	13*	55	31	69	4	16
1964	29	71	355	11	89	18*	102	*no data available*			
1968	34	66	450	12	88	22*	94	10	90	24*	31
1970	44	56	249	19	81	25*	37	*no data available*			
1979	37	63	412	30	70	7	101	29	71	8	48
1985	34	66	258	23	77	11*	83	17	83	17*	35
1988	35	65	264	29	71	6	66	18	82	17*	34
1991	39	61	195	32	68	7	68	32	68	7	31
1994	34	66	171	24	76	10	50	41	59	-7	22

Moderate Party

	voters			members				active members			
	work	mid	n	work	mid	diff.	n	work	mid	diff.	n
1960	20	80	164	11	89	9	46	0	100	20	7
1964	16	84	257	6	94	10*	69	*no data available*			
1968	17	83	265	12	88	5	60	17	83	0	12
1970	18	82	103	19	81	-1	32	*no data available*			
1979	16	84	490	7	93	9*	55	11	89	5	18
1985	20	80	479	6	94	14*	66	12	88	8	17
1988	17	83	340	7	93	10*	54	0	100	17	11
1991	23	77	472	11	89	12*	37	8	92	15	13
1994	17	83	421	7	93	10*	41	21	79	-4	14

Comment: Source: Swedish Election Studies. Work = working class. Mid = middle class. Categories based on 8-fold occupational classification. Students excluded from percentage base. 'Diff.' = difference in percentage points between membership stratum (total, individual and active members respectively) and the electorate or a party's voters. Positive difference = middle class over-represented among members, and vice versa. (*) = difference significant on 05 level or higher (one-tailed Z test). Students excluded from the percentage base. Members include members of women's and youth organisations (if any) from 1979 onwards. Members included among electorate and voters. See also note 47 in this chapter.

The total (including collective) members category has followed this development. The middle class has always been over-represented and the working class under-represented among the total members, but the differences have mostly been very small and the national trends have been followed. If collective members are excluded, however, the situation becomes different. There, the proportions of working class and middle class have not changed in any particular direction. The middle class has always constituted about two-thirds of the individual members. This stability means that the representation of the respective classes among the members has changed. In the 1960s, workers were clearly under-represented among the members, and the middle class over-represented. The degree of these discrepancies with the electorate has decreased continually, however, and in the 1990s both the working class and middle class is proportionally represented among individual members on the aggregate national level.

The difference between total and individual members is perhaps not surprising, since the collective members have been predominantly working class, which compensates for the middle class domination among individual members. This, in turn, explains why the class distribution among total members has been more similar to that of the electorate.[49] A more intriguing observation is that the class distribution among individual members has remained so constant over time, despite ongoing changes in society at large. If collective members are included, class representativeness among party members has always been high. If only individual members are taken into account, there has been a clear increase. This is because reality has caught up with the members, not vice versa. The middle class has consistently dominated also among the active members (except in 1960). Also here, this means that the representativeness has increased.

The class distribution of Social Democratic voters and members has developed in directions similar to the electorate as a whole. The voters used to be overwhelmingly dominated by the working class. This domination has decreased continuously, but in 1994 workers still constituted a narrow majority of the voters. The decreased working class dominance is reflected also among the party's members. In the 1960s, 80 per cent of the total members were working class; in 1988 the proportion had decreased to 63 per

---

[49] On the time points where it is possible to distinguish among collective and individual members, the following percentages of the solely collectively enrolled members have been reported to be working class: 1968: 93%. 1970: 96%. 1979: 80%. 1985: 82%. 1988: 78%.

cent. Thus, the majority of total members were still working class at the time when collective membership was abolished.

The individual Social Democratic members have followed a similar pattern, although it has not been totally continuous. The percentage of workers increased between 1979 and 1988. In the 1990s, however, this short term trend was sharply reversed and in 1994 the middle class again overtook the workers, after having done so first in 1979. The active members, on the other hand, have been quite evenly split between working and middle class since 1979. In 1960 and 1968, however, they were overwhelmingly dominated by workers. The traditional party for the Swedish working class is changing in its class composition on the electoral as well as organisational level. In the 1990s, the party's members and activists resemble their voters more closely than before. Again, this is primarily because the voters have caught up with the members instead of vice versa. Until 1985, the party's individual and active members were middle class to a higher extent than the voters. Since 1988, they are fairly class representative.

The class distribution has remained fairly stable in the Centre and Moderate parties. They have both been dominated by the middle class, on electoral, membership and activist level. This dominance is especially strong in the Moderate Party. The middle class has frequently tended to be over-represented among members and activists in both parties. However, the size of this discrepancy has not gone in the same direction. In the Centre Party, the members are have become more class representative of their voters after 1970. In the Moderate Party, the situation is less clear cut. In the 1980s and 1990s, the middle class dominance among Moderate members was more accentuated than in 1968 and 1970. Counting from 1960, however, there is no clear and continuous trend. The smallest percentage difference are observed in 1968 and 1970, and the development is perhaps best described as curvilinear.

So far, the presented evidence suggests that party members in Sweden have become more class representative over time. On the party level, this national development is echoed in the Social Democratic and Centre parties. Rather than making these conclusions final, however, the evidence will be extended. The middle class category used so far is very crude. It includes very diverse professions and does not very well reflect the changes in social groups in Sweden since 1960. The group variable, mentioned above, distinguishes among three sub-categories of the middle class -- salaried employees, self-employed and farmers. This will better take into account the different social profiles of the three parties and also make possible a more refined account of the longitudinal development.

The social group distributions appear in Table 7.6. The discussion in connection with the table will concentrate on the three separated middle classes. Together, they add up to the middle class proportions in Table 7.5, and the proportion working class is the same in both tables.[50] Unlike Tables 7.1, 7.4 and 7.5, Table 7.6 does not specify the percentage differences between members and voters. This is because it includes more categories than any of the earlier tables. The representativeness of the party members can be more easily studied in Table 7.7, which presents the aggregate differences between the percentage distributions in Table 7.6.

Before elaborating on group representativeness, some observations will be made on the group distribution of the party members and voters. Of the three separated middle class categories, the proportion of salaried employees has doubled among the electorate between 1960 and 1994. The proportion of farmers has been reduced by two-thirds, while the proportion of self-employed has remained constant. The salaried employees have always been the largest of the three middle class groups. In the 1960s, farmers and other self-employed were neck and neck in second place, but since the late 1970s the drastically decreasing number of farmers has meant that they are now clearly the smallest of the three middle class groups.

On the membership level, the salaried employees have always been the biggest middle class group. Since 1979, they have even outnumbered the workers (among individual members). This also applies to the active members. The farmers were very evident among the members in the 1960s. Since then they have decreased, but they have constantly been over-represented among members compared to the electorate. The changes among the electorate have been reflected among the members and activists. Even though the developments year by year have not followed identical patterns, the direction of the changes -- the increases of the salariat, the stability of self-employed and the decrease of the farmers -- have by and large corresponded.

---

[50] There are some minor variations because of rounding errors.

Table 7.6 **Social group distribution of Swedish electorate, party voters, party members and activists, 1960-1994. Percentages**

Nation

	electorate					total members					ind. members					active members				
	wrk	sal	sep	frm	n	wrk	sal	sep	frm	n	wrk	sal	sep	frm	n	wrk	sal	sep	frm	n
1960	56	24	10	10	1342	50	23	9	18	244	*no data available*					53	21	4	22	53
1964	51	29	9	11	2803	48	23	8	21	491	*no data available*					*no data available*				
1968	53	33	7	7	2785	50	24	7	19	446	31	31	10	28	307	47	24	1	28	97
1970	55	32	6	7	1262	47	30	6	17	168	37	34	7	22	135	*no data available*				
1979	46	40	8	6	2696	42	37	6	15	417	32	42	7	19	331	36	41	5	18	174
1985	43	43	10	4	2636	42	37	10	11	431	30	44	12	14	330	29	48	8	15	155
1988	43	45	9	3	2530	42	38	11	9	327	39	40	11	10	304	29	47	11	13	120
1991	41	46	10	3	2444	*no collective members*					37	44	8	11	258	33	47	3	17	98
1994	41	47	9	3	2294	*no collective members*					33	44	10	13	248	38	42	10	10	98

Social Democrats

	voters					total members					ind. members					active members				
	wrk	sal	sep	frm	n	wrk	sal	sep	frm	n	wrk	sal	sep	frm	n	wrk	sal	sep	frm	n
1960	76	18	4	2	613	80	15	5	0	116	*no data available*					80	16	4	0	25
1964	71	23	4	2	1242	80	16	3	1	248	*no data available*					*no data available*				
1968	71	25	4	0	1398	80	18	2	0	234	61	35	4	0	95	80	20	0	0	46
1970	70	25	4	1	546	71	29	0	0	77	61	39	0	0	46	*no data available*				
1979	67	29	3	1	1123	61	36	2	1	216	48	47	4	1	130	49	50	1	0	86
1985	60	35	4	1	1074	65	30	4	1	225	51	42	6	1	124	46	47	6	1	72
1988	57	38	4	1	1010	63	32	5	0	166	61	34	5	0	143	51	45	4	0	49
1991	55	41	4	0	820	*no collective members*					54	45	0	1	109	47	50	0	3	36
1994	52	43	4	1	956	*no collective members*					49	44	6	1	124	48	46	4	2	46

Centre Party

	voters					members					active members				
	wrk	sal	sep	frm	n	wrk	sal	sep	frm	n	wrk	sal	sep	frm	n
1960	35	10	7	48	181	22	5	2	71	55	31	0	0	69	16
1964	29	14	10	47	355	11	7	3	79	102	*no data available*				
1968	34	28	9	29	450	12	7	8	73	94	10	10	3	77	31
1970	44	26	8	22	249	19	14	5	62	37	*no data available*				
1979	37	31	8	24	412	30	16	3	51	101	29	17	2	52	48
1985	34	31	8	27	258	23	20	10	47	83	17	17	12	54	35
1988	35	34	11	20	264	29	21	12	38	66	18	26	15	41	34
1991	39	37	7	17	195	32	18	12	38	68	32	20	3	45	31
1994	34	32	12	22	171	24	16	10	50	50	41	14	13	32	22

Moderate Party

	voters					members					active members				
	wrk	sal	sep	frm	n	wrk	sal	sep	frm	n	wrk	sal	sep	frm	n
1960	20	45	21	14	164	11	59	19	11	46	0	86	0	14	7
1964	16	56	15	13	257	6	61	17	16	69	*no data available*				
1968	17	57	12	14	265	12	58	13	17	60	17	66	0	17	12
1970	18	54	15	13	103	19	47	19	15	32	*no data available*				
1979	15	62	17	7	490	7	62	18	13	55	11	39	22	28	18
1985	20	54	22	4	479	6	70	23	1	66	12	76	6	6	17
1988	17	58	22	3	340	7	63	26	4	54	0	82	18	0	11
1991	23	55	18	4	472	11	65	19	5	37	8	69	8	15	13
1994	17	60	20	3	421	7	68	17	8	41	21	72	7	0	14

Comment: Sources: Swedish Election Studies. Wrk = working class. Sal = salaried employees. Sep = self-employed. Frm = farmers. The categories have been made out of an eight category occupational classification which has been re-coded in the 1960, 1964, 1968 and 1970 Election Studies to enable comparisons over time (see also note 47 in this chapter). Students are excluded from the percentage base. Members include members of women's and youth organisations (if any) from 1979 onwards. Members are included among electorate and party voters.

As was already observed in connection with Table 7.5, the social profile of the Social Democrats has changed substantially over time. Table 7.6 adds little new information in this respect. The proportion of farmers and self-employed has constantly been low, and the entire increase of the middle class among the party's voters can be attributed to the increased number of salaried employees. The same applies to the party's members and activists. The long term changes take place among the workers and the salaried employees.

In the Centre and Moderate parties, however, Table 7.6 adds valuable new information. The Centre Party is by tradition a party of farmers. The decreased proportion of farmers in the nation is reflected also among the Centre Party members and activists but they have still remained over-represented compared to the electorate as a whole. In 1994, half of the party's members were still farmers, compared to 13 per cent of the aggregate total of party members, and 3 per cent of the electorate. The Moderate Party is dominated by salaried employees, but is also notable for disproportionate number of self-employed, on electoral as well as membership level. The party used to have a sizeable minority of farmers, but they have diminished after 1970.

The overall group representativeness of party members and activists, measured as the aggregate size of the percentage differences between members and voters, is shown in Table 7.7. The measure can vary between 0 (the two percentage distributions are identical) and 100 (means that there is a maximum difference).[51] Thus, the lower the figure, the more representative the members/activists. Because of the many categories, this aggregate measure cannot indicate the direction of the difference between the two percentage distributions. The measure cannot take into account that, for example, workers are over-represented, but self-employed under-represented, among the members. Such information is found in Table 7.6.

---

[51] For two percentage distributions with four categories, the maximum measure of 100 would be the result if the distributions among two groups were as follows:

Group 1: 50   0   50   0
Group 2: 0 50   0 50

Table 7.7 **Development of social group representativeness of Swedish party members and activists, 1960-1994. Differences between percentage distributions: the lower the figure, the higher the representativeness.**

	Nation tot.	Nation ind.	Nation act.	SD tot.	SD ind.	SD act.	C memb.	C act.	M memb.	M act.
1960	8	---	12	5	---	4	23	21	14	41
1964	10	---	---	9	---	---	32	---	10	---
1968	12	24	21	9	10	9	44	48	5	12
1970	10	18	---	5	14	---	40	---	7	---
1979	9	15	13	7	19	21	27	28	8	26
1985	7	13	16	5	9	14	22	31	17	24
1988	8	9	14	7	5	7	19	25	10	24
1991	---	8	15	---	5	12	26	28	12	25
1994	---	11	8	---	3	4	28	18	13	16

Comment: The table is based on Table 7.6. Nation tot. = total (including collective) members in the whole nation compared to the electorate. Nation ind. = all individual party members in the nation compared to the electorate. Nation act. = all active party members in the nation compared to the electorate. SD tot. = Members of the Social Democratic Party (including collective members) compared to Social Democratic voters. SD. ind. = individual members of the Social Democratic Party compared to Social Democratic voters. SD act. = active members of the Social Democratic Party compared to Social Democratic voters. C memb. = members of the Centre Party compared to Centre Party voters. C act. = active members of the Centre Party compared to Centre Party voters. M memb. = members of the Moderate Party compared to Moderate Party voters. M act. = active members of the Moderate Party compared to Moderate Party voters. The entries of the table are the differences between the respective percentage distributions in Table 7.6. The differences are calculated as follows: The differences between each category (e.g. the difference between the per cent working class among the electorate and the per cent working class among total members in the nation, and so on with salaried employees, self-employed and farmers), are all added together and the resulting sum is divided by two. This is a simplified version of Kent Asp's correspondence coefficient for differences between percentage distributions (Asp 1986:135f). The same method has been used in a study on the representativeness of Swedish parliamentarians (Holmberg and Esaiasson 1988:137) and a comparative study on the representativeness of party members in Europe (Widfeldt 1995, see explanatory note on p. 148).

Table 7.7. tells us that, on the aggregate national level, individual members have become more representative over time. So have individual Social Democratic members (and activists between 1979 and 1994). Members of both the Centre and Moderate parties display trendless fluctuation. Nor can any clear trend can be attributed to Centre and Moderate activists, but in both cases their representativeness was high in 1994 compared to earlier years. Few of these observations are in blatant contradiction to the differences between class dichotomies in Table 7.5, except, possibly, the Centre Party, where there is less evidence of increased representativeness in terms of group than in the dichotomous class variable. The Social Democrats have the most representative members of the three studied parties, in terms of class as well as group. The combined evidence from the class dichotomy and the four category group classification, shows that party members in Sweden are more class representative in the 1990s than before.

Conclusion and comparative outlook

The development of the social representativeness of the Swedish party members is summarised in Figure 7.1. With the exception of the age variable, it is hard to find clear cases of decreased representativeness, neither on the aggregate national level, nor among the different parties.[52] Therefore, the findings in this chapter show little evidence of a decline in social representativeness.

Figure 7.1 The development of social representativeness of party members and activists in Sweden 1960-1994

	Gender	Age	Education	Class	Group
Sweden (nation) total members	(increase)	(decline)	(decline)	increase	no trend
Sweden (nation) individual members	no trend	decline	no trend	increase	increase
Sweden (nation) active members	(increase)	decline	no trend	increase	(increase)
Social Democrats total members	increase	increase	(decline)	no trend	stability
Social Democrats individual members	(increase)	no trend	stability	increase	increase
Social Democrats active members	(increase)	decline	no trend	increase	increase
Centre Party members	no trend	decline	decline	increase	no trend
Centre Party active members	(increase)	(decline)	(decline)	no trend	(increase)
Moderate Party members	(increase)	decline	no trend	no trend	no trend
Moderate Party active members	(decline)	(increase)	(decline)	no trend	(increase)

Comment: The entries in the cells are summaries of the trends for the respective party membership stratum. Brackets indicate that the evidence of an increase or decline is inconclusive. The row 'Gender' is based on Table 7.1. The row 'Age' is based on Table 7.2. The row 'Education' is based on Table 7.4. The row 'Class' is based on Table 7.5. The row 'group' is based on Tables 7.6 and 7.7. The summarised trends for total (i.e. including collective) members in the nation and of the Social Democrats are based on the development between 1960 and 1988. The summarised trends for individual members in the nation and of the Social Democrats are based on the development between 1968 and 1994. The summarised trends for members of the Centre and Moderate parties are based on the development between 1960 and 1994. The summarised trends for active members in the nation and of all parties are based on the development between 1979 and 1994 (data on active members from 1960 and 1968 are not taken into account because of inconsistent operationalisations of activity).

---

[52] The recent development in education, where party members are now marginally less educated than the electorate, could if it continues mean that members are becoming less representative in this respect. The size of the differences between individual members and the electorate has not changed much between 1970 and 1994, however, and have been significant only in 1970.

This conclusion is not least valid for active members on the national level. Their development over time has been similar to that of the totality of individual members. However, they are also showing signs of increasing gender representativeness. Thus, from a representational perspective, where activity is implied, the conclusion of no decline is accentuated.

Despite the general conclusion of no overall decline, there are some variations among the different parties. There most encouraging signs are for the Social Democrats, who have become less representative in only one of the five studied variables (Social Democratic activists in terms of age). The situation is somewhat more ambiguous for the Centre Party and the Moderates, as they have both become less representative in terms of age and, at least the Centre Party, in education.

Whether this leads to a more negative conclusion for the Centre and Moderate parties is open to question. In neither of the two parties is there a clear decline in a majority of the studied indicators. If we begin to put different weights to the different variables, there is again room for a positive conclusion. It could be argued that the two variables where a decline has been observed for the two parties, age and education, are less crucial from a linkage perspective than gender, class and group, where there is no clear case of a decline.

Besides the overall conclusion, the evidence presented allows several additional observations. The typical Swedish party member is male. This has constantly been so between 1960 and 1994, and while the gender difference among the members has not increased, it has remained. It does, however, seem to have narrowed among the activists. Furthermore, the Swedish party member is middle-aged, and has constantly been older than the average citizen, a difference which has become more accentuated in recent years. He has constantly belonged to the middle class. He is not highly educated, although the proportion of highly educated members is increasing. Thus, although it would be incorrect to describe the social profile of Swedish party members as stable during the 1960-1994 period, the main social characteristics of the average member have remained quite similar.

Of the three different parties, the Moderates tended to be the most representative until 1970. Their members displayed comparatively low differences against the party's voters in terms of class, age and gender. They were also competitive in terms of education. It is a somewhat surprising observation that the most cadre-like of the three parties was the most representative of its voters at a time which was characterised by traditional class cleavages to a higher extent than in the 1990s. Of course, the Moderate Party was not more representative compared to the electorate, only to their own voters. It is still interesting to note that there tended to be bigger differences between voters and members in the two parties with movement origins.

In the 1990s, however, the picture has changed. The Social Democrats are now the most representative in terms of class and education. They are also comparing well in the age variable but less so in terms of gender. The Moderates are very gender representative, and comparable to the other parties in terms of age, but are decidedly less representative in terms of education and class. Thus, the Social Democrats have now gained the relative position that they might have been expected to have had all along. This has happened because their voters have become more middle class and, hence, caught up with the members, where the class distribution has been stable over time.

The Centre Party has, at times, been competitive in terms of gender representativeness. However, it has developed from the most to the least representative in terms of age. A similar development can be observed in the education variable. The party's representativeness in terms of group and class has increased but in terms of group it was in 1994 the least representative of the three parties.

It is of interest to note that there is no general tendency for the different social profiles of the parties' voters to be exaggerated among the members or activists. There are examples of such a social exaggeration effect, such as the disproportionate percentage of farmers among Centre Party members and activists, and the amount of self-employed on the organisational level of the Moderate Party. However, workers tend to be under-represented among individual Social Democratic members.

Comparability problems mean that longitudinal comparisons with the active members only stretch back to 1979. The Centre Party activists seem to fare better than the members on the gender variable but that apart, available evidence suggests that the patterns and developments among members remain among activists.

In a comparative study on the representativeness of party members in Western Europe, Swedish members were not found to be particularly socially representative in an international perspective. On the aggregate national level, class was the variable where Sweden was most representative, but much less so in terms of gender and age. Overall, Sweden was somewhere in the middle among the 15 investigated countries. Among the 37 parties included in the study, the Swedish Centre Party was the fifth most socially representative. The Social Democrats were 10th and the Moderate Party 20th.[53]

If, despite the warning signs for the Centre Party and the Moderates, the general conclusion of this chapter is no overall decline in social representativeness, then the mentioned comparative study is a caveat against too rosy a picture. With the exception of the class variable, Swedish party members are not proven to be socially representative in an international comparison. Thus, there is cause for restraint. The findings in this chapter do not point towards a decline in social representativeness for the Swedish parties during the past 35 years. The international comparison suggests that the picture could change with other reference points.

From the perspective of this study, however, the conclusion is somewhat more positive. There are differences in social composition between members and voters. The conditions for the parties to use their members as 'ambassadors to the community' are not ideal. But, and this is the important thing, they have not become worse since the 1960s.

---

[53] Widfeldt 1995:164f. This is not identical to their relative positions in this study at the same time point (1988). The reasons are that the comparative study used different operationalisations of some variables, that the education variable was not taken into account when making the overall comparison due to lack of comparable data, and that side organisation members were not included, to ensure comparability with other countries.

8 Opinion Representativeness of Party Members and Activists

Introduction

The evidence presented so far, with declines in party membership and activism, means that two of the necessary conditions for participatory linkage have not been met. The fact that there has been found no evidence of a decline in social representativeness does not alter this general conclusion. Therefore, the first part of the main question of this study must be given a negative answer: The Swedish parties have suffered a participatory linkage decline.

Attention now shifts from participatory to representative linkage. If the parties seem to be failing to provide linkage between citizens and the state by getting the citizens to participate, how well to they represent the people? Can they, after all, provide linkage in the sense that their members and activists are representative of the voters in terms of opinion? As has been argued in Chapters 2 and 7, representativeness in terms of opinion is a necessary condition for representative linkage. Since the two other necessary conditions for representative linkage, openness and internal membership influence (which are necessary conditions for both participatory and representative linkage), have been found to be met in Chapter 3, at least on the aggregate national level, opinion representativeness will be decisive.

One of the most recurrent criticisms against political parties is that they have distanced themselves from the public. Popular discontent against politics and parties is often based on a notion of parties as unresponsive and out of touch with the general public. In Sweden, the proportion of the electorate that agrees when confronted with statements like "the parties are only concerned with the winning of votes, not the thoughts and feelings of ordinary people" has increased quite drastically over time.[1]

Such criticism can include the perception of parties as being unrepresentative. It is not necessarily that straightforward, however. Otto Kirchheimer's critical account of the development of catch-all parties is partly based on the observation that, in the quest for vote maximisation, the

---

[1] Gilljam and Holmberg 1995:85. In 1968, 37 per cent agreed with such a statement; in 1994, the proportion had increased to 69 per cent.

parties have adopted standpoints so similar and so vague that they can hardly be distinguished from each other. It is somewhat unclear whether he means that this constitutes a lack of actual opinion representativeness, or that the parties are failing to pursue the actual interests of their voters and supporters, as opposed to their manifest opinions.[2]

Michels's position on the problem was élitist. His criticism against the oligarchy in parties was not based on a notion of ordinary citizens as deprived of rightful influence. His view was that the 'masses' were often so unsophisticated in their outlook that representative parties were not desirable at all. At the same time he acknowledged that this would be different if the general educational level and popular sophistication increased, which he anticipated would happen.[3] Still, several decades later, J. A. Schumpeter, and B. R. Berelson et al. argued that the majority of voters were so superficial and unknowledgeable that their opinions were not fit to be transformed into policies.[4] Even today, similar arguments exist based on the assumption that popular opinions are simplistic and intransitive.

At the same time, it is not difficult to find arguments to the contrary. In a political system which to a very large extent is based on representation, and where the parties are still considered as key actors, lack of opinion representativeness would be detrimental to their legitimacy. It can be argued that the knowledge of the general public has now reached a level high enough to disqualify any arguments based on lack of sophistication. Russell Dalton argues that "citizen-élite agreement is the normal standard for judging the representativeness of a political system", and goes even further when he concludes that similarity in opinion between decision makers and the public is a "basic goal for democracy".[5] Huber and Bingham Powell subscribe to the same view in their declaration, "...we do think that congruence between the preferences of citizens and the actions of policy-makers constitutes a major claim and goal of liberal democracy."[6]

The concept of opinion representativeness is not unambiguous. Even if representativeness is accepted as a basic goal, it is not necessarily desirable that the representatives are the mirror image of the opinions of the

---

[2] Kirchheimer 1966.

[3] Michels 1915/1968:369f.

[4] Schumpeter 1942/1952. Berelson, Lazarsfeld and McPhee 1954/1986.

[5] Dalton 1996:241.

[6] Huber and Bingham Powell 1992:2.

represented at any given time. Because the representatives are more frequently involved in politics and have more time to study the complexities of the issues, they may come to certain conclusions before the public has had time to do so. It is then the task of the representatives to convey these conclusions to the represented, and seek their subsequent approval. According to this perspective, the representatives are *opinion leaders*. According to the opposite perspective, where the representatives register the popular opinion and then act according to it, they are *opinion followers*. Thus, opinion congruence at any given time needs not be a categorical requirement, because it can be argued that a time lag between the views of representatives and represented should be allowed. Still, any notion of opinion representativeness as a norm should imply that the opinions converge at some point, sooner or later.

It is also appropriate to bear in mind that the definition of representation, discussed in the previous chapter, assumes some sort of action. We might or might not have opinion congruence, but it is how the representatives act which at the end of the day determines the extent to which they provide representative linkage. Nevertheless, to assume that representatives act according to their opinions is not unreasonable -- it is at least more plausible than to assume, for example, that they act in a certain way because they have certain social or demographic characteristics.

Opinion representativeness, also referred to as opinion congruence or opinion correspondence, can be divided into two levels. First, similarity between the representatives and the represented on the aggregate national level, something which has been labelled *collective correspondence*. An obvious example is the opinion correspondence between the totality of a nation's parliamentarians and its voters.[7] This is a very crude concept, however. Political representation is not a collective process. Representatives and represented are better divided into bilateral representational segments. The second level of opinion representativeness, *dyadic correspondence*, consists of such bilateral relationships.

In some political systems, notably the USA, dyadic representational bonds are primarily regarded as geographical, between a legislator and the voters in his/her respective electoral constituency. This is the way Weissberg uses the concept.[8] In most other systems, however, political representation is not primarily geographical, but instead based on ties to the political parties.

---

[7] Dalton 1996:240-244.

[8] Weissberg 1978.

Thus, the dyadic correspondence we should be looking for in Sweden can be found in the relationships between the voters and the representatives of individual parties. Russell Dalton argues that in Western Europe, where representation is largely structured around parties, dyadic correspondence is more based on representation between parties and voters than between legislators and constituents. In countries characterised by the 'Party Government Model', where people are primarily represented by parties, "(d)yadic correspondence is based more on a voter-party model than a district-legislator model."[9] This is the way the concept of dyadic correspondence will be used here.

With few exceptions, studies on opinion representativeness have employed a mass-élite perspective, where the representatives are regarded as political élites. Most commonly, the representatives have been elected legislators,[10] but there are also several examples where election candidates and party conference delegates have been given an analogous position.[11] The perspective here is similar, but not identical. The majority of party members cannot be assumed to be political élites. Most of them will never be a national party conference delegate, nor a candidate for public office. It would seem plausible that party members, on average, are comparatively more politically aware and knowledgeable than the public at large, but it would be going too far to equate them with political élites in the way the latter are usually defined. Indeed, it was shown in the previous chapter that there has not tended to be a significant over-representation of the highly educated among Swedish party members.

The arguments for the relevance of opinion correspondence between parties and the public are still relevant to party members, however. They constitute the party organisations and are the organisational backbone on which most modern parties are built. Not all members have actual influence in the parties (they need at least to be active for that) but, as was shown in Chapter 3, the rules of the Swedish parties give them some influence

---

[9] Dalton 1996:247.

[10] E.g. Converse and Pierce 1986 (France), Holmberg 1974 and Esaiasson and Holmberg 1996 (Sweden), Barnes 1977 (Italy) and Miller and Stokes 1963/1972 (USA).

[11] Dalton 1996, Chapter 11, presents data on collective as well as dyadic correspondence between voters and candidates in the 1979 election to the European Parliament in Great Britain, Germany and France. There are also studies of the opinions of party conference delegates and how they compare to the voters, e.g. Norris (1995).

potential. Even passive members can be attributed the role as the parties' 'ambassadors to the community' if they make no secret of their membership.[12]

A framework for the study of dyadic correspondence has been presented in a famous study by Warren Miller and Donald Stokes. They distinguish between four central components in the representational process. The first component, the constituents' attitude, has two connections: to the representative's own attitude and the representative's perception of the constituents' attitude. The two latter components are also connected to the final component, the representative's action (i.e. roll- call vote in parliament). These four components and their inter-connections are graphically depicted in the shape of a diamond, hence the well-known label 'Diamond Model'.[13]

Miller and Stokes apply their model to representatives in the US Congress. The Diamond Model is general enough to be applicable to Party Government systems and the relations between members and voters. The data used in this study do not allow such an analysis, however. The dependent variable, actual actions (the equivalent to what Miller and Stokes called roll-call behaviour) is not possible to operationalise via Election Studies data. Nor are indicators of party members' perceptions of voters' opinions, or vice versa, available.

A more directly relevant analytical concept is the law of curvilinear disparity, often referred to as 'May's Law' after its founding father, John D. May.[14] For the purposes of this study, May's Law has the advantage that it explicitly refers to party members. The Law postulates that the party activists will be the most ideologically extreme level (or stratum) in the party, while there will be a comparatively high degree of opinion correspondence between the party's leaders and the voters and passive members. The reasons are several. One is that ideologically extreme party followers are more likely to become party activists. Another reason is differential incentives inside the parties. Leaders have the incentive to be re-elected, while activists have no material incentives, only ideological.[15] May's Law has been given a lot of attention. The most recent contribution is by

---

[12] The term 'ambassadors to the community' has been coined by Susan Scarrow 1991 (it first appears already in the abstract) and has been taken up by others (e.g. Seyd and Whiteley 1992:37).

[13] Miller and Stokes 1963/1972. The Diamond Model is graphically depicted on p. 551.

[14] May 1973. The complete name of the Law is The Special Law of Curvilinear Disparity (May 1973:139).

[15] May 1973:146-150.

Pippa Norris, who raises important conceptual question marks and also finds that the Law does not find empirical support in Great Britain.[16]

Although not uncontroversial, May's Law can be expected to remain relevant and familiar. The questions raised against it do not obscure the fact that it offers a logically coherent and immediately intelligible framework. The Law bears relevance to much of the debate, general as well as academic, about political parties. Examples are criticism against ideologically diffuse party leaderships as well as criticism against extreme party activists. As Norris has pointed out, however, the Law requires more than a comparison between two levels. At least three levels need to be taken into account before one can claim to be testing the Law of curvilinear disparity. Even though this study operates with three levels, activists, members and voters, it cannot claim to meet the three-level criterion. This is because the élite level is missing, a stratum which is crucial to the rationale of the Law.[17] May's Law is a useful concept, which has relevance to the findings in this chapter, but it will not be subject to an actual test.

Data and method

Sören Holmberg has identified two main models of opinion representativeness. The *majority model* is based on the majority rule, the formal rule most commonly used in democratic systems and organisations. The majority model measures whether the respective majorities of the representatives and the represented share the same opinion.[18] The *mirror model* has a wider perspective and takes into account how the opinion is distributed within the group in question.[19]

The measures used in this chapter will be most closely related to the mirror model, although the majority model will also be given some consideration. The reason for this emphasis is that the majority model is a very crude measure. Potentially, it may hide quite substantial differences in

---

[16] Norris 1995.

[17] In her test of May's Law, Norris has not included data on passive members. She argues that the largest opinion differences can be expected to be between 'sub-leaders' and voters (Norris 1995:44, n.8). The inclusion of passive members in this study is not *per se* inconsistent with the Law. The crucial difference is that the élite level is missing.

[18] Holmberg 1974:65-69. The term majority here refers to absolute, or simple, majority, i.e. at least one more than half of the persons in question.

[19] Holmberg 1974:65, 69-84.

opinion distribution. Consider, for example, a situation in which 51 per cent of the represented share the same opinion, compared to 75 per cent of the representatives. According to the dichotomous majority model, such a situation would be regarded as presence of representativeness, full stop. The thus hidden difference in opinion is substantively important. In the case of members versus voters, it has implications for a party if the members are so much closer to unanimity on an issue whereas it is much more finely balanced among the voters. The internal party debate would then be likely to be insignificant, and a decision on the issue in the party would be a foregone conclusion. The mirror model is able to register such a situation.

This chapter will deal both with collective correspondence, between the Swedish electorate and the aggregate total of party members, and dyadic correspondence, between members and voters of individual parties. This method is not free of problems. On the national level, it hides the obvious fact that the totality of voters and members are divided according to party. On the party level, it does not take into account different factions and divisions in the party. In some parties, it could be argued that it should be sub-divided into several 'dyads', geographical or ideological.

The justification on the national level is that it is not irrelevant to see the extent to which the aggregate opinion situation among the public is reflected among party members as a collective. If the totality of members are unrepresentative it says something relevant about the party system. On the party level, it is reasonable to regard the Swedish parties as the dyadic units. Referring to Dalton's reasoning cited above, they are the most important units of political identification, and sufficiently coherent, to justify this approach. If the members of a party are unrepresentative, it says something relevant about the party.

The focus will be set on the size of the differences between members and voters. If 75 per cent of the members share the same opinion, compared to 70 per cent of the party's voters, then that party is more representative than a party where 10 per cent of the members have the same opinion compared to 30 per cent of the voters. In the latter case, the difference in percentage points is larger than in the former (note that the majority model would not register any differences). As in all other chapters, the main perspective is longitudinal. The intention is to find out whether the representativeness, that is the percentage differences between members and voters, has decreased over time. If this is the case, then we have an indication of a representative decline; if not, no such decline. The direction of the differences will be noted and discussed, but the main perspective is the size of the differences and whether it has declined over time.

It is difficult to find opinion variables that are comparable over a time period as long as between 1960 and 1994. The Election Studies have included a multitude of questions which have been designed to measure the opinion concerning concrete policies as well as general political outlook. However, only a handful of questions stretch across the time frame between the 1960s and the 1990s. Three questions have been chosen. First, respondents have been asked whether they agree or do not agree with the statement that society ought to have more influence over the banks and the industry. Second, they have been asked if they agree or not with a statement that social reforms have gone too far. Third, they have been asked to place themselves on a left-right scale from 0 (left) to 10 (right). The first two questions have the advantage that they have been asked in every Swedish Election Study since 1960. The third has fewer time points, 1968 and 1979 onwards, but has other advantages which will be discussed further on in this chapter.

These questions all are designed to measure the left-right dimension. The first tests whether respondents agree with a leftist statement, the second whether they agree with a rightist statement and the third is a more general measure of left-right ideology. The first two can be regarded as objective indicators, because the left-right ideological dimension is left implicit. The third indicator is subjective, because it is based on a question which explicitly mentions, and asks respondents to consider, the left-right dimension.[20]

Despite many shifts, twists and turns during the 35 years between 1960 and 1994, the left-right dimension has remained supreme in Swedish politics. It is the only attitudinal cleavage among Swedish voters that meets the criteria of a political dimension, at the same time as it structures the party

---

[20] In their study on Swedish parliamentarians, Sören Holmberg and Peter Esaiasson distinguish between subjective and objective ideological location. Subjective location is operationalised as a left-right scale, on which the respondents are explicitly asked to place themselves. Objective location is a summarising index of how respondents have answered a series of questions that comply with the left-right dimension, such as their opinions on taxation, privatisation etc. The distinction between subjective and objective is thus, that the former is the respondent's own self judgement, while the latter is based on the analyst's overall assessment, irrespective of the respondent's self perception. See Holmberg and Esaiasson 1988, Ch. 4 and Esaiasson and Holmberg 1996, Ch. 5.

political cleavages. It shapes attitudes which are consistent, among each other and over time, and it is independent of opinions which theoretically belong to other dimensions.[21]

The left-right dimension in Sweden is structured around a number of familiar ideological controversies. Its main components are issues related to taxes, distribution of wealth, the size of the public sector, privatisation and the welfare state. It is, however, not empirically connected to certain other issues, which are often described as left-right conflicts, such as immigration and law and order.[22]

There have been attempts to claim that the superior position of the left-right dimension has been challenged, or even overtaken, by other political dimensions. These claims have often focused on the growth of a green, or ecological, political dimension. As has been shown by Martin Bennulf, however, such claims do not hold up to empirical scrutiny. Green attitudes exist, but do not meet the necessary criteria to constitute an independent political dimension.[23] Thus, the left-right dimension is very suitable to measure opinion correspondence between members and voters. It has remained important in Swedish politics, it structures political thought and political conflict and it is well known among the public.

The data will be presented using the same principles as in the previous chapter on social representativeness. Voters will be compared to party members and activists. Three membership strata, or membership categories, will be used. Total members include collective, individual and active members. Individual members include individual and active members. Active members include only those who have answered that they are active in their party. Party members have not been removed from the voters. Thus, as in the previous chapter, members are compared to the entire electorate and the totality of their own party's voters, not only with non-members. Due to data limitations, only the three largest membership parties, the Social Democrats, the Centre Party and the Moderate Party, will be included.

Objective opinion congruence: leftist statement

The first test of opinion congruence is based on a leftist statement. The exact wording and response alternatives were slightly different in the Election

---

[21] Bennulf 1994:203f.

[22] Gilljam and Holmberg 1993:134ff.

[23] Bennulf 1994:221.

Studies of the 1960s, but the variations have not been substantively important. The statement is: "Leading banking and industry people will get far too much influence unless society is given the possibility to control private business and industry."

This is an example of the left-right conflict of whether private capitalism should be subject to public control. The question is carefully worded. The words 'possibility to control' are chosen to avoid the subject of nationalisation, which may have run the risk of appearing too leftist even for many Social Democrats. The issue of nationalisation of banks and large industries has been on the agenda in the Social Democratic Party, but it has never been fully approved by the party conferences, let alone embraced by Social Democratic governments.[24] Legislation concerning industrial relations, the allocation of government grants to banks and industries and actively affecting the interest rate can be considered as examples of the type of governmental control referred to in the question. Thus, the question covers a conflict issue which has had practical and symbolic relevance in Swedish politics for a long time. The Social Democratic and Left parties have tended to be more open to state control of banks and industries than the non-socialist parties.[25]

Table 8.1 reports the percentages that agree completely, or agree on the whole, with the 'public control' statement. The opinion congruence, operationalised as percentage differences, can be found in the 'diff.' columns. A negative difference means that the members are relatively more to the left on the issue than the voters. This is to increase the conformity among all the tables in this chapter. Negative differences always mean that the members are further to the left. Differences which are significant at the 95 per cent level or higher have been marked with an asterisk.

Among the entire electorate, between 63 and 83 per cent of the voters have agreed with the statement. The levels have fluctuated back and forth, but since 1988 the trend has been increasing, and 83 per cent in 1994 is an all-time high. This can be explained by the events in the 1990s, when several of the major Swedish banks were on the verge of bankruptcy and

---

[24] Pierre 1986:138-152.

[25] This is not to say that the policies of the two ideological blocs can easily be divided into two discrete types. Non-socialist governments have sometimes interfered with banks and industries, and the Social Democrats have never adopted a strict control policy. There has been a systematic difference in emphasis, however, a difference which arguably remains in the mid 1990s, despite a trend towards de-regulation in Social Democratic governments.

Table 8.1   Opinion representativeness of Swedish party members/ activists: per cent agreeing with leftist statement about public control over banks and industry. 1960-1994

Nation

	Electorate per cent	n	total members per cent	diff.	n	individual members per cent	diff.	n	active members per cent	diff.	n
1960	65	844	57	8*	199	no data available			64	1	42
1964	69	2237	68	1	434	no data available			no data available		
1968	73	2449	69	4*	429	61	12*	293	74	- 1	92
1970	64	1032	63	1	147	56	8*	116	no data available		
1979	70	2343	68	2	396	62	8*	312	73	- 3	168
1985	63	2334	68	-5*	403	64	- 1	314	73	-10*	155
1988	73	2215	73	0	304	72	1	282	75	- 2	117
1991	73	2116	no collective members			69	4	239	73	0	94
1994	83	2082	no collective members			83	0	247	81	2	100

Social Democrats

	Voters per cent	n	total members per cent	diff.	n	individual members per cent	diff.	n	active members per cent	diff.	n
1960	85	383	77	8*	96	no data available			90	-5	20
1964	81	967	88	-7*	226	no data available			no data available		
1968	91	1218	90	1	231	93	- 2	95	96	-5	46
1970	81	438	90	-9*	70	90	- 9	41	no data available		
1979	94	955	95	-1	209	99	- 5*	125	98	-4	84
1985	86	911	90	-4	206	96	-10*	117	94	-8*	71
1988	88	861	88	0	156	90	- 2	134	92	-4	49
1991	89	694	no collective members			91	- 2	100	94	-5	35
1994	94	840	no collective members			99	- 5*	121	100	-6*	46

Centre Party

	Voters per cent	n	members per cent	diff.	n	active members per cent	diff.	n
1960	55	104	46	9	39	55	0	11
1964	67	281	59	8	81	no data available		
1968	60	394	58	2	85	64	- 4	25
1970	56	215	45	11	31	no data available		
1979	54	347	42	12*	83	49	5	43
1985	56	220	58	- 2	74	68	-12	34
1988	71	221	60	11	53	69	2	29
1991	79	154	75	4	55	88	- 9	26
1994	88	146	87	1	47	82	6	22

Moderate Party

	Voters per cent	n	members per cent	diff.	n	active members per cent	diff.	n
1960	20	114	22	- 2	41	0	20	6
1964	35	225	28	7	68	no data available		
1968	32	249	27	5	59	17	15	12
1970	27	97	18	9	28	no data available		
1979	33	451	17	16*	59	17	16	18
1985	30	460	15	15*	65	21	9	19
1988	34	325	29	5	51	9	25*	11
1991	47	432	17	30*	42	19	28*	16
1994	57	400	44	13	41	36	21	14

Comment: Source: Swedish Election Studies; 1960 q. 12, 1964 q. 13C, 1968 q. 19D, 1970 q. 9D, 1979 q. 23A, 1985 q. 21A, 1988 q. 21A, 1991 q. 24A, 1994 q. 18A. Question: "Leading banking and industry people will get far too much influence unless society is given the possibility to control private business and industry". 'per cent' = proportion answering 'agree entirely' or 'agree on the whole'. 'diff' = difference in percentage points between membership stratum and electorate or party voters. Negative difference = members are to the left of voters, and vice versa. (*) = difference is significant at .05 level (one-tailed Z test.)

needed financial backing by the government to avoid closure. As a consequence, public confidence in banks collapsed.[26] Although the question does not deal only with banks, the inclusion of banks in the wording is likely to have had an effect on the answers. Party members have followed the trend among the electorate. Total, individual and active members all display a late and quite sharp increase in the percentage agreeing with the 'public control' statement.

The majority of the differences between voters and members on the national level are too small to be significant at the 95 per cent level. Over time, there has been a tendency for individual Swedish party members to change from being to the right of the electorate (a smaller percentage agreeing about increased state control of the banks and private industry) in the 1960s and 1970s, to virtual agreement with the electorate in the 1980s and 1990s. Among the total members, the fluctuations vary back and forth and are mostly very small. The active members have been close to the electorate all along, with 1985 as the only exception.

Thus, the collective correspondence for the leftist statement has increased. Among individual members the development towards higher correspondence is unambiguous. Individual members used to be more reluctant to accept state control than citizens in general. In 1985, the electorate moved slightly to the right, where they met up with the members. Since then, they have followed the same path.

Of course, the figures on the national level hide party variations. Social Democratic voters and members have been disproportionately open to state control throughout the research period. Consistently, more than 80 per cent of voters and members -- total, individual and active -- have agreed with the statement (the only exception is the total members in 1960). The level of agreement has not undergone a notable trend over time. The very high percentages in 1994 are in fact virtually identical to those in 1979. Thus, in this case we can say that the opinion among the Swedish electorate as a whole has come closer to the Social Democratic opinion, although it has not quite caught up with it.

The Social Democratic members have consistently been to the left of the party's voters. There are exceptions if the total (including collective)

---

[26] Elliot 1993, 1994. There was a simultaneous, if not as sharp, decrease in confidence in major companies and industries, which constitute the second part of the question used in Tables 8.1 and 8.2.

members are taken into consideration, notably in 1960, but the individual and active members have invariably agreed with the leftist statement to a higher extent than the voters. The size of the percentage differences varies between 2 and 10 points for the individual members, and between 4 and 8 for the activists. They are significant only on three occasions for the former and twice for the latter, something which leaves little room for far-reaching conclusions. The systematically negative differences still indicate some left radicalism among the party's individual members and activists. There is no systematic tendency for activists to be more radical than individual members in general, however.

With respect to the main perspective, the size of the differences and their development over time, the Social Democratic members show no signs of decreasing representativeness. There is no apparent trend over time in the percentage differences between the voters and any of the three membership strata. The fact that the differences increased in 1994 is not enough to refute this conclusion. The 1994 differences are not larger than they were in 1979 and it is too early to tell whether the recent decrease in representativeness is the beginning of a more long term decline.

After having been somewhat more reluctant until the 1980s, the Centre Party voters, members and activists have developed a high degree of agreement with the leftist statement. In 1994 over 80 per cent of the voters as well as members and activists agreed that banks and industries ought to be subject to some level of public control. The members followed the interventionist trend among the voters in the late 1980s and 1990s, but they did so at a somewhat slower pace. In 1994, however, they caught up. Thus, the members of the Centre Party have in the past been to the right of their voters and they have been more reluctant to follow the general trend towards a more positive attitude to public control. The sharp decrease in percentage differences to four points in 1991 and one point in 1994 means that the opinion among Centre Party members and voters must now be considered very similar, if not identical.[27]

---

[27] It could be argued that the differences between Centre Party members and voters have always been small, because they have only been significant once, in 1985. However, it is especially difficult to attribute significant percentage differences to a party like the Centre Party. Confidence intervals vary, not only according to the number of cases, but also according to how even the percentage distribution is. If the number of cases is held constant, a percentage of 50 has a larger confidence interval than a percentage of 90. Thus, other things being equal, it can be expected to be harder to find significant percentage differences between members and voters in parties whose policies are in the middle of a

The active Centre Party members have followed the general trend towards acceptance of state intervention, with notable increases in 1985 and 1991. These sharp increases were followed by the voters and, later, by the totality of the party's members. In other words, the Centre Party activists can claim to be opinion leaders. With the exception of 1994, the activists have always been more prone to agree with the leftist statement than the members as a whole, but they display very unsystematic differences to the voters. There is no evidence of activist radicalism, or conservatism, in the Centre Party. In 1979 and 1988 the activists were placed between the members and voters, in 1985 they were furthest to the left and in 1994 they were the stratum which on aggregate was least enthusiastic about state intervention, i.e. furthest to the right.

The Moderate voters have followed the general trend. In 1960 20 per cent of them agreed that banks and industries should be subject to some sort of state control. In 1994 the proportion had increased almost three-fold. At the same time it should be noted that the 57 per cent proportion agreeing with the leftist statement in Table 8.1 is still more than 30 points lower than in the Centre Party and nearly 40 points lower than among Social Democratic voters. Thus, although all parties have moved to the left on the issue, there are still substantial inter-party differences which makes the issue relevant to the left-right dimension.

The Moderate members and activists are consistently to the right of the party's voters. There is a positive difference between voters and members on every time point except in 1960, and the differences are significant in 1979, 1985 and 1991. The active members are to the right of the voters on every available time point. The percentage differences are mostly quite large, and even with the very small number of cases for the members, the differences are large enough to be statistically significant on two occasions.

Both the members and the activists in the Moderate Party have followed the trends towards a relatively more positive attitude to public control of banks and industry. However, they have done so quite reluctantly. The rise from 17 to 44 per cent agreement among Moderate members between 1991 and 1994 still leaves them 13 points behind the voters. The development has been similar among the active members. Even though most of the percentage differences are not significant, they are systematically

---

scale, or dimension. The decreasing differences after 1988 do constitute a break with the apparent pattern up to that year, something which points in the direction of increased representativeness. It is admitted that this is only an educated guess.

positive. This means that we can speak of some radicalism among Moderate members and activists. There is no systematic tendency for the activists to be more radical than the generality of members but both groups have consistently been to the right of the aggregate opinion among Moderate voters.

The Moderate members and activists have, on the whole, been the least representative among the three parties in the table. The Moderate Party is the only party to display percentage differences of over 20 points. The Moderate members are, furthermore, the only case where a tendency towards decreased representativeness can be detected. The percentage differences have fluctuated, but have on average been larger between 1979 and 1994 than between 1960 and 1970, and the statistically significant differences are concentrated towards the end of the research period. No other party displays an increase in percentage differences, i.e. decrease in representativeness. The same can be said of the Moderate activists. They have always been clearly further to the right than the voters, sometimes more so than the totality of the party's members. Like the members, the activists appear to have become less representative of the party's voters, even though the evidence is less conclusive.

The contention that Moderate voters and members have been the least representative can be modified somewhat. According to the majority model, the majorities among the party's different strata have been identical every year except in 1994, when, for the first time, a majority of the voters agreed with the leftist statement, while still minorities of members and activists did so. In the Centre Party, the majorities have been different between voters and members on three occasions. On the other hand, the last time this happened was in 1979, while the Moderates had conflicting majorities for the first time in 1994. Thus, the evidence of decreased representativeness in the Moderate Party is reinforced. The Social Democratic members and voters have, with their very high agreement levels, always had consistent majorities.

In Table 8.1 two levels of agreement ('agree entirely' and 'agree on the whole') have been collapsed into one agreement category. To get an appreciation of the more detailed opinion distributions among members and voters, an index ranging from 1 (far Left) to 5 (far right) has been constructed. Low figures indicate agreement with the statement of state control, i.e. a leftist outlook, and vice versa. The resulting averages for members and voters are presented in Table 8.2. The comment under the table includes more detailed information of how the index has been constructed.

Table 8.2 **Opinion representativeness of Swedish party members/ activists: averages of five point index of leftist statement, 1=left, 5=right. 1960-1994**

Nation

	Electorate			total members				individual members				active members			
	average	StD	n	average	diff.	StD	n	average	diff.	StD	n	average	diff.	StD	n
1960	2.4	1.9	844	2.6	.2	1.9	199	no data available				2.4	0	1.9	42
1964	2.3	1.5	2237	2.4	.1	1.5	434	no data available				no data available			
1968	2.2	1.3	2449	2.3	.1	1.4	429	2.6	.4*	1.5	293	2.3	.1	1.4	92
1970	2.6	1.7	1032	2.4	-.2	1.7	147	2.7	.1	1.7	116	no data available			
1979	2.4	1.3	2343	2.4	0	1.5	396	2.6	.2*	1.5	312	2.2	-.2*	1.4	168
1985	2.6	1.3	2334	2.5	-.1	1.4	403	2.6	0	1.4	314	2.2	-.4*	1.3	155
1988	2.4	1.2	2215	2.3	-.1	1.3	304	2.3	-.1	1.3	282	2.2	-.2	1.3	117
1991	2.4	1.2	2116	no collective members				2.4	0	1.3	239	2.3	-.1	1.3	94
1994	2.1	1.1	2082	no collective members				2.0	-.1	1.1	247	2.1	0	1.2	100

Social Democrats

	Voters			total members				individual members				active members			
	average	StD	n	average	diff.	StD	n	average	diff.	StD	n	average	diff.	StD	n
1960	1.6	1.4	383	1.9	.3*	1.6	96	no data available				1.4	-.2	1.2	20
1964	1.9	1.2	967	1.7	-.2*	1.1	226	no data available				no data available			
1968	1.7	1.0	1218	1.6	-.1	1.0	231	1.5	-.2*	0.8	95	1.5	-.2*	0.7	46
1970	1.9	1.4	438	1.5	-.4*	1.1	70	1.5	-.4*	1.1	41	no data available			
1979	1.7	0.8	955	1.5	-.2*	0.8	209	1.3	-.4*	0.5	125	1.4	-.3*	0.6	84
1985	2.0	1.0	911	1.8	-.2*	0.9	206	1.6	-.4*	0.7	117	1.5	-.5*	0.8	71
1988	1.9	1.0	861	1.8	-.1	1.0	156	1.8	-.1	1.0	134	1.7	-.2	0.9	49
1991	1.9	0.9	694	no collective members				1.7	-.2*	0.9	100	1.5	-.4*	0.8	35
1994	1.7	0.8	840	no collective members				1.4	-.3*	0.5	122	1.4	-.3*	0.5	46

Centre Party

	Voters			members				active members			
	average	StD	n	average	diff.	StD	n	average	diff.	StD	n
1960	2.8	2.0	104	3.1	.3	2.0	39	2.8	0	2.1	11
1964	2.5	1.4	281	2.7	.2	1.5	81	no data available			
1968	2.7	1.3	394	2.8	.1	1.3	85	2.8	.1	1.3	25
1970	2.8	1.7	215	3.0	.2	1.7	31	no data available			
1979	2.9	1.3	347	3.2	.3*	1.3	83	3.0	.1	1.4	43
1985	2.9	1.3	220	2.7	-.2	1.3	74	2.4	-.5*	1.3	34
1988	2.4	1.2	221	2.7	.3	1.3	53	2.4	0	1.3	29
1991	2.3	1.1	154	2.4	.1	1.2	55	2.1	-.2	0.9	26
1994	2.0	0.9	146	2.0	0	0.9	47	2.2	.2	1.0	22

Moderate Party

	Voters			members				active members			
	average	StD	n	average	diff.	StD	n	average	diff.	StD	n
1960	4.2	1.6	114	4.0	-.2	1.6	41	4.7	.5	0.8	6
1964	3.5	1.5	225	3.8	.3	1.4	68	no data available			
1968	3.6	1.4	249	3.8	.2	1.3	59	4.2	.6	1.1	12
1970	3.8	1.5	97	4.1	.3	1.4	28	no data available			
1979	3.5	1.3	451	4.1	.6*	1.1	59	4.2	.7*	1.1	18
1985	3.6	1.2	460	4.2	.6*	1.0	65	3.9	.3	1.1	19
1988	3.4	1.3	325	3.6	.2	1.3	51	4.2	.8*	0.9	11
1991	3.1	1.3	432	3.9	.8*	1.0	42	3.9	.8*	1.0	16
1994	2.9	1.3	400	3.3	.4*	1.3	41	3.8	.9*	1.4	14

Comment: Source and question wording, see Table 8.1 Averages based on response alternative index: Agree completely = 1, Agree on the whole = 2. Disagree on the whole = 4. Disagree completely = 5. In 1960, 'ambivalent' was coded 3. Other years, only four response alternatives existed. 'diff' = difference in average index between membership stratum and electorate or party voters. Negative difference = members to the left of voters, and vice versa. (*) = difference is significant at .05 level (T test for significance between two means). StD = standard deviance.

There is nothing in Table 8.2 which blatantly contradicts the observations from the more crude measure used in Table 8.1. In fact, the patterns are, if anything, accentuated, due to the higher number of statistically significant differences. Thus, the suspicion that the Moderate members have become less representative since 1979 is strengthened.

The first test of opinion representativeness has resulted in no general indication of a representational decline. The Swedish party organisations have followed the general development towards acceptance of state control. The exception is the Moderate members -- possibly also the Moderate activists -- who have followed the same trend, but with so much reluctance that they have become less representative over time. The question used can be criticised because the general political development has made public interference, at least with banks, comparatively uncontroversial in the 1990s. Indeed, it was a Moderate-led government, with a Moderate deputy Minister of Finance as the mainly responsible person, that was forced to intervene and save important parts of the Swedish banking system in 1992. Nevertheless, there have remained important and systematic differences between the parties so that the issue has not lost its relevance to the left-right dimension. In 1994, less than half of the Moderate members and activists agreed about state control, compared to 99 and 100 per cent of their respective Social Democratic counterparts. Among the voters, the remaining differences are smaller, but still notable; 57 per cent of the Moderates compared to 94 per cent of the Social Democrats.

Objective opinion congruence: rightist statement

The second objective indicator is a question where respondents have been confronted with the statement: "Social reforms in this country have gone so far that the state ought to *reduce* rather than increase social benefits and support for people." It highlights the conflict about the size and scope of the welfare state which has been an important topic in the Swedish political debate for several decades. The parties on the left have advocated and defended social spending, while the non-socialist parties have been somewhat less enthusiastic, at times very critical. The conflict lines have remained constant for a long period, despite the fact that the actual size of social benefits and support has not been constant. Even in the 1990s, when Social Democratic governments have made important welfare cuts, the issue has not lost relevance. Even if the size of the welfare state has been subject to increased reassessment and debate, the conflict lines between the parties have remained the same.

The percentage agreeing, entirely or on the whole, with the rightist statement among voters and members appears in Table 8.3. As in the previous indicator concerning public control over banks and private industries, the Swedish voters have tended to agree with the anti-welfare statement, although somewhat less decidedly so. More than half of the electorate has agreed with the welfare sceptical statement on every time point except in 1968. This general agreement still allows for some variations over time. Between 1964 and 1968 there was a drop in agreement of over 20 percentage points. In 1979 the proportion had increased to 71 per cent. The highest percentage, 73 per cent, occurred in 1991, the election in which a Moderate-led government took office and the right populist New Democracy entered the Riksdag. Three years later, when the Social Democratic government returned amid a general swing back to the left, the proportion went down by five percentage points.

The total (including collective) members have always been to the left of the electorate on the issue, as is shown by the constantly negative differences. More than half of them have agreed with the statement every year except in 1968, but the percentage agreeing has always been lower than among the electorate. In 1979 and 1985 the differences were particularly large. Because the difference between total and individual members on the national level consists of collective Social Democrats, it is not surprising to find that individual members are relatively more likely to agree about cuts in welfare spending. Except in 1968, which was an exceptional year, roughly two-thirds of the individual members have agreed with the anti-welfare statement. Since 1979, the individual members have on aggregate placed themselves slightly to the left of the electorate. The active members have consistently been the group furthest to the left. In 1960 and 1968 less than half of the activists agreed to cut social spending. In 1979 and 1985 the proportion was around 50 percent, followed by an increase to over 60 per cent in the 1990s.

The overall representativeness of party members has not decreased during the research period. The total members are a partial exception, as there was a tendency towards larger differences to the electorate in 1979 and

Table 8.3　Opinion representativeness of Swedish party members/ activists: per cent agreeing with rightist statement about welfare expenditure. 1960-1994

Nation

	Electorate		total members			individual members			active members		
	per cent	n	per cent	diff.	n	per cent	diff.	n	per cent	diff.	n
1960	54	⌐1316	52	-2	246	no data available			42	-12*	55
1964	66	2723	63	-3	489	no data available			no data available		
1968	45	2610	41	-4	433	48	3	298	37	- 8	96
1970	63	1220	60	-3	158	68	5	125	no data available		
1979	71	2517	63	-8*	410	65	-6*	326	54	-17*	173
1985	68	2453	60	-8*	414	62	-6*	320	50	-18*	157
1988	67	2296	62	-5*	315	61	-6*	295	55	-12*	119
1991	73	2270	no collective members			70	-3	239	68	- 5	88
1994	68	2142	no collective members			65	-3	243	64	- 4	97

Social Democrats

	Voters		total members			individual members			active members		
	per cent	n	per cent	diff.	n	per cent	diff.	n	per cent	diff.	n
1960	32	597	21	-11*	116	no data available			8	-24*	26
1964	53	1203	44	- 9*	245	no data available			no data available		
1968	31	1305	21	-10*	229	14	-17*	46	16	-15*	45
1970	51	524	35	-16*	74	37	-14*	43	no data available		
1979	57	1010	44	-13*	213	36	-21*	129	27	-30*	86
1985	50	962	39	-11*	213	28	-22*	119	23	-27*	71
1988	57	888	45	-12*	159	40	-17*	139	31	-26*	49
1991	60	728	no collective members			54	- 6	99	39	-21*	31
1994	60	858	no collective members			46	-14*	116	43	-17*	42

Centre Party

	Voters		members			active members		
	per cent	n	per cent	diff.	n	per cent	diff.	n
1960	72	174	81	9	54	76	4	17
1964	80	343	80	0	102	no data available		
1968	60	427	61	1	93	61	1	31
1970	74	250	92	18*	36	no data available		
1979	88	391	87	- 1	94	87	- 1	47
1985	84	243	88	4	78	83	- 1	35
1988	78	242	80	2	60	78	0	32
1991	80	169	91	11*	58	93	13	27
1994	77	159	82	5	50	77	0	22

Moderate Party

	Voters		members			active members		
	per cent	n	per cent	diff.	n	per cent	diff.	n
1960	88	172	88	0	50	86	- 2	7
1964	85	256	80	- 5	71	no data available		
1968	75	255	75	0	56	64	-11	11
1970	83	105	86	3	28	no data available		
1979	94	473	96	2	56	100	6	17
1985	92	470	94	2	66	95	3	19
1988	90	345	100	10*	53	100	10	10
1991	93	461	95	2	41	93	0	15
1994	91	414	95	4	40	100	9	14

Comment: Sources: Swedish Election Studies; 1960 q. 13, 1964 q. 13B, 1968 q. 19I, 1970 q. 9C, 1979 q. 23A, 1985 q. 21B, 1988 q. 21B, 1991 q. 24B, 1994 q. 18B. Question: "Social reforms in this country have gone so far that the state ought to *reduce* rather than increase social benefits and support for people". 'per cent' = proportion answering 'agree entirely' or 'agree on the whole'. 'diff' = difference in percentage points between membership stratum and electorate or party voters. Negative difference = members are to the left of voters, and vice versa. (*) = difference is significant at .05 level (one-tailed Z test).

1985.[28] The individual members, however, display consistently small differences and a tendency towards a decrease in the 1990s. A similar development can be observed among the activists. The very large differences between 1979 and 1988 went down clearly in the 1990s.

Social Democratic voters have undergone an interesting development. Their level of acceptance of the welfare sceptical statement has fluctuated, but the general tendency is clearly increasing. In 1960, 32 per cent agreed. In 1991 the proportion was 60 per cent, a level which was maintained in 1994. The members have developed in the same direction. However, they have done so with some hesitation. On only one occasion have more than 50 per cent among any of the three membership strata agreed with the statement (individual members in 1991). The total, individual and active Social Democratic members are all further to the left on the issue than the party's voters on every available time point; on most occasions the differences are significant. The activists have constantly been furthest to the left (at least since 1979), total members furthest to the right and individual members have tended to be placed in a position between the other two.

Although it does not exactly indicate extremism, it is an important finding that Social Democratic members are much less open than the party's voters to suggestions that the welfare state has gone too far. There is no trend in the size of the differences between members, total or individual, and voters; but the defensive attitude increases with activism. Social Democratic activists are still a core of support for social spending, even if they slowly follow the general trend. Throughout the 1960-1994 period they deviate significantly from the party's voters, even if the sizes of the differences have decreased steadily since 1979.

The lack of representativeness in the Social Democratic Party is emphasised if the majority model is taken into account. Every year except in 1960 and 1968, more than 50 per cent of Social Democratic voters have agreed with the welfare sceptical statement. The only time that any of the three other strata has reached this level of agreement was individual members in 1991. In the other parties, the majorities coincide every year.

The opinion among Centre Party voters has varied. Compared to the Social Democrats, however, they have consistently been clearly more

---

[28] The representativeness of the total members increased again in 1988. The abolition of collective membership had begun by then, however, and the number of solely collectively affiliated members in the sample was very small that year.

positive to the welfare sceptical statement. The same applies to the members and activists: clearly positive but with no time trend. The members have mostly, if not always, been to the right of the voters. Only in 1970 and 1991 is the difference large enough to be statistically significant, but every year except in 1964 and 1979 the members have agreed with the statement to a greater extent than the voters. The active members have mostly been very close to the voters. The only exception is in 1991, when they made a huge leap to the right, only to return to absolute correspondence with the voters three years later. Thus, the activists are not as a rule more radical on the issue than the voters. The most radical Centre Party stratum is the members, who have agreed with the rightist statement to a greater extent than the activists in most years, and also tended to be more welfare sceptical than the party's voters. Over time, there are no trends with respect to the representativeness of members and activists. Among the members, the fluctuations between different years are sometimes large, but there is no trend. Rather, the pattern is reminiscent of a roller coaster ride. With the exception of 1991, the representativeness of the active members has constantly been high and stable.[29]

The two investigated non-socialist parties share some characteristics. They have both always had clear majorities in favour of the welfare-sceptical statement. However, the Moderate Party is further to the right than the Centre Party. The voters, members and activists have consistently been overwhelmingly positive to cutting social spending. Since 1979 more than 90 per cent have agreed with the statement, and this is true of all three strata. There has been a trend towards a more positive attitude, but it has been sharper among members and activists than among the voters. Moderate members have been to the right of the party's voters since 1970. As a rule, the activists have been even further to the right. In both cases, however, the differences have mostly been quite small. With a temporary exception in 1988, the representativeness of Moderate members has been relatively constant over time. There are no signs of a decrease, neither among the members nor among the activists.

As in the previous section about attitudes to a leftist statement, the evidence will be complemented with a left-right index based on the answers to the rightist statement about welfare cuts. The index averages for members

---

[29] The difference between active Centre Party members and Centre Party voters in 1991 is not significant on the .05 level. It falls only marginally short, however, and is significant on the .10 level.

Table 8.4 Opinion representativeness of Swedish party members/ activists: averages of five point index of rightist statement. 1=left, 5=right. 1960-1994

Nation

	Electorate			total members				individual members				active members			
	ave	StD	n	ave	diff.	StD	n	ave	diff.	StD	n	ave	diff.	StD	n
1960	3.4	1.8	1316	3.2	-.2	1.9	246	*no data available*				2.8	-.6*	2.0	55
1964	3.4	1.5	2723	3.3	-.1	1.6	489	*no data available*				*no data available*			
1968	2.8	1.5	2610	2.7	-.1	1.5	433	2.9	.1	1.5	298	2.6	-.2	1.4	96
1970	3.4	1.6	1220	3.3	-.1	1.6	158	3.5	.1	1.6	125	*no data available*			
1979	3.7	1.4	2517	3.4	-.3*	1.5	410	3.5	-.2*	1.5	326	3.1	-.6*	1.6	173
1985	3.5	1.3	2453	3.3	-.2*	1.4	414	3.4	-.1	1.5	320	3.0	-.5*	1.5	157
1988	3.5	1.3	2296	3.3	-.2*	1.5	315	3.3	-.2*	1.5	295	3.1	-.4*	1.5	119
1991	3.7	1.2	2270	*no collective members*				3.6	-.1	1.2	239	3.5	-.2	1.3	88
1994	3.5	1.3	2142	*no collective members*				3.4	-.1	1.3	243	3.3	-.2	1.4	97

Social Democrats

	Voters			total members				individual members				active members			
	ave	StD	n	ave	diff.	StD	n	ave	diff.	StD	n	ave	diff.	StD	n
1960	2.5	1.8	597	2.0	-.5*	1.6	116	*no data available*				1.3	-1.2*	1.1	26
1964	3.0	1.5	1203	2.6	-.4*	1.6	245	*no data available*				*no data available*			
1968	2.3	1.4	1305	2.0	-.3*	1.2	229	1.8	-.5*	1.0	94	1.9	-.4*	1.0	45
1970	2.9	1.6	524	2.4	-.5*	1.6	74	2.5	-.4	1.6	43	*no data available*			
1979	3.2	1.4	1010	2.8	-.4*	1.5	213	2.6	-.6*	1.4	129	2.3	-.9*	1.3	86
1985	2.9	1.4	962	2.6	-.3*	1.3	213	2.3	-.6*	1.2	119	2.1	-.8*	1.2	71
1988	3.1	1.3	888	2.7	-.4*	1.4	159	2.7	-.4*	1.4	139	2.3	-.8*	1.3	49
1991	3.2	1.3	718	*no collective members*				3.1	-.1	1.2	99	2.7	-.5*	1.2	31
1994	3.2	1.3	858	*no collective members*				2.8	-.4*	1.3	116	2.7	-.5*	1.3	42

Centre Party

	Voters			members				active members			
	ave	StD	n	ave	diff.	StD	n	ave	diff	StD	n
1960	4.0	1.6	174	4.3	.3	1.5	54	4.3	.3	1.4	17
1964	3.9	1.3	343	4.0	.1	1.2	102	*no data available*			
1968	3.3	1.5	427	3.4	.1	1.4	93	3.6	.3	1.3	31
1970	3.9	1.4	250	4.3	.4*	1.0	36	*no data available*			
1979	4.2	1.0	391	4.3	.1	1.1	94	4.3	.1	1.2	47
1985	4.0	1.0	243	4.2	.2*	0.9	78	4.1	.1	1.1	35
1988	3.9	1.2	242	4.0	.1	1.3	60	3.9	0	1.3	32
1991	3.8	1.1	169	4.1	.3*	0.8	58	4.0	.2	0.7	27
1994	3.8	1.2	159	3.9	.1	1.1	50	3.7	-.1	1.1	22

Moderate Party

	Voters			members				active members			
	ave	StD	n	ave	diff.	StD	n	ave	diff.	StD	n
1960	4.6	1.1	172	4.6	0	1.0	50	4.7	.1	0.8	7
1964	4.1	1.1	256	4.1	0	1.3	71	*no data available*			
1968	3.8	1.3	255	3.8	0	1.2	56	3.6	-.2	1.4	11
1970	4.2	1.2	105	4.2	0	1.1	28	*no data available*			
1979	4.4	0.8	473	4.4	0	0.7	56	4.4	0	0.5	17
1985	4.3	0.9	470	4.4	.1	0.8	66	4.4	.1	0.8	19
1988	4.3	0.9	345	4.6	.3*	0.5	53	4.6	.3	0.5	10
1991	4.3	0.8	461	4.4	.1	0.8	41	4.3	0	1.0	15
1994	4.2	0.9	414	4.5	.3*	0.8	40	4.6	.4*	0.5	14

Comment: Sources and question wording, see Table 8.3. Averages based on response alternative index: Agree completely = 5. Agree on the whole = 4. Disagree on the whole = 2. Disagree completely = 1. In 1960, 'ambivalent' was coded 3. Other years, only four response alternatives have existed. 'diff.' = difference in average between membership stratum and the electorate or the party. Negative difference = members are to the left of the voters, and vice versa. (*) = difference significant at .05 level (T test for significance between two means). 'ave' = average. StD = standard deviance.

and voters are presented in Table 8.4. Again, the observations based on more crude categorisations (Table 8.3) are reinforced. The most interesting additional information is a more noticeable tendency towards decreased representativeness for members of the Moderate Party. Unlike the percentages in Table 8.3, the index accounts for intensity in opinion, because it differentiates between those who answer 'agree entirely' and 'agree on the whole'. Table 8.4 reveals a weak but observable increase in the differences between Moderate members and voters.

To summarise, the indicator used in Tables 8.3 and 8.4 has discriminated among the parties the way one would expect from a left-right issue. The Social Democrats are furthest to the left, the Moderate Party furthest to the right and the Centre Party in between. The two flank parties, the Social Democrats and the Moderates, show evidence of membership radicalism. The members are, respectively, further to the left and right of their party's voters and the active members are even further out towards the ideological flanks (although the evidence for Moderate activists is statistically weak).

In the Centre Party, the situation is more ambiguous. The members are to the right of the voters, but the activists are sometimes between the voters and members. Of course it is somewhat dubious to speak of Centre 'radicalism'. The party is generally regarded as ideologically located between the Social Democrats and the Moderates. An extreme Centre Party person would presumably be in the very middle of the left-right scale. This cannot be measured the way the data in Tables 8.1 through 8.4 are presented, but the problem will be returned to in the next section. The data in Tables 8.3 and 8.4 indicate that despite shifts over time, all levels in the Centre Party have constantly agreed to a very large extent that welfare spending has gone too far. In that perspective, radicalism could be expected to be to the right, even in the Centre Party. There is, however, no category in the Centre Party which is constantly more radical than the others. Members and activists tend to be slightly to the right of the voters, but the differences are often very small, sometimes even negligible.

The membership representativeness varies among the parties. The Social Democratic members and activists are the least representative. The most representative strata are the Moderate members and the Centre activists; on the whole the Moderate Party is arguably the most representative of the three parties, closely followed by the Centre Party.

There is no clear case of decreasing representativeness, collective or dyadic. Thus, the evidence in this section does not suggest a representational decline. This conclusion must be qualified for the Moderate Party, however. In the previous section, which was based on a leftist statement, the Moderate members and activists showed signs of decreasing representativeness. The explanation why that finding is not repeated in this section could be that the voters are already so far to the right when confronted with the rightist statement that the remaining radicalism space is too small. Thus, low representativeness is not possible. Other questions, where the members are more towards the middle, might have discriminated better. On the other hand, it is a relevant finding that members and voters are both so far to the right on the issue. Even if there is not much space to spare to the right, the members could have deviated in the other direction. Another problem is the crude agreement categorisation in Table 8.3. The index in Table 8.4, which takes the intensity of agreement and disagreement into account, suggests that the representativeness of Moderate members may, after all, have decreased somewhat. The pattern of decreased representativeness for the Moderate members in Table 8.4 is not overwhelming, but noticeable enough to justify the suspicion of a representational decline.

The overall evidence, using objective indicators of ideological representativeness and using leftist as well as rightist statements, indicates that party members and activists in Sweden are no less representative in the 1990s than they were in the 1960s. The Moderate Party is a partial exception. The focus will now shift to a subjective indicator of left-right ideology.

Subjective opinion congruence: left-right self-placement

The subjective indicator of opinion representativeness is self-placement on a scale from left to right. The respondents have been asked to think in terms of a left-right dimension and then to place themselves on a scale between 0 to 10, where low numbers indicate a position on the left and high numbers a position on the right.[30] Thus, the focus is set on the respondents' self-

---

[30] Respondents have been asked: "Political parties are often thought of as being possible to place from left to right, according to their political outlook". The interviewer then shows a scale from 0 to 10, and instructs the respondent that a low number indicates an ideological position to the left and a high number an ideological position to the right. The mid point, 5, is explicitly described to the respondent as neither left nor right. After first being asked to place the parties on the scale, the respondent is asked to place him/herself. In 1968, the

perception. If the last two sections dealt with concrete policy opinions, with no reference to what respondents thought of the ideological implications, this indicator concentrates on how respondents perceive their own ideological position, without reference to its consistency with their more concrete policy opinions.

The reduction of the complex left-right dimension into a scale, what Dieter Fuchs and Hans-Dieter Klingemann refer to as a 'left-right schema', involves several assumptions. The schema should be recognised and understood by the public. It should have a limited number of possible meanings, which should be generaliseable and follow a binary structure of association (i.e. be possible to classify as either left or right). After testing the schema in Germany, the Netherlands and the USA, Fuchs and Klingemann conclude that the schema meets these criteria, at least in the two European countries. They conclude that it is an indicator which measures generalised political positions.[31]

In an article dealing with 17 Western democracies, Francis Castles and Peter Mair have found that it is possible to place the majority of parties on a left-right scale, after asking a number of national political experts to do so.[32] In Sweden, left-right self-placement is largely consistent with party vote and opinions on relevant separate political issues.[33] In conclusion, the left-right scale, or schema, is widely accepted as measurement of political outlook, suitable for cross-national as well as longitudinal studies.

A conceptual problem is that the meaning of left and right may not have been constant over time. For example, it could be argued that in 1968, the first year where the left-right schema was used in the Swedish Election Studies, left and right was primarily related to nationalisation of industries and issues related to class interests, while in the 1990s left and right is more related to the size of the public sector and the welfare state. Even if this is true, the left-right schema is still defensible as a general measure of ideological location. It measures the ideological attitude according to the issues that respondents consider most important at a given time. If leftism has meant different things in 1968 and 1994, the schema can be seen as a

---

scale presented to the respondents was different, but it has been re-coded to correspond with the questions from 1979 to 1994.

[31] Fuchs and Klingemann 1990:209, 216-222, 233.

[32] Castles and Mair 1984.

[33] Peter Esaiasson and Sören Holmberg found that subjective left-right placement correlates strongly and positively with standpoints on concrete political issues, among Swedish parliamentarians as well as among the voters. Esaiasson and Holmberg 1996:102.

measure which controls for such changes. 'Old' left-right issues need not have ceased to be left-right, they are only less salient, and have been succeeded by other more salient issues.

If this argument is accepted, it is meaningful to compare left-right self-placement between the 1960s and 1990s. A change in any direction is meaningful, even if the interpretation has to be made with some care. To use Fuchs and Klingemann's criteria, the possible meanings of left and right may vary, but if these meanings are generaliseable on both time points, follow a binary structure on both time points and do not contradict each other between the respective time points, changes according to the left-right schema are meaningful and interpretable. The analytical focus will be set on differences between voters and party members. The relative sizes of these differences, and their changes over time, are interpretable because they measure difference in opinions related to what is perceived as left and right at a certain point in time.

Two technical aspects deserve attention. The first is the number of points on the scale. Some international studies, for example the Eurobarometers, use a ten point scale ranging between 1 and 10. Such a scale does not have a natural mid-point, as it is not possible for respondents to use decimals in their answers. The Swedish Election Studies have used eleven point scales between 0 and 10, where 5 is the mid point. The existence of a mid point is potentially relevant. Its non-existence can be regarded as useful because it forces respondents to take a stand on the left-right scale, to press them into the left or right side. On the other hand, it is conceptually meaningful to be exactly in the middle of the scale, and therefore it should be possible. A related problem is that many respondents are likely to think of 5 as the mid point, regardless whether it is a 10 or 11 point scale. Thus, some answers on a ten point scale can be misleading in the sense that they are registered as slightly to the left when respondents have intended to place themselves exactly in the middle.

The second technical aspect is how the aggregate position of a number of individuals can best be measured. The most common measure is the mean.[34] However, it has its problems. First, it is possible that no single respondent is placed on the exact position of the mean. This would be the case in a polarised party, where two major factions cluster on two separate

---

[34] See Esaiasson and Holmberg 1996:102f, Widfeldt 1995.

positions some points apart.[35] Second, the mean position gives disproportional weight to individuals who place themselves at a distance from the majority.[36]

Alternatives exist. Huber and Bingham Powell argue that the median measure is preferable, since it avoids the disproportional impact of individual outliers.[37] Another possibility is the modal value, i.e. the value which represents the highest number of respondents. The median and modal measures neglect the spread of the respondents, however. Even if nobody is actually placed on the mean value, it makes a substantively important difference if the respondents are evenly spread along the scale, or clustered around two points. In the latter case, it makes a difference where these two points are. In both cases, the mean value will vary in a meaningful and interpretable way, because the point of gravity is affected. Of course, it is not without importance if the respondents are spread out or centred around the mean. Therefore, the standard deviations will be presented. The problem with outliers is there no matter which method is used. It can be problematic to let a few individual outliers affect the mean. But is it better to leave them out? It is relevant information that a political party does have members, or voters, who are ideologically so far apart.[38]

The means and standard deviations of voters' and party members' left-right self-placement between 1968 and 1994 are presented in Table 8.5. The Swedish electorate has on aggregate consistently been positioned very close to the middle of the scale. In no year has the mean of the electorate deviated from 5 with more than half a scale step. The total members and the activists have consistently been further to the left. The individual members, on the other hand, were to the right of the electorate between 1968 and 1985, but since 1988 they have moved to a position slightly to the left. No stratum has developed in a particular direction. Both the individual and active

---

[35] In practice, a mean value will almost certainly have several decimals. Thus, nobody will by definition be on the mean position, since it is not allowed for respondents to indicate decimals in their answers. However, the reasoning is also applicable to the whole number which is nearest to the mean.

[36] Huber and Bingham Powell 1992:2f.

[37] Huber and Bingham Powell 1992:2f. John D. May uses the median as measure of opinion in a particular party stratum when presenting his Law of Curvilinear Disparity (May 1973:139).

[38] This reasoning does not take into account the possibility that some outliers are simply errors, due to coding mistakes and so forth. However, risks of such a nature exist in all research, not only when using of the left-right schema.

members moved rather clearly to the left between 1991 and 1994, but before then the patterns have been very topsy-turvy.

The Social Democratic voters have fluctuated within a range between 3.4 and 3.9 on the left-right scale, what can be characterised as 'moderate left'. All three membership strata have been to the left of the voters. This applies to every year and, with one isolated exception (total members in 1985), the differences are significant. Thus, there is clear evidence of membership radicalism in the Social Democratic Party. Furthermore, the radicalism increases with activity. The total members are the closest to the voters, the individual members slightly further away to the left, and the activists are furthest out on the left end of the scale.

Total Social Democratic members, i.e. including collective members, moved slightly to the right between 1968 and 1988. The individual members display a curvilinear movement, and in 1994 they were back in virtually the same position as in 1968. The activists moved slightly to the left between 1968 and 1994. Given that the party's voters have moved slightly to the right during the same period, this means that the individual members and, in particular, the activists have become less representative over time. They have always been to the left of the voters but the size of the difference has increased. Among individual members, the development has not been continuous, but the difference of a full scale step in 1994 is the biggest ever. If the time frame had been between 1968 and 1991, the pattern would have been curvilinear. Taking 1994 into account, however, there is some justification to speak of a decline in representativeness. The activists display a continuous decline up until 1991. In 1994 the difference decreased somewhat, but their ideological distance to the voters in the 1990s is twice as big as in the 1960s.

The Centre Party has lived up to its name. The voters, members and activists have always been within one and a half scale step from the mid-point of the scale, i.e. 5. It should be noted, however, that the deviations from the mid-point have always been to the right. The Centre Party membership categories range between a minimum of 5.6 (activists in 1960) and a maximum of 6.5 (activists in 1985). Thus, the party can be located somewhat to the right of centre. The differences between voters, members and activists are small; none falls outside the margin of error. However, there is a fairly consistent tendency for members and activists to be slightly to the right of the voters. The differences are very small and the rule is not without

Table 8.5 Opinion representativeness of Swedish party members and activists: average self-placement on left-right scale from 0 to 10, 1968-1994

Nation

	Electorate			total members				individual members				active members			
	ave	StD	n	ave	diff.	StD	n	ave	diff.	StD	n	ave	diff.	StD	n
1968	4.7	2.3	2523	4.6	-0.1	2.7	441	5.3	0.6*	2.7	304	4.4	-0.3	2.6	98
1979	4.9	2.3	2548	4.6	-0.3*	2.5	423	5.0	0.1	2.6	333	4.3	-0.6*	2.6	175
1985	5.2	2.3	2531	4.9	-0.3*	2.6	425	5.3	0.1	2.7	327	4.6	-0.6*	2.7	156
1988	5.0	2.2	2425	4.7	-0.3*	2.6	326	4.8	-0.2	2.6	303	4.6	-0.4*	2.4	123
1991	5.5	2.1	2344	*no collective members*				5.2	-0.3*	2.5	246	5.1	-0.4	2.6	95
1994	4.9	2.2	2183	*no collective members*				4.6	-0.3*	2.6	253	4.6	-0.3	2.6	102

Social Democrats

	Voters			total members				individual members				active members			
	ave	StD	n	ave	diff.	StD	n	ave	diff.	StD	n	ave	diff.	StD	n
1968	3.4	1.8	1307	2.9	-0.5*	1.8	234	2.6	-0.8*	1.5	97	2.8	-0.6*	1.6	46
1979	3.4	1.6	1048	3.0	-0.4*	1.5	219	2.7	-0.7*	1.3	129	2.6	-0.8*	1.3	87
1985	3.6	1.7	1011	3.4	-0.2	1.8	221	2.9	-0.7*	1.7	123	2.7	-0.9*	1.8	71
1988	3.7	1.7	966	3.2	-0.5*	1.9	166	3.1	-0.6*	1.8	143	2.6	-1.1*	1.4	49
1991	3.9	1.7	771	*no collective members*				3.1	-0.8*	1.4	104	2.7	-1.2*	1.6	34
1994	3.7	1.7	882	*no collective members*				2.7	-1.0*	1.5	125	2.6	-1.1*	1.4	47

Centre Party

	Voters			members				active members			
	ave	StD	n	ave	diff.	StD	n	ave	diff.	StD	n
1968	5.7	1.6	411	5.9	0.2	1.6	93	5.6	-0.1	1.8	31
1979	5.9	1.4	395	6.1	0.2	1.5	98	6.2	0.3	1.6	48
1985	6.2	1.5	248	6.4	0.2	1.5	80	6.5	0.3	1.7	35
1988	5.9	1.3	248	6.0	0.1	1.4	63	6.1	0.2	1.4	34
1991	6.1	1.3	176	6.3	0.2	1.4	57	6.0	-0.1	1.2	28
1994	5.8	1.3	156	5.7	-0.1	1.4	50	6.0	0.2	1.7	23

Moderate Party

	Voters			members				active members			
	ave	StD	n	ave	diff.	StD	n	ave	diff.	StD	n
1968	7.9	1.7	253	8.4	0.5*	1.3	59	8.5	0.6	1.0	12
1979	7.3	1.5	488	8.1	0.8*	1.4	60	8.0	0.7*	1.5	18
1985	7.7	1.5	475	8.3	0.6*	1.3	66	8.2	0.5*	1.1	19
1988	7.7	1.4	354	8.3	0.6*	1.3	53	8.5	0.8*	1.0	12
1991	7.5	1.4	470	8.3	0.8*	1.1	42	8.3	0.8*	0.9	16
1994	7.3	1.4	421	8.2	0.9*	1.2	42	8.2	0.9*	1.1	14

Comment: Sources: Swedish Election Studies; 1968 q. 44B, 1979 q. 27B, 1985 q. 30B, 1988 q. 28B, 1991 q. 31B, 1994 q. 26B. Respondents have been asked the following question: "Political parties are sometimes thought of as being possible to place on a scale from left to right, according to their political outlook". Then, after being asked to place the parties, the respondents are asked the follow-up question "Where on the scale would you place yourself?". The respondents are shown a card with the scale from 0 to 10 printed on it, and instructed by the interviewer that low figures indicate a leftist outlook and high figures a right-wing outlook. NB: In 1968, the original scale ranged from -5 (left) to 5 (right), with 0 as the mid point. The answers have been re-coded to ensure comparability with the questions from 1979 to 1994. The differences indicate the difference in average left-right self-placement between the respective membership stratum and the electorate (on national level) or the party's voters (on party level). A negative difference means that the members are to the left of the voters, and vice versa. An asterisk (*) after the difference indicates that, even though the size of the difference is a rough estimation, there is a difference between the two averages which is significant at the .05 level, according to a T test for significance between two means. StD = standard deviance.

exception, but there is enough to speak of a pattern. The relationship between members and activists is less clear. The active members of the Centre Party are, as a rule, slightly to the right of the party's voters, but they do not systematically deviate from the members.

The Centre Party members and activists are the most representative among the three studied parties. The differences in mean self-placement have never exceeded 0.3 scale step, and have changed very little during the research period. Thus, the ideological representativeness in the Centre Party is high and stable.

A possible weakness in this conclusion is that the subjective left-right schema does not discriminate in the Centre Party. The Centre Party encompasses political thoughts, some of which do not fit the left-right dimension. This argument does not lack merit, but there are counter-arguments. The observations in the previous section, that the party is to the right rather than to the left in concrete left-right policy issues, and the fact that voters, members and activists do on aggregate place themselves slightly to the right, indicate that the left-right dimension is not entirely irrelevant in the Centre Party. The party can be ascribed a place to the right of centre, if only slightly so. It is therefore no trivial observation that the Centre Party members and activists are the most representative of the three parties studied. They are somewhat to the right of the voters, but the differences are mostly so small that they are not significantly separated from zero.[39]

The Moderate Party is furthest to the right of the Swedish parties. In 1968, the average self-placement of Moderate voters was 7.9. Since then, they have moved marginally towards the left, at most to 7.3.[40] Thus, there is a slight de-radicalisation tendency among Moderate voters. The same can, with a bit of stretching, be said of the members and activists; neither have ever been further to the right than they were in 1968, even if the fluctuations are too erratic to speak in terms of a trend. There is, however, clear evidence

---

[39] In a study on the party of the centre in British politics, the Liberal Democrats, Lynn Bennie, John Curtice and Wolfgang Rüdig have found that members of the party tended to place themselves to the left rather then right of centre of a left-right schema ranging from 1 to 9 (Bennie, Curtice and Rüdig 1996:143f). Thus, the Liberal Democrats could be labelled centre-left, while the evidence from Table 8.5, as well as the whole of this chapter, suggests that centre-right is a better label for the Swedish Centre Party.

[40] The voters of the only possible competitor, New Democracy, had an average left-right self placement of 6.3 in 1991 and 6.0 in 1994. The party's members are too few to allow meaningful calculations.

that the members and activists have consistently been to the right of the voters. This has been so every year for which data are available, and only once, activists in 1968, the differences fail to be significant at least at the 95 per cent level.[41] Furthermore, the voters have moved further towards the left than the members and activists, a development which means that the latter two have become less representative over time. The difference in 1994 is bigger than ever before for both members and activists, and at least the activists display systematically bigger differences in the 1990s than before. The members and activists have been very close to each other, but they have always been to the right of the voters. They have not become more radical in absolute terms; that is, the members and activists have not moved to the right on the ideological scale. Relative to the voters, however, they are more radical in the 1990s than in the 1960s due to the fact that the distance between members and voters has increased.

Up to now the focus has been on the means. The standard deviations give the additional information of how spread the respective stratum is around that mean. According to the information extracted so far, members and activists of the two flank parties are more polarised than the members in the sense that their means are further out towards the respective ends of the left-right schema. The standard deviations reinforce the conclusion of membership polarisation. The members and activists of the Social Democratic and Moderate parties tend to have lower standard deviations than their respective voters. This pattern is most evident in the Moderate Party, where there also is a systematic pattern of further decreased standard deviations among activists compared to the members. In the Social Democratic Party, there is an analogous pattern between voters and members although there are exceptions in 1985 and 1988. The pattern does not extend to the Social Democratic activists, however, who tend to have lower standard deviations than the party's voters but mostly not compared to the individual members.

In the Centre Party, the standard deviations among the different strata are very similar, often even identical. Among the three studied parties, the deviations from the means are smallest among the Moderate members and activists. The relative differences in means between voters and members are bigger between the Social Democratic Party voters and members, but the

---

[41] The differences for the activists are significant according to a T test, which can be used to test differences between mean values of small samples. This test assumes equal variance among the two different means, something which does not hold up to scrutiny. The figures and differences for Moderate activists should be treated with caution.

standard deviations are lower in the Moderate Party. In their own right, both these observations suggest a pattern of membership radicalism.

To conclude this section, the subjective indicator does not show decreased ideological representativeness on the national level, between the combined total of party members and activists on the one hand, and the electorate on the other. The Centre Party members and activists have also remained at a stable -- and small -- distance from the party's voters.

On the party level, the situation is different. The members and activists of the Moderate and Social Democratic parties have become less representative. They have always been more radical than their respective voters, but in relative terms their radicalism has increased. Voters, members, and activists of the Moderate and Social Democratic parties have all moved towards the middle of the left-right scale. The voters have moved further, however, leaving their respective members and activists behind. Thus, although the members and activists have become less radical compared to themselves over time, they have become more radical relative to their respective voters.

Party members and the Swedish EU accession

The indicators of representativeness used so far in this chapter have been chosen with the purpose to measure the members' representativeness in terms of left-right ideology and its development over a longer period. This is only a part of the linkage relevance of political parties. Politics often concern issues which are short term. A political issue can turn up on the agenda, become very important and then change its meaning, sometimes even disappear completely. Furthermore, a political issue needs not belong to the left-right dimension.

The issue of Swedish accession to the European Community/European Union has been on the agenda since the early 1960s.[42] After the Social Democratic government's announcement in October 1990 of their intention to submit an application for full membership, the 'European issue' has been at the centre of attention in Swedish politics. The EU issue has left-right relevance. Many of the arguments for and against accession followed these lines. It was not as easy as that, however. There have been

---

[42] For the historical background and an account of the development of the issue in the Swedish parties, see Widfeldt 1996.

notable instances of EU criticism among people on the right, as well as EU enthusiasm among people on the left.

The EU issue has been problematic for the political parties in Sweden. The Social Democrats, Centre Party and Christian Democrats have all been severely split. The wounds have not been healed after Sweden voted in favour of accession in a referendum in November 1994. Other parties, such as the EU positive Moderates and People's Party Liberals and the EU critical Left and Green parties, have been more united, but no party has been totally unhurt.

This section will investigate development of the EC/EU opinion on different party levels between 1991 and 1994, and in connection herewith study the development of the representativeness of party members and activists. The data used are taken from the SOM Studies, conducted at Göteborg University. The fact that the SOM Studies take place annually makes it possible to follow the short term development, and also to merge data from consecutive years, to increase the number of cases for parties with few members. This means that members of the People's Party Liberals and the Left Party, who have not otherwise been separately studied in this and the previous chapter, will be included. In addition, the data allow the distinction of not only party activists, but also members with commissions in the parties. The proportions in favour of Swedish EU accession between 1990 and 1994 are presented in Table 8.6.[43]

By the time of the Swedish membership application in July 1991, the Swedish public was fairly positive to accession. The proportion of the population who were positive to accession did not command an outright majority, but outnumbered those who were directly negative (this cannot be seen in the table). Then, however, the opinion took a sharp turn, and the Swedish public was decidedly sceptical to accession in 1992 and 1993. In fact, although the opinion began shift back when the referendum came closer, it had not returned to the 1991 level in the autumn of 1994.[44]

In 1991, there was a relatively high degree of correspondence between party members and the general public about EU accession. The

---

[43] The comparison is made between members and the sympathisers of the respective party (answers to the question "Which party do you like best today?"), instead of party voters. This is to ensure comparability over time. There were no elections in 1992 and 1993.

[44] The data of the 1994 SOM Study were collected between October 1994 and January 1995. The referendum in which the Swedish voters approved EU accession took place on 13 November, 1994.

Table 8.6 Opinions about Swedish EU accession on four party levels 1991-1994. Per cent positive to Swedish EC/EU accession

Nation

	Population	members	diff.	active members	diff.	members with commissions	diff.
1991	46 (1552)	51 (205)	5	51 (91)	5	53 (66)	7
1992	31 (1864)	35 (194)	4	37 (59)	6	30 (37)	-1
1993	30 (1836)	36 (198)	6*	39 (61)	9	45 (31)	15*
1994	39 (1677)	43 (174)	4	48 (61)	9	50 (34)	11

Social Democrats

	Partisans	members	diff.	active members	diff.	members with commissions	diff.
1991	36 (444)	34 (71)	-2	16 (48)	20*	13 (22)	-23*
1992	18 (736)	23 (75)	5	25 (24)	7	24 (17)	6
1993	18 (766)	22 (86)	4	34 (29)	16*	44 (16)	26*
1994	29 (682)	34 (65)	5	43 (23)	14	45 (11)	16

Centre Party

	Partisans	members	diff.	active members	diff.	members with commissions	diff.
1991	25 (101)	28 (32)	3	37 (16)	12	67 (9)	42*
1992	23 (99)	22 (27)	-1	36 (11)	13	33 (9)	10
1993	13 (91)	19 (26)	6	18 (11)	5	20 (5)	7
1994	36 (117)	41 (34)	5	55 (11)	19	50 (6)	14

Moderate Party

	Partisans	members	diff.	active members	diff.	members with commissions	diff.
1991	78 (301)	91 (45)	13*	93 (14)	15	89 (9)	11
1992	65 (372)	70 (43)	5	89 (9)	24	67 (3)	2
1993	62 (366)	73 (49)	11	88 (8)	26	75 (4)	13
1994	72 (350)	87 (31)	15*	83 (12)	11	78 (9)	6

1991-1994 merged

	Population	members	diff.	active members	diff.	members with commissions	diff.
Nation	36 (6929)	41 (771)	5*	44 (272)	8*	50 (155)	14*

	Population	members	diff.	active members	diff.	members with commissions	diff.
Social Democrats	24 (2628)	31 (297)	7*	39 (109)	15*	43 (66)	19*
Centre Party	25 (408)	29 (119)	4	37 (49)	12*	45 (29)	20*
Moderates	69 (1389)	89 (168)	20*	88 (43)	19*	80 (25)	11
People's Party Liberals	58 (309)	57 (46)	- 1	65 (17)	7	82 (11)	24
Christian Democrats	35 (274)	21 (38)	-14*	29 (14)	- 6	50 (6)	15
Left Party	11 (293)	8 (25)	- 3	2 (14)	- 9	---	---

Comment: Data are taken from the SOM studies 1991 (question 18), 1992 (q. 20), 1993 (q. 21) and 1994 (q. 24). The questions are phrased "What is your opinion about Swedish membership of the EC/EU?" Respondents have been given three choices: "On the whole for Swedish EC/EU membership", "On the whole against Swedish EC/EU membership" and "No definite opinion on the issue". Percentages in the table indicate the proportion answering the first alternative "On the whole for...". The number of cases of the percentage base for each percentage appears in brackets. Respondents have been asked about party membership, activity and whether they have commissions in the party, but not of which party they are members. Therefore, the members have been broken down by party sympathy, i.e. answers to the question "Which party do you like best today?". This question is also the basis for the category 'Partisans'. The 'diff.' columns indicate the differences in percentage points between members and partisans (on the party level) or population (on the national level). A negative difference means that the members are less positive to EU accession than the population or partisans, and vice versa. An asterisk (*) after the difference means that, although the size of the difference is a rough estimation, there is a difference between the two percentages which, according to a one-tailed Z test, is significant on the .05 level or higher. Figures for the 'population' include people aged between 15 and 80.

members tended to be somewhat more positive, but the differences were not substantial. On the national level, party members and activists have constantly been more EU positive, although the differences were significant only in 1993. It is, however, possible to interpret the figures so that the members and activists are seen as opinion leaders, as the leaderships in six of the eight nationally relevant parties worked to ensure a popular majority for accession. In 1993, party members and members with commissions were significantly more EU positive than the public. A year later, the public had almost caught up.

This observation is particularly applicable to the Social Democratic Party. Before 1990, the party had been sceptical about EC accession and had often been criticised by the Liberals and Moderates for this. This is still reflected in the figures for 1991, when all membership strata were more sceptical to accession than the party's sympathisers. In fact, the scepticism increased with activity, and the members with commissions were the least willing to accept Swedish accession to the then EC. In 1992 and, especially, 1993 the situation had been reversed. Party members also became more sceptical to accession, but not to the same extent as the supporters. In 1992, 1993 and 1994, all three membership strata were more positive than Social Democratic partisans. In addition, the positive attitude now increased with activity. In 1991, the proportion positive to accession decreased continuously from partisans via members and active members to members with commissions. In 1993 and 1994 this pattern was exactly reversed.

Thus, while the Social Democratic leadership had a difficult job in convincing their sympathisers of the advantages with accession, they were rather more successful inside the party organisation. It has been shown that a crucial number of the Yes voters in November 1994 were Social Democratic late deciders.[45] It could be guessed that the leadership of the Social Democratic Party succeeded in convincing its activists and members who, in turn, worked as opinion leaders to convince sceptical and hesitant supporters of the party.[46]

---

[45] This was indicated by an exit poll conducted by *Sveriges Television* (VALU 94). See also Holmberg 1996b.

[46] It is admitted that this is speculation based on weak statistical foundations. Another factor, which can be supported by deductions from the table, is that the number of activists decreased during this spell. It could then be guessed that it was mainly the EU positive members that stayed active and that EU sceptical members became passive, or left the party. This would cast doubt on the theory of the leadership managing to persuade the members and activists.

In the Centre and Moderate Parties, members and activists have tended to be more EU positive than the respective partisans, but the differences are seldom statistically significant. The Social Democrats and the Centre Party members have been quite representative of their parties' sympathisers throughout the 1991-1994 period, while the Moderate members have tended to be more markedly EU positive than their (already positive) party supporters. No party displays a trend in any direction with respect to the representativeness of their members or activists.

The merged data from 1991 through 1994 should be interpreted with care. As is apparent from the year by year data from on the national level and from the Social Democratic, Centre and Moderate parties, the EU opinion has fluctuated during the period, something which makes the data unsuitable for merging. With this caveat in mind, it is nevertheless interesting to note that party members and activists were more EU positive than the general public during the 1991-1994 period. This deviation from the public towards a more positive attitude increased with activity, so that the members with commissions were the most positive. All these differences are statistically significant.

The least representative party according to the merged data is the Moderate Party. All levels, from partisans to members with commissions, are very positive, but the three different membership strata are overwhelmingly dominated with EU enthusiasts. All three membership strata of the Social Democratic Party are also more EU positive than their party's supporters to a significant extent, especially the activists and members with commissions. There is a similar pattern in the Centre Party, although the members do not deviate from the partisans to a significant extent. The most representative members can be found in the EU positive People's Party Liberals and in the EU critical Left Party.

Conclusion and comparative outlook

The evidence presented in this chapter has shown that the members of two of the three studied parties are more radical than the party's voters. The members and activists of the Moderate Party are further to the right than the party's voters; in the Social Democratic Party the situation is analogous. The membership radicalism applies to all the three indicators used, objective as well as subjective. It can be observed virtually throughout the 1960-1994 research period.

When opinion representativeness between different party levels has been studied in previous research, two patterns have tended to emerge. First, a pattern where the 'élite' level is consistently to the left of the 'ordinary' level in all parties -- left, right and centre -- a pattern which can be labelled the 'élite leftism model'.[47] Second, an 'élite conflict model', where the 'élites' are more polarised than ordinary citizens. Elites of parties on the left are further to the left than their voters, and vice versa in parties on the right. Empirical evidence has tended to support the elite leftism model. According to subjective indicators, party élites (mostly parliamentarians) in France, Italy, Denmark, Germany and the Netherlands have been found to be further to the left than the voters of their respective parties.[48]

The Swedish case is not quite so straightforward. In the 1960s, objective indicators strongly supported the élite leftism model. Using an index of five left-right issues, Sören Holmberg found that Swedish parliamentarians in 1969 were to the left of their respective voters in 1968.[49] They were also to the left of their voters according to the two objective indicators used in this chapter, the statements regarding state control over banks and industry and reduction in social spending. Likewise, a study of local government politicians in 1966 showed that they were more to the left than their respective voters when asked to choose between prioritising tax cuts or more services provided by local governments.[50]

In the late 1970s and the 1980s, the picture had changed. The élite conflict model had become the best description of the relationship between voters and parliamentarians. Westerståhl and Johansson's retake of the local government study in 1979 showed that Moderate local politicians had moved to the right of their voters, while Social Democratic and Left Party politicians were still to the left of theirs. Holmberg and Esaiasson's study of parliamentarians in 1985 gave the same result, both when a summary index and the two statements were used as indicators.[51]

---

[47] 'Leftism' is here to be understood in a relative sense. The élites in a conservative party are of course not 'leftist', only less to the right than their voters.

[48] Converse and Pierce 1986:128f (France), Barnes 1977:102f (Italy), Kristensen 1980 (Denmark), Schmitt 1984 (West Germany), van de Geer and de Man 1974 (Netherlands), Dalton 1996:241f (Britain, West Germany and France).

[49] Holmberg 1974:87. The finding is also depicted graphically on the book cover.

[50] Strömberg 1974:116.

[51] Esaiasson and Holmberg 1996:93f, Holmberg and Esaiasson 1988:95, 98.

It should be emphasised that all these findings were made using comparable indicators, which lends support to the conclusion that an actual shift had taken place. The élite conflict model also applied to the relationship between parliamentarians and voters in 1985 if subjective left-right self-placement was used.[52] Based on the same indicator, the élite conflict model has been shown to fit opinion patterns between members and supporters of 37 West European parties in 1988/89.[53]

The findings in this chapter are quite unambiguously consistent with the élite conflict model. All three indicators, objective as well as subjective, point in the same direction. Social Democratic members and activists are to the left of Social Democratic voters, and Moderate members and activists are to the right of Moderate voters. With a few exceptions, this observation applies to the entire research period.[54] Thus, the shift in the relationship between parliamentarians and local politicians, on the one hand, and their voters on the other, is not repeated when the focus is set on party members. The relationship between members and voters has not changed, but it has been analogous with the élite conflict model throughout the research period. As has been argued before, party members cannot be regarded as political élites. The relationship between members and voters in Sweden can therefore be labelled the *membership conflict model.*

What are the potential consequences of this finding? A positive interpretation is that the ideological diversity inside the party organisations gives the voters clearer alternatives to choose from. It can also be argued that in a democracy, it is fully legitimate for ideologically aware and committed persons to join political parties in an attempt to change society in their desired direction.

There are also more negative interpretations. The ideologically aware members do not reflect the situation among the electorate. If their extreme views are reflected in actual behaviour, the parties will not be responsive. Robert McKenzie's assertion that party democracy is incompatible with societal democracy is supported.[55] The radical members

---

[52] Esaiasson and Holmberg 1996:101ff.

[53] Widfeldt 1995:166-170.

[54] There are isolated exceptions in the Moderates in the 1960s, but the differences are never statistically significant.

[55] McKenzie 1982:195.

could also alienate other citizens from joining and participating in party activities.

The extreme members may cause problems for the party leaderships, who are likely to see the situation as an obstacle against electoral success. That is, of course, assuming that the top party élites are less radical than members and activists. This brings us back to May's Law. It should be emphasised that May's Law has not been, and will not be, tested in this study, because élites above active members will not be analysed. The findings are not inconsistent with May's Law, but not enough to prove it. In fact, when Holmberg and Esaiasson applied May's Law to the Swedish parties in 1985, the Élite Conflict model applied to every party except one, all they way up to the level of the parliamentarians. In the Left, Social Democratic and Moderate parties, there was a consistent pattern of increased radicalism from the voters via members and activists up to the parliamentarians -- something which is not consistent with May's Law.[56]

It may be somewhat questionable to conclude that the party leaderships see radical members as a problem if they are even more radical themselves. On the other hand, the totality of a party's parliamentarians is not equal to the party's leadership. Only a handful can be expected to be really influential, or members of leading party bodies. Thus, while the findings reported by Holmberg and Esaiasson are relevant with respect to May's Law in the way it has been formulated, they do not answer the question of whether there is an ideological conflict between party élites and members which could be detrimental to internal party democracy, because the real élites have not been measured.

The membership conflict model deals primarily with parties on the flanks of the left-right scale. The third studied party is secondary in this respect. In this study, a high degree of opinion correspondence has been found in the Centre Party. The members and activists have tended to be slightly to the right of the party's voters, especially on objective indicators, but on the whole the party is the most representative of the three studied. Previous research has come up with inconsistent findings about the Centre Party. They have always been placed between the Moderates and Social

---

[56] Esaiasson and Holmberg 1996:97ff; Holmberg and Esaiasson 1988:102. This pattern was not found in the Centre Party and the People's Party Liberals. In the Centre Party, members were to the right of the voters but activists were slightly to the left of the members. The parliamentarians were slightly to the right of the voters. The People's Party showed a zig-zag pattern where the voters and the activists were relatively to the left and the members and parliamentarians more to the right.

Democrats on élite as well as rank-and-file level. The relative positions of the two levels have varied; sometimes the élites have been to the left of the voters,[57] sometimes to the right.[58] They have not always been the most representative party.

The results in this chapter offer some additional information about the Centre Party. It is the overall most opinion representative of the three investigated parties. This is not consistent with some of the studies on parliamentarians, where the Moderate Party has sometimes been more representative. The mentioned comparative study of party members in Western Europe in the late 1980s shows that the centre/agrarian parties in Finland, Norway and Sweden are among the most opinion representative of the studied parties, with minuscule or no differences in average left-right self-placement between members and supporters. Thus, the high representativeness of the Centre Party seems to apply to the membership level, but does not extend to the parliamentary level.

As has been argued above, the reason for the high representativeness in the Centre Party could be that the left-right dimension is not suitable to discriminate among different groups in parties which are located in the middle, and that other dimensions could therefore be more appropriate. A possible example is the growth/ecology dimension. One counter-argument has already been mentioned, i.e. that the Centre Party in Sweden is essentially a non-socialist party and that in left-right issues 'extreme centrism' would, after all, be equal to a deviation towards the right. If this is true, we would expect the Centre Party to join the Moderates in the 'Élite Conflict' model, at least when based on objective indicators. On the other hand, the self-image of a '*centerpartist*' is still very much in the middle, leaving no space for extremism based on subjective indicators. Empirical evidence does not seem to support this interpretation, however. Objective indicators used here and in other studies do not point towards a general tendency that the 'élite' level in the Centre Party is to the right of the voters.

---

[57] Local politicians in 1966 and 1979 (Westerståhl and Johansson 1981:86), parliamentarians in 1968 according to objective left right index based on 15 issues and the statement about reduction in social benefits, and parliamentarians in 1985 according to left-right self-placement (Holmberg and Esaiasson 1988:95, 98, 105; Esaiasson and Holmberg 1996:94f, 103).

[58] Parliamentarians in 1985 according to objective left-right index based on 12 issues, and to statement about state control over banks and industry (Holmberg and Esaiasson 1988:95; Esaiasson and Holmberg 1996:94f).

The party's activists and parliamentarians are sometimes found to be to the left of the voters. Again, the findings in this study suggests that the membership level in the Centre Party is different to the parliamentary level. Centre Party members and activists are further to the right, and more representative of the voters, than Centre Party parliamentarians.

Voters and members of the three studied parties have not been stable in their opinions between the 1960s and 1990s. It should be noted, however, that they have tended to go in the same direction. There are individual exceptions to this rule, but there is no case where the long time trends conflict; more often than not they converge. However, the pace of the opinion shift is, as a rule, not such that members and voters eventually meet. If the voters go to the left, so do the members, and vice versa on the right. Their respective rates may vary, so that the representativeness decreases or increases, but if they were apart at the beginning of the research period, they do not usually meet at the end. The only possible exception is the opinion correspondence between Centre Party voters and members based on the leftist statement in Tables 8.1 and 8.2. There, it was the members that followed the voters rather than vice versa.

This means that cases of opinion leadership, or following, in the sense that members or voters have taken the lead in a development which has led to full agreement, are rare. Besides the just mentioned example from the Centre Party, instances where it might be relevant to speak of opinion leadership, or opinion following, can be found only with a bit of creative reading. The proportion Social Democratic individual members and activists agreeing with the leftist statement of state control over banks and industries (Table 8.1) has always been at least 90 per cent. The party's voters were below that level in 1960, 1964 and 1970. Thus, the voters could be said to have followed the members.[59] Another example of possible opinion leadership on behalf of the members and activists in the EU issue (see Table 8.6). On the other hand, Social Democratic members and activists have clearly lagged behind the opinion development among the party's voters concerning the welfare sceptic statement in Tables 8.3 and 8.4.

Using the same reasoning, Moderate members and activists followed, rather than led, the shift towards a more positive attitude to public control over banks and industries. At least 30 per cent of the voters agreed with the statement in Table 8.1 every year except 1960 and 1970; the

---

[59] It should be pointed out that this is not supported by Table 8.2 which is based on a more fine-tuned index.

members and activists did not reach this level until 1994. Thus, there are more cases where the members are opinion followers rather than opinion leaders. This is positive in the sense that they are responsive. On the other hand, some of their attributed roles in the party organisations can be questioned. They do not seem to fill the role as 'megaphones', where they bring out the party's message to the public. The Social Democrats, a party known and feared for its ability to mobilise its membership for propaganda purposes,[60] offers only limited and disputable exceptions.

The key question is yet unanswered: are the Swedish parties in a state of representational decline? The findings from the three indicators are summarised in Figure 8.1. The Moderate and Social Democratic members have already been shown to be more ideologically extreme than their voters. This relative extremism has increased to some extent. The Moderate Party members have become less representative according to the leftist statement. There are also, albeit less conclusive, signs of a decline in terms of the rightist statement and left-right self-placement. The Social Democrats display no decreased representativeness in any of the two objective indicators. According to the rightist statement, their active members have in fact become more representative over time (although if the majority model is taken into account, it could be argued that conflicting majorities between members and voters have been more common after 1970). In terms of subjective left-right self-placement, there are signs of a decline in representativeness among individual and, more clearly, active Social Democratic members.

The Centre Party is the only party with no sign of decline at all. There are sometimes quite substantial fluctuations over the years, but there is no way the fluctuations can be regarded as a trend with decreasing opinion congruence between members and voters. A comparison between the first and the last available time points for the Centre Party members and activists in Tables 8.1 through 8.5 corroborates this conclusion. It is, furthermore, quite rare to find statistically significant differences between Centre Party members/activists and voters at any time.

---

[60] E.g. Adelsohn 1987. See also Esaiasson 1990:408f.

Figure 8.1 The development of opinion representativeness of party members and activists in Sweden 1960-1994

	objective, leftist statement	objective, rightist statement	subjective, left-right self placement
Sweden (nation) total members	No trend	(Decline)	(Decline)
Sweden (nation) individual members	Increase	No trend	No trend
Sweden (nation) active members	No trend	Increase	No trend
Social Democrats total members	No trend	Stability	No trend
Social Democrats individual members	No trend	No trend	(Decline)
Social Democrats active members	Stability	Increase	Decline
Centre Party members	(Increase)	No trend	Stability
Centre Party active members	No trend	No trend	Stability
Moderate Party members	Decline	(Decline)	(Decline)
Moderate Party active members	(Decline)	No trend	(Decline)

Comment: The entries in the cells are summaries of the trends for the respective party membership stratum. Brackets indicate that the evidence of an increase or decline is inconclusive. The row 'Objective, leftist statement' is based on Tables 8.1 and 8.2. The row 'Objective, rightist statement' is based on Tables 8.3 and 8.4. The row 'Subjective, left-right self-placement' is based on Table 8.5. The summarised trends for total (i.e. including collective) members in the nation and of the Social Democrats are based on the development between 1960 and 1988. The summarised trends for individual members in the nation and of the Social Democrats are based on the development between 1968 and 1994. The summarised trends for members of the Centre and Moderate parties are based on the development between 1960 and 1994. The summarised trends for active members in the nation and of all parties are based on the development between 1979 and 1994 (data on active members from 1960 and 1968 are not taken into account because of inconsistent operationalisations of activity).

It is the parties on the flanks that are the least representative. It is also in those parties that any signs of a representational decline can be found. It should be noted that, according to the subjective indicator of left-right self-placement, the distance between Social Democrats and Moderates has not increased; neither among voters, nor among members.

Thus, it is not justified to conclude that the Swedish party system has become more polarised. In fact, the Social Democrats and the Moderates have moved closer to each other on the left-right schema. However, this contraction has not been equal on the different party strata. It has been bigger among voters than among members and activists. This has meant that the intra-party distances between voters and members of the two flank parties have increased. In that respect, members are more polarised relative to the voters of the same party in the 1990s than they were in the 1960s. The membership conflict model has strengthened its hold.

Collective opinion correspondence, between the totality of party members and the entire electorate, has not decreased over time. The reason for this is partly that the intra-party developments cancel each other out, and partly that members of other parties than the three studied separately are included among members and activists on the national level. It is not irrelevant that the party members on the national level show no evidence of a representational decline. If all party members were assembled into a large meeting, they would be as representative of the Swedish electorate in the 1990s as they have been in the past. But that is not the way the political system works. Party members meet in their own parties and influence the decisions taken there. The most important lesson in this chapter is therefore to be found in the development of dyadic correspondence.

The overall conclusion from the data just analysed is not straightforward. What we can say, is that there are some signs of a decline in representativeness. It is not a general decline among all parties, and it is not obvious on every indicator. The most conspicuous finding is the polarisation between members and voters in the two biggest electoral parties, the Social Democrats and the Moderates.

Other research has reported somewhat contradicting findings concerning opinion representativeness in Sweden. Holmberg and Esaiasson's study of the opinion correspondence between voters and parliamentarians in Sweden resulted in two conclusions. On the one hand, they showed that the degree of opinion correspondence was lower than would have been the case if the representatives, the members of the Swedish Riksdag, were randomly selected among the public; in other words that there were statistically significant differences between voters and parliamentarians.[61] In this respect, the results in this chapter are similar. Especially in the Social Democrats, but also relatively often in the Moderates, differences between members and voters are significant. On the other hand, Esaiasson and Holmberg found that the opinion correspondence between Swedish voters and parliamentarians had not decreased between the late 1960s and late 1980s.[62] Thus, according to the perspective in this study, where the focus is set on decline or no decline, Esaiasson and Holmberg's findings can be interpreted positively.

---

[61] Esaiasson and Holmberg 1996:111.

[62] Esaiasson and Holmberg 1996:108ff.

Similarly, the opinion representativeness of the Social Democratic, Moderate and, especially, Centre Party members compared rather favourably with other European parties in the late 1980s.[63]

The conclusion of this chapter is somewhat less positive. There is not enough evidence to speak of an overall representational decline. But there are signs that the members and activists of the two electorally biggest Swedish parties are distancing themselves from their respective voters.

Finally, a few words about the relationship between social representativeness and representativeness in terms of opinion. In the comparative study on European party memberships, it was found that a party's social representativeness says little about its opinion representativeness, and vice versa. Esaiasson and Holmberg have come up with a similar conclusion in their study on Swedish parliamentarians.[64] The circumstantial evidence that can be extracted from Chapters 7 and 8 above, supports the negative findings. The Centre Party has declined in terms of age and educational representativeness, but has a high and stable degree of opinion representativeness. The Social Democrats have become more representative in terms of class, group and to some extent also gender. Yet, they are showing signs of a decline in subjective left-right placement. The Moderate social representativeness has not changed much, while the opinion representativeness has declined. The evidence is by no means conclusive, but it is hard to find signs of a relationship between social and opinion representativeness in the material examined in this study.

---

[63] Widfeldt 1995:166-170.
[64] Widfeldt 1995:171, Holmberg and Esaiasson 1988:99ff.

9 Conclusion: Has There Been Linkage Decline?

The findings

According to the perspective of this study, party membership is a vital aspect of democracy. By being open and voluntary membership organisations, the political parties provide participatory and representative linkage between citizens and the state. The purpose has been to empirically investigate whether there has been a linkage decline in these respects. The time has now come to recapitulate the findings from Chapters 3 through 8 and put them into context. Are the parties providing less linkage in the 1990s than they were in the 1960s? This summary will follow the linkage conditions that appear in Figure 2.2 above.

In Chapter 3 it was shown that the parties have, by and large, remained open organisations. The obstacles to becoming a member are few and do not extend beyond obvious requirements, like not simultaneously being a member of another party. The obligations required to remain a member are also few, and do not go much further than the payment of membership dues. In these respects there are no substantial differences among the eight parties included in the study, and with the exception of the Left (formerly Communist) Party, there have been no important changes between 1960 and 1994.

The formal conditions for membership influence vary among the parties. At the end of the research period, the Green and Christian Democratic parties are the parties where the rules give the members the most opportunity to influence party business. The influence in the Green Party has decreased, however, because the rules were changed in 1992 so that all central decision making bodies are no longer directly elected by the party congress, and the National Council was downgraded to an advisory organ. The influence index in Table 3.11 has decreased also in the Centre Party and the People's Party Liberals. The opposite development, increased influence, can be observed in the Moderate Party, New Democracy, the Christian Democrats and the Left Party. The Christian Democrats is the most notable case of an increase, and in 1994 it came level with the Greens on the influence index. The Social Democrats have remained at a constantly low level of membership influence between 1960 and 1994. On the whole, the members' potential for influence in the Swedish parties is at least as big today as it was in the 1960s. The entries of new parties in the party system have helped to increase the average influence. There have also been positive changes in two of the older parties.

This means that two fundamental linkage conditions, openness and internal membership influence, are met. The formal rules of the parties allow popular participation and membership influence to at least as high an extent in the 1990s as in the 1960s. Thus, the Swedish party system has met two of the conditions for both participatory and representative linkage.

There are, however, less encouraging findings with regard to membership strength and activity. Party membership, the subject of Chapter 4, has decreased over time. On the face of it, individual membership remained quite stable between the 1960s and the mid 1990s. The detailed development varies according to whether party records or survey data are used, but all parties had a combined individual membership of around 600,000 in the 1960s, a figure which remained relatively similar as recently as in 1994. There are two reasons why a membership decline was a justified conclusion even then. First, the increased size of the electorate. Thus, although the absolute number of individual members has been relatively stable, their proportion of the electorate has decreased from 11 to 12 per cent in the 1960s to 9 to 10 per cent in 1994 (depending on whether party records or election studies data are used).

The second argument is that it would be wrong to discount all collective members of the Social Democratic Party. It is plausible that a large proportion of the collectively enrolled members of the Social Democratic Party were 'genuine' members, who would have joined the party as individual members if that had been the only possibility. Thus, the relatively limited decrease in observable individual membership hides a clearer membership decline. This applies to the absolute number of members (the M count), as well as their proportion of the electorate (the M/E count), and to the aggregated membership of all parties as well as the Social Democratic Party.

This conclusion is of course corroborated by the very sharp membership decline according to Party Records in 1995, 1996 and 1997. During this short period, total party membership in Sweden has fallen to a total of 456,000, or under seven per cent of the electorate. This is by far the lowest membership level throughout the time frame used in this book.

The membership drop has to some extent affected almost every party. The Liberal, Moderate and Centre parties have been severely hit and, in recent years, also the Social Democrats. The two former parties have seen their memberships more than halved since the early 1960s. The membership of the Centre Party has undergone a curvilinear development, but has experienced a steady and increasingly sharp decline since the early 1980s, and in the 1990s the membership is lower than ever before during the 1960-1997 period. The only possible exceptions from the general trend are the Christian Democrats and, to some extent, the Green Party. The membership decline has also affected the side organisations for women and youth of virtually every party, with a particularly sharp decline in the 1990s (see Appendix II).

Party activity has also declined. As was admitted in Chapter 5, comparable data exist only from the late 1970s onwards, but during that period the overall decrease is clear. In 1979 nearly six and a half per cent of the electorate were active in a party or a side organisation. In the mid 1990s, the figure has sunk to just below four per cent. It is difficult to register variations over time in the different parties because their respective proportions of members of the entire electorate have always been so small. Nevertheless statistically significant decreases in activity during the 1979 through 1994 period can be attributed to the Social Democratic and Centre parties.[1]

It can thus already be established that, according to the conditions for linkage set out in Chapter 2, there is a participatory linkage decline in the Swedish party system. Each and every one of the given conditions for the respective type of linkage has to be met. Now that two conditions, membership and activity, have found not to be met, that means that a participatory linkage decline is the inevitable conclusion.

The evidence presented in Chapter 7 suggests that there has been no overall decline in social representativeness, among party members nor activists. Five indicators of social representativeness have been studied: gender, age, education, class and group. Age is the only indicator of social representativeness with a clear overall decline. Party members and activists have become decidedly older than the public, on the national level as well as among the three parties. In terms of gender, the situation is different. Women

---

[1] There are also signs of a decline in activity in the Left Party and the Christian Democrats. These changes are statistically significant at the .05 level, but we are dealing with changes from A/E percentages of about 0.3 down to slightly below 0.1. This means that they must be taken with a couple of grains of salt.

remain under-represented among party members, but the extent has not increased. Active members are almost fully representative in terms of gender in the 1990s. None of the three parties whose representativeness it has been possible to study, defy this trend. The only possible exception is Moderate activists and this is in fact because women appear to have become over-represented.[2]

Educational representativeness has remained stable. Swedish party members have followed the general trend towards an increasing educational level among the public. The only clear case of decline in representativeness is the Centre Party. Class and group representativeness have in fact increased, among all party members and activists and in the Social Democratic Party, with no signs of decline anywhere.

If the observations from the five indicators of social representativeness are combined, the totality of Swedish party members, and even more so activists, are at least as socially representative in the 1990s as they were at the first available time point. Despite a decline in some cases -- notably age -- there is no case, on the national or party levels, where it can be justified to speak of an overall representational decline. Party members in Sweden in the 1990s represent societal and demographic groups at least as well as they used to in the past. Since their number and activity are decreasing, however, they are nevertheless in a state of participatory decline.

But what about representative linkage? Figure 2.2 identifies three conditions: openness, membership influence and opinion representativeness. It has already been asserted that the first two have been met. The third was studied in Chapter 8. Three indicators were used, all intended to measure left-right ideology. Two are objective measures: responses to a leftist statement that banks and industries should be controlled by society and responses to a rightist statement that welfare spending has gone too far. Finally, the subjective measure of self-placement on a left-right scale has been used.

On the aggregate national level, there is no sign of a representational decline for individual or active members (although there are traces of a decline for total members in two of the three indicators). The only party to which a decline can be attributed is the Moderates, whose members have become less representative in all three indicators, and their activists show the

---

[2] This observation is based on very few observations and should be interpreted with care. If the 1991 and 1994 Election Studies are merged, 57.5 per cent of the Moderate activists are women (based on a total number of 31 observations), compared to 41.5 per cent of the party's voters.

same tendency in two of the indicators. In the Centre Party, on the other hand, there is no sign of a decline in any of the operationalisations of opinion representativeness. The Social Democrats are in an intermediate position, with signs of a decline in representativeness in terms of left-right self-placement, but not in any of the two objective indicators.

In Chapter 8, it was argued that there is not enough evidence to be able to speak of an overall decline in opinion representativeness. There are, however, quite strong indications that the members and activists of the Social Democratic and, especially, Moderate parties have become less representative in terms of left-right self-placement. The development suggests that there has been a process of polarisation in the two electorally biggest Swedish parties. It is not a new phenomenon that Social Democratic members are to the left of Social Democratic voters and that Moderate members are to the right of Moderate voters. What has happened is that the differences between members and voters have increased in both parties, leaving the respective voters ideologically further away from the organisations of their preferred party.

The results of chapters 3, 4, 5, 7 and 8 are summarised in Figure 9.1 below. The entries are summaries of the combined evidence for each of the conditions for political linkage, on the aggregate national level and among the eight parties. Out of necessity, some entries in the figure are simplifications. The reasoning behind the simplifications should, however, be apparent from the discussion in the respective chapters (see comment below the figure).

Due to difficulties with data, it has not always been possible to reach all the way back to the starting point of 1960 in this study. Individual membership figures are not available before 1967 (with Party Records) or 1968 (with survey data). Comparable figures on activity exist only from 1979 onwards. Still, there is enough evidence to conclude that there has been a decline in the participatory linkage provided by the Swedish parties between 1960 and 1994. The negative development in membership and activity makes this an inevitable conclusion, which is reinforced by the negative development in membership and activity between 1995 and 1997. There has been decline on the aggregate national level, and most political parties have been affected. The only possible exception is the Christian Democrats, but it should be pointed out that due to data restrictions, it has not been possible to study the development of the party's social representativeness.

Figure 9.1   Overall trends in participatory and representative linkage provided by Swedish parties, 1960-1994

Participatory linkage:

Party	Openness	Membership influence	Membership strength	Membership activity	Social representativeness	Overall development
Sweden (nation)	Stability	Increase	**Decline**	**Decline**	No overall trend	**Linkage decline**
Social Democrats	Stability	Stability	**Decline**	**Decline**	Increase	**Linkage decline**
Centre Party	Stability	**Decline**	**Decline** .	**Decline**	No overall trend	**Linkage decline**
Moderate Party	Stability	Increase	**Decline**	Stability	No overall trend	**Linkage decline**
People's Party Liberals	Stability	**Decline**	**Decline**	Stability	*No data*	**Linkage decline**
Christian Democrats	Stability	Increase	Increase	Stability	*No data*	*Not testable*
Green Party	Stability	**Decline**	Stability	Stability	*No data*	**Linkage decline**
Left Party	Increase	Increase	**Decline**	**Decline**	*No data*	**Linkage decline**
New Democracy	Stability	Increase	**Decline**	Stability	*No data*	**Linkage decline**

Representative linkage:

Party	Openness	Membership influence	Opinion representativeness	Overall development
Sweden (nation)	Stability	Increase	No overall trend	No linkage decline
Social Democrats	Stability	Stability	No overall trend	No linkage decline
Centre Party	Stability	**Decline**	No overall trend	**Linkage decline**
Moderate Party	Stability	Increase	**Decline**	**Linkage decline**
People's Party Liberals	Stability	**Decline**	*No data*	**Linkage decline**
Christian Democrats	Stability	Increase	*No data*	*Not testable*
Green Party	Stability	**Decline**	*No data*	**Linkage decline**
Left Party	Increase	Increase	*No data*	*Not testable*
New Democracy	Stability	Increase	*No data*	*Not testable*

Comment: This Figure relates to Figure 2.2, which outlines the conditions for linkage. 'Openness' refers to the restrictions and obligations of party membership (see Chapter 3). 'Membership influence refers to the formal membership influence (see Chapter 3, especially Table 3.11). 'Membership strength' refers to the development of the size of individual party membership (see Chapter 4). 'Activity' refers to the development of the number of active party members between 1979 and 1994 (see Chapter 5). 'Social representativeness' refers to the development of social representativeness, and is a combination of the development of representativeness in terms of gender, age, education, class and group (see Chapter 7, summarised in Table 7.8). 'Opinion representativeness' refers to the development of opinion representativeness, and is a combination of the development of representativeness according to two objective and one subjective indicators of left-right ideological outlook (see Chapter 8, summarised in Table 8.7). In the columns of social and opinion representativeness, the entries have taken into account both the development among the totality of individual members and the active members of the respective party. The time frame between 1960 and 1994 does not apply to parties which were formed after 1960. In such cases the time frame begins the year the party was formed, i.e. 1964 (Christian Democrats), 1981 (Green Party) and 1991 (New Democracy).

The Green Party has not suffered a proven decline in membership and activity, but has declined in terms of membership influence. It may seem a bit harsh to attribute a linkage decline to a party for what some might regard as mere organisational modernisation. The counter-argument is that the reorganisation nevertheless does represent a decline. The Green Party started off from a very high degree of membership influence, scoring maximum points on the influence index in Table 3.11. The fact that the party has decided to do away with its previous organisational structure, where every central organ was directly elected by the congress, and the National Council was the highest decision-making organ between congresses, is relevant information. It suggests that the party is moving away from its original grass roots oriented organisation, something which represents a participatory linkage decline, even if it is limited, and from a high starting level compared to the other parties.

There is not sufficient evidence to be able to ascertain an overall decline also in representative linkage. Opinion representativeness has fluctuated, on the aggregate national level as well among the three parties where it has been possible to study this linkage type. As a rule, however, these fluctuations are trendless. The only clear case of a representational decline is the Moderate Party. Overall, the combined evidence suggests some traces of a representational decline, at least the development in left-right self-placement, but it is not enough to constitute an overall decline.

The Centre Party can also be attributed a representative linkage decline, because of the decline in membership influence. This may seem somewhat harsh. Just as in the case of the Green Party decline in participatory linkage, however, it must be borne in mind that we are not talking about no linkage, or low linkage. What has been found is a decline, which is a relevant finding even if the Centre Party is the most opinion representative of the studied parties. The influence potential of the Centre Party members has declined. This means that, even though the members are representative of the party's voters, their capacity to channel the opinions that they represent into the party organisation has decreased.

It could be that a more refined analysis of membership influence than the one based on the formal party rules in Chapter 3, would have led to a different conclusion for the Green and Centre parties. The changes in the party rules towards decreased formal influence do, however, mean that the rank-and-file members have less potential to channel public opinions into the party organisations. Thus, the ability for these two parties to provide linkage has declined, even though they both compare favourably with several other parties.

Possible explanations and consequences

As was noted in Chapter 2, many of the traditional characteristics attributed to the Swedish political system have either changed, or disappeared. Cracks have started to appear in the once stable party system. The welfare system is being fundamentally reassessed. The hey day of the 'Swedish model' and the Swedish welfare state is over. Can this be expected to have had a negative effect on the parties?

On the one hand, it might be expected that a political and economic crisis could make people more likely to join political parties, in order to try and change the situation with political activity. On the other hand, the political and economical difficulties faced by Sweden are closely connected with the old and established political parties. It might not be appealing for a disgruntled Swedish citizen, who wants to the welfare state back, to join the Social Democratic Party, under whose rule the welfare system has suffered a profound crisis. Indeed, none of the major Swedish parties sees any way back to the traditional welfare model. In short, it could be expected to be easier to get support for politics of growth and expansion oriented reforms, than for politics of cutbacks and austerity.

The evidence presented in Chapters 4 and 5 is clearly more in support of the latter hypothesis. A political and economic decline does not create conditions favourable for the parties' ability to provide participatory linkage. Swedish citizens have not responded to the economic difficulties by joining political parties.

At the same time, it should be emphasised that the new parties which have challenged the established party system have not been able to halt the negative membership development. It is interesting to note that the two Swedish parties to have mounted an organisational challenge to the established parties have not been particularly successful in membership recruitment. The Green Party has offered a grass roots oriented, flat, and direct democratic organisation. New Democracy, on the other hand, has provided the opposite alternative, with strong leadership and an organisation designed to allow quick and unbureaucratic decision-making. In neither case has the membership reached 10,000. In fact, the most successful of the three newest parties included in the study, the Christian Democrats, is organised along quite traditional lines.

Does this mean that people are beginning to reject Party as a phenomenon, rather than specific types of parties? That alternative party organisations do not help, and that Party as such is out of date? The findings in this study do not support such a radical conclusion. If, however, the observed trends continue, a much more serious situation may be approaching.

It could be noted that there is no evidence of a general decline in political interest, or in political participation outside the political parties. The Swedish electorate has become more interested in politics. Swedes are also more competent and confident to express themselves, and they try to influence decision-makers more than before.[3] In 1994, 10 per cent of the electorate were members of a political party. At the same time, 45 per cent had signed a petition, 35 per cent had donated money for a political cause and 19 per cent had contacted an official in local or central government.[4]

It may be a bit rash to conclude that Party as a phenomenon is out of date, but the development is not encouraging. According to Holmberg's findings, today's Swedish citizens are as politically active and competent as in the past. However, the evidence presented in this book suggests their activity does not primarily take place in political parties. The Swedish parties had more members when the welfare state was expanding and the disaffection with parties was not a great as is the case in the 1990s. Thus, when the welfare state is on the retreat, and trust in parties and politicians is lower than ever, the public response has been an increasing tendency to stay outside the parties. Although the incentives for joining political parties have not been studied here, a tentative interpretation could be that party membership is more an expression of support for a party than a conscious means towards a political end.

But is the negative development something which is deplored by the parties themselves? It might be expected that they could not care less. The public subsidies to political parties, introduced in the 1960s and increasingly generous over the years, made the parties financially virtually independent of their members. If, as the findings in Chapter 8 suggest, the members are ideologically extreme and not representative of the party's voters, then the

---

3 Gilljam and Holmberg 1995:175-184. The findings are based on Swedish Election Studies data, between 1960 and 1994.

4 Gilljam and Holmberg 1995:180.

leading party officials may not wish to keep recruiting large numbers of members.

This does not hold up to scrutiny, however. As was shown in Chapter 4, the parties show the utmost concern for their membership size. The findings in Chapter 3, where it is shown that the parties' openness has remained stable, and that there has been no general decrease in membership influence, reinforce this picture. Although it has not been systematically investigated here, there is much to suggest that the Swedish parties would like to have more members.

It is also interesting to note that some Swedish parties have made conscious attempts to renew their organisations, in order to attract members and activists. The People's Party Liberals, for example, have tried to open the party for participation by non-members. In 1988, furthermore, the party formed a side organisation for immigrants.[5] There is no sign that these attempts at organisational renewal have been successful.

Thus, it is plausible to assume that the development is contrary to the ambitions of most parties. The two parties attributed a mass tradition, the Social Democrats and the Centre Party, are the two with the largest memberships; but they have lost members. It is not only traditional movement parties that are losing members, however. Parties of all ages, origins, organisational types and ideologies are losing members. The only partial exceptions are the Green and Christian Democratic parties.

A bit tentatively, it could be said that party members in Sweden have become fewer and ideologically radicalised; in other words that party membership is becoming a small radical clique. True, the members of the Moderate and Social Democratic parties have actually moved towards the middle of the left-right scale, but the increased distances between members and voters in these two parties is a relevant finding.

Does all of the above suggest a crisis for the Swedish parties? It depends on whether the linkage decline is so serious that it has reached the level of crisis. It is of course not easily determined where this level is. Many of the conclusions summarised in Figure 9.1 are marginal rather than extreme declines. It is undeniable that there has been a decline in party membership but it is a matter of judgement whether the decrease has yet become critical. The same can be said about party activity. Nor is the decline in opinion representativeness among members and activists entirely

---

[5] For a study of the Liberal Immigrants' Organisation (*Liberala invandrarförbundet*), see Rodrigo Blomqvist 1996.

Epilogue[9]

In the summer of 1946, some 13 years after having been recruited in the street, Herbert Tingsten left the Social Democratic Party. He had undergone a profound political development and come to seriously question the advantages of socialism. On 12 June he openly declared his anti-socialist conviction in a public debate broadcast on radio. Tingsten did not at the time consider actively leaving the party. A few days later, however, he received a request by the party to pay his membership dues, something he had failed to do for a couple of years. Tingsten writes that it is possible that the approach was prompted by his radio appearance but he is not certain; it could also have been a coincidence. The sum demanded by the party was over 100 Swedish Kronor, quite a substantial amount at the time. Tingsten decided that this was too expensive for the privilege to remain a member of a party whose ideology he had come to question so profoundly. A few months later, Herbert Tingsten was appointed editor of the liberal morning newspaper *Dagens Nyheter*. In this capacity, he soon became a leading critic of the Social Democratic Party. But he never joined a political party again.

---

[9] This section is exclusively based on Tingsten 1962:361f.

Sources

MASS DATA SURVEYS

Swedish Election Studies, Department of Political Science, Göteborg University: Second Chamber Elections 1956, 1960, 1964 and 1968. Riksdag Elections 1970, 1979, 1985, 1988, 1991 and 1994.

VALU94, Exit poll by Swedish Television at the EU referendum, 13 November 1994:

Referendum Study, Department of Political Science, Göteborg University of the Referendum on Nuclear Energy 1980.

SOM Studies, Göteborg University, Department of Political Science and Department of Journalism and Mass Communication. National SOM Studies 1986-1997.

PUBLIC STATISTICS

Election Statistics, Parliamentary Elections:

SOS (Sveriges Officiella Statistik), Allmänna val. Riksdagsmannavalen: 1959-1960 I, 1961-1964 I and 1965-1968 Del 1.

SOS (Sveriges Officiella Statistik), Allmänna valen: 1970 Del 1, 1973 Del 1, 1976 Del 1, 1979 Del 1, 1982 Del 1, 1985 Del 1, 1988 Del 1, 1991 Del 1 and 1994 Del 1.

Election Statistics, Regional Elections:

SOS (Sveriges Officiella Statistik), Allmänna val. Kommunala valen: 1962 and 1966.

SOS (Sveriges Officiella Statistik), Allmänna valen: 1970 Del 2, 1973 Del 2, 1976 Del 2, 1979 Del 2, 1982 Del 2, 1985 Del 2, 1988 Del 2, 1991 Del 2 and 1994 Del 2.

C. PRINTED PARTY DOCUMENTS

Left Party (and predecessors):
Partistadgar (Party Rules): 1957, 1964, 1967, 1969, 1972, 1975, 1978, 1981, 1985, 1990 and 1993.

Verksamhetsberättelser (annual reports to Party Congress): 1964-1966 (to 1967 congress), 1967-1968 (to 1969 congress), 1969-1971 (to 1972 congress), 1972-1974 (to 1975 congress), 1975-1977 (to 1978 congress), 1979-1980 (to 1981 congress), 1981-1983 (to 1985 congress), 1984-1986 (to 1987 congress), 1987-1989 (to 1990 congress) and 1990-1992 (to 1993 congress).

Kongresshandlingar (Congress documents): VPKs 29e kongress 23-26 maj 1990, häfte 1-6. (29th congress 1990, booklets 1-6) Vänsterpartiets kongress 5-9 januari 1993, häfte 1-6. (1993 congress, booklets 1-6).

Other printed party documents and publications: Organisationsöversyn, maj 1992. Internal report on the party organisation.

SOCIAL DEMOCRATS:
Partistadgar (Party Rules): 1956, 1964, 1968, 1975, 1984, 1987, 1990 and 1993.

Verksamhetsberättelser (annual reports to Party Congress): 1969 (Presented to 1972 congress).Stockholm: Socialdemokraterna 1970. 1990-1992 (Presented to 1993 congress). Stockholm: Socialdemokraterna 1993.

Other printed party documents and publications:

Utveckling av organisation och verksamhet. Rapport från arbetsgruppen i organisationsfrågor. Stockholm: Tiden. (Organisational report to 26th Party Congress 1975).

Folk i rörelse. Förslag till organisatoriskt program. Stockholm: Socialdemokraterna. (Organisational programme proposal submitted to local and regional party organisations, 1989).

Aktuellt i Politiken (party periodical), special editions published during 1993 congress.

CENTRE PARTY:

Partistadgar (Party Rules): 1960, 1967, 1969, 1971, 1972, 1977 and 1992.

Verksamhetsberättelser (annual reports to Party Congress): 1985 (to 1986 congress), 1986 (to 1987 congress), 1987 (to 1988 congress), 1988 (to 1989 congress), 1989 (to 1990 congress), 1990 (to 1991 congress), 1991 (to 1992 congress), 1992 (to 1993 congress), 1993 (to 1994 congress), 1994 (to 1995 congress).

C 4. PEOPLE'S PARTY LIBERALS (and predecessors):

Partistadgar (Party Rules): 1964, 1966, 1967, 1969, 1971, 1974, 1977, 1980, 1987, 1990 and 1993. (1960: see "Other Party Sources").

Verksamhetsberättelser (annual reports to Party Congress): 1984-1986 (Presented to 1987 congress). 1987-1989 (Presented to 1990 congress). 1990-1993 (Presented to 1993 congress).

Other printed party documents and publications: Politik i praktiken - en handbok för dig som jobbar i folkpartiet. (Handbook for party activists). Stockholm: Folkpartiet 1984.

MODERATE PARTY (and predecessors):

Partistadgar (Party Rules): 1964, 1969, 1972, 1974, 1978, 1984, 1987, and 1993. (1950: see Other Party Sources).

Verksamhetsberättelser (annual reports to Party Congress): 1958-1960 (Presented to 1960 congress), 1960-1962 (Presented to 1962 congress), 1962-1964 (Presented to 1964 congress), 1964-1965 (Presented to 1965 congress), 1965-1967 (presented to 1967 congress), 1984-1986 (Presented to 1987 congress), 1987-1989 (Presented to 1990 congress) and 1990-1992 (Presented to 1993 congress).

Stämmohandlingar (Congress documents): Extra partistämma, Stockholm 1995: Stämmohandlingar. (Extra congress 1995)

CHRISTIAN DEMOCRATIC PARTY (and predecessors):

Partistadgar (Party Rules): 1964-1980: See Other Party Sources. 1984-1994: Printed in annuals (see *Other printed party documents and publications*).

Verksamhetsberättelser (annual reports to Party Congress): 1968 (presented to 1969 congress), 1990/91 (presented to 1991 congress) and 1991/92 (presented to 1992 congress).

Other printed party documents and publications: Årsböcker (annuals): 1984/85, 1985/86, 1988/89, 1990/91, 1993, 1994 and 1995.

GREEN PARTY (and predecessors):

Partistadgar (Party Rules): 1982, 1984, 1986, 1987, 1988, 1992, 1993 and 1994.

Verksamhetsberättelser (annual reports by Förvaltningsutskottet to party congress): 1982 (presented to 1983 congress), 1984 (presented to 1984 congress), 1985-1986 (presented to 1986 congress), 1986-1987 (presented to 1987 congress), 1987 (presented to 1988 congress), 1987 (presented to 1988 congress), 1988 (presented to 1989 congress), 1989 (presented to 1990 congress) and 1990 (presented to 1991 congress).

Other printed party documents and publications: <u>Lilla Gröna</u> 1987 (Party handbook). Morjärv: Börja Nu Förlaget.

NEW DEMOCRACY:

Partistadgar (Party Rules): 1992 and 1993.

OTHER PARTY SOURCES

PEOPLE'S PARTY LIBERALS:
"Utredning med förslag till organisationsplan för folkpartiets riksorganisation och huvudbyrå", avgiven den 29 september 1959 på uppdrag av folkpartiets organisationsdelegation. (Organisational report; contains proposed changes of the Party Rules; the Party Rules of 1960 are based on this document). Deposited at Riksarkivet, Stockholm (Folkpartiet Liberalernas arkiv); photocopy with the author.

"Medlemsstatistik 1960-1986". Compiled by Lennart Jörenborg, People's Party Archive, and given to the author, September 1989. Contains membership figures between 1960 and 1986.

MODERATE PARTY:
"Stadgar för högerns riksorganisation, ändringsförslag utarbetade av stadgekommittén 1949 med ändringar vidtagna av arbetsutskottet" (Party Rules as of 1949 with proposed changes before 1950 congress; the Party Rules of 1950 are based on this document and also on Albinsson 1986). Deposited at Riksarkivet, Stockholm (Moderata samlingspartiets arkiv); photocopy with the author.

Membership statistics 1968-1994. Kept at Moderate Party Central Office, Stockholm.

Telephone interview with organisational director Claes Weidstam, 10 December 1993.

CHRISTIAN DEMOCRATS:
Congress Minutes 1964, 1965, 1974, 1975, 1978, 1979 and 1980 contain changes and revisions of Party Rules. Deposited at Riksarkivet, Stockholm (Kristdemokraternas arkiv); photocopy with the author.

GREEN PARTY:
Membership statistics for 1989 (as of 24 October 1989). Supplied by Green Party Central Office.

NEW DEMOCRACY:
Telephone interview with Kristina Wahlberg, New Democracy Central Office, 23 March 1995.

Fax letter from John Holck-Bergman (formerly employed at New Democracy Central Office) to Dr. Paul Taggart, University of Sussex, 8 August 1995. Contains membership figures from 1991 to 1995.

Bibliography

Adelsohn, U. (1987): *Partiledare. Dagbok 1981-1986.* Stockholm: Gedins.

Albinsson, P. (1986): *Skiftningar i Blått. Förändringar i Moderata Samlingspartiets Riksorganisation 1960-1985.* Lund: Kommunfakta Förlag.

Almond, G. A. and Bingham Powell, G. (1966): *Comparative Politics. A Developmental Approach.* Boston (Mass.): Little, Brown and Company.

Andersson, L. (1984): "Urval och datainsamling". Appendix A in Erikson, R. and Åberg, R., eds.: *Välfärd i förändring. Levnadsvillkor i Sverige 1968-1981.* Stockholm: Prisma.

Arter, D. (1994): "The War of the Roses: Conflict and Cohesion in the Swedish Social Democratic Party". In Bell, D. S. and E. Shaw, eds.: *Conflict and Cohesion in Western European Social Democratic Parties.* London: Pinter.

Asp, K. (1986): *Mäktiga massmedier. Studier i politisk opinionsbildning.* Stockholm: Akademilitteratur.

Assarsson, J. (1993): "Bör partierna vara internt demokratiska?". *Statsvetenskaplig Tidskrift,* vol. 96, no. 1, pp. 39-68.

Back, P.-E. and Berglund, S. (1978): *Det svenska partiväsendet* (4th ed.). Stockholm: AWE/Gebers.

Bardi, L. and Morlino, L. (1992): "Italy". In Katz, R. S. and P. Mair, eds.: *Party Organizations. A Data Handbook on Party Organizations in Western Democracies, 1960-1990.* London: Sage.

Barnes, S. (1977): *Representation in Italy.* Chicago: University of Chicago Press.

Bartolini, S. (1985): "The Membership of Mass Parties. The Social Democratic Experience, 1889-1978". In Daalder, H. and P. Mair, eds.: *Western European Party Systems. Continuity and Change.* London: Sage.

Bartolini, S. and Mair, P. (1990): *Identity, Competition and Electoral Availability. The Stabilisation of European Electorates 1885-1985.* Cambridge (UK): Cambridge UP.

Bennie, L. G., Curtice, J. and Rüdig, W. (1996): "Party Members". In McIver, D., ed.: *Liberal Democrats*. London: Harvester Wheatsheaf.

Bennulf, M. (1994): *Miljöopinionen i Sverige*. Stockholm: Dialogos.

Berelson, B. R., Lazarsfeld, P. F., and McPhee, W. N. (1954/1986): *Voting. A Study of Opinion Formation in a Presidential Campaign*. Chicago: University of Chicago Press (Midway Reprint).

Berglund, S., and Lindström, U. (1978): *The Scandinavian Party System(s)*. Lund: Studentlitteratur.

Berglund, S. and Wörlund, I. (1990): "Partiorganisation som determinant till röstningsbeteendets regionala variationer". In Djupsund, G. and Svåsand, L., eds.: *Partorganisationer. Studier i strukturer og prosesser i finske, norske og svenske partier*. Turku: Åbo Academy Press.

Bergqvist, C. (1994): *Mäns makt och kvinnors intressen*. Uppsala: Acta Universitatis Upsaliensis (distributed by Almqvist and Wiksell international).

von Beyme, K. (1985): *Political Parties in Western Democracies*. Aldershot (UK): Gower.

Bille, L. (1992): "Denmark". In Katz, R. S. and P. Mair, eds.: *Party Organizations. A Data Handbook on Party Organizations in Western Democracies, 1960-1990*. London: Sage.

Bille, L. (1994): "Denmark: The Decline of the Membership Party?". In Katz, R. S. and P. Mair, eds.: *How Parties Organize: Change and Adaptation in Party Organizations in Western Democracies*. London: Sage.

Blondel, J. (1991): "Party Government: Normative and Empirical Aspects". In Wiberg, M., ed.: *The Political Life of Institutions. Scripta in Honorem Professoris Jaakko Nousiainen Sexagesimum Annum Complentis*. Helsinki: The Finnish Political Science Association.

Broomé, B. and Eklundh, C. (1973): *Ny regeringsform - ny riksdagsordning. Presentation av och kommentar till den nya författningen*. Stockholm: Aldus/Bonniers.

Butler, D. and Kitzinger, U. (1976): *The 1975 Referendum*. London and Basingstoke: Macmillan.

Bäck, H. (1995): "Partikrisen, den nya politiken och den nya högern". *Statsvetenskaplig Tidskrift*, vol. 98, no. 1, pp. 51-54.

Bäck, M. (1984): *Partier och organisationer i Sverige*. Stockholm: Publica.

Bäck, M. and Möller, T. (1990): *Partier och organisationer*. Stockholm: Allmänna Förlaget.

Castles, F. G. and Mair, P. (1984): "Left-Right Political Scales: Some 'Expert' Judgments". *European Journal of Political Research*, vol. 12, no. 1, pp. 73-88.

Childs, Marquis W. (1936/1948): *Sweden - the Middle Way. The Story of a Constructive Compromise between Socialism and Capitalism*. New York: Pelican Books.

Converse, P. and Pierce, R. (1986): *Political Representation in France*. Cambridge (US): The Belknap Press.

Crewe, I., Day, N. and Fox, A. (1991): *The British Electorate 1963-1987: A Compendium of Data from the British Election Studies*. Cambridge (UK): Cambridge UP.

Daalder, H. (1992): "A Crisis of Party?". *Scandinavian Political Studies*, vol. 15, no. 4, pp. 269-288.

Dahlerup, D. (1989): *Vi har väntat länge nog - handbok i kvinnorepresentation*. Copenhagen: Nordisk Ministerråd.

Dalton, R. J. (1996): *Citizen Politics. Public Opinion and Political Parties in Advanced Industrial Democracies (Second Edition)*. Chatham, New Jersey: Chatham House.

Dalton, R. J., Flanagan, S. C. and Beck, P. A. (1984): "Political Forces and Partisan Change". In Dalton, R. J., S. C. Flanagan and P. A. Beck, eds.: *Electoral Change in Advanced Industrial Democracies. Realignment or Dealignment?* Princeton (US): Princeton UP.

Dalton, R. J. and Kuechler, M, eds. (1990): *Challenging the Political Order. New Social and Political Movements*. New York: Oxford UP.

Deschouwer, K. (1994): "The Decline of Consociationalism and the Reluctant Modernization of Belgian Mass Parties". In Katz, R. S. and P. Mair, eds.: *How Parties Organize: Change and Adaptation in Party Organizations in Western Democracies.* London: Sage.

van Deth, J. W. and Horstman, R. (1989): *Dutch Parliamentary Elections Studies Sourcebook 1971-1986.* Amsterdam: Steinmetz Archive.

Duverger, M. (1951/1964): *Political Parties.* London: Methuen.

Elder, N., Thomas, A. H. and Arter,D. (1988): *The Consensual Democracies? The Government and Politics of the Scandinavian States (revised edition).* Oxford (UK): Basil Blackwell.

Elklit, J. (1991): "Faldet i medlemstal i danske politiske partier". *Politica,* vol. 23, no. 1, pp. 60-83.

Elliot, M. (1993): "Tilltro på tillväxt?". In Holmberg, S. and L. Weibull, eds.: *Vägval.* Göteborg: The SOM Institute. (SOM report no. 11).

Elliot, M. (1994): "Förnyat samhällsförtroende". In Holmberg, S. and L. Weibull, eds.: *Det gamla riket.* Göteborg: The SOM Institute. (SOM report no. 13).

Elmbrant, B. (1991): *Fälldin.* Stockholm: T. Fischer & Co.

Epstein, L. D. (1967): *Political Parties in Western Democracies.* New York: Praeger.

Erikson, R. and Åberg, R. eds. (1984): *Välfärd i förändring. Levnadsvillkor i Sverige 1968-1981.* Stockholm: Prisma.

Esaiasson, P. (1985): *Partiledarna inför väljarna. Partiledarnas popularitet och betydelse för valresultatet.* Göteborg: Department of Political Science. Forskningsrapport 1985:4.

Esaiasson, P. (1990): *Svenska valkampanjer 1866-1988.* Stockholm: Publica.

Esaiasson, P. and Holmberg, S. (1996): *Representation from Above. Members of Parliament and Representative Democracy in Sweden.* Aldershot (UK): Dartmouth.

Farrell, D. (1992): "Ireland". In Katz, R. S. and P. Mair, eds.: *The Development of Party Organizations in Western Democracies, 1960-1990: a Data Handbook.* London: Sage.

Fisher, J. (1996): *British Political Parties.* Hemel Hempstead: Prentice Hall.

Fuchs, D. and Klingemann, H.-D. (1990): "Partisanship and Political Behavior". In Jennings, M. K. and van Deth, J. W., eds.: *Continuities in Political Action.* Berlin: de Gruyter.

Fuchs, D. and Klingemann, H.-D. (1995): "Citizens and the State: A Changing Relationship?". In Klingemann, H.-D. and Fuchs, D., eds.: *Citizens and the State.* Oxford: Oxford UP.

van de Geer, J. and de Man, H. (1974): *Analysis of Responses to Issue Statements by Members of the Dutch Parliament.* Leiden: University of Leiden.

Gidlund, G. (1989): "Folkrörelsepartiet och den politiska styrelsen. SAPs organisationsutveckling". In Misgeld, K., K. Molin and K. Åmark, eds.: *Socialdemokratins samhälle 1889-1989. SAP och Sverige under 100 år.* Stockholm: Tiden.

Gidlund, G. (1991): "Public Investments in Swedish Democracy - Gambling with Gains and Losses". In Wiberg, M., ed.: *The Public Purse and the Political Parties. Public Financing of Political Parties in Nordic Countries.* Helsinki: The Finnish Political Science Association.

Gilljam, M. (1990): "Valrörelsen 1988". In Gilljam, M. and S. Holmberg, eds.: *Rött Blått Grönt. En bok om 1988 års riksdagsval.* Stockholm: Bonniers.

Gilljam, M. and Holmberg, S. (1993): *Väljarna inför 90-talet.* Stockholm: Norstedts juridik.

Gilljam, M. and Holmberg, S. (1995): *Väljarnas val.* Stockholm: Norstedts juridik.

Goul Andersen, J. (1993): "Politisk deltagelse i 1990 sammenlignet med 1979". In Andersen, J., Christensen, A.-D., Langberg, K., Siim, B. and Torpe, L.: *Medborgerskab. Demokrati og politisk deltagelse.* Herning: Forlaget Systime.

Hagård, B. (1966): *Socialdemokratien och fackföreningsrörelsen.* Stockholm: Forum för Borgerlig Debatt no. 3.

Heclo, H. and Madsen, H. (1987): *Policy and Politics in Sweden: Principled Pragmatism.* Philadelphia: Temple University.

Heidar, K. (1986): "Party Organizational Elites in Norwegian Politics: Representativeness and Party Democracy". *Scandinavian Political Studies,* vol. 9, no. 3, pp. 279-290.

Hirschman, A.O. (1970): *Exit, Voice and Loyalty. Responses to Decline in Firms, Organizations and States.* Cambridge (US): Harvard UP.

Holmberg, S. (1974): *Riksdagen representerar svenska folket.* Lund: Studentlitteratur.

Holmberg, S. (1996a): "Svensk åsiktsöverensstämmelse". In Rothstein, B. and B. Särlvik, eds.: *Vetenskapen om politik. Festskrift till professor emeritus Jörgen Westerståhl.* Göteborg: Department of Political Science.

Holmberg, S. (1996b): "Partierna gjorde så gott de kunde". In Gilljam, M. and S. Holmberg, eds.: *Ett knappt ja till EU. Väljarna och folkomröstningen 1994.* Stockholm: Norstedts Juridik.

Holmberg, S. and Asp, K. (1984): *Kampen om kärnkraften. En bok om väljare, massmedier och folkomröstningen 1980.* Stockholm: Publica/Liber Förlag.

Holmberg, S. and Esaiasson, P. (1988): *De folkvalda. En bok om riksdagsledamöterna och den representativa demokratin.* Stockholm: Bonniers.

Huber, J. D. and Bingham Powell Jr, G. (1992): "Congruence between Citizens and Policymakers in Two Visions of Liberal Democracy". Ann Arbor and Rochester: Department of Political Science, University of Michigan and University of Rochester. (Working paper).

Håkansson, A. (1995): "Kris för de svenska partierna?". *Statsvetenskaplig Tidskrift,* vol. 98, no. 1, pp. 45-51.

Häll, L. (1996): "Färre aktiva partimedlemmar". *Välfärdsbulletinen,* no. 2 1996.

Isberg, M. (1992): "The Two Waves of Party Reform: How State Decisions Have Shaped the Organization of Swedish Legislative Parties". Stockholm: Department of Political Science. (Report no. 1 from the research project "Party Groups in the Swedish Parliament").

Janda, K. (1980): *Political Parties. A Cross-National Survey.* New York: The Free Press.

Johansson, S. (1971): *Politiska resurser. Om den vuxna befolkningens deltagande i de politiska beslutsprocesserna.* Stockholm: Allmänna Förlaget.

Katz, R. S. (1990): "Party as Linkage: A Vestigial Function?" *European Journal of Political Research,* vol. 18, no. 1, pp. 143-161.

Katz, R. S. and Mair, P. (1992): "Introduction: The Cross-National Study of Party Organizations". In Katz, R. S. and P. Mair, eds.: *Party Organizations. A Data Handbook on Party Organizations in Western Democracies, 1960-1990.* London: Sage.

Katz, R. S. and Mair, P. eds. (1992): *Party Organizations. A Data Handbook on Party Organizations in Western Democracies, 1960-1990.* London: Sage.

Katz, R. S. and Mair, P. *et al.* (1992): "The Membership of Political Parties in European Democracies, 1960-1990". *European Journal of Political Research,* vol. 22, no. 3, pp. 329-345.

Katz, R. S. and Mair, P. (1995): "Changing Models of Party Organization: The Emergence of the Cartel Party". *Party Politics,* vol. 1, no. 1, pp. 5-28.

Kennerström, B. (1974): *Mellan två internationaler. Socialistiska Partiet 1929-1937.* Lund: Arkiv. (Arkiv Avhandlingsserie 2).

Key, V. O. (1967): *Public Opinion and American Democracy.* New York: Albert A. Knopf.

Kirchheimer, O. (1966): "The Transformation of the Western European Party Systems." In LaPalombara, J. and M. Weiner, eds.: *Political Parties and Political Development. Princeton: Princeton UP.*

Kitschelt, H. (1990): "New Social Movements and the Decline of Party Organization." In Dalton, R. J. and M. Kuechler, eds.: *Challenging the Political Order. New Social and Political Movements.* New York: Oxford UP.

Kristensen, O. (1980): "Den politisk-bureaukratiske beslutningsproces som medvirkende årsak til væksten i den offentlige sektor". *Nordisk Administrativt Tidskrift,* vol. 61, pp. 80-102.

Larsson, H. A., ed., (1985): *Från bonderörelse till centerrörelse. Jubileumsboken 1985.* Stockholm: Centerns riksorganisation. (Publication in commemoration of the 75th anniversary of the Centre Party).

Lawson, K. (1988): "When Linkage Fails". In Lawson, K. and P. Merkl, eds.: *When Parties Fail. Emerging Alternative Organizations.* Princeton: Princeton UP.

Lawson, K. and Merkl, P. (1988): "Alternative Organizations: Environmental, Supplementary, Communitarian and Antiauthoritarian". In Lawson, K. and P. Merkl, eds.: *When Parties Fail. Emerging Alternative Organizations.* Princeton: Princeton UP.

Lawson, K. and Merkl, P., eds., (1988): *When Parties Fail. Emerging Alternative Organizations.* Princeton: Princeton UP.

Lewin, L. (1970): *Folket och Eliterna.* Stockholm: Almqvist & Wiksell.

Lewin, L. (1977): *Hur styrs facket? Om demokratin inom fackföreningsrörelsen.* Stockholm: Rabén och Sjögren.

Listhaug, O. (1989): *Citizens, Parties and Norwegian Electoral Politics 1957-1985. An Empirical Study.* Trondheim: Tapir.

Lundgren, Å. (1991): "Miljöpartiet - en alternativ partiorganisation?". *Statsvetenskaplig Tidskrift,* vol. 94, no. 1, pp. 55-76.

Maguire, M. (1985): "Is There Still Persistence? Electoral Change in Western Europe, 1948-1979." In Daalder, H. and P. Mair, eds.: *Western European Party Systems. Continuity and Change.* London: Sage.

Mair, P. (1994): "Party Organizations: From Civil Society to the State". In Katz, R. S. and P. Mair, eds.: *How Parties Organize: Change and Adaptation in Party Organizations in Western Democracies.* London: Sage.

May, J. D. (1965): "Democracy, Organization, Michels". *American Political Science Review,* vol. 59, no. X, pp. 417-429.

May, J. D. (1973): "Opinion Structure of Political Parties: The Special Law of Curvilinear Disparity". *Political Studies,* vol. 21, no. 2, pp. 135-151.

McKenzie, R. T. (1982): "Power in the Labour Party: The Issue of Intra-Party Democracy". In Kavanagh, D., ed.: *The Politics of the Labour Party*. London: George Allen & Unwin.

Michels, R. (1915/1968): *Political Parties. A Sociological Study of the Oligarchical Tendencies of Modern Democracy.* New York: The Free Press.

Miller, W. E. and Stokes, D. E. (1963/1972): "Constituency Influence in Congress". In Nimmo, D. D. and C. M. Bonjean, eds.: *Political Attitudes and Public Opinion.* New York: David McKay Company.

Milner, H. (1990): *Sweden: Social Democracy in Practice.* Oxford: Oxford UP.

Molin, B. (1965): *Tjänstepensionsfrågan. En studie i svensk partipolitik.* Göteborg: Akademiförlaget (Scandinavian University Books).

Molin, K. (1989): "Partistrid och partiansvar. En studie i socialdemokratisk försvarsdebatt". In Misgeld, K., K. Molin and K. Åmark, eds.: *Socialdemokratins samhälle 1889-1989. SAP och Sverige under 100 år.* Stockholm: Tiden.

Morgan, G. (1986): *Images of Organization.* London: Sage.

Müller, W. C. (1992): "Austria". In Katz, R. S. and P. Mair, eds.: *Party Organizations. A Data Handbook on Party Organizations in Western Democracies, 1960-1990.* London: Sage.

Müller, W. C. (1994): "The Development of Austrian Party Organizations in the Post-War Period". In Katz, R. S. and P. Mair, eds.: *How Parties Organize: Change and Adaptation in Party Organizations in Western Democracies.* London: Sage.

Müller-Rommel, F. (1990): "New Political Movements and 'New Politics' Parties in Western Europe." In Dalton, R. J. and M. Kuechler, eds.: *Challenging the Political Order. New Social and Political Movements.* New York: Oxford UP.

Norris, P. (1987): *Politics and Sexual Equality.* Brighton: Wheatsheaf.

Norris, P. (1993): "Conclusions: Comparing Legislative Recruitment". In Lovenduski, J. and P. Norris, eds.: *Gender and Party Politics.* London: Sage.

Norris, P. (1995): "May's Law of Curvilinear Disparity Revisited: Leaders, Officers, Members and Voters in British Political Parties". *Party Politics,* vol. 1, no. 1, pp. 29-47.

Oscarsson, V. (1976): "Politiskt deltagande". *Statsvetenskaplig Tidskrift,* vol. 79, no. 3, pp. 185-208.

Oskarson, M. (1994): *Klassröstning i Sverige. Rationalitet, lojalitet eller bara slentrian.* Stockholm: Nerenius och Santérus förlag.

Oskarson, M. and Wängnerud, L. (1995a): *Kvinnor som väljare och valda.* Lund: Studentlitteratur.

Oskarson, M. and Wängnerud, L. (1995b): "Vem representerar kvinnorna?" In Rothstein, B. and Särlvik, B., eds.,: *Vetenskapen om politik. Festskrift till professor emeritus Jörgen Westerståhl.* Göteborg: Department of Political Science.

Panebianco, A. (1988*): Political Parties: Organization and Power.* Cambridge (UK): Cambridge UP.

Parry, G., Moyser, G. and Day, N. (1992): *Political Participation and Democracy in Britain.* Cambridge (UK): Cambridge UP.

Peterson, C. G. (1975): *Ungdom och politik. En studie av Sveriges Socialdemokratiska Ungdomsförbund.* Stockholm: Frihets Förlag.

Petersson, O. (1994): *Swedish Government and Politics.* Stockholm: Publica.

Petersson, O., A. Westholm and G. Blomberg (1989): *Medborgarnas makt.* Stockholm: Carlsson Bokförlag.

Pierre, J. (1986): *Partikongresser och regeringspolitik. En studie av den socialdemokratiska partikongressens beslutsfattande och inflytande 1948-1978.* Lund: Kommunfakta förlag.

Pierre, J. (1990): "Organisationsstrukturen i svenska politiska partier". In Djupsund, G. and L. Svåsand, eds.*: Partorganisationer. Studier i strukturer og prosesser i finske, norske og svenske partier.* Turku: Åbo Academy Press.

Pierre, J. and Widfeldt, A. (1992): "Sweden". In Katz, R. S. and P. Mair, eds.: *Party Organizations. A Data Handbook on Party Organizations in Western Democracies, 1960-1990.* London: Sage.

Pierre, J. and Widfeldt, A. (1994): "Party Organizations in Sweden: Colussuses with Feet of Clay or Flexible Pillars of Government?". In Katz, R. S. and P. Mair, eds.: *How Parties Organize: Change and Adaptation in Party Organizations in Western Democracies.* London: Sage.

Pierre, J. and Widfeldt, A. (1995): "Partikris i Sverige?". *Statsvetenskaplig Tidskrift,* vol. 98, no. 1, pp. 41-45.

Pitkin, H.F. (1967): *The Concept of Representation.* Berkeley and Los Angeles: University of California Press.

Poguntke, T. (1994): "Parties in a Legalistic Culture: The Case of Germany". In Katz, R. S. and P. Mair, eds.: *How Parties Organize: Change and Adaptation in Party Organizations in Western Democracies.* London: Sage.

The Riksdag in Figures 1994/95. Stockholm: Riksdagens förvaltningskontor.

Rodrigo Blomqvist, P. (1996): "Liberala invandrarförbundet - Respons på partikrisen? En fallstudie av folkpartiet och dess sidoorganisation liberala invandrarförbundet". Göteborg: Department of Political Science, Göteborg University (undergraduate dissertation, *C-uppsats*).

Rohrschneider, R. (1991): "Iron Law of Oligarchy or Soft Law of Democracy? Robert Michels and National Party Delegates in Eleven West European Democracies". Bloomington: Department of Political Science, University of Indiana. (Working paper).

Roth, P. A. (1996): *Riket, valkretsen och hemkommunen.* Göteborg: Göteborg University.

Rüdig, W, Bennie, L.G. and Franklin, M. (1991): *Green Party Members: A Profile.* Glasgow: Delta Publications.

Rönström, A. (1995): "SOM-undersökningen 1994. Genomförande och tillförlitlighet". In Holmberg, S. and L. Weibull, eds.: *Det gamla riket.* Göteborg: The SOM Institute. (SOM report no. 13).

SCB 1994: Föreningslivet i Sverige - en statistisk belysning. Levnadsförhållanden, rapport nr. 86. (Living conditions, report 86, publ. by Statistics Sweden).

SCB 1996: Politiska resurser och aktiviteter 1978-1994. Levnadsförhållanden, rapport nr. 90. (Living conditions, report 90, publ. by Statistics Sweden).

Sainsbury, D. (1993): "The Politics of Increased Women's Representation: The Swedish Case". In Lovenduski, J. and P. Norris, eds.: *Gender and Party Politics.* London: Sage.

Sartori, G. (1976): *Parties and Party Systems. A Framework for Analysis.* New York: Cambridge UP.

Scarrow, S. E. (1991): *Organizing for Victory: Political Party Members and Party Organizing Strategies in Great Britain and West Germany, 1945-1989.* Ph.D dissertation at Yale University (unpublished mimeograph).

Scarrow, S. E. (1996): *Parties and their Members. Organizing for Victory in Britain and Germany.* Oxford (UK): Oxford UP.

Schmitt, H. (1984): "Zur Links-Rechts-Polarisierung in Mittlerer Führungsschicht und Wählerschaft in 10 Westeuropäischen Parteiensysteme". In Falter, J. W. *et al.,* eds.: *Politische Willensbildung und Interessenvermittlung.* Opladen: Westdeutscher Verlag.

Schmitt, H. and Holmberg, S. (1995): "Political Parties in Decline?". In Klingemann, H.-D. and D. Fuchs, eds.: *Citizens and the State.* Oxford: Oxford UP.

Schumpeter, J. A. (1942/1952): *Capitalism, Socialism and Democracy.* London: George Allen and Unwin.

Seyd, P. and Whiteley, P. (1992): *Labour's Grass Roots.* Oxford: Clarendon Press.

Strömberg, L. (1974): *Väljare och valda. En studie av den representativa demokratin i kommunerna.* Göteborg: Department of Political Science. (Kommunforskningsgruppens avhandlingsserie nr. 32; unpublished mimeographed PhD dissertation).

Svåsand, L. (1994): "Change and Adaptation in Norwegian Party Organizations". In Katz, R. S. and P. Mair, eds.: *How Parties Organize: Change and Adaptation in Party Organizations in Western Democracies.* London: Sage.

Svensson, P. (1974): "Support for the Danish Social Democratic Party 1924-1939 - Growth and Response". *Scandinavian Political Studies,* vol. 9. pp. 127-146.

Taggart, P. A. (1993): *The New Populism and the New Politics: Transformations of the Swedish Party System in Comparative Context.* Ph.D dissertation at the University of Pittsburgh (unpublished mimeograph).

Taggart, P. A. (1996*): The New Populism and the New Politics: New Protest Parties in Sweden in a Comparative Perspective.* Basingstoke: Macmillan.

Taggart, P. A. and Widfeldt, A. (1993): "1990s Flash Party Organization: The Case of New Democracy in Sweden". Paper presented to the Annual Conference of the Political Studies Association of the UK (Panel on Scandinavian Politics), University of Leicester, 20-22 April 1993.

Thermeanius, E. (1933): *Sveriges politiska partier.* Stockholm: Hugo Gebers.

Tingsten, H. (1962): *Mitt liv. Mellan trettio och femtio.* Stockholm: Norstedts.

Togeby, L. (1992): "The Nature of Declining Party Membership in Denmark: Causes and Consequences". *Scandinavian Political Studies,* vol. 15., no. 1, pp. 1-19.

Webb, P. D. (1992a): *Trade Unions and the British Electorate.* Aldershot: Dartmouth.

Webb, P. D. (1992b): "The United Kingdom". In Katz, R. S. and P. Mair, eds.: *Party Organizations. A Data Handbook on Party Organizations in Western Democracies, 1960-1990.* London: Sage.

Webb, P. D. (1994): "Party Organizational Change in Britain: The Iron Law of Centralization?". In Katz, R. S. and P. Mair, eds.: *How Parties Organize: Change and Adaptation in Party Organizations in Western Democracies.* London: Sage.

Webb, P. D. (1995): "Are British Political Parties in Decline?". *Party Politics,* vol. 1, no. 3, pp. 299-322.

Webb, P. D. and Widfeldt, A. (1996): "Quantitative Trends in European Party Membership" (manuscript).

Weissberg, R. (1978): "Collective versus Dyadic Representation in Congress". *American Political Science Review,* vol. 72, no. 2, pp. 535-547.

Wellhofer, E. S. and Hennessey, T. M. (1974): "Models of Political Party Organisation and Strategy: Some Analytical Approaches to Oligarchy". In Crewe, I., ed.: *Elites in Western Democracy. (British Political Sociology Yearbook, vol. 1).* London: Croom Helm.

Westerståhl, J. and Johansson F. (1981): *Medborgarna och kommunen. Studier av medborgerlig aktivitet och representativ folkstyrelse.* Stockholm: Kommundepartementet. (Departementsserien: Ds Kn 1981:12).

Whiteley, P., Seyd, P. and Richardson, J. (1994): *True Blues. The Politics of Conservative Party Membership.* Oxford: Clarendon Press.

Widfeldt, A. (1995): "Party Membership and Party Representativeness". In Klingemann, H.-D. and D. Fuchs, eds.: *Citizens and the State.* Oxford: Oxford UP.
Widfeldt, A. (1996): "Sweden and the European Union. Implications for the Swedish Party System". In Miles, L., ed.: *The European Union and the Nordic Countries.* London: Routledge.

Winqvist *et al.* (1972): Winqvist, K.-V., Wickléus, J.-Å., Uddman, P., Bengtsson, L. and Lundström, B.-O.: *Svenska partiapparater. De politiska partiernas organisatoriska uppbyggnad.* Stockholm: Aldus/Bonniers.

Wright, W. E. (1971): "Comparative Party Models: Rational-Efficient and Party Democracy". In Wright, W. E., ed.: *A Comparative Study of Party Organization.* Columbus (Ohio): Charles E. Merrill Publishing Company.

NEWSPAPER ARTICLES:

Dagens Nyheter, 29 June 1997.
Expo, no. 1, 1996.
Göteborgs-Posten, 5 June 1994, 20 June 1996.
Tidningen Z, no. 15, July 1991.

Appendix I. Key to the Swedish parties

English name used in book: Centre Party.
Name in Swedish: *Centerpartiet* or *Centern*. Year of formation: 1921 (predecessor formed in 1913).
Previous names: Farmer's League (*Bondeförbundet*) 1921-1957. Centre Party Farmer's League
(*Centerpartiet Bondeförbundet*) 1957-1958.
Ideological location: Centre.

English name used in book: Christian Democrats.
Name in Swedish: *Kristdemokraterna*. Year of formation: 1964.
Previous names: Christian Democratic Coalition (*Kristen demokratisk samling*) 1964-1987, Christian
Democratic Society Party (*Kristdemokratiska samhällspartiet*) 1987-1996.
Ideological location: Christian Democratic.

English name used in book: Green Party.
Name in Swedish: *Miljöpartiet de gröna*. Year of formation: 1981.
Previous names: Environmentalist Party (*Miljöpartiet*) 1981-1985.
Ideological location: Green, new politics.

English name used in book: Left Party.
Name in Swedish: *Vänsterpartiet*. Year of formation: 1917 (split from Social Democrats).
Previous names: Left Social Democratic Party of Sweden (*Sveriges socialdemokratiska vänsterparti*)
1917-1921. Communist Party of Sweden (*Sveriges kommunistiska parti*) 1921-1967. Left Party
Communists (*Vänsterpartiet kommunisterna*) 1967-1990.
Ideological location: 1920s to 1960s communist (member of 3rd international 1919-1943). 1960s to
1980s Euro-communist. 1990s left socialist, new politics.

English name used in book: Moderate Party.
Name in Swedish: *Moderata samlingspartiet* or *Moderaterna*. Year of formation: 1904.
Previous names: National membership organisation called General League of Voters (*Allmänna
valmansförbundet*) 1904-1938, National Organisation of the Right (*Högerns riksorganisation*) 1938-
1952 and National Organisation of the Right Party (*Högerpartiets riksorganisation*) 1952-1969. Until
1969 the party was generally referred to as 'the Right' (*Högern*).
Ideological location: Conservative.

English name used in book: New Democracy.
Name in Swedish: *Ny demokrati*. Year of formation: 1991.
Previous names: None.
Ideological location: Right wing populist.

English name used in book: People's Party Liberals.
Name in Swedish: *Folkpartiet liberalerna*. Year of formation: 1934 (predecessor formed in 1902).
Previous names: People's Party (*Folkpartiet*) 1934-1990.
Ideological location: Liberal.

English name used in book: Social Democratic Party, Social Democrats.
Name in Swedish: *Sveriges socialdemokratiska arbetareparti* or *Socialdemokraterna*.
Year of formation: 1889.
Previous names: None.
Ideological location: Social democratic.

Appendix II. Membership figures of Swedish parties and side organisations, 1960-1997. Party Records

II a) Social Democrats

year	total members	ind. members	women's org.	tot. members incl. women's org.	ind. members incl. women's org.	youth org.	students' org.	Christian org.
1960	730305	n/a	70763	801068	n/a	54713	966	n/a
1961	740608	n/a	68209	808817	n/a	53969	1215	10204
1962	768292	n/a	67720	836012	n/a	49132	1319	10219
1963	799173	n/a	67913	867086	n/a	50721	1500	10614
1964	814780	n/a	66255	881035	n/a	56469	2000	10816
1965	809533	n/a	63491	873024	n/a	58560	2000	10871
1966	824616	n/a	61216	885832	n/a	59793	1868	n/a
1967	831712	163212	59738	891450	222950	61124	n/a	10500
1968	830146	n/a	58148	888294	n/a	61680	3016	10500
1969	849382	n/a	58120	907502	n/a	70402	n/a	n/a
1970	835721	n/a	54349	890070	n/a	66490	---	n/a
1971	857941	n/a	51199	909140	n/a	72067	---	n/a
1972	889582	n/a	48733	938315	n/a	70583	---	n/a
1973	905136	n/a	47583	952519	n/a	70585	---	n/a
1974	935379	214379	46399	1001406	260788	72110	---	n/a
1975	986862	n/a	45357	1032219	n/a	72300	---	8200
1976	1028574	n/a	45921	1074495	n/a	65300	---	n/a
1977	1082226	n/a	47235	1129461	n/a	72000	---	8300
1978	1114806	n/a	47222	1162028	n/a	70126	---	8300
1979	1141847	n/a	47112	1188959	n/a	72800	---	n/a
1980	1159655	n/a	45597	1205252	n/a	73649	---	n/a
1981	1159970	n/a	45094	1205064	n/a	69880	---	n/a
1982	1184321	n/a	45382	1229703	n/a	66320	---	6666
1983	1188574	n/a	44592	1233166	n/a	63180	---	6741
1984	1170482	n/a	43078	1213560	n/a	63705	---	6666
1985	1160707	n/a	43078	1203785	n/a	68000	---	6380
1986	1166410	n/a	40973	1207383	n/a	68000	---	6399
1987	1124164	n/a	39391	1163555	n/a	69130	---	6367
1988	1077876	n/a	38342	1116218	n/a	44217	---	6208
1989	978265	n/a	36300	1014565	n/a	44219	---	6192
1990	804386	n/a	33484	837870	n/a	40890	n/a	6014
1991	---	229095	31251	---	260346	37778	n/a	5727
1992	---	232468	29137	---	261605	34247	n/a	5753
1993	---	232723	27165	---	259888	35319	1050	5077
1994	---	233498	25610	---	259108	25632	1016	5059
1995	---	206203	22225	---	228428	21544	1200	4906
1996	---	183517	19201	---	202718	20769	1100	4522
1997	---	172337	16567	---	188904	n/a	1486	n/a

Comment: In the party's statistics, members of women's organisation are included in the party total, the same as in the 5th and 6th columns. In the 2nd and 3rd columns, the number of members of women's organisation is subtracted from the total figures in the party statistics. Women's and Christian organisations are ancillary, i.e. all their members are also members of the party. Youth and student's organisations are affiliated, i.e. there is no such complete overlap. *Sources:* Social Democrats, annual report 1990-1992 pp. 314-319. Figures from 1993 to 1997 supplied by central office of the party and women's organisation. Youth org. 1993-1996 supplied by *Ungdomsstyrelsen*. Students' org. 1993-1996: E-mail from Therese Svanström, 10 Sep. 1998. Christian org.: Annual reports of Christian Social Democratic organisation. Figures separating individual and collective members taken from Social Democratic Organisational Report to 1975 congress, p. 28. Collective membership abolished in 1990.

II b) Left Party

year	party	youth org.
1960	19834	n/a
1961	n/a	n/a
1962	n/a	n/a
1963	19907	n/a
1964	n/a	n/a
1965	n/a	8000
1966	17511	10000
1967	n/a	n/a
1968	16211	n/a
1969	n/a	n/a
1970	14368	n/a
1971	14740	n/a
1972	n/a	n/a
1973	15338	n/a
1974	15399	15388*
1975	n/a	18342*
1976	15461	18612*
1977	15010	19542*
1978	15883	19702*
1979	17483	20914*
1980	18157	19846*
1981	17793	19537*
1982	17320	19352*
1983	16761	18419*
1984	15976	16363*
1985	15696	16315*
1986	14379	15574*
1987	13699	16236
1988	13517	16092
1989	12935	14705
1990	12279	14528
1991	11821	14721
1992	11104	13758
1993	10691	12978
1994	10700	12419
1995	11313	11383
1996	11652	11490
1997	11916	n/a

Comment: The youth organisation is affiliated, which means that there is no total membership overlap between the organisation and the party. *Sources:* Party: Winqvist et at. (1972) page 296f , annual reports (*Verksamhetsberättelser*) to congresses 1964-1993, telephone information from party central office. See also Hermansson 1986: Youth organisation: Back and Berglund 1967:55. Winqvist et al. 1972:293. *Ungdomsstyrelsen* statistics 1974-1996 (*=includes only members aged up to 25 years. Total membership figures not available for these years).

II c) Centre Party

Year	party	women's org.	party incl. women's org.	youth org.	students' org.
1960	119012	60092	179104	91290	267
1961	118297	61394	179691	89921	306
1962	116911	61957	178868	87359	n/a
1963	116133	62128	178261	78086	337
1964	113996	62305	176301	72018	368
1965	113411	62111	175522	66243	385
1966	114113	63149	177262	58749	460
1967	113880	63141	177021	53654	533
1968	114106	63946	178052	50899	600
1969	114503	64667	179170	47749	523
1970	116798	65639	182437	45019	532
1971	119017	66212	185229	45899	n/a
1972	125248	68073	193321	47181	---
1973	130984	70233	201217	46223	---
1974	133984	71207	205191	44481	---
1975	135576	72209	207785	42924	---
1976	138978	73491	212469	42451	---
1977	139959	74325	214284	41711	---
1978	141344	74798	216142	40995	---
1979	141208	74886	216094	40949	---
1980	137057	73307	210364	37106	---
1981	133082	72058	205140	44917	---
1982	130638	71566	202204	40098	---
1983	130218	71151	201369	41183	---
1984	129081	70497	199578	39123	n/a
1985	125318	69599	194917	30112	n/a
1986	120941	67887	188828	28614	430
1987	119550	66894	186444	27022	425
1988	116515	65119	181634	24479	517
1989	112848	63071	175919	23087	521
1990	110406	60718	171124	19042	508
1991	105101	58004	163105	14589	430
1992	98580	54789	153369	12634	425
1993	93769	51305	145074	11342	365
1994	88588	47878	136466	10201	447
1995	83656	44392	128048	n/a	n/a
1996	76398	40674	117072	8286	n/a
1997	70971	37300	108271	n/a	n/a

Comments: All side organisations are affiliated, which means that their members are not automatically members of the Centre Party. *Sources:* Party: Larsson, ed., 1985 page 162. Annual reports (*Verksamhetsberättelser*) to party congress 1985-1994. Women's org.: Larsson, ed., 1985, page 163. Annual reports (*Verksamhetsberättelser*) to congress of Women's organisation, telephone information from central office of Women's organisation. Youth organisation: Larsson, ed., 1985, page 163. Annual reports (*Verksamhetsberättelser*) to Centre youth org. congresses 1985 and 1986. *Ungdomsstyrelsen* statistics 1987-1996. Students' organisation: *Ex Ante* (Periodical of Centre Party Student's organisation) issue 2, 1989 (vol. 5). Annual reports (*Verksamhetsberättelser*) to Centre Party congress 1990 and 1991. Fax message (24 November 1995) to the author from Centre Party Student's organisation.

II d) People's Party Liberals

Year	party	women's org.	party incl. women's org.	youth org.	students' org.	immigrants' org.
1960	89528	n/a	89528	n/a	386	---
1961	88845	n/a	88845	n/a	595	---
1962	85136	n/a	85136	n/a	742	---
1963	89833	n/a	89833	n/a	667	---
1964	88542	n/a	88542	n/a	899	---
1965	87368	n/a	87368	n/a	1095	---
1966	86232	n/a	86232	n/a	863	---
1967	85287	n/a	85287	18728	n/a	---
1968	85356	n/a	85356	18614	n/a	---
1969	80564	n/a	80564	n/a	781	---
1970	76335	n/a	76335	27500*	320	---
1971	75673	n/a	75673	27250*	---	---
1972	70439	n/a	70439	29000*	---	---
1973	69241	n/a	69241	n/a	---	---
1974	62795	n/a	62795	28510*	n/a	---
1975	59405	n/a	59405	17697*	255	---
1976	59474	n/a	59474	17810*	1500	---
1977	57174	n/a	57174	17896*	2600	---
1978	55717	n/a	55717	18013*	3000	---
1979	54320	n/a	54320	17854*	4000	---
1980	50553	n/a	50553	16956*	3500	---
1981	47556	n/a	47556	14368*	n/a	---
1982	46891	4800	51691	11770*	n/a	---
1983	43665	4936	48601	10804*	n/a	---
1984	42446	4417	46863	11172*	n/a	---
1985	45225	4035	49260	12093*	n/a	---
1986	44613	4968	49581	11954*	n/a	---
1987	45776	5009	50785	12391	270	---
1988	46490	4426	50916	12233	345	400
1989	43061	3885	46946	10665	300	230
1990	40416	n/a	n/a	11873	n/a	425
1991	37869	3500	41369	15276	n/a	421
1992	34404	2458	36862	14823	n/a	505
1993	31113	3033	34146	13287	n/a	521
1994	28854	3037	31891	11419	n/a	560
1995	26201	2720	28921	4628		600
1996	24387	2187	26574	2357		550
1997	23785	1825	25610	1160		500

Comments: All side organisations are affiliated, which means that their members are not automatically members of the People's Party Liberals. Between circa 1964 and 1982 the Women's organisation did not keep membership records. *Sources:* Party: Annual reports (*Verksamhetsberättelser*) to party congress 1961-1994. Complemented by statistics supplied by party central office. Women's org.: Supplied by central office of People's Party Liberals women's organisation. Youth organisation: Annual reports (*Verksamhetsberättelser*) to People's Party 1967, 1968. *Ungdomsstyrelsen* statistics 1970-1994 (*=only members aged up to 25 included. Total membership figures not available for these years). Youth org. 1995-1997: E-mail from Erik Wallenberg 14 September 1998. Students' organisation: supplied by central office of Liberal Student's organisation. Immigrants' organisation: Rodrigo Blomqvist 1996 and e-mail message from Tuula Rudbäck, 25 August 1998.

II e) Moderate Party

year	party	women's org.	party incl. women's org.	youth org.
1960	133443	73170	206613	40475
1961	n/a	n/a	n/a	n/a
1962	127658	71795	199453	30907
1963	n/a	n/a	n/a	n/a
1964	108303	62676	170979	25923
1965	88305	66520	154825	23640
1966	n/a	n/a	n/a	n/a
1967	n/a	n/a	n/a	n/a
1968	67122	67494	134616	14186
1969	64381	64852	129233	12815
1970	61014	62237	123251	12042
1971	61547	60432	121889	12750
1972	57488	59741	117229	13171
1973	60148	61375	121523	16001
1974	59772	60629	120401	15616
1975	59740	61127	120867	16040
1976	63942	64525	128017	24548
1977	62333	63630	125963	22214
1978	63084	63103	126187	22969
1979	64134	64655	128789	28250
1980	63955	63780	127735	30060
1981	64464	62720	127184	28247
1982	68142	65107	133249	33961
1983	71005	66989	137994	40960
1984	90444	52218	142662	41503
1985	96338	52450	148788	43328
1986	89831	51112	140943	34582
1987	83820	47472	131292	29921
1988	80572	44364	124936	29643
1989	77393	41185	118578	24022
1990	78730	39863	118593	23199
1991	78757	37383	116140	22557
1992	72317	35307	107624	19323
1993	66304	32229	98533	17545
1994	65896	27852	93748	15078
1995	61877	24695	86572	13092
1996	61714	23182	84896	11065
1997	66845	21248	88093	10874

Comments: Both side organisations are ancillary, which means that all their members are also members of the Moderate Party. Until 1983, all female party members were automatically made members of the women's organisation. Thus the figures in the first column include only men until that year. *Sources:* Party: Annual reports (*Verksamhetsberättelser*) to party congress 1960-1993. Complemented by statistics supplied by party central office. Women's org.: ditto, complemented with figures supplied by Moderate Party women's organisation. Youth org.: ditto, complemented by figures supplied by Moderate Party youth organisation.

II f) Christian Democrats

Year	party	women's org.	party incl. women's org.	youth org.	senior org.
1964	12000	---	12000	---	---
1965	n/a	---	n/a	---	---
1966	13311	---	13311	1000	---
1967	14811	---	14811	1000	---
1968	13409	---	13409	2000	---
1969	13805	---	13805	2000	---
1970	13587	---	13587	2345	---
1971	14471	---	14471	3287	---
1972	16112	---	16112	4041	---
1973	20981	---	20981	4500	---
1974	21668	---	21668	5135	---
1975	22580	---	22580	5027	---
1976	23578	---	23578	4824	---
1977	22589	---	22589	5066	---
1978	22250	---	22250	5259	---
1979	22439	---	22439	5758	---
1980	22041	---	22041	6094	---
1981	22898	---	22898	6345	---
1982	23860	1775	25635	6299	---
1983	24721	2377	27098	6674	---
1984	26763	2814	29577	6396	---
1985	26672	2677	29349	6621	---
1986	26122	3010	29132	n/a	---
1987	24943	3117	28060	6594	---
1988	24365	3326	27691	6645	---
1989	24005	3457	27462	6581	---
1990	24949	3527	28206	6535	---
1991	27605	3592	31197	6528	---
1992	29346	3666	33012	6772	n/a
1993	28703	3743	32446	5262	n/a
1994	27041	3884	30925	4987	n/a
1995	25328	3602	28930	5024	n/a
1996	23505	3187	26692	5031	n/a
1997	22793	3100	25893	5027	ca. 1600

Comments: Both side organisations are affiliated, which means that their members are not necessarily members of the Christian Democratic Party. *Sources:* Party: KDS Annual (*Årsbok*) 1985/86, p/ 90. Complemented with figures supplied by Christian Democratic Party central office. Women's org.: KDS Annual (*Årsbok*) 1985/86, p. 90. Complemented with figures supplied by Christian Democratic Women's organisation central office. Youth org.: KDS Annual (*Årsbok*) 1985/86, p. 90. *Ungdomsstyrelsen* statistics, e-mail from Robert Lisborg, 9 October 1998.

II g) Green Party

Year	party	youth org.
1981	1979	---
1982	5800	---
1983	2500	---
1984	3000	---
1985	4000	---
1986	5000	---
1987	6000	---
1988	8857	300
1989	7000	1134
1990	7000	1288
1991	6900	n/a
1992	6400	n/a
1993	5300	n/a
1994	6500	n/a
1995	5600	n/a
1996	6950	1133
1997	7500	1318

Comment: Youth organisation is ancillary, which means that its members are also members of the Green Party. *Sources:* Party: Annual reports (*Verksamhetsberättelser*) to party congress 1982-1988. Complemented by statistics supplied by party central office. Youth org.: Supplied by Green Party youth organisation.

II h) New Democracy

Year	party
1991	4735
1992	9125
1993	6850
1994	2675
1995	445

Source: Fax message (3 August 1995) from John Holck-Bergman (former administrative director of New Democracy) to Paul Taggart, University of Sussex.

Appendix III. Election results of the Swedish parties, 1960-1994, in absolute numbers and percentages

Social Democrats

year	votes	per cent
1960	2,033,016	47.8
1962	2,044,976	50.5
1964	2,006,923	47.3
1966	1,858,506	42.2
1968	2,420,277	50.1
1970	2,256,369	45.3
1973	2,247,727	43.6
1976	2,324,603	42.7
1979	2,356,234	43.2
1982	2,533,250	45.6
1985	2,487,551	44.7
1988	2,321,826	43.2
1991	2,062,761	37.7
1994	2,513,905	45.2

People's Party Liberals

year	votes	per cent
1960	744,142	17.5
1962	694,629	17.1
1964	720,733	17.1
1966	736,782	16.7
1968	688,456	14.3
1970	806,667	16.2
1973	486,028	9.4
1976	601,556	11.1
1979	577,063	10.6
1982	327,770	5.9
1985	792,268	14.2
1988	655,720	12.2
1991	499,356	9.1
1994	399,556	7.2

Centre Party

year	votes	per cent
1960	579,007	13.6
1962	529,589	13.1
1964	559,632	13.4
1966	602,380	13.7
1968	757,215	15.7
1970	991,208	19.9
1973	1,295,246	25.1
1976	1,309,669	24.1
1979	984,589	18.1
1982	859,618	15.5
1985	564,710	10.1
1988	607,240	11.3
1991	465,175	8.5
1994	425,153	7.7

Moderate Party

year	votes	per cent
1960	704,365	16.5
1962	627,534	15.5
1964	582,609	13.7
1966	646,831	14.7
1968	621,031	12.9
1970	573,812	11.5
1973	737,584	14.3
1976	847,672	15.6
1979	1,108,406	20.3
1982	1,313,337	23.6
1985	1,187,335	21.3
1988	983,226	18.3
1991	1,199,394	21.9
1994	1,243,253	22.4

Left Party

year	votes	per cent
1960	190,560	4.5
1962	155,299	3.8
1964	221,746	5.2
1966	283,402	6.4
1968	145,172	3.0
1970	236,659	4.8
1973	274,929	5.3
1976	258,432	4.8
1979	305,420	5.6
1982	308,899	5.6
1985	298,419	5.4
1988	314,031	5.8
1991	246,905	4.5
1994	342,988	6.2

Christian Democrats

year	votes	per cent
1960	---	---
1962	---	---
1964	75,389	1.8
1966	78,957	1.8
1968	72,377	1.5
1970	88,770	1.8
1973	90.388	1.8
1976	73,844	1.4
1979	75,993	1.4
1982	103,820	1.9
1985	126,548	2.3
1988	158,182	2.9
1991	390,351	7.1
1994	225,974	4.1

Green Party

year	votes	per cent
1982	91,787	1.7
1985	83,645	1.5
1988	296,935	5.5
1991	185,051	3.4
1994	279,042	5.0

New Democracy

year	votes	per cent
1982	---	---
1985	---	---
1988	---	---
1991	368,281	6.7
1994	68,663	1.2

Sources: SOS (Sveriges Offentliga Statistik): Allmänna val, riksdagsmannavalen 1959-60, 1961-1964 and 1965-1968. Allmänna val, kommunala valen 1962 and 1966. Allmänna val 1970, 1973, 1976, 1979, 1982, 1985, 1988, 1991 and 1994. The percentages are based on the total number of valid votes. The figures from 1962 and 1966 are from regional elections. The figures from 1960, 1964 and 1968 are from elections to the second chamber of the Riksdag. The figures from 1970, 1973, 1976, 1979, 1982, 1985, 1988, 1991 and 1994 are from elections to the unicameral Riksdag. The electorate was extended, due to lowering of the minimum voting age, in 1968, 1970 and 1976.